Golf
Resorts

Where to Play in the USA
Canada, Mexico, Costa Ri
& the Caribbean

3rd Edition

Jim & Barbara Nicol

HUNTER

Hunter Publishing, Inc.
130 Campus Drive
Edison, NJ 08818-7816
☎ 732-225-1900 / 800-255-0343 / Fax 732-417-1744
Web site: www.hunterpublishing.com
E-mail: hunterp@bellsouth.net

IN CANADA:
Ulysses Travel Publications
4176 Saint-Denis, Montréal, Québec
Canada H2W 2M5
☎ 514-843-9882 ext. 2232 / Fax 514-843-9448

IN THE UNITED KINGDOM:
Windsor Books International
The Boundary, Wheatley Road, Garsington
Oxford, OX44 9EJ England
☎ 01865-361122 / Fax 01865-361133

ISBN 1-58843-122-3
© 2001 Jim & Barbara Nicol

The publisher, author, affiliated individuals and companies disclaim any responsibility for any injury, harm, or illness that may occur to anyone through, or by use of, the information in this book. Every effort was made to insure the accuracy of information in this book, but the publisher and author do not assume, and hereby disclaim, any liability or any loss or damage caused by errors, omissions, misleading information or potential travel problems caused by this guide, even if such errors or omissions result from negligence, accident or any other cause.

Prices, hours of operation, amenities and conditions change over the course of time, and readers are advised to contact the locations prior to planning a visit. The restaurants, markets, shops and other businesses listed in this book have been reviewed over a period of time and reflect the personal experiences of the author and other contributors to this guide. The author, contributors, and publisher cannot be held responsible for the experiences of the reader with regard to the establishments listed herein. We welcome comments and suggestions from our readers for future editions.

Maps by Kim André, Lissa K. Dailey & Toni Carbone,
© 2001 Hunter Publishing, Inc.

Cover: Chateau Whistler Resort, British Columbia
Back cover: The Homestead, Hot Springs, Virginia

Contents

Introduction

In this edition we have added many new resorts, including some in Canada, the Caribbean, Mexico, as well as the United States. Please keep in mind that the rates quoted for the Canadian destinations are in Canadian dollars. Rates for all other locations, including Mexico, are in US dollars.

Clearly, some resorts and golf courses are a notch or two above the others; we have frequently been asked which resorts were our favorites. The list below gives what we consider to be the top 50 resorts. The list is in alphabetical order and does not try to indicate who is number one and who is number 50. It is based on the quality of lodgings, the amenities and general ambience, as well as the quality of the golf facilities.

The Top 50 Resorts

Amelia Island Plantation – Amelia Island, FL
American Club, The – Kohler, WI
Balsams Grand Resort Hotel, The – Dixville Notch, NH
Banff Springs Hotel – Banff, Alberta, Canada
Boulders, The – Carefree, AZ
Broadmoor, The – Colorado Springs, CO
Casa De Campo Resort – La Romana, Dominican Republic
Cloister, The – Sea Island, GA
Colonial Williamsburg Inn – Williamsburg, VA
Eagle Ridge Inn & Resort – Galena, IL
Fairmont Scottsdale Princess – Scottsdale, AZ
Four Seasons Punta Mita – Nayarit, Mexico
Four Seasons Resort & Club – Irving, TX
Four Seasons Resort, The – Nevis, West Indies
Greenbrier, The – White Sulphur Springs, WV
Homestead, The – Hot Springs, VA
Kiawah Island Resort – Charleston, SC
Kingsmill Resort – Williamsburg, VA
La Costa – Carlsbad, CA
La Quinta Resort & Club – La Quinta, CA
Las Brisas Resort – Acapulco, Guerrero, Mexico
Las Hadas – Manzanillo, Colima, Mexico

Le Chateau Montebello – Montebello, Quebec, Canada
Lodge at Koele, The – Lanai, HI
Lodge at Pebble Beach, The – Pebble Beach, CA
Lodge Of Four Seasons, The – Lake Ozark, MO
Loews Ventana Canyon Resort – Tucson, AZ
Manele Bay Hotel – Lanai, HI
Marriott at Sawgrass Resort – Ponte Vedra Beach, FL
Marriott's Camelback Inn – Scottsdale, AZ
Marriott's Grand Hotel Resort – Point Clear, AL
Marriott's Rancho Las Palmas Resort – Rancho Mirage, CA
Mauna Kea Beach Hotel – Kohala Coast, Hawaii, HI
Mauna Lani Bay Hotel – Kohala Coast, Hawaii, HI
Mauna Lani Islands & Point Condos – Kohala Coast, Hawaii, HI
Ojai Valley Inn & Country Club – Ojai, CA
Palmilla Resort Hotel – San Jose del Cabo,BSC Sur, Mexico
Phoenician Resort, The, Scottsdale, AZ
Pinehurst Hotel & Country Club – Pinehurst, NC
Princeville Hotel – Princeville, Kauai, HI
Quail Lodge – Carmel, CA
Resort at Longboat Key Club, The – Longboat Key, FL
Ritz–Carlton Kapalua – Maui, HI
Saddlebrook Golf & Tennis Resort – Wesley Chapel, FL
Tides Lodge, The – Irvington, VA
Westin La Paloma, The – Tucson, AZ
Westin Rio Mar Beach Resort, The, Rio Grande, Puerto Rico
Wigwam Resort & Country Club, The – Litchfield Park, AZ
Wintergreen – Wintergreen, VA
Wyndham El Conquistador Resort – Fajardo, Puerto Rico

How To Use This Book

The following abbreviations are used throughout this book:

- **EP:** European Plan. No meals are included in the rate shown.
- **BP:** British Plan. Breakfast only is included.
- **MAP:** Modified American Plan. Two meals are included, usually breakfast and dinner.
- **FAP:** Full American Plan. All three meals are included.

◉ **GREEN FEES:** Rates shown are per person. When two rates are indicated (for example $35/$45), the first is for weekdays and the second is for weekends or holidays. Rates shown are for guests of the resort, not walk-ons.

◉ **CART FEES:** Rates are for two players for 18 holes.

◉ **LODGING FEES:** All rates are for double occupancy during the resort's peak golf season unless otherwise noted. In most cases, fees are lower at other times of the year. All resorts reserve the right to change rates without prior notice, so there may be a variation between the rates we show and those in effect when you make a reservation. The figures are given as a guideline only. None of the rates include taxes or gratuities unless so stated. Many resorts automatically attach a service charge to your bill covering gratuities. When making reservations ask what is covered by the service charge. In a few cases you will find that it includes check-in and check-out baggage handling. Many resorts offer short-term specials. When making reservations ask if any such discounts are available.

◉ **CREDIT CARDS:** While the great majority of resorts/hotels accept credit cards, this is not always the case. Check when booking.

◉ **TEE TIMES:** Be sure to set up tee times at least for the first day you wish to play when you make your reservations.

◉ **GOLF PACKAGES:** Package plans generally represent savings. Keep in mind, however, that you may not have time to play on the days of arrival or departure.

◉ **TRAVEL AGENCIES:** We urge you to use a travel agency once you have decided which resort you'll be visiting. There is no fee and you will find it to be a hassle-free procedure.

◉ **PETS:** Few resorts allow pets. In some instances you may find a kennel in a nearby town. Ask when making your reservations.

Alabama

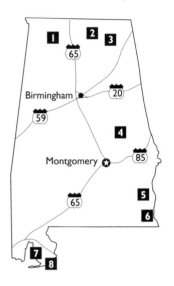

1. Joe Wheeler State Park
2. Four Points Hotel
3. Lake Guntersville State Park Resort
4. Still Waters Resort
5. Lakepoint State Park Resort
6. Dothan National Golf Club
7. Marriott's Grand Hotel
8. Gulf State Park Resort

Dothan National Golf Club

Box 6108, Highway 231 South, Dothan, AL 36302

(334) 677-3321; (800) 214-1150

ACCOMMODATIONS: 96-room motel.

AMENITIES: Indoor mineral pool, exercise room, steam room and saunas, and eight tennis courts (four lighted). They have a distinguished dining room and lounge.

GOLF: The Olympia Spa course, a Bob Simmons design, has been rated one of the top five golf courses in Alabama. It has been host to many top professional and amateur tournaments since its completion in 1968. Parring at 72/73, it measures a monstrous 7,315/6,793/5,947 yards. It is interesting and challenging, with tree-lined fairways and a creek that seems to be everywhere (seven holes).

RATES: (EP) Lodgings - $60/$85. Green fees - $22/$29, carts $22. Golf packages are available. Rates are for February-March.

ARRIVAL: By air - Dothan (15 minutes). By car - five miles from Dothan on US 231.

Four Points Hotel

1000 Glen Hearn, Huntsville, AL 35824

(256) 772-9661; (800) 241-7873

ACCOMMODATIONS: 148 rooms and suites.

AMENITIES: Outdoor pool, two lighted tennis courts, an exercise room and saunas. Dining is in the Bayou Grille and The Lunch Pad (lighter fare).

GOLF: The course, adjacent to the hotel, plays 6,720/6,320/5,625 yards, parring at 72. It offers the challenge of very large greens and water on three holes.

RATES: (EP) Lodgings - $99/$109. Green fees - $25/$35 including cart.

ARRIVAL: By air - Huntsville Jetplex.

Alabama

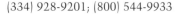

Marriott's Grand Hotel Resort

Scenic Highway 98, Point Clear, AL 36564

(334) 928-9201; (800) 544-9933

The Grand Hotel has been selected as one of the Top 50 resorts. As you drive to the resort you will see some of the finest Southern estates and summer homes to be found anywhere in this country.

Built in 1847, the hotel was demolished in the hurricane of 1893 and mauled again by Hurricane Frederick in 1979. Each time the Grand has come back a better and more beautiful facility. Its 550 acres are full of ancient magnolias and venerable moss-draped oak trees. Most of the property either fronts on or has a magnificent view of Mobile Bay.

ACCOMMODATIONS: 306 rooms and suites in the Main Hotel, Bay House or Cottages. All rooms have air-conditioning and cable TV; suites have built-in bar, refrigerator with icemaker, and a wide-screen TV.

AMENITIES: Beautiful sand beaches, a 40-slip marina, eight Rubico tennis courts (two lighted), jogging paths, and a huge swimming pool. Almost every type of water sport imaginable is offered: sailing, paddleboats, fishing, windsurfing, and charter yachts. They also have stables and over five miles of riding trails, with instruction available. A children's program is offered during the summer for ages five through 12.

Grand Dining Room has a rather formal setting (jackets required after 6 PM, but not ties), and a spectacular view of Mobile Bay. Other options are the Bayview Dining Room and, for casual meals, the Lakewood Golf Club is open for lunch only. For a change of pace, try The Wash House Restaurant, about a mile from the resort on Scenic Highway 98. They have great seafood. Reservations are necessary; call (334) 928-1500.

GOLF: The Azalea Course, a par 72, reaches out a substantial 6,770/6,292/6,000/5,307 yards. The Dogwood Course measures 6,676/6,331/5,532 yards and pars at 71/72. Undulating terrain, many sand bunkers, massive oaks and several lazy creeks turn these layouts into a most interesting golfing experience. While not easy, they are not back-breakers either, and are fun to play.

 Several resident alligators inhabit this golf complex. While they generally will not bother you, it is best to leave them alone. After all, the morning you meet them could well be their "grouchy" morning.

RATES: (EP) Lodgings - $180/$279 and up. Green fees - $75, including cart. Golf package – includes (lodgings, breakfast, golf with cart for each night of stay) $219/$279 per couple per night. Rates are for April-September.

ARRIVAL: By air - Mobile (35 miles). Private aircraft - Fairhope, a 5,200-foot blacktop strip (five minutes). By car - from Mobile, take I-10 to US 98 and head east to Alternate 98, which brings you to Point Clear.

Still Waters Resort

1816 Still Waters Drive, Dadeville, AL 36853

(205) 825-7021; (888) 797-3767

ACCOMMODATIONS: One- to three-bedroom villas with either golf or lake locations. Two- and three-bedroom units feature two baths. The Lake Villas are equipped with fireplaces, washer/ dryer, living room, dining room, fully equipped kitchen, and patio with barbecue grill.

AMENITIES: Six lighted tennis courts, pool, bicycle rentals and, of course, golf. The 40,000-acre freshwater lake, with over 750 miles of shoreline, offers spectacular fishing, sailing, and sandy beaches. There is a full-service 132-slip marina with a restaurant and shops. For dining, try the newly refurbished Fox's Den Tavern (referred to as the 19th Hole), which has a beautiful view of Lake Martin. Another restaurant was recently added at the water's edge.

GOLF: The Still Waters Legend course, which fronts the lake, is a George Cobb design. Measuring 6,407/5,903/5,449/5,287 yards, it pars at 72. The wooded and rolling terrain, tree-lined fairways, and water hazards make it an intriguing layout. A second course now in play is named The Tradition. Rolling out 6,906/6,519/5,753/5,048 yards, it also plays to a par of 72. While a traditional layout with trees and traps it adds the challenge of tri-level greens and elevation changes.

RATES: (EP) Lodgings - $159/$179/$189. Green fees - $65 including carts. Several golf packages are available. Rates are for mid-March to November.

ARRIVAL: By air - Montgomery (60 miles). By car - from Dadeville, take 49 south for six miles. At Lake Martin Grocery take a right and drive two miles. The entrance is on your left.

Alabama State Parks

While the state of Alabama operates many parks, only four have a full 18-hole golf course, restaurant and inn, cabins, or motel units. The telephone number given for each park will connect you with the inns. Many locations offer improved campsites (with facilities), as well as some primitive camping sites. The Alabama State Parks System, like so many state park systems in the country, represents one of the best buys for your vacation dollar. For in-depth information on any of the parks, call (800) 252-2262 nationwide; within Alabama, (800) 392-8096. You can also call each resort on its own toll-free line.

Gulf State Park Resort

HC 79 Box 9, Gulf Shores, AL 36542

(334) 968-7531; (800) 544-4853.

ACCOMMODATIONS: A 144-room inn, 21 cabins.

AMENITIES: 2½ miles of white sand beach, 825 foot fishing pier, tennis courts, boat rentals, a restaurant and bar.

GOLF: Parring at 72, the course measures 6,563/6,171/5,310 yards.

RATES: (EP) Lodgings - $118/$219. Green fees - $30/$35, including cart. Rates are for April 20-September 2.

ARRIVAL: By car - the resort is south of I-10 off SR 59, on the Gulf of Mexico.

Lake Guntersville State Park Resort

State Route 63, Box 224, Guntersville, AL 35976

(205) 571-5440; (800) 548-4553

ACCOMMODATIONS: A combination of inn rooms and chalets on the ridge top as well as lakeview cottages.

AMENITIES: A beach complex, tennis courts, fishing, boating, restaurant and lounge.

GOLF: A championship 18-hole layout playing 6,824/6,286/5,802 yards and parring at 72.

RATES: (EP) Lodgings - $65/$105. Suites - $125. Chalets (one to six persons) - $119. Green fees - $18, carts $20. Rates are for April 1-October 1.

ARRIVAL: By car: six miles northeast of Guntersville off Highway 227.

Lakepoint State Park Resort

Route 2, Box 94, Eufaula, AL 36027

(334) 687-8011; (800) 544-5253.

ACCOMMODATIONS: 101 rooms at the Inn, plus 29 air-conditioned cabins fully equipped for housekeeping.

AMENITIES: Fishing and swimming in Lake Eufaula, a 200-slip marina, 10 lighted tennis courts, dining room and bar.

GOLF: A par 72 layout reaching out 6,752/6,531/5,363 yards. While generally flat, the fairways are tree-lined with water coming into play on eight holes.

RATES: (EP) Lodgings - $62/$122. Green fees - $16, carts $20. Rates are for mid-April to October 31.

ARRIVAL: By car - seven miles north of Eufaula, off Highway 431.

Alabama

Arizona

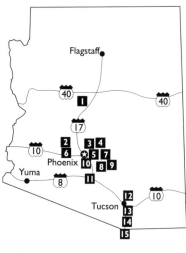

1. Bell Rock Inn
2. Rancho De Los Caballeros
3. The Boulders/Four Seasons at
   Troon NorthRenaissance Cottonwoods
4. Rio Verde-Tonto Verde Resort
5. Arizona Biltmore/The
   Phoenician Resort/The Pointe
   Hilton at Tapatio Cliffs/The Pointe
   Hilton on South Mountain
6. The Wigwam Resort
7. Hyatt Regency Scottsdale/
   Marriott's Camelback Inn/
   Marriott's Mountain Shadows/
   Orange Tree Resort/Rancho Pima
   Golf Resort/Regal McCormick
   Ranch/Radisson Resort/
   Fairmont Scottsdale Princess
8. The Arizona Golf Resort/Dobson
   Ranch Inn
9. The Gold Canyon Resort
10. Sheraton San Marcus/Ventana
    Canyon Golf & Racquet Club
11. Francisco Grande Resort
12. Loews Ventana Canyon Resort/
    Sheraton Tucson/El Conquistador/
    The Omni Tucson National Resort
    & Spa/Westin La Paloma
13. Starr Pass Golf Club
14. Tubac Golf Resort
15. Rio Rico Resort

The Arizona Biltmore

24th Street and Missouri, Phoenix, AZ 85016

(602) 955-6600; (800) 950-0086

ACCOMMODATIONS: 600 rooms, including several wings and courts. An extravagant and lavishly landscaped resort completed in the late 1920s, it has not lost its stately atmosphere nor its quiet gentility.

AMENITIES: Eight lighted tennis courts, three pools, health center, sauna, and therapy pools. There are two dining areas plus the Adobe Golf Restaurant.

GOLF: Two 18-hole golf courses are adjacent to the property. The Links Course (par of 71), playing at 6,300/5,726/4,912 yards, offers a typical resort layout. The longer Adobe Course, older and more traditional, measures 6,767/6,455/6,094 and pars at 72/73. Although we have played and enjoyed both, we found the Links to be the better of the two.

RATES: (EP) Lodging - $330/$395/$495. Villas - $1,200. Green fees - $165, including cart. Customized golf packages are available and include several other golf courses in the area. Rates quoted are for January-May.

ARRIVAL: By air - Phoenix. By car - I-17 to Squaw Peak Parkway, then north to Highland exit. Head east to 24th Street, north to Missouri and the entrance to the hotel.

The Arizona Golf Resort

425 South Power Road, Mesa, AZ 85206

(602) 832-3202; (800) 528-8282

ACCOMMODATIONS: 150 rooms, some with kitchenettes, as well as one- and two-bedroom suites.

AMENITIES: Four tennis courts, Olympic-size pool, and access to a nearby health club (within a half-mile; additional fee). Dining facilities include Anabelle's Restaurant, a lounge, and the "19th Green," which offers a coffee shop menu and cocktail service.

GOLF: The resort's course has more than enough water hazards and bunkers to keep you honest. With a par of 711, it reaches out 6,574/6,195/5,782/5,124 yards.

RATES: (EP) Rooms - $149/$340. Green fee - $65, including cart. Golf package (one night/one day, including daily breakfast, one rounds of golf, cart), $300 per couple. Rates are for January 1-April 30.

ARRIVAL: By air - Phoenix Airport (35 minutes). By car - Maricopa Freeway to Superstition Freeway. Exit on Power Road and continue north to resort.

The Bell Rock Inn

6246 Highway 179, Sedona, AZ 86336

(520) 282-4161; (800) 881-7625

ACCOMMODATIONS: 47 rooms and suites. This resort has a spectacular setting within the region's startling red rock cliffs.

AMENITIES: Swimming pool, two tennis courts; horseback riding available nearby. For dining, there is the Bell Rock Restaurant and lounge. Make time to sightsee in this area or you will miss an outstanding experience. Be sure to visit the many shops and art galleries.

GOLF: Guests of the Bell Rock play on The Sedona Golf Resort course, about a mile away. Designed by architect Gary Parks, it enjoys an outstanding visual setting. It reaches out 6,642/6,126/5,637/5,030 yards with a par of 71. Although water comes into action on only three holes, the greens are extremely fast. For tee times, call (602) 284-9355.

There is a second 18 available: the Oakcreek Country Club, designed by Robert Trent Jones. Built on undulating terrain and using the ever-present, beautiful rekd mountains as a backdrop, it covers 6,854/6,286/5,555 yards and pars at 72. For tee times, call (602) 284-1660.

RATES: (EP) Rooms - $90/$160. Golf package (one night/one day, including lodging, one round of golf with cart, one breakfast), $209/$219 per couple.

ARRIVAL: By air - Flagstaff (45 miles) or Phoenix Sky Harbor Airport (90 miles). By private aircraft/charter flights - Sedona Airport (5,100-foot paved runway, lighted, radio equipped).

The Boulders

PO Box 2090, Carefree, AZ 85377

(602) 488-9009; (800) 553-1717

The Boulders has been judged one of the Top 50 resorts. It is set in the desert foothills northeast of Phoenix in an area of saguaro cactus, Indian paintbrush, hollyhocks and giant boulders shaped by water, wind and thousands of years. To say that it is beautiful and impressive is an understatement

ACCOMMODATIONS: 160 individual casitas built with natural wood, Mexican glazed tile, and adobe plaster surfaces. Each casita features a full-size woodburning fireplace, a private patio or deck. Now there are also 35 Pueblo Villas (private homes). One-, two- and three-bedroom units come completely equipped for housekeeping.

AMENITIES: Freeform pool, six plexi-cushioned tennis courts, picturesque trails to hike, ride or stroll, off-road bicycling, hot air ballooning, rock climbing clinics, the Sonoran Spa, a full service program and a magnificently equipped fitness center along with a lap-pool. Another recent addition is El Pedregal, a festival marketplace featuring 40 boutiques, restaurants, a museum, art galleries and so on. Dining is provided in the Palo Verde, the Latilla Dining Room and the lovely Boulders Club (much more than a 19th hole), the Bakery Café and finally Cantina del Pedregal featuring, of course, Mexican cuisine.

GOLF: The resort's 36-hole complex is a Jay Morrish design. The Boulders North Course reaches out a respectable 6,717/6,277/ 5,440/4,893 yards and pars at 72. The South plays 6,589/6,073/ 5,141/4,715 yards with a par of 71. These are both beautiful as well as demanding golf courses. With the desert, cactus, huge boulders and a profusion of sand traps, you will find them all you can handle. The Director of Golf Operations is Stuart Stubbs.

It is not at all unusual to spot coyotes or javelinas – although neither will let you get very close.

RATES: (EP) Casitas - $565. Green fees, including cart - $185. Golf package (four nights/four days, including lodging, MAP, golf with cart), $3,568 per couple plus tax and gratuities. Rates are for January through mid-May.

ARRIVAL: By air - Phoenix (33 miles) - Scottsdale Airport (13 miles). By car - take I-17 north to Carefree Highway. Travel east to Scottsdale Road, then head north for less than a mile.

Dobson Ranch Inn

1666 South Dobson Road, Mesa, AZ 85202

(602) 831-7000; (800) 528-1356

ACCOMMODATIONS: 212 oversize guest rooms and 10 suites.

AMENITIES: Fitness center, swimming pool (which is the focal point of the resort), and G. Willikers Restaurant. While the restaurant is modest in size, it offers an excellent and very diverse menu.

GOLF: The Dobson Ranch Golf Course is about one mile away. The par 72 course reaches out 6,593/6,176/5,598 yards.

RATES: (EP) Rooms - $122/$155 (add $15 for a poolside room). Green fees - $75, including cart. Golf packages available.

ARRIVAL: By air - Phoenix Sky Harbor Airport (20 minutes). By car - south on I-10. Exit to Superstition Freeway (I-60) east. Take the Dobson Road Exit and you will see the resort signs on your right.

Fairmont Scottsdale Princess

7575 East Princess Drive, Scottsdale, AZ 85255

(480) 585-4848; (800) 866-5577

The Scottsdale Princess has been judged one of the Top 50 resorts. Built on a slightly raised area, it seems to loom up out of the desert somewhat like a huge Mexican estate. The beautiful McDowell Mountains serve as a backdrop. The general motif of Old Mexico, complemented by earth tones, old brick courtyards, cottonwoods, and even a bell tower, all combine to produce a quiet, pastoral setting.

ACCOMMODATIONS: 400 rooms and suites, 125 casitas near the tennis complex and 75 golf villas. Each of the rooms has three phones, a mini-bar, an iron and ironing board and a private terrace. The casitas have a living room with a working fireplace (additional logs are just outside your door), a large bedroom, a walk-in closet and a bathroom big enough to hold the NBA play-offs.

AMENITIES: Nine tennis courts, including a stadium court; a health and fitness center with racquetball and squash courts; aerobics and weight rooms; three pools; and a very sophisticated spa program (saunas, steambaths, loofahs, herbal wraps, and much more). Adjacent to the resort is a 400-acre equestrian center with a four-mile cross-country course and two polo fields.

There are four dining rooms and six cocktail lounges. The Marques is in a class by itself, featuring unusual Southwestern cuisine. There is also La Hacienda, for authentic Mexican fare (and, I hasten to add – it is outstanding), Las Ventanas, adjacent to the pool; and the Grill at TPC. Don't pass up the excellent grill at the course itself.

GOLF: The Stadium Course, home of the Phoenix Open, has one of the better layouts in the country. Stretching 6,992/6,508/6,049/5,567 yards, it pars at 71. A Tom Weiskopf and Jay Morrish design, it is a links type affair, with rolling terrain, multi-level greens, over 70 traps (a few six or seven feet deep) and water coming into play on seven holes. While fun to play, it is anything but a pushover. The Desert Course is a more relaxing option. Again, this is a Tom Weiskopf/Jay Morrish design. Measuring a more modest 6,552/5,908/5,339 yards, it also pars at 71.

RATES: (EP) Rooms - $429/$659. Green fees - (Stadium Course), $181; Desert Course - $48, including cart. Rates are for January through April.

ARRIVAL: By air - Sky Harbor (approximately one hour). By private aircraft (including private jets) - Scottsdale Municipal Airport (10 minutes away). By car: the resort is about a quarter-mile north of the intersection of Bell Road and Scottsdale Blvd.

Four Seasons Resort at Troon North

10600 Crescent Moon Drive, Scottsdale, AZ 85255

(480) 515-5700; (800) 332-3442

Adjacent to the famous Troon golf facility and located in the high Sonoran Desert, the resort offers guest a view of Pinnacle Peak as well as a portion of Phoenix.

ACCOMMODATIONS: Consist of a total of 210 rooms and suites located in one and two story casitas. Featuring walk-in closets, wall safes and gas burning fireplaces. Suites feature outdoor private plunge pools, outdoor garden showers and kiva fireplace (Native-American-style fireplace).

AMENITIES: In addition to the magnificent golf facilities there is a fitness center, a 12,000 square-foot full-service spa program, four tennis courts (two lighted), a 6,000 square-foot swimming pool, and a shallow children's pool as well as a complimentary "Kids for All Seasons program.

GOLF: The Monument Course opening in 1990 was designed by Tom Weiskopf and Jay Morrish. Playing to a par of 72, it reaches out a bruising 7,028/6,636/6,247/5,901/5,050 yards. Following the success of the Monument layout, Mr. Weiskopf designed the Pinnacle 18-hole course, once again introducing a very substantial 7,044/6,719/6,302/5,765/4,980 yards, also parring at 72. A collection of steep arroyos, and the general views of the Sonoran Desert will challenge your ability to concentrate on your game. Guests also have privileges at the clubhouse.

RATES: Casitas - $500/$650. 1 Bedroom suites $1,150/$1,500. Green fees - $250 including cart. Rates are for high season mid-December through mid-May.

ARRIVAL: By air - Phoenix or Scottsdale Airports. By car - take Scottsdale Blvd, north to Pinnacle Peak, turn right and follow signs.

Francisco Grande Resort

PO Box 326, Casa Grande, AZ 85222

(520) 836-6444; (800) 237-4238

ACCOMMODATIONS: Multi-level hotel with 112 guest rooms and suites.

AMENITIES: Huge swimming pool, modern lighted Laykold tennis courts and, of course, golf. Dining is now offered in the Palo Verde Room or in a more informal setting on the veranda.

GOLF: The course has undergone extensive renovation with added trees and traps. Its length, however, remains awesome; it reaches out 7,320/6,975/6,454/5,554 yards and pars at 72.

RATES: (EP) Lodging - $99/$139/$250. Green fees - $55/$65, including cart. Golf package (three nights/four days, including room, green fees and cart, daily breakfast), $740.

ARRIVAL: By car - Midway between Phoenix and Tucson; from I-10, turn west at Exit 194 and drive to Casa Grande. The resort is four miles west on Highway 84.

The Gold Canyon Resort

6100 South Kings Ranch Road, Apache Junction, AZ 85219

(602) 982-9090; (800) 624-6445

The natural beauty of this part of Arizona is legendary. Speaking of legends, Apache Junction is reputed to be the location of the fabled Lost Dutchman Mine. As the story goes, the mine is somewhere in the Superstition Mountains. Although many have sought and, in fact, are still seeking it, the mine's location remains unknown.

ACCOMMODATIONS: 100 Southwestern-style rooms and suites. There are also some casitas available. Several new suites have been added.

AMENITIES: Tennis, swimming, trail rides (with an experienced wrangler to assist), and guided tours. Overnight campouts and cookouts can also be arranged. The clubhouse dining room features a varied menu.

GOLF: The 18-hole Dinosaur Course pars at 70/72 and extends 6,584/6,008/5,498/4,921 yards. Water comes into play on only two holes. A very nice change of pace. By the time you read this book a second layout called The Sidewinder Course will be in play. Parring at 72/74, it rolls out 6,230/6,016/5,563/4,529 yards.

RATES: (EP) Lodgings - $200/$230. Green fees - $135, including cart. Golf packages are available. Sidewinder Course green fees - $55/$65. Rates are from January to May 15th.

ARRIVAL: By air - Phoenix. By car - Highway 60 east to Apache Junction; continue seven miles southeast on 60 to Kings Ranch Road. Turn left to the resort.

Hyatt Regency Scottsdale

7500 East Doubletree Ranch Road, Scottsdale, AZ 85258

(602) 991-3388; (800) 233-1234

An impressive art collection is showcased in and around the hotel. It includes sculpture, wall friezes, paintings and carvings. Some of the artifacts date back to 700 B.C.

ACCOMMODATIONS: 493 guest rooms within the main structure and a VIP wing (The Regency Club) on the third and fourth levels. Seven lakeside casitas are also available.

AMENITIES: Tennis on eight surfaced courts (four lighted), a health and fitness center, saunas, massage rooms, therapeutic massage, croquet and a four-mile jogging and cycling trail laid out over the 580-acre Gainey Ranch property. Horseback riding is available nearby. There is a water playground consisting of a half-acre of pools with waterfalls, three-story water slide and sand beach. Dining facilities include The Golden Swan, an indoor/outdoor restaurant; The Squash Blossom, with a beautiful view of the cascading fountain area; and Sandolo, for casual dining.

GOLF: The Gainey Ranch Golf Club offers golf on 27 holes designed by Benz and Poellot. The nine-hole Arroyo features a meandering desert look. The Lakes is a showcase nine. The Dunes, with its rolling moor-like terrain, is reminiscent of Scottish courses. Using a crossover system, the Arroyo/Lakes stretches out a substantial 6,800/6,252/5,790/5,312 yards. The Dunes/Lakes combination measures 6,614/6,019/4,993 yards, and the Arroyo/Dunes reaches out 6,662/6,113/5,681/5,151 yards. The dining facilities at the golf club are far more than a 19th-hole affair. You should consider at least one evening meal here.

RATES: (EP) Lodging - $405/$455/$515. Green fees - $155, including cart. Golf packages available. Rates are for January through May.

ARRIVAL: By air - Phoenix Sky Harbor Airport (45 minutes). By car - from the airport take 44th Street north to Camelback Road. Turn right on Camelback and proceed east to Scottsdale Road, where you turn left and drive north to DoubleTree Ranch Road.

Loews Ventana Canyon Resort

7000 North Resort Drive, Tucson, AZ 85715

(520) 299-2020; (800) 234-5117

Loews Ventana Canyon Resort has been judged one of the Top 50 resorts. It is situated in one of the prettiest parts of Arizona, the Sonoran Desert, a world of rock spires guarded by stately saguaro cacti.

ACCOMMODATIONS: 400 rooms and suites in a quiet park-like setting. Each room has a private balcony, refrigerator and mini-bar. The hotel is built into the surrounding mountains. Walkways, set above the unusual selection of flora, take you from wing to wing. The natural growth includes almost every type of cactus as well as many desert flowers and shrubs. Indigenous wildlife is also profuse. Bird lovers have not been overlooked – there are cardinals, owls, road runners, hawks and doves, along with about 12 species of hummingbirds.

AMENITIES: Nature trails, two pools with hot tubs, jogging, a tennis complex (10 lighted courts), Jacuzzis, saunas, a health club and, of course, golf. You will not want for food or entertainment as there are several restaurants, including the outstanding Ventana, The Canyon Café, and The Flying V Bar and Night Club for dining and entertainment.

GOLF: The Canyon Course, with a par of 72, measures some 6,818/6,282/5,756/4,919 yards. Although the front nine might well be considered conservative, the back side will challenge any golfer. While water becomes a factor on only two holes, the fact that there is little or no rough becomes important. Should you stray off the lush green fairway you will find yourself in raw desert, home to rock, sand, sagebrush, lizards and, on occasion, snakes. Trying to hit a shot from here may elicit a new and not very pretty vocabulary. The fabulous Mountain Course is once again available. A Fazio design, it reaches out a substantial 6,948/6,356/5,618/4,709 yards with a par of 72. It's a wonderful layout.

RATES: (EP) Rooms - $245/$385/$405/$750. Green fees - $170, including cart. Golf package (one night/one day, including lodging, breakfast, one day green fees, cart, bag storage, tax), $685 per couple. Rates given are for January 1st to April 30th.

ARRIVAL: By air - Tucson. By car - from the airport, head north to Valencia Road, turn right (heading east). Travel to Alvernon Road and turn left (north). Drive to Golf Links and turn right (east) to Swan Road, then turn left (north). Go to Sunrise Drive and turn right (east) to Kolb Road, then turn left (north). Proceed 1½ miles and look for a large rock with the resort name on it.

Marriott's Camelback Inn Resort

5402 E. Lincoln Drive, Scottsdale, AZ 85253

(602) 948-1700; (800) 242-2635

Marriott's Camelback Inn is one of our Top 50 resorts. The inn dates back to 1936, and has been a favorite of many celebrities. Although constantly updated and renovated, Camelback has not lost its grace or subdued splendor. The inn is one of only 21 hotels or resorts in the United States to have continually earned the Mobil Five Star Award.

ACCOMMODATIONS: 423 rooms, including many adobe casitas decorated in a Southwestern motif (seven with private pools). The rooms and suites are beautifully decorated. There is a washer/dryer complex for guest use – an uncommon extra.

AMENITIES: Three pools, 10 tennis courts (five lighted) with a professional to assist, horseback riding nearby, whirlpool baths and a relatively new, 25,000-square-foot European-style health spa. The resort shops are interesting. The dining rooms are among the finest in the Southwest. The Chaparral, while a bit formal, is superb (jackets required, ties optional). The Navajo Room, less formal but also outstanding, is available for all three meals. There is also the North Pool for casual dining. Should you have an early tee time, consider breakfast at the country club. Again, both the service and the food are excellent.

GOLF: Realizing that their golf facilities were aging and in need of updating, Marriott invested $16 million in the golf courses and in construction of an outstanding new 22,000-square-foot clubhouse.

The Indian Bend layout, now called the Club Course, lies in the shadow of Mummy Mountain and underwent little change. Parring at 72, it reaches out a monstrous 7,014/6,486/5,917 yards. There is little water in play here, but the undulating fairways, trees and fast greens will more than keep your attention.

The Padre Course, now called the Resort Course, was redesigned by Arthur Hill. He rebuilt every tee, green and bunker, removed many trees and planted others. Don't be misled; he did not make it easier. But, with some deep pot bunkers and other innovations, he surely made it more interesting. Playing to par of 72, it reaches out 6,868/6,421/6,014/5,069 yards.

RATES: (EP) Lodging - $419/$725. MAP or FAP plans and golf packages are offered. Green fees - $137/$195, including cart. Rates are for January-May.

ARRIVAL: By air - Sky Harbor International Airport. By car - north on Scottsdale Road, left on Lincoln Drive.

Marriott's Mountain Shadows

641 E. Lincoln Drive, Scottsdale, AZ 85253

(602) 948-7111; (800) 782-2123

ACCOMMODATIONS: 354 rooms, including six suites. The resort lies in a beautiful setting, literally in the shadow of Camelback Mountain.

AMENITIES: Eight lighted tennis courts, a steam room, sauna, masseur/masseuse, two pools, and a fitness center. Horseback riding is available nearby. For dining, choose from Shells Restaurant or Cactus Flower. The restaurant at the country club is also open to guests of Mountain Shadows.

GOLF: Their 18-hole, par-56 course comes complete with a stream (some refer to it as a waterfall), which is highly unusual for this desert area. You can also play on the two fabulous Camelback golf courses. For details on the Resort Course and Club Course, see the listing for Marriott's Camelback Inn.

RATES: (EP) Lodging - $240/$820. Golf packages are offered. Green fees - Mountain Shadows, $60/$74, including cart;. Camelback, $137/$172, including cart. Rates are for January through May.

ARRIVAL: By air - Sky Harbor International Airport (approximately 20 minutes). By car - from Scottsdale Road, turn west onto Lincoln Drive.

The Omni Tucson National Resort & Spa

2727 West Club Drive, Tucson, AZ 85741

(520) 297-2271; (800) 528-4856

ACCOMMODATIONS: 51 casita rooms, 116 villas and a townhouse, all with private patios, wet bars and refrigerators. Twenty-seven of the Executive Casitas have a living room, bedroom and kitchen.

AMENITIES: Few spas in the world offer the variety of services available at the National, with deluxe massages, facials, herbal wraps, and special therapies. Dining is provided in the casual setting of the Fiesta.

GOLF: There are 27 holes to play, the Gold, Orange and the Green nines. When inter-joined to form 18 holes, you have Orange/Gold at 7,108/6,549/5,764 yards with a par of 72/73. The Green/Orange combination weighs in at 6,692/6,215/5,428 yards, parring at 72. The Gold/Green nines play 6,860/6,388/5,502 and par at 72/73. Water hazards and bunkers make each an interesting and challenging affair.

RATES: (EP) Lodging - $300/$335/$390. Green fees - $125, including cart. Rates are for January-May 15.

ARRIVAL: By air - Tucson (30 to 45 minutes). By car - take I-10 to Cortaro exit, travel 3½ miles and you are there.

Orange Tree Golf Resort

10601 North 56th Street, Scottsdale, AZ 85254

(602) 948-6100; (800) 228-0386

ACCOMMODATIONS: 160 oversize, soundproofed rooms and two executive suites. Following a Southwestern architectural style, the rooms have been arranged in a series of two-story villas, with the majority enjoying a view of the course. There is a 27" cable-equipped TV set in each room plus a 9" TV in the bathroom so you won't miss your favorite soap while relaxing in the two-person whirlpool spa. Each of the rooms has either a private patio or a deck. Opened in January of 1989, this golf and conference center was developed on a beautiful 128-acre site.

AMENITIES: 25,000 square-foot Racquet & Fitness Club, 16 lighted, all-weather tennis courts, eight racquetball courts, aerobics center, Nautilus workout equipment, heated pool, therapy spas and a sauna. Dining is offered in Joe's American Grill & Bar. There is also the more casual Fairway Pavilion at the course itself.

GOLF: Designed by Johnny Bulla, the Orange Tree Golf Course stretches 6,837/6,398/5,618 yards and pars at 72. While relatively flat, it is well trapped and has enough trees to create a definite series of challenges.

RATES: (EP) Rooms - $175/$200. Green fees - $88/$105, including cart. Golf package (one night/one day, including lodging, one round of golf with cart, club storage, all taxes and gratuities), $428 per couple.

ARRIVAL: By air - Phoenix Sky Harbor Airport (13 miles) or Scottsdale Municipal (four miles). By car - from Scottsdale Airport, drive south to Shea Blvd. Turn west and drive to north 56th. Turn right (north) for one block.

The Phoenician Resort

6000 East Camelback Road, Scottsdale, AZ 85251

(602) 941-8200; (800) 888-8234

The Phoenician Resort has been judged one of our Top 50 resorts. The Resort is southeast of Camelback Mountain. With its profusion of plantings, along with pools and waterfalls, it seems to belie its desert setting.

ACCOMMODATIONS: 567 guest rooms, 73 suites and seven villas. All with patios or balconies. To say these accommodations are deluxe may well be the understatement of the year.

AMENITIES: Health spa, 12 tennis courts (including a stadium court), eight swimming pools, a 22,000-square-foot fitness center along with steam, sauna, whirlpool and Swiss showers. Horseback riding is available nearby. The various restaurants include Mary Elaine's Dining Room (jackets for men required at this dining room only), the Outdoor Terrace, and The Windows on the Green.

Lighter fare is also available poolside and at the Oasis. One of several lounges, this one located in the lobby, has been named "The Thirsty Camel." There is also a children's program for ages five to 12.

GOLF: The course was originally designed by Homer Flint with an additional nine added by Ted Robinson, Sr. Using a crossover system, you can choose from several combinations. The Desert/Canyon 18 plays 6,068/5,691/4,777 yards. The Desert part of this combination brings water into contention on only one hole, while the Canyon nine shows you wet stuff on four. The Canyon/Oasis reaches out 6,258/5,839/4,871 yards, with the Oasis nine bringing water into play on eight holes. The final joining of nines, the Oasis/Desert, plays 6,310/5,482/5,024 yards. They represent an exceptionally tailored and manicured golf facility. The entire layout is well bunkered and enjoys undulating terrain. No matter how you match the various nines you wind up with a par of 70.

RATES: (EP) Lodging - $525/$665. Suites - $1,350 and up. Green fees - $170, including cart. There are many different package plans available. Rates are for January through June.

ARRIVAL: By air - Phoenix Sky Harbor Airport (nine miles).

The Pointe Hilton on South Mountain

7777 S. Pointe Parkway, Phoenix, AZ 85044

(602) 438-9000; (800) 934-1000

ACCOMMODATIONS: Two-room, presidential, or concierge-level suites (638 in total), each with refrigerator, honor bar, two phones, two TV sets and private balcony. Built adjacent to South Mountain preserve, the resort is just minutes from the airport and the valley's business center. The resort is Mediterranean in style, with shaded walkways, fountains, and very impressive grounds.

AMENITIES: Seven outdoor pools, 10 Plexipave tennis courts, indoor racquetball courts, weight machines, LifeCycles, StairMasters, rowers and treadmills. They also offer a sports medical clinic, massage therapy, steam rooms and saunas. The resort has its own stable and the surrounding area presents excellent riding conditions. There are several dining options: Rustler's Roost; Aunt Chilada's; Another Pointe in Tyme; and the Sports Club, for lighter fare.

GOLF: The Pointe Golf Club reaches out a modest 6,003/5,400/ 4,700 yards and pars at 70. The designers were extremely careful to maintain the character of the Sonora landscape; they included over 100 different species of wildflowers and every form of cactus known to exist in Arizona. These include 300-year-old saguaros, some weighing up to eight tons.

RATES: (EP) Suites - $159/$239/$259. Green fees - $100/$150, including cart. Golf packages are available. Rates shown are for January through April and are substantially less at other times.

ARRIVAL: By air - Sky Harbor Airport (Phoenix). By car - from the airport, take I-17 south. Get off at Baseline and drive to 58th Street, where you turn right. The resort is on your left.

The Pointe Hilton at Tapatio Cliffs

11111 North 7th Street, Phoenix, AZ 85020

(602) 866-7500; (800) 934-1000

ACCOMMODATIONS: 584 suites, 230 of which are built into the surrounding mountainside. Each air-conditioned unit features a private patio or balcony, two phones, two TV sets, and a stocked mini-bar. Some have a woodburning fireplace. A washer/dryer facility is available for guest use. Laid out much like a small village, the Tapatio Cliffs resort is in the northeast end of the valley.

AMENITIES: 15 tennis courts, four racquetball courts, six pools, (including a lap-pool), horseback riding, fitness center with state-of-the-art equipment, steam, sauna and massage therapy. There are three different dining facilities: the Different Pointe of View, the Chuckwagon Saloon and the clubhouse Pointe In Tyme.

GOLF: The Lookout Mountain course plays a respectable 6,617/ 5,834/4,552 yards, with a par of 72. There are only three holes with water, but the unexpected and numerous elevation changes will give you all the challenge you might wish for.

RATES: (EP) Two-room suites - $169/$289. Green fees - $142, including cart. Golf package (two nights/two days, including lodging, two rounds of golf with cart, bag storage, full breakfast), $843 per couple. Rates are for January through April.

ARRIVAL: By air - Sky Harbor Airport (Phoenix). By car - take I-10 to I-17 north and exit at Thunderbird Road east. Drive to 7th Street and turn right. The resort is on your left.

The Radisson Resort

7171 North Scottsdale Road, Scottsdale, AZ 85253

(602) 991-3800; (800) 333-3333

ACCOMMODATIONS: 318 rooms, including 34 suites, all of which are impeccably furnished. There are complimentary in-room movies. All rooms have a mini-bar and most have wet bars and refrigerators. There are two coin-operated washer/dryer complexes on the property.

AMENITIES: 21 tennis courts (all lighted), horseback riding nearby, three pools and a health spa. The restaurants include La Champagne, open seasonally, and Café Brioche for more casual dining. There is 24-hour room service.

GOLF: There are two 18-hole layouts. The Pines, with a par of 72, plays at 7,013/6,346/5,963/5,367 yards. Water comes into play on six or seven holes and the course has more than its share of trees. The Palms course reaches out a substantial 7,032/6,279/5,820/5,210, also parring at 72. With water in contention on nine holes and some of the toughest par-3 holes you would ever want to tangle with, this is a real challenge.

RATES: (EP) Lodging - $259/$309. Green fees - $129 including cart. Golf packages are available. Rates are for January to mid-May.

ARRIVAL: By air - Phoenix. By car - from the airport, take 44th Street north to Lincoln. Turn right (east) and drive to your right.

Rancho De Los Caballeros

1551 S Vulture Mine Road, Wickenburg, AZ 85358

(520) 684-5484; (800) 684-5036

ACCOMMODATIONS: Rooms in the inn, plus 14 one- to four-bedroom bungalows decorated with memories of the Old West. There are a total of 79 spacious rooms and suites. It can get quite cool in the evenings, so warm clothing (sweater or jacket) is recommended. The name is appropriate, as the resort is set on 20,000 acres of rolling foothills and was at one time a working ranch. It is open only October through May each year.

AMENITIES: Riding (80-horse stable), desert cookouts, complimentary tennis on four courts, skeet/trap shooting, square dances, swimming and, of course, golf. Meals are served in the main dining room, which offers an imaginative and varied menu.

GOLF: Played on the Los Caballeros 18-hole course. With a yardage of 6,965/6,577/5,896, it pars at 72/73. The course circles the entire resort and comes complete with lakes, traps and trees.

RATES: (FAP) Lodgings - $359/$499. Green fees - $90, including cart. Golf package (three nights/four days, including lodging in a Ranch Room, FAP, golf or riding each day), $1,896 per couple. Rates quoted are for February-May.

ARRIVAL: By air - Phoenix. By private aircraft - Wickenburg (4,200-foot paved runway) or the Rancho (2,600 feet). By car - an hour's drive northwest of Phoenix on Highway 60/89, two miles west of Wickenburg on Highway 60.

Regal McCormick Ranch

7401 North Scottsdale Road, Scottsdale, AZ 85253

(602) 948-5050; (800) 243-1332

Once internationally known for breeding and training Arabian horses, the McCormick Ranch has an unusual setting for the desert. It is located on the shores of a lake.

ACCOMMODATIONS: 125 rooms and suites, plus 51 fully equipped two- and three-bedroom condominium villas. These villas are quite large, with some ranging up to 2,200 square feet.

AMENITIES: Heated pool, a whirlpool, four lighted tennis courts, horseback riding nearby, biking, sailing and fishing on 40-acre Camelback Lake. Dining is provided in the Piñon Grille and the colorful terrace. Food and service here are well above average.

GOLF: The Palm Course reaches out a substantial 7,032/6,279/5,820/5,210 yards with a par of 72. The Pine Course, stretching out 7,013/6,346/5,963/5,367 yards, also pars at 72. There is enough water on both courses for you to increase your sailing skills.

RATES: (EP) Hotel - $279/$299. Green fees - $125/$135, including cart. Golf packages are available. Rates are for January to through April.

ARRIVAL: By air - Phoenix (25 minutes). By car - from the airport take 44th Street north to McDonald. Turn right (east) and drive to Scottsdale Blvd. A left turn will bring you to the resort's entrance on your right.

Renaissance Cottonwoods Resort

6160 North Scottsdale Road, Scottsdale, AZ 85253

(602) 991-1414; (800) 468-3571

ACCOMMODATIONS: 170 casitas plus a 2,200-square-foot hacienda. The units range from a basic bedroom to the deluxe Phoenix suite arrangement with a fully equipped kitchen, living room, a beehive woodburning fireplace, mini-bar, and a private patio with a hot tub.

AMENITIES: Four all-weather tennis courts (two lighted), two pools, ping pong, shuffleboard, bicycle rentals, desert mountain jeep tours, and jogging on the Paracourse Trail. Horseback riding is nearby. There is an excellent restaurant (Moriah), serving classic Southwestern specialities.

GOLF: The resort has a working arrangement with four nearby courses (less than two miles away). Two beautiful Camelback Resort courses and the two great 18-hole layouts at the Regal McCormick Ranch Resort are at your disposal. For details on these refer to the appropriate resort in this book.

RATES: (EP) Lodging - $258/$335. Green fees, including cart - McCormick Ranch, $135; Camelback Golf Club, $135.

ARRIVAL: By air - Phoenix Airport. By car - from the airport take Exit 44 north to McDonald. Turn east and travel to Scottsdale Road. Turn left (north); the resort is at the intersection of Rose Lane and Scottsdale Road.

The Resort Suites

7677 E. Princess Blvd., Scottsdale, AZ 85255

(602) 585-1234; (800) 858-5786

ACCOMMODATIONS: One- to four-bedroom suites, each fully equipped for housekeeping. Two- and four-bedroom units also have

Arizona

a washer/dryer. Located on the grounds of the Scottsdale Princess Hotel, the suites enjoy a wonderful setting.

AMENITIES: Three swimming pools, bicycle rentals, dining room and lounge. The outstanding dining facilities at the Princess Hotel are also at your disposal.

GOLF: The Scottsdale Princess courses are less than a quarter-mile away. For details, refer to the text on the Princess Resort. The Resort Suites has made arrangements for guests to play on a selection of some 40 different layouts, ranging from the Wigwam to the Sedona and many others.

RATES: (EP) Lodgings - $235/$475. Golf packages are also available. They offer a golf school package.

ARRIVAL: By air - Scottsdale or Phoenix.

Rio Rico Resort & Country Club

1069 Camino Caralampi, Rio Rico, AZ 85648

(520) 281-1901; (800) 288-4746

ACCOMMODATIONS: 180 rooms and suites. The magnificent scenery provided by the Santa Cruz Mountains is one of the more spectacular sights in Arizona.

AMENITIES: Four lighted tennis courts, an Olympic-size pool, riding and trap shooting. The hotel dining room serves Mexican cuisine, seafood and steaks.

GOLF: The Robert Trent Jones, Jr. course stretches out an awesome 7,119/6,426/5,577 yards and pars at 72/71. It has an interesting layout with undulating terrain on the back side, a rather flat front nine and a liberal supply of water coming into play.

RATES: (EP) Lodging - $165/$185. Green fees - $55, including cart. Golf package (one night/one day, including lodging, MAP, golf with cart, bag storage), weekdays $260 per couple. Rates are for January-April.

ARRIVAL: By car - 57 miles south of Tucson and 12 miles north of Nogales on I-19, Calabasas exit.

Rio Verde/Tonto Verde Resort

18815 Four Peaks Boulevard, Rio Verde, AZ 85263

(480) 471-1962; (800) 233-7103

ACCOMMODATIONS: Private homes located either on or near one of the three 18-hole courses. They range in size from two to three bedrooms and have two baths, a kitchen (fully equipped for housekeeping), a barbecue unit and a washer/dryer. The backdrop of the beautiful McDowell, Superstition and Mazatzal mountains provides a spectacular setting.

AMENITIES: Six tennis courts (two lighted) and two pools. The new 17,000-square-foot clubhouse features a cocktail lounge and restaurant.

GOLF: Reaching out 6,524/6,228/5,558 yards, the Quail Run course pars at 72. It is well bunkered, with water hazards in play on eight holes. The second 18, the White Wing Course, measures 6,456/6,053/5,465 yards, with a par of 71. Both courses operate from the new pro shop. For tee times, call (602) 471-9420.

While the Quail and White courses are fun, neither is of championship caliber. The new Tonto Verde Golf Course, designed by David Graham and Gary Panks, is most definitely a championship affair. Playing to a yardage of 6,737/6,342/5,952/5,376/4,791, it pars at 72. It is supported by a 28,000-square-foot clubhouse and surrounded by an 18-hole putting course. If you have not played this type of putting layout, you might try it – not only for fun but to help your putting game.

RATES: (EP) Casa Bonita - $900/$1,100 weekly. Hacienda - $1,100/$1,700 weekly. Green fees - $90, including cart. Rates are for mid-December to mid-April. Golf packages are available.

ARRIVAL: By air - Phoenix. By car - take Scottsdale to Shea Blvd., turn east (right) and travel 13 miles to Fountain Hill Blvd. Take a left, continue 12 miles to Forrest Road and you have arrived.

Scottsdale Pima Suites

7330 North Pima Road, Scottsdale, AZ 85258

(602) 948-3800; (800) 344-0262

ACCOMMODATIONS: 93 air-conditioned rooms, including 53 two-room suites, each with a guest service bar and private patio.

Suites have fully equipped kitchens and feature dining spaces and private covered patios.

AMENITIES: Heated pool. Horseback riding and hayrides can be arranged nearby. Dining is available in The Patio Room, with cocktails served in The Sand Trap Lounge.

GOLF: A championship layout is across the street. Playing 6,952/6,449/5,722, it pars at 72/73. This layout is fun to navigate. The course is well bunkered and brings water into play on 10 holes.

RATES: (EP) Rooms - $99/$114/$149. Green fees - $75, including cart. Rates are for January through April.

ARRIVAL: By air - Phoenix. By car - North Pima Road runs north and south and is due east of Scottsdale Road.

Sheraton San Marcus

1 San Marcus Place, Chandler, AZ 85224

(602) 963-6655; (800) 325-3535

ACCOMMODATIONS: 295 rooms and suites, 45 overlooking the golf course and 250 in the new sections. There are also 11 executive suites. The original San Marcus structure was completed in 1912.

AMENITIES: Tennis, two pools, whirlpool, horseback riding nearby, jogging, bicycling and a fitness center. The restaurants include the 1912 Room and A.J.'s Café. There is also Mulligan's Bar & Grill adjacent to the 18th green.

GOLF: A traditional layout with a par of 72/73, the course reaches out 6,501/6,172/5,386 yards. While not heavily trapped, there is more than enough sand and, as usual, it seems to be in the wrong place. Water in play on eight holes is also a factor.

RATES: (EP) Rooms - $255/$275/$425. Green fees - $55/$75, including cart.

ARRIVAL: By air - Sky Harbor International. By car - Exit I-10 at Chandler Blvd. Travel east to the intersection of Chandler Blvd. and Arizona Avenue. Turn right and the resort is one block on your right.

Sheraton Tucson El Conquistador

10000 North Oracle Road, Tucson, AZ 85737

(520) 544-5000; (800) 325-7832

ACCOMMODATIONS: 428 rooms, suites and casitas, all done in a beautiful and impressive Western Spanish architectural style.

AMENITIES: 16 lighted tennis courts, four racquetball courts, health club with a full spa program, a pool and riding stables. Dining facilities include the White Dove, the Last Territory and the Sundance Café.

GOLF: Played on the El Conquistador nine, a par-3 course contiguous to the hotel, and the Canada Hills Country Club course, a few miles away. The Club layout plays 6,698/6,215/5,316 yards and pars at 72. Relatively open, the course is both fun and demanding.

RATES: (EP) Lodging - $249/$398. Suites - $329/$1,000. Green fees - $99, including cart. Golf packages available. Rates are for January-May.

ARRIVAL: By air - Tucson. By car: take I-10 north, turn off at Miracle, then head east to Oracle Road, then north.

Starr Pass Golf Club

3645 West Starr Pass Blvd. (West 22nd Street), Tucson, AZ 85745

(520) 670-0500; (800) 503-2898

ACCOMMODATIONS: 115 rooms. The casitas range from one-bedroom suites, two-bedroom units (equipped for housekeeping, and with fireplace and washer/dryer) to master suites, also with fireplace and washer/dryer. Starr Pass enjoys a picturesque setting with a beautiful view of Tucson.

AMENITIES: Tennis courts, complete fitness center, hiking trails, horseback riding, a very large pool and a delightful dining room and lounge.

GOLF: Situated on undulating terrain, the Starr Pass course was designed by Robert Cupp. It reaches 6,910/6,193/5,665/5,071 yards with a par of 71. It is well bunkered, with the usual desert distraction of large cactus growth and raw desert area.

RATES: (EP) - $179/$309/$429 per couple. Golf Package (two nights/two days, including lodging, unlimited golf with cart for one round, bag storage), $641/$757 per couple.

ARRIVAL: By air - Tucson Airport (13 miles). By car - from I-10, exit at Starr Pass Boulevard (west 22nd Street). Drive three miles west to resort.

Tubac Golf Resort

PO Box 1297, Tubac, AZ 85646

(520) 398-2211; (800) 848-7893

ACCOMMODATIONS: Casitas with woodburning fireplace, one bedroom, and living room; some with full kitchen. There are also two-bedroom/two-bath villas, each with living room and kitchen. The full villas are handled by a local real estate firm; call (602) 398-2701 for information. The inn is situated on the original Otero Spanish Land Grant in the lush Santa Cruz Valley, just 25 miles from the Mexican border.

AMENITIES: Tennis court, large pool and horseback riding. The Otero and Santa Cruz Dining Rooms are well known throughout the area for their food and service.

GOLF: The Santa Cruz River forms the main challenge of this course, bringing water into play on five holes. Trees and many traps also keep your attention. Reaching out a strong 6,957/6,408/5,847/5,504 yards, it pars at 72/71.

RATES: (EP) Lodging - $185/$195. Weekly/monthly rates and golf packages available. Green fees - $65, including carts. Rates are mid-January to April 15th.

ARRIVAL: By air - Tucson or Nogales. By car - head south from Tucson on Highway 19. Get off at Exit 34.

Ventana Canyon Golf & Racquet Club

6200 N Clubhouse Lane, Tucson, AZ 85715

(520) 577-1400; (800) 828-5701

This 1,100-acre property north of Tucson is set high in the Sonoran Desert, using the Santa Catalina Mountains as a spectacular backdrop.

ACCOMMODATIONS: 49 suites within the clubhouse. Each of the one- or two-bedroom units features a fully equipped kitchen and a living/dining area.

AMENITIES: 12 lighted all-weather tennis courts, a pool, aerobic and exercise facilities, saunas, steam baths and whirlpool baths. The two restaurants in the clubhouse are the Terrace Lounge (casual dining) and the Main Dining Room.

GOLF: The Ventana Canyon Mountain course, a Tom Fazio design, reaches a substantial 6,948/6,356/5,618/4,709 yards and pars at 72. While water only comes into play on two holes, the desert terrain, complete with a tremendous number of cacti and trees, plus a profusion of traps, more than makes up for the water oversight. I would particularly like to warn you about hole number three. This par 3 plays a short 104 yards, with the green at least 70 feet below the tee. It is easy to misjudge distance and to do so can lead to disaster.

The par-72 Canyon Course is also a Fazio design. A bit more modest, it measures 6,818/6,282/5,756/4,919 yards. Something that becomes a problem on both courses is the fact that there is really no rough. Should you stray off that beautiful green stuff you will come into contact with raw desert rocks, sand, cactus, frustration and, very possibly, bad language.

RATES: (EP) Suites - $349/$499. Green fees - $169, including cart. Golf packages are available.

ARRIVAL: By air - Tucson International Airport. By car - from the airport head north to Valencia Road and turn right (east). Turn left (north) onto Alvernon Road and then right (east) onto Golf Links Road. Turn left on Swan Road, go to Sunrise Drive and turn right (east). Proceed to Kolb Road and turn left (north). Drive about ¾ of a mile; the entrance is on your right.

Arizona

The Westin La Paloma

3800 East Sunrise, Tucson, AZ 85718

(520) 742-6000; (800) 937-8461

The Westin La Paloma has been judged one of our Top 50 resorts. The Southwestern furnishings complement the architecture and suggest a relaxing oasis in the desert. There is a great deal of wildlife to observe.

ACCOMMODATIONS: 487 guest rooms (including 40 suites) arranged in a village setting.

AMENITIES: 12 tennis courts (10 lighted), along with a tennis clubhouse, a racquetball court, two pools (one with swim-up bar), spa, a fully equipped health club, jogging and cycling paths. Dining is provided in The Desert Garden, La Villa and The Courtside Deli. The 35,000-square-foot golf clubhouse has another lovely dining facility.

GOLF: The Country Club's 27-hole golf course is a Jack Nicklaus Signature layout. When played in combination they are as follows: the Hill/Ridge nines reach out 7,017/6,464/5,984/4,878 yards; the Ridge/Canyon nines play an awesome 7,088/6,635/6,011/5,125 yards; the final combination of the Canyon and Hill nines weighs in at 6,997/6,453/5,955/5,057 yards. Each pars at 72. For tee times, call (800) 222-1249. Something different: the resort can provide a "forecaddy" who stays with you throughout your round. He can save his weight in golf balls (and you no small amount of frustration) by directing you away from the hazards, some of which are not readily visible until **after** you have struck the ball.

RATES: (EP) Lodging - $450/$490. Green fees - $165, including cart. Golf package (one night/one day, including lodging, one round of golf, cart, and a caddy) - $525/$565 per couple.

ARRIVAL: By air - Tucson. By car - driving from Phoenix, Exit I-10 at Ima Road and travel east. Ima changes its name to Skyline and later to Sunrise Road. The resort is on your right. Take the second entrance.

The Wigwam Resort

300 Indian School Lane, Litchfield Park, AZ 85340

(623) 935-3811; (800) 327-0396

The Wigwam has been judged one of the Top 50 resorts. They seem to do everything right, and the fact that this magnificent destination resort has also earned the Mobil Five Star Award is no surprise. The property has 475 acres of manicured lawns and flower beds.

ACCOMMODATIONS: 331 rooms, suites or casitas located near either the pool, tennis, golf course, or gardens.

AMENITIES: Patio, large pool (a delightful place for lunch), nine lighted tennis courts and a stadium court, horseback riding and hayrides (from their own stables), complete health club with massage facility and exercise rooms, sauna, and whirlpool. You can also try your hand at skeet and trap shooting. Bicycles, ping-pong tables, and shuffleboard are all complimentary. A second pool has been added adjacent to the newly constructed casitas. The centrally located Main Lodge houses the new Terrace Dining Room. Another recent addition is the Arizona Kitchen restaurant. Jackets are required in the Terrace Room, but the Arizona Kitchen is less formal. Additional dining is offered in the Grille on the Greens, located in the country club.

GOLF: There are three golf courses. The Gold Course stretches out 7,047/6,504/5,567 yards and pars at 72. The West Course, also with a par of 72, reaches out 6,865/6,307/5,808 yards. The Blue Course plays 5,960/5,178 yards and pars at 70. The Gold and Blue courses are Robert Trent Jones, Sr. designs, while the West was designed by the late Robert Lawrence.

RATES: (EP) Lodging - $330/$525 per couple. Green fees - $100/$130, including cart. Golf package mid-week (one night/one day, including lodging, green fees, cart and club storage), $512/$727 per couple. Rates shown are for January to mid-May.

ARRIVAL: By air - Phoenix Sky Harbor Airport (23 miles). By car - take I-10 17 miles west to the Litchfield Road exit. Travel north to Indian School Road and turn east to the resort.

Arizona

Arkansas

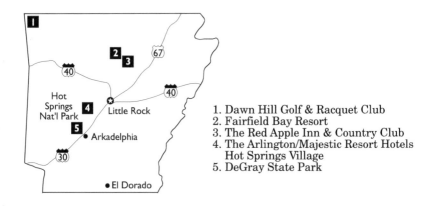

1. Dawn Hill Golf & Racquet Club
2. Fairfield Bay Resort
3. The Red Apple Inn & Country Club
4. The Arlington/Majestic Resort Hotels
   Hot Springs Village
5. DeGray State Park

The Arlington/Majestic Resort Hotels

Hot Springs National Park, AR 71901

Arlington Hotel – (501) 623-7771; (800) 643-1502

Majestic Hotel – (501) 623-5511; (800) 643-1504

ACCOMMODATIONS: This resort complex consists of two hotels – the Arlington and the Majestic. The Arlington has 488 guest rooms, including suites; the Majestic has 310.

AMENITIES: Eight tennis courts (four lighted), pools, sundecks, jogging paths, exercise rooms, game rooms and racquetball. Good fishing is found in the lakes of Hot Springs National Park, including Lake Hamilton and Lake Ouachita. The hotels have long been known for their thermal mineral baths and massages. Dining facilities at the Arlington consist of the Fountain Room, Venetian Room and the Captain's Tavern (a coffee shop). The Majestic offers dining in the H. Grady Dining Room and the more casual Grady's Grill.

GOLF: The Arlington course, reaching out 6,646/6,393/6,206 yards, pars at 72/74. The Majestic course pars at 72 and plays 6,667/6,286/5,541 yards. There is also a nine-hole, par-3 layout, measuring 2,929/2,717 yards.

RATES: (EP) Arlington - $86/$112/$172/$395. The Majestic - $65/$95. Green fees - $56, including carts. Golf packages are available.

ARRIVAL: By air - Little Rock (53 miles). By car - from Little Rock take I-30, connecting with State Highway 70 west. Turn north on Highway 7 and continue past Bath House Row to the resort.

Dawn Hill Golf & Racquet Club

PO Box 1289, Siloam Springs, AR 72761

(501) 524-5217; (800) 423-3786

ACCOMMODATIONS: Two- and three-bedroom townhouse clusters, featuring natural stone fireplaces, loft bedrooms and fully equipped kitchens. Private homes are also available.

AMENITIES: Four lighted tennis courts and a pool. If you decide to dine out, there is a restaurant and cocktail lounge.

GOLF: The Dawn Hill Golf Course. Reaching out 6,768/6,434/5,307 yards, it pars at 72. It is an open layout with little water coming into play.

RATES: (EP) Townhouses - $115/$135. Green fees - $20/$25, carts $22. Golf package (two nights/three days) includes lodging golf, cart breakfast), $236/$276.

ARRIVAL: By air - Siloam Springs (six miles). By car - Route 68 near the Oklahoma border.

DeGray State Park

Box 490, Bismarck, AR 71923

(501) 865-2851; (800) 737-8355

ACCOMMODATIONS: 96 rooms plus full camping facilities. The Lodge, fashioned from redwood and stone, rises magnificently from an island on beautiful DeGray Lake.

AMENITIES: Tennis courts, pool and a 110-boat marina (boats and motors are available to rent). The lake, which covers some 13,500 acres, offers excellent fishing. The Lodge has an outstanding restaurant.

Arkansas

GOLF: Weighing in at a pretty fair 6,930/6,417/5,731 yards, De-Gray State Park Golf Course carries a par of 72. Water comes into play on eight holes.

RATES: (EP) Rooms - $65/$75. Green fees - $15/$16, carts $18.

ARRIVAL: By air - Hot Springs (21 miles). By car - from I-30, exit to Highway 7 and head northwest for six miles.

Fairfield Bay Resort

PO Box 3008, Fairfield Bay, AR 72088

(501) 884-3333

ACCOMMODATIONS: 350 bedrooms, suites, villas and condominiums. Villas and condos are equipped for housekeeping. Fairfield Bay Resort is in the foothills of the Ozarks.

AMENITIES: Ten tennis courts (four lighted), two pools, health club, racquet club, horseback riding, youth recreation center, marina (180 boat slips), beach area, and two restaurants.

GOLF: The Mountain Ranch golf course has a par of 72 and plays 6,780/6,280/5,760/5,325 yards. Its tree-lined fairways, with water coming into play on only two holes, are a nice change from the "Pacific Ocean" type of course. The Indian Hills Country Club layout, parring at 71, weighs in at 6,437/5,727/4,901 yards. Water presents a challenge on seven holes.

RATES: (EP) Lodgings - $125/$155/$230. Green fees - $47/$52, including carts. Golf packages are available.

ARRIVAL: By air - Little Rock. By car - 80 miles north of Little Rock. Entrance is on Highway 16 west of Highway 65.

Hot Springs Village

Box 970, Hot Springs Village, AR 71909

(501) 922-3333; (800) 872-8381

ACCOMMODATIONS: Townhouses or homes, fully equipped for housekeeping, which may be rented by the day, week or month. Some have a fireplace and washer/dryer. Hot Springs Village, 16 miles north of Hot Springs, is a large recreational community.

AMENITIES: 11 tennis courts, two recreational centers with pools and game rooms, and a clubhouse. There is also a marina on

Lake DeSoto. For dining there is the Village Bakery & Sandwich Shop, Mary Lee's Restaurant, the DeSoto Clubhouse and Lounge, the 19th Hole and the Wood-N-Iron Restaurant.

GOLF: There are four 18-hole courses – The DeSoto, The Cortez, The Coronado and the newer Balboa. Three are full 18-hole championship courses, while the Coronado is an executive affair. Eight other courses are within a few miles.

RATES: (EP) Townhouses - $85/$150. Green fees - $45, carts $25. Excellent monthly golf rates are also available.

ARRIVAL: By air - Hot Springs. By car - via Highway 7, approximately 21 miles northeast of Hot Springs.

The Red Apple Inn & Country Club

Eden Isle, Heber Springs, AR 72543

(501) 362-3111; (800) 733-2775

Arkansas

Nestled in the rolling hills of Arkansas and surrounded by 35,000-acre Greers Ferry Lake, the Red Apple Inn is one of the better resorts. Muted and handsome, sprinkled with works of art, fireplaces, patios, fountains and tapestries, it is a delightful place.

ACCOMMODATIONS: Rooms and suites appointed with hand-carved furniture from Italy and Spain. There are also one- to three-bedroom condominiums, each featuring fireplace, living room/dining room, fully equipped kitchen and private deck.

AMENITIES: Water-skiing, sailing, lake swimming, five tennis courts (three lighted), two pools and fishing. A Spanish gate, retrieved from an ancient castle, welcomes you to the After Five Room for cocktails. Once you experience the main dining room's touch of French cuisine with a Southern accent, you will understand why the restaurant has earned the Mobil Four Star Award. The same kitchen now serves a second dining room, so you can choose from either a formal (jacket and tie required) or casual atmosphere.

GOLF: Stretching out to 6,431/6,006/5,137 yards and parring at 71, the Red Apple's course brings water into play on five holes on the front nine. Architect Gary Parks blended the rolling terrain and tree-lined fairways to create an interesting layout.

RATES: (EP) Lodgings - $99/$115/$145. Green fees - $35, carts $22. Rates are for April-October.

ARRIVAL: By air - Little Rock. By car - take Highway 65 to Highway 25 and turn right.

California

Northern California

1. Northstar at Tahoe
2. Resort at Squaw Creek
3. Bodega Bay Lodge/The Inn At The Tides
4. Sonoma County Hilton
5. Silverado
6. Half Moon Bay Lodge
7. Pasatiempo Inn
8. Carmel Valley Ranch Resort/Quail Lodge/Hyatt Regency Monterey/ The Inn & Links at Spanish Bay/ The Lodge at Pebble Beach
9. Furnace Creek Inn & Ranch Resort

Bodega Bay – Sonoma Coast Area

The history of this coastal area goes back a long way. Claimed by Sir Francis Drake in 1579, by Juan Francisco de la Bodega in 1775, later by Russia, and eventually by the US in 1846, it is a world apart. The marshy seaside area teems with birds and wildflowers and is one of the few peaceful, laid-back places left in this extremely busy state.

There are many outstanding places to eat here as well as a number of wineries to visit. Rather than golfing, one could spend days perusing the historic buildings, restored villages, art galleries and antique stores.

The **Bodega Harbour Golf Links** was created by Robert Trent Jones, Jr. While there are virtually no trees on the course, this is more than compensated for by 58 pot bunkers on the first nine and 38 on the back side. Using the undulating terrain, multi-level greens and prevailing winds off the ocean, Mr. Jones introduced some unique challenges. All in all, this course is one of the most fun layouts we have experienced in California. Parring at 70/71, it reaches out a modest 6,220/5,630/4,833 yards. For tee times, call (707) 875-3538.

Accommodations are available in two motels. Both are close by and offer golf packages. Details on the Bodega Bay Lodge and The Inn at the Tides are listed below.

Bodega Bay Lodge

103 Coast Highway 1, Bodega Bay, CA 94923

(707) 875-3525; (800) 368-2468, Ext. 5

ACCOMMODATIONS: 78 rooms, most with fireplace, vaulted ceilings, cooler/refrigerator, wet bar, and wicker and oak furnishings.

AMENITIES: Glass-walled whirlpool spa, pool, sauna, and exercise room. Located nearby are facilities for deep-sea fishing and whale watching (in season). There are also bicycle trips and beachcombing. Dining is in the Ocean Club Restaurant.

GOLF: Bodega Harbor Golf Links.

RATES: (EP) Lodgings - $200/$400/$475. Green fees - $55/$65, carts $30. Golf package (one night/one day, including lodging, one round of golf, tax) - midweek only, $295.

ARRIVAL: By air - San Francisco International Airport (two hours), or Santa Rosa Airport (35 minutes). By car - from San Francisco, cross the Golden Gate Bridge (Highway 101) and continue to Petaluma. Take E. Washington Street/Bodega Avenue west to Highway 1.

The Inn at the Tides

800 Coast Highway 1, Bodega Bay, CA 94923

(707) 875-2751; (800) 541-7788

ACCOMMODATIONS: 86 rooms, each with a small refrigerator, coffee maker, TV and a woodburning fireplace.

AMENITIES: Indoor/outdoor pool, sauna, whirlpool. Beachcombing is popular along this fabulous coast. The Bayview Restaurant serves a wide variety of dishes, but highlights fresh seafood. Directly across the highway from the entrance is the Tides Wharf & Restaurant.

GOLF: Bodega Harbor Golf Links.

RATES: (EP) Rooms - $159/$239. Green fees - $55/$65, carts $30. Golf package – one night/one day, including lodging, 18 holes per person, continental breakfast – $240 per couple. Rates are for June-September.

ARRIVAL: By air - San Francisco (two hours) or Santa Rosa (40 minutes). By car - from San Francisco, cross the Golden Gate Bridge (Highway 101) and continue to Petaluma. Take E. Washington Street/Bodega Avenue west to Highway 1.

The Monterey Peninsula Area

Monterey, Pacific Grove, Carmel and Carmel Valley represent a treasure box of intriguing shops, along with restaurants that utterly destroy your will to remain slim. There are a seemingly infinite number of art galleries, photographic studios, antique shops and more. Many of the items are made by talented local artists. But then, not everyone likes to shop. So how about a visit to Monterey's museums of history, literature (including the John Steinbeck Library) and art?

You can tour the exciting Monterey Aquarium or any of the numerous wineries. If music is your thing, there is the Carmel Bach Festival, the Monterey Symphony, the Chamber Music Society, the Monterey Jazz Festival or the Monterey Mozart Festival. And you should not miss the famous Carmel Mission.

If none of these activities appeals to you, then consider sailing or kayaking in magnificent Monterey Bay, hot air ballooning, or a helicopter tour over Big Sur and the entire Peninsula. There is also Steinbeck's Cannery Row, Fisherman's Wharf, whale watching, fishing, and the beaches of fabled Carmel-by-the-Sea.

I have saved the best for the last – a ride along the enchanting 17 Mile Drive. It takes in the beach area of Carmel, the white sand, deer so sure of themselves they almost come to you, quail, ducks, and rabbits, and the overwhelming Pacific Ocean.

California

Adding to the magic of this area are five fabulous resorts: Carmel Valley Ranch, Hyatt Regency Monterey, the Inn & Links at Spanish Bay, the Lodge at Pebble Beach, and Quail Lodge.

Carmel Valley Ranch

One Old Ranch Road, Carmel, CA 93923

(831) 625-9500; (800) 422-7635

On 1,700 acres in the scenic Carmel Valley, the entire complex is nestled high above the clubhouse and the front nine. One of the most remarkable architectural achievements was the siting of the buildings within a huge grove of venerable old oak trees. It is an outstanding part of the resort.

ACCOMMODATIONS: 100 luxurious suites, as well as a beautiful main lodge. The suites, built in clusters of four to five, feature fully stocked wet bars (including refrigerators with icemakers). Each also has a living room, woodburning fireplace (some in the bedrooms), cathedral ceilings throughout, and private decks with views of the mountains, fairways and the valley. Eight of the one-bedroom suites include a private outdoor spa. Plans call for several new clusters to be added. All in all they are extremely posh.

AMENITIES: Tennis program (13 courts), two freeform pools and six spas. A dining room and lounge as well as the golf clubhouse are available for breakfast, lunch and afternoon cocktails. Now luncheon can be enjoyed poolside at the main lodge.

GOLF: The course, a Pete Dye design, plays 6,234/5,563/5,046/4,337 yards with a par of 70. A typical Dye layout, it has small greens, some surrounded by sand traps with railroad ties forming a border. There are also three man-made lakes and the Carmel River, which runs alongside four additional fairways. The back nine has been substantially modified and improved. In fact, holes 11, 12, and 13 are now a pleasure to navigate. The course takes full advantage of the elevation changes as well as the rolling terrain. The one adjective you won't use to describe the Ranch Course is "easy." The golf facilities are under the direction of Director of Golf Andy Cude.

RATES: (EP) Suites - $390/$575/$605/$800. Green fees - $135, including cart. Golf packages are available.

ARRIVAL: By air - Monterey. By car - take US Highway 1 south just past the turnoff to Carmel and take a left (east) onto Carmel Valley Road. Continue for six miles and exit to the right onto Robinson Canyon Road. This turnoff is difficult to find. It is just beyond the shopping center on your right.

Hyatt Regency Monterey

One Golf Course Drive, Monterey, CA 93940

(831) 372-1234; (800) 233-1234

The hotel has one of the loveliest settings we've seen, surrounded by cypress, pine and gnarled oaks.

ACCOMMODATIONS: Located in 26 guest buildings are 575 guest rooms, some quite lavish.

AMENITIES: Two pools and six tennis courts (two lighted). Although you are in "Steinbeck Country," where superb food is commonplace, the Peninsula Restaurant at the hotel more than holds its own. A nice extra: there are coin-operated laundry facilities available.

GOLF: In May of 1997 the course celebrated its 100th year of operation and is the oldest course west of the Mississippi. It has hosted such famous players as Vardon, Hagen, Hogan and Bobby Jones. Playing 6,339/6,069/5,526 yards, it pars at 72/74. It is lined heavily with trees and is one of the most beautiful courses in the area. While it is extremely well trapped - a real plus - there is no water in play. Several other golf layouts, including Pebble Beach and Spyglass, are at your disposal, provided tee times are available – which can sometimes be very difficult.

RATES: (EP) Lodgings - $210/$245. Green fees -$70, carts $36. The Hyatt offers special room rates from time to time. Be sure to check.

ARRIVAL: By air - Monterey. By car - take Pacific Grove exit from Highway 1. Travel on Del Monte Road to Sloat Avenue, turn left and continue to entrance of the Hyatt Regency Monterey.

California

The Inn & Links at Spanish Bay

17 Mile Drive, Pebble Beach, CA 93953

(831) 647-7500; (800) 654-9300

ACCOMMODATIONS: 270 rooms, including 16 suites. Each has a gas-burning fireplace and mini-bar. All feature a deck or balcony with views of the grounds, forest or ocean. In addition, there are 80 privately owned condominiums a bit north of the clubhouse.

AMENITIES: A spa, eight tennis courts (two lighted), a lap pool, saunas and steam rooms. There are three dining rooms, ranging from the rather formal Bay Club to the more casual Dunes Restaurant. The Clubhouse Bar & Grill is another option. As one might well expect, the food and service are excellent.

GOLF: Combining their talents, designers Robert Trent Jones, Jr., Tom Watson and Frank "Sandy" Tatum used narrow, rolling fairways and large sand dunes to create a distinctly Scottish-style golf course. The natural beauty of the area, which has some restored coastal marshes, adds a unique dimension. The course is positioned directly along the ocean with a portion of the famous 17-Mile Drive passing through. It is not unusual to have people stop their cars to watch your tee shot. If you enjoy strong breezes, and I mean constant wind, you will fall in love with this layout. The course plays 6,820/6,078/5,287 yards, parring at 72. The resort can also arrange for guests to play on Pebble Beach and Spyglass.

RATES: (EP) Lodgings - $375/$425/$625 and up. Green fees - $185 (includes cart). Guests of Spanish Bay Inn also have access to golf at Pebble Beach ($300) and Spyglass Hill ($225).

ARRIVAL: By air - Monterey. By car - enter the 17 Mile Drive at the Pacific Grove entrance.

The Lodge at Pebble Beach

17 Mile Drive, Pebble Beach, CA 93953

(831) 624-3811; (800) 654-9300

The Lodge at Pebble Beach has been judged one of the Top 50 resorts. Many things have contributed to its mystique. Perhaps it is the location on the incomparable 17-Mile Drive, the view of the famous Lone Cypress (reputed to be between 200 and 300 years old), an occasional mist and the sound of a distant foghorn, the murmur of the surf, the quiet solitude, or the nostalgia of the Crosby Tournament. Or it may be the extraordinary list of famous guests who have stayed here. Until 1977, it was called The Del Monte Lodge. It is somewhat formal, but that too can be a refreshing change of pace. In recent years, it has actually relaxed somewhat and ties are no longer required in the evening. It has, however, lost none of its charm or elegance since opening in 1919.

ACCOMMODATIONS: 161 guest rooms, including 10 suites. Most are in low-rise buildings and many feature a brick hearth fireplace stocked with almond wood logs. A trip by cart around the course, even if only one of you plays, is well worth the time. The backs of the homes are easy to see without the interference of gates and trees. These homes, many built in the heyday of the flamboyant 20s (before income taxes), are truly something to behold.

AMENITIES: Outdoor heated pool, beach, 14 tennis courts (including a stadium court), two paddle tennis courts, hiking, bicycling, exercise rooms, saunas, massage, steam rooms, aerobics classes, and sailing. The equestrian center is considered one of the best, with 34 miles of bridle paths, rings for dressage and a regulation polo field. You may choose to dine in The Cypress Room, with its magnificent views of Carmel Bay, or try patio dining at Club XIX (jackets required at both restaurants). For a more casual atmosphere, I recommend a visit to The Tap Room, where entertainment and relaxed dining is provided nightly.

GOLF: The fabled Pebble Beach Golf Links plays 6,799/6,357/5,197 yards, parring at 72. Designed by Jack Neville in 1919, it is one of the premier golf layouts in the world. Depending on how the wind changes, it can turn from tough to monstrous.

The Del Monte Forest abounds with deer, and it is not at all unusual to have them cross in front of you on the course. Until a few years ago, Pebble Beach was the home of the Bing Crosby Tournament. It is now the location of the AT&T Pebble Beach National.

If you are a guest of the Lodge, Spyglass Hill (one of the most difficult courses around) is also at your disposal. Rounds can also be arranged at Del Monte (the oldest golf layout west of the Mississippi, circa 1897) and the Links at Spanish Bay.

RATES: (EP) Lodgings - $425/$475/$575. Green fees (for registered guests, including cart) - Pebble Beach, $300; Spyglass, $225; The Links at Spanish Bay, $185. No golf packages are available.

ARRIVAL: By air - Monterey. By car - US 101 to Carmel; San Francisco (130 miles); Los Angeles (330 miles).

California

Quail Lodge

8205 Valley Greens Drive, Carmel, CA 93923

(831) 624-1581; (800) 538-9516

Quail Lodge has been judged one of the Top 50 resorts. Situated in the relative shelter of the Carmel Valley, the Lodge remains warm and sunny on many days when Carmel and Monterey are foggy and cold.

ACCOMMODATIONS: Quail provides a unique choice of lodgings. There are a total of 100 guest accommodations, including 14 suites. The cottage units have five rooms that can be personalized to meet your specific needs: one or two bedrooms plus sitting room, or all five as bedrooms. Each suite has a fireplace, fully-stocked bar and refrigerator, stereo unit with tape deck and a TV. The Executive Villas also feature private outdoor hot tubs.

AMENITIES: Two pools, four tennis courts, or forget the rest of the world, at least for a little while, and enjoy a few moments in an outdoor hot tub. The Covey Restaurant, with its superb selection and quality of food, is one of the reasons that Quail has received the Mobil Five Star Award year after year. Herbs are picked fresh from the chef's courtyard garden minutes before the meal is prepared. The results are wonderful. While the dress code is informal, men are requested to wear jackets when dining in the Covey. A second restaurant in the clubhouse serves breakfast and lunch.

GOLF: A Robert Muir Graves design, the course measures 6,521/6,141/5,453 yards, with a par of 71. A meticulously manicured layout it features strategically placed lakes and bunkers, with the Carmel River wandering throughout. Some of its most delightful distractions are the many deer and birds who, at times, appear to be critiquing your swing. But perhaps I'm getting too sensitive about my game.

RATES: (EP) Lodgings - $305/$900. Green fees - $125, including cart. Golf package (one night/one day, including lodging, golf with cart, breakfast, club storage) - $578 per couple. Package plan rate is available Sunday through Thursday only.

ARRIVAL: By car - South from Monterey, left on Carmel Valley Road, 3½ miles to Valley Greens Drive. Turn right to the Lodge.

Napa Valley Area

Napa Valley is home to a great number of California's best vineyards. Many of these venerable old wineries crafted from hand-hewn stone are worth a visit. I believe there are over 100 of them.

From Napa and Yountville with St. Helena on the north, many excellent and unusual eating experiences await you. A few that I would especially recommend are Domaine Chandon, pricey but outstanding, (707) 944-2892, and Mama Nino, not pricey but delightful, (707) 944-2112.

Silverado

1600 Atlas Peak Road, Napa Valley, CA 94558

(707) 257-0200; (800) 532-0500

ACCOMMODATIONS: Studios to one-, two- or three-bedroom condos. Each condo has a fully equipped kitchen, living room with fireplace, and a balcony.

AMENITIES: Several pools, 23 Plexipave tennis courts (three lighted). Other amenities (boating, horseback riding, racquetball and health center) are quite some distance from the resort. There are two restaurants, The Vintners Court and The Royal Oak.

GOLF: The North Course, stretching out 6,896/6,351/5,857 yards, pars at 72. The South layout measures 6,632/6,213/5,672 yards and also pars at 72. We have played both and found each of them all we could handle. Golf carts are mandatory for guests and, unfortunately, are restricted to the cart paths. **Note:** Members are allowed to walk.

RATES: (EP) Lodgings - $165/$255/$325/$435. Green fees - $125, including cart. Golf package (one night/one day, including lodging and green fees with cart) - $280/$370/$440 per couple.

ARRIVAL: By air - San Francisco (62 miles) or Oakland (50 miles). By private aircraft - Napa (five miles). By car - north end of Napa, east on Trancas Boulevard then left on Atlas Peak Road.

California

Sonoma County Hilton

3555 Round Barn Boulevard, Santa Rosa, CA 95401

(707) 523-7555; (800) 445-8667

The Sonoma County Hilton is in the heart of California's wine country, some 55 miles north of San Francisco.

ACCOMMODATIONS: 247 larger-than-average guest rooms with oversized desks, several phones, and cable TV.

AMENITIES: Pool, whirlpool, and jogging path. Located at the golf course are five tennis courts. Horseback riding is nearby.

GOLF: The Fountain Grove Country Club course stretches out 6,797/6,380/5,644 yards and pars at 72. While winding up and down these beautiful hills is not easy, it is a fun layout to play. Should the course prove too much, there are always the wineries.

RATES: (EP) Lodgings - $96/$115. Green fees - $95, carts included.

ARRIVAL: By air - San Francisco. By car - from San Francisco travel north on Highway 101. Take the Old Redwood Highway/ Mendocino Avenue exit. Stay right. At the first light, swing left up the hill, then take the first left again (up the hill).

Other Northern California Resorts

Furnace Creek Inn & Ranch Resort

PO Box 1, Death Valley, CA 92328

The Inn: (760) 786-2361; (800) 236-7916

Furnace Creek Resort is quite different for a variety of reasons. Although its location in Death Valley is 200 feet below sea level, the lowest point in the contiguous 48 states, you can see the highest point from here as well – Mt. Whitney. Its beauty is highlighted by the valley, one of the bleakest, most inhospitable places on earth.

There is much to do and see here, including the Borax Museum, the visitor's center and the fascinating geology. Due to the arid conditions, the landscape has remained virtually unchanged for thousands of years. If at all possible, schedule time to visit Scotty's Castle.

ACCOMMODATIONS: The inn enjoys a spectacular setting. It is a Spanish villa-style hotel built directly into the mountain, well above the Ranch, with sheer cliffs rising behind the entire structure. The guest rooms are at various levels.

AMENITIES: Fully equipped health room, a lovely pool (the spring-fed water is at a constant 83°), horseback and bicycle riding as well as hiking. The dining room is, to say the very least, outstanding. We dined at the Inn Dining Room and found the food and service excellent.

GOLF: The course is an 18-hole layout playing 5,750/4,977 yards, with a par of 70/71. The many palm trees and the lush greenery provide a startling contrast to the desert. While the course is not long, it does pose its own special challenges.

RATES: (EP) The Inn - $230/$325 per couple. The Ranch - $94/$144. Green fees - $50, carts $22. The season is November-May.

ARRIVAL: By air - Las Vegas Airport (140 miles). By private aircraft - Furnace Creek (3,040-foot surfaced runway). By car - from Las Vegas take I-95 north to Lathrop Wells, then Highway 373 west to Death Valley Junction. Drive Highway 190 north to Furnace Creek.

California

Half Moon Bay Lodge

2400 South Cabrillo Highway, Half Moon Bay, CA 94019

(650) 726-9000; (800) 368-2468, Ext. 3

ACCOMMODATIONS: 83 rooms, some with fireplaces, all with either private balconies or patios.

AMENITIES: Enclosed whirlpool spa and a swimming pool. In addition to the recreation offered by numerous nearby parks and beaches, there is riding, tennis and fishing. Papa George's Restaurant is located next door. About seven miles north you will find one of the best seafood restaurants anywhere, The Shore Bird. The San Francisco crowd knows good food when they find it, and this place has been discovered! Make reservations.

GOLF: Designed by Francis Duane and Arnold Palmer and making full use of the picturesque setting, this layout brings water, barrancas (ravines) and bluffs into play. It has been rated third in Northern California. Parring at 72, it plays 7,116/6,447/5,710 yards. This course is one of the more beautiful and challenging layouts we have come across.

RATES: (EP) Lodgings - $175/$225. Green fees - $95/$115/$135, including cart.

ARRIVAL: By air - San Francisco Airport (30 minutes). By car - from San Francisco, take Highway 92 to Highway 1, then head south. The resort is two miles south of Half Moon Bay.

Northstar at Tahoe

PO Box 129, Truckee, CA 96160

(530) 587-1010; (800) 466-6784

Situated in one of the more scenic areas in the US, Northstar is just seven miles from the California/Nevada border. Basically a winter-oriented resort, it also offers a wide range of activities during the summer months.

ACCOMMODATIONS: 230 units divided between Village Lodge rooms and one- to four- bedroom condos. The condos are fully equipped for housekeeping, with dishwasher and either gas log or woodburning fireplaces.

AMENITIES: 10 tennis courts, Olympic-size pool, horseback riding (barbecue dinner or breakfast rides can be arranged), and mountain biking through beautiful forest. The various streams and lakes are a fisherman's paradise. There is also a Minors' Camp for children between two and 10. Northstar offers super skiing during the winter. It has 2,200 vertical feet of downhill, 65 kilometers of cross-country trails, and a 100-instructor ski school.

GOLF: This is a Robert Muir Graves design, reaching up to 6,000 feet above sea level and providing some spectacular views. The yardage is 6,897/6,337/6,015/5,470, with a par of 72. Surrounded by aspens and pines, the course also has a creek wandering throughout the area. Water, as a matter of fact, forms a good part of the challenge on 14 holes. There is a clubhouse, complete with pro shop and a restaurant open for breakfast and lunch.

RATES: (EP) Lodgings - $99/$119//$139/$159. There are also homes for rent. Green fees -$75, including cart. Golf packages are available. Rates are June-September.

ARRIVAL: By air - Reno (40 minutes). By private aircraft - Truckee-Tahoe, a 6,400-foot strip. By car - Highway 267 between Truckee and the north shore of Lake Tahoe (approximately six miles).

Pasatiempo Inn

555 Highway 17, Santa Cruz, CA 95060

(831) 423-5000; (800) 834-2546

A beautiful "Spanish Mood" structure overlooking Pasatiempo Golf Course.

ACCOMMODATIONS: 54 recently refurbished rooms.

AMENITIES: An excellent restaurant and cozy cocktail lounge. There are also two fine dining facilities on the golf course.

GOLF: The Pasatiempo Golf & Country Club, bordering the Inn, is one of the older and finer courses in the state. Little wonder, as it was designed by Dr. Alistair MacKenzie, the same man responsible for St. Andrews in Scotland, the Masters course in Augusta, and Cypress Point at Monterey. It has been judged by *Golf Digest* as having one of the top 100 layouts in the United States. The course plays 6,483/6,154/5,647 yards, parring at 71/72. In addition to the deep barrancas, sand traps and oak trees bordering the fairways, you can enjoy breathtaking views of shimmering Monterey Bay or the Santa Cruz Mountains. You will find this a challenging layout and one that can test your vocabulary, on occasion, as well.

RATES: (EP) Rooms - $117/$148/$195. Green fees - $135, including cart. Golf packages can be arranged.

ARRIVAL: By car - from the north take Highway 17 (I-880) south to the Pasatiempo Drive exit. The resort will be on your right.

California

Resort at Squaw Creek

1000 Squaw Creek Road, Olympic Village, CA 96146

(530) 583-6300; (800) 327-3353

The Resort at Squaw Creek is in the high country of the Sierra Nevada Mountains of Northern California. The main group of buildings includes the lobby, with its vaulted ceilings, marble floors, and a massive granite fireplace.

ACCOMMODATIONS: 405 rooms and suites. All rooms have views of the beautiful valley and feature mini-bar, refrigerator and cable TV.

AMENITIES: Two outdoor heated pools (a lap pool and a water slide plunge pool), three outdoor spas, a health and fitness center, eight tennis courts (including the High Camp Tennis Club) an ice-skating pavilion and a golf shop. Trout fishing in this area is outstanding and fly-fishing clinics can be arranged. There are three restaurants: Gussandi; Cascades; and the Hardscramble Bar & Grill, which has a bistro atmosphere and is open for lunch and dinner. Bullwhackers Pub serves cocktails. For your edification (should you not be aware), a bullwhacker was a mule or oxen driver – rough, tough, profane and usually mean.

GOLF: The course was designed by Robert Trent Jones II. It runs along the floor of the valley and is relatively flat. The back side, however, begins to skirt the edge of the valley and will take you through some definite elevation changes. Modestly trapped, it brings water into contention on four holes. Playing 6,931/6,453/6,010/5,097 yards, the course pars at 71.

RATES: (EP) Lodgings - $209/$375/$1,000. Green fees - $115/$125, including cart. Golf packages are available. Rates are for summer season from mid-June through mid-September.

ARRIVAL: By air - Reno, Nevada (42 miles). By car - from Reno travel Highway 395 north to I-80; west on I-80 to Highway 89. Take 89 south to the entrance of Squaw Valley. You are about 200 miles from San Francisco and 100 miles from Sacramento, California.

Seascape Resort & Conference Center

One Seascape Resort Drive, Aptos, CA 95003

(831) 688-6800; (800) 929-7727

Seascape enjoys an excellent setting along the bluffs overlooking the northern end of Monterey Bay. It is 31 miles north of Monterey and 72 miles south of San Francisco. Seascape is quite large – spread out over several acres.

ACCOMMODATIONS: 28 studios plus 56 one-bedroom suites. Each unit has a gas fireplace, a balcony and a fully equipped kitchen-ette (small refrigerator, surface unit and microwave). The great majority of the rooms offer an ocean view.

AMENITIES: 12 tennis courts, bicycle riding, pool and Jacuzzi. Beach activities, including surfing and sailing, are nearby, as is the golf course. The resort has a lovely restaurant specializing in fresh seafood and locally grown fruits and vegetables.

GOLF: The course was originally known as the Rio Del Mar Country Club. In operation for many years, it is a fully mature, lush and lovely layout. Reaching out a modest 6,116/5,576 yards, with a par of 72, it serves up a nice change of pace, with undulating terrain, trees, and water coming into play on only one hole. It has, however, more than its share of sand bunkers.

RATES: (EP) Lodgings - $219/$449/$489. Green fees - $61/$86, including cart $26. Golf packages are available.

ARRIVAL: By air - San Jose Airport. By car - from San Jose, drive Highway 17 to Highway 1. Turn south on Highway 1 to the Sea-scape/San Andreas exit. Turn right onto Seascape Boulevard.

California

Southern California

1. Rio Bravo Resort
2. The Inn at Morro Bay
3. The Resort at Stallion Springs
4. The Inn at Silver Lakes
5. The Alisal
6. Ojai Valley Inn & CC
7. Residence Inn at River Ridge
8. Sheraton at Industry Hills Resort

The Alisal

1054 Alisal Road, Solvang, CA 93463

(805) 688-6411; (800) 425-4725

While The Alisal is a mere two miles from Solvang, it has a definite country setting enhanced by hundreds of wild deer, raccoons, bobcats and other wildlife. A visit to the nearby town of Solvang is a must. With its picturesque shops and Danish-style architecture, it has great charm.

ACCOMMODATIONS: 73 units ranging from studios, two-room suites, two-room loft suites, or private bungalows, all with woodburning fireplaces.

Note: There are no phones or TV's in the rooms. However, a large color TV is in the recreation room along with one for adult viewing in the attractive library. There is a coin-operated laundry.

AMENITIES: Horseback riding, including breakfast rides (riding instruction can also be arranged); a spa; pool; badminton; volleyball; croquet; and seven tennis courts. There is a 96-acre private lake with sailing, windsurfing, pedal boats, and fishing (all tackle as well as boats are available – no license is needed). They operate a summer children's program. The food and service here are excellent. Jackets are required in the evening and smoking is not allowed in the dining areas.

GOLF: The Alisal Golf Course, studded with oaks, is both beautiful and challenging. Parring at 72/73, it measures 6,286/5,919/5,594 yards. While the course is not monstrous in length, its many trees and wandering creek will more than keep your attention. The golf course is supported by a new and enlarged pro shop with locker rooms, a restaurant and a lounge.

A second layout, the River Course, is situated along the Santa Ynez River just south of the town of Solvang. Reaching out 6,830/ 6,451/6,117/5,815 yards, it carries a par of 72.

RATES: (MAP) Lodgings - $375/$400/$425/$450. Green fees - $75, cart $28. Some package plans are available from late September through mid-June.

ARRIVAL: By air - Santa Barbara (40 miles). By private aircraft - Santa Ynez. By car - take US 101 to Buellton; turn off to Solvang. In Solvang, turn right on Alisal Road and go two miles to the resort.

The Inn at Morro Bay

State Park Road, Morro Bay, CA 93442

(805) 772-5651; (800) 321-9566

The seaside town of Morro Bay is a quaint fishing village. The clean, fresh ocean air, the wispy fog cover, the sound of the surf, the unhurried fishing boats coming and going from the marina, join to create a delightful setting.

ACCOMMODATIONS: 96 guest rooms, some with fireplaces and sweeping views of the bay, others with a pool or garden view.

AMENITIES: A heated outdoor pool, miles of hiking trails, and the world-renowned Hearst Castle at San Simeon some 30 miles north. A fascinating pastime is simply to watch a band of sea otters cavort through the kelp. There are also many wineries to be visited. The inn calls their lifestyle "life in the slow lane." The Morrow Bay Dining Room is recognized throughout the area for its food and service and has, in fact, won several awards.

GOLF: The course lies across the road from the Inn. It plays to a modest yardage of 6,113/5,727 and pars at 71. Do not let the humble mileage lead you astray. This small, tight layout on undulating terrain along with difficult greens will more than keep your attention. Situated in Morrow Bay State Park, it offers the added distraction of fabulous views of the Pacific Ocean and Morro Bay. Tee times can be difficult to set up. Call (805) 772-4560 for the starter.

RATES: (EP) Lodgings - $109/$129/$259. Green fees - $50, including cart.

ARRIVAL: By air - San Louis Obispo (12 miles). By car - from the north, exit Highway 101 onto Highway 46 at Paso Robles. Continue

California

25 miles to Highway 1. From the south, exit Highway 101 onto Highway 1 and travel 15 miles to Morro Bay Boulevard.

The Inn at Silver Lakes

PO Box 26, Helendale, CA 92342

(760) 243-4800; CA (800) 228-7209

ACCOMMODATIONS: 40 guest rooms, each with either private patio or balcony.

AMENITIES: A large pool, a sauna, Jacuzzis, and four lighted tennis courts. There is also a dining room and lounge.

GOLF: The course consists of 27 holes. When played in combination, they measure as follows: The North/East nines reach 6,689/6,328/5,465 yards; the South/North are 6,822/6,428/5,564 yards; the East/South combination plays 6,747/6,374/5,633 yards. No matter how you mix them, they come out to a par of 72. These are intriguing layouts, with water in play on several holes of each nine.

RATES: (EP) Rooms - $70/$105. Golf packages are available. Green fees - $25/$50, carts $22.

ARRIVAL: By car - off I-15 between Victorville and Barstow, on the National Trails Highway about 95 miles from Los Angeles.

Ojai Valley Inn & Spa

Country Club Road, Ojai, CA 93023

(805) 646-5511; (800) 422-6524

The Ojai Valley Inn & Country Club has been judged one of the Top 50 resorts. It has also received many additional well-deserved accolades.

The Valley's snow-capped mountains (specifically Topa/Topa Mountain, a part of the Sierra Madre range), were the setting for the mythical paradise of Shangri-la in the movie *Lost Horizon* (circa 1937). If you saw this movie during its original showing, back up and ask for extra strokes.

The charming Inn, with its quiet and idyllic setting, is 14 miles from the Pacific Ocean and about 90 minutes northwest of Los Angeles. It is, however, a million miles from Los Angeles in gentility and culture.

ACCOMMODATIONS: 218 beautifully decorated guest rooms, each air-conditioned and equipped with a mini-bar. The 15 suites have parlors and most include fireplaces. All lodgings have a terrace. The general motif is one of warm Spanish/American design that blends into the surrounding area. We suggest that you take the time to look at the quaint village of Ojai. Its Spanish mission-style architecture, along with the boutiques, shops, galleries and museum are more than worth the time.

AMENITIES: Eight newly resurfaced tennis courts (four lighted), two pools, exercise equipment and fitness classes, jogging trails, complimentary use of bicycles, and lawn croquet. Recently added is a comprehensive spa program, one of the best in the country. If you have biked or hiked into the village and have just plain run out of gas, you can catch the shuttle bus from Ojai's shopping arcade back to the Inn. Dining in the Vista Room, the more informal Oak Grill & Terrace, or The Club can be a delightful experience.

GOLF: The course, originally designed by George C. Thomas, Jr. in 1923 and put together by Billy Bell, has long been regarded as one of the better layouts in California. To bring it up to date and still maintain its almost legendary reputation, Jay Morrish, a leading designer, was engaged. The restoration, including a modern irrigation system, is now complete. Playing 6,235/5,892/5,225 yards, the Ojai course pars at 70/71. With its lush fairways and rolling terrain, it is in a class by itself. While the front nine is fun, the back nine is something else. It is one of the most unusual courses we have tried. Wandering through the foothills, the back side takes advantage of every tree (and there are more than enough of them), every ravine, gully and hill, to turn this nine into a shotmaker's course. There is a well-equipped pro shop and an excellent professional staff under the supervision of the Director of Golf, Mark Greenslit.

RATES: (EP) Lodgings - $245/$280/$320 per couple. Deluxe suites - $390/$440. Green fees - $110, including cart. Golf package mid-week (two nights/two days, including lodging, two rounds of golf with cart, tax and gratuity) - $712/$854 per couple.

ARRIVAL: By air - Santa Barbara (30 miles). By car - take US 101 south to Route 150. Turn east (left) onto 150 and travel into the town of Ojai. Turn right onto Country Club Drive.

California

Residence Inn at River Ridge

2101 West Vineyard, Oxnard, CA 93030

(805) 278-2200; (800) 331-3131

ACCOMMODATIONS: 250 residential-style suites spread over a total of 32 buildings. Each suite has a full kitchen, cable TV, cassette player, and all the equipment needed for housekeeping. There are also some two-story loft suites featuring woodburning fireplaces.

AMENITIES: Five lighted tennis courts, two pools, three hot tubs, along with exercise and massage facilities. There is a restaurant, Mullarkey's Food & Spirits.

GOLF: The course, adjacent to the hotel, reaches out 6,543/6,111/5,525 yards and carries a par of 72. It sports an island par 3, number 14, playing 158 yards from the regular tees. Surrounded by water, the green can be reached only by a small foot bridge. There are also several holes running directly along the Santa Clara River.

RATES: (EP) Lodgings - $114/$159. Golf packages are available. Green fees - $39/$54, carts $24. Rates are for peak summer golf season.

ARRIVAL: By air - Oxnard (five minutes away). By car - the resort is just a few blocks off US Highway 101. Take the Vineyard exit and drive west for one and a half miles.

The Resort at Stallion Springs

18100 Lucaya Way, Tehachapi, CA 93561-32766

(661) 822-5581; (800) 244-0864

ACCOMMODATIONS: 84 guest rooms (including housekeeping cottages). Guest rooms are studio kings, loft suites and double bedrooms, all with a panoramic view of tall pines, greens and fairways. The lodge crowns a mountaintop in the rugged Tehachapi range. It is one of the most unusual settings we have seen.

AMENITIES: Five lighted tennis courts, a heated pool, locker rooms with saunas and an equestrian center with instruction and supervised trail rides. The attractive dining room has an outstanding view.

GOLF: Horse Thief Golf Course is a well-maintained, 18-hole layout. Parring at 72, it reaches out 6,650/6,317/5,723 yards.

RATES: (EP) Lodgings - $75/$130/$155. Golf packages are available. Green fees - $28/$48, carts $24.

ARRIVAL: By air - Tehachapi. By car - 56 miles from Bakersfield, 118 miles from Los Angeles. Located 16 miles west of Tehachapi on Route 202, it is not easy to get to this resort. Get local directions in Tehachapi and have patience

Rio Bravo Resort

11200 Lake Ming Road, Bakersfield, CA 93306

(805) 872-5000; (888) 517-5500

Rio Bravo is adjacent to a 110-acre lake. In this desert-like part of the San Joaquin Valley, water in any form is a rare commodity.

ACCOMMODATIONS: Each room has a private balcony or patio. There are also some one- and two-bedroom units with sitting area, fireplace and wet bar.

AMENITIES: 18 tennis courts (14 lighted), professional tennis staff, two pools, a very complete and sophisticated fitness center, saunas, whirlpools, and sailing on Lake Ming. Whitewater rafting, kayaking or fishing on the nearby Kern River can be arranged. The two dining areas are excellent.

GOLF: There are two golf courses available. The private Rio Bravo Country Club course, a Robert Muir Graves design plays to a substantial 6,993/6,521/5,704 yards, with a par of 72. There are only two holes where water comes into play. The Kern River Course, a public affair plays 6,458/6,258/5,971 yards and pars at 70. While several holes border the lake, there is no water coming into play.

RATES: (EP) Lodgings - $128/$165/$225. Kern River green fees - $12/$15, carts $20. Rio Bravo, $52 including cart.

ARRIVAL: By air - Bakersfield Airport. By private aircraft - Rio Bravo (3,000-foot runway, three minutes away). By car - from Highway 99 north of Bakersfield, take State Highway 178 east to Alfred Harrell Highway. Turn back in a westerly direction to resort.

California

Sheraton at Industry Hills Resort

One Industry Hills Parkway, City of Industry, CA 91744

(626) 810-4455; (800) 325-3535

ACCOMMODATIONS: 295 rooms and suites within this 11-story structure. Located on a hill, the hotel comes packaged with indoor fountains, liberal use of marble and stained glass.

AMENITIES: 17 tennis courts, 15 miles of riding trails, three pools, whirlpools, saunas and billiards. A few years back they added an equestrian center, with a covered arena. There are three restaurants.

GOLF: Two 18-hole courses are available: the Dwight D. Eisenhower and the Babe Zaharias layouts. The Eisenhower 18, parring at 72/73, stretches 6,712/6,287/5,967/5,637 yards. The Babe Zaharias Course, a bit shorter, plays 6,481/5,994/5,426 and pars at 71. You will enjoy the view provided by the St. Andrews station and the golf funicular, which operates on the Eisenhower course, lifting you from the ninth green up to the 10th tee.

RATES: (EP) Lodgings - $140/$165/$350. Green fees - $60, carts $24. Golf packages are available.

ARRIVAL: By car - Highway 60 (Pomona Freeway) to the Azusa Avenue exit; then north to Industry Hills Parkway.

San Diego Area

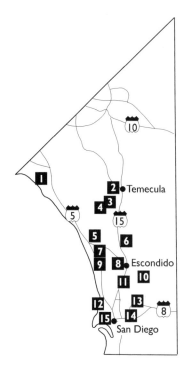

1. Ritz-Carlton Laguna Niguel
2. Temecula Creek Inn
3. Pala Mesa Resort
4. San Luis Rey Downs
5. Oceanside Days Inn
6. Lake San Marcus Resort
7. La Costa/Four Seasons Aviara
8. Lawrence Welk Resort
9. Whispering Palms Lodge & CC
10. San Vincente Inn & CC
11. Rancho Bernado Inn
12. La Jolla Hilton Torrey Pines
13. Carlton Oaks Lodge & CC/Warner Springs Ranch
14. Singing Hills CC & Lodge
15. Carmel Highlands DoubleTree Resort/Handlery Hotel & CC

California

Carlton Oaks Lodge & Country Club

9200 Inwood Drive, Santee, CA 92071

(619) 448-4242; (800) 831-6757

Bordered on one side by the 6,500-foot-high Laguna Mountains, and with rolling hills on the other side, the atmosphere here is one of relaxation.

ACCOMMODATIONS: Air-conditioned rooms in the lodge, with a view of the course or tennis courts. A few are equipped with either a full kitchen or a kitchenette.

AMENITIES: The resort's location in northeastern San Diego County (20 miles from downtown San Diego) gives you access to the beaches, watersports, Sea World, and the Mexican border. In addition to the heated pool, there are four lighted tennis courts. The casual dining room and lounge offer entertainment and dancing on the weekends.

GOLF: This Pete Dye course reaches out a substantial 7,109/ 6,613/6,084/5,772/4,817 yards, with a par of 72. The challenging features are found in a creek that meanders throughout the entire complex, aided and abetted by menacing ponds, rolling terrain and, of course, Mr. Dye's penchant for railroad ties.

RATES: (EP) Rooms - $73/$83. Green fees - $65/$75, including cart. Golf packages are available.

ARRIVAL: By air - San Diego. By car - from Highway 15 turn east on Highway 8, then north on Mission Gorge Road.

Carmel Highland/ DoubleTree Resort

14455 Penasquitos Drive, San Diego, CA 92129

(858) 672-9100; (800) 222-8733

ACCOMMODATIONS: 172 guest rooms, including 14 suites overlooking or adjacent to the golf course. The Highlands has an ideal location approximately 30 minutes north of San Diego.

AMENITIES: Six lighted tennis courts, two pools, a 5,500- square-foot health and fitness center equipped with state-of-the-art weight systems and providing massage, saunas, and steam baths. There is a washer/dryer facility adjacent to the pool. Trents is their primary evening dining room; there is also the less formal Terraces Café.

GOLF: Reaching out 6,521/6,108/5,488 yards, the course pars at 72/73. With all the recent improvements, water comes into contention on only two holes.

RATES: (EP) Rooms - $109/$132. Green fees - $65/$75, including cart. Golf packages are available.

ARRIVAL: By air - San Diego International Airport. When making reservations you can arrange a pickup at the airport by Super Shuttle. By car - take I-15 north to the Carmel Mountain Road exit. Turn left. At the third traffic light turn right onto Penasquitos Drive.

Four Seasons Resort Aviara

7100 Four Seasons Point

Carlsbad, CA 92008

(760) 603-6800; (800) 332-3442

The Resort Aviara is situated on a plateau overlooking the Batiquitos Lagoon Wildlife Reserve and the Pacific Ocean.

ACCOMMODATIONS: 331 rooms and 25 suites, as well as a total of 240 vacation villas in the planning stage.

AMENITIES: Include six tennis courts (four lighted), a fitness center, swimming pools (3,200 square feet, freeform) and a spa program. The five restaurants range from northern Italian to California-style cuisine with a French accent, and include poolside and golf course dining. There is also 24-hour room service available.

GOLF: While the resort opened in mid-1997, the course came into play in July of 1991. An 18-hole championship layout, it was designed by Arnold Palmer and sculpted around three natural valleys. The traditional layout is well bunkered and tree lined, with undulating terrain and water. Playing to a par of 72 it rolls out substantial 7,007/6,591/6,054/5,007 yards. The course is supported by a 32,000-square-foot clubhouse.

RATES: (EP) Lodging - $365/$400/$475. Suites - $585/$8750. Green fees - $160/$180, including cart. For villa information and rates, call (800) 828-4466.

ARRIVAL: By air - San Diego Airport. By car - take I-5 north and exit to Poinsettia Lane. Turn right onto Aviara Parkway. At third street, turn right.

California

Hotel Del Coronado

1500 Orange Avenue, Coronado, CA 92118

(619) 435-6611; (800) 468-3533

The Coronado, opened in 1888, is reputed to be one of the largest wooden structures in the world. When it opened, Grover Cleveland was in the White House and Wyatt Earp was in Tombstone. This elegant Victorian structure is directly across the bay from San Diego.

ACCOMMODATIONS: The Ocean Towers houses 214 rooms and the poolside addition has 97 guest rooms. The original 400 guest rooms (now 700) have been upgraded.

AMENITIES: Two lovely pools, six lighted tennis courts, men's and women's spas, bicycle rentals, white sand beaches, sailing and fishing. The Galleria Shops offer a variety of merchandise. You are 10 miles from Tijuana, Mexico, a short distance from the San Diego Zoo and the Wild Animal Park. The resort also offers a family "Summer Camp" with a variety of activities for children aged four to 17. Dining facilities include the Crown-Coronet Room; the Prince of Wales, with traditional and nouvelle cuisine (dinner only, jackets required); the Ocean Terrace; the Burger Bar; the Palm Court (coffee and croissants); and the Ocean Terrace Lounge.

GOLF: This course was designed by Jack Daray. Bordered on one side by San Diego Bay and another by Glorietta Bay, it actually brings water into action on only three holes. Although it is a flat layout, the course is well-trapped and heavily treed. The par-72 layout reaches out a relatively modest 6,633/6,317/5,784 yards. There are many other golf facilities within a few miles.

RATES: (EP) Lodgings - $205/$250/$595. Modern Complex - $245/$850. Green fees - $55, including cart.

ARRIVAL: By air - San Diego International Airport. By car - from I-5 take Coronado Exit #75. Drive west across the Bay Bridge. At the first light take a left (onto Orange Avenue) and drive 1½ miles.

Days Inn

3170 Vista Way, Oceanside, CA 92056

(760) 757-2200; (800) 458-6064

ACCOMMODATIONS: 42 one- and two-bedroom units, some with living rooms and dining areas. A few have either kitchens or kitchenettes. Guests of the inn can enjoy all the services of a private country club.

AMENITIES: Two pools, seven tennis courts (two lighted). The clubhouse dining room affords a commanding view of the course and the rolling hills beyond.

GOLF: The club's 18-hole course reaches out 6,774/6,439/5,831 yards, parring at 72. While water comes into play on only three holes, traps are strategically placed around the greens.

RATES: (EP) Rooms - $85/$105. Green fees - $79, including cart.

ARRIVAL: By air - San Diego (35 minutes); Los Angeles (90 minutes). By car - I-5 to 78 east, then El Camino Real north to Frontage Road.

The Handlery Hotel & Country Club

950 Hotel Circle, San Diego, CA 92108

(619) 298-0511; (800) 448-8355

ACCOMMODATIONS: 217 rooms plus four suites in a four-story hotel.

AMENITIES: Lighted handball and racquetball courts, steam rooms, massage, beauty and barber shops, eight tennis courts (four lighted), golf and swimming. Dining takes place in The Crane Room, specializing in steak and seafood. There is also a 24-hour coffee shop.

GOLF: Golf is offered on 27 holes. Using a crossover system, you can play three 18-hole layouts. The Lake/River nines reach out 6,602/6,309/5,734 yards; the Valley/Lake combination plays 6,655/6,357/5,797 yards; and the River/Valley combo weighs in at 6,645/6,356/5,871 yards. All three combinations par at 72. There is also a par-3 nine available.

RATES: (EP) Lodgings - $129/$149. Green fees - $75, including cart. Golf packages are available. Rates are June 16 - September 15.

ARRIVAL: By air - San Diego. By car - located in the Mission Valley Hotel Circle, near Highways I-5 and I-8.

La Costa

Costa Del Mar Road, Carlsbad, CA 92008

(760) 438-9111; (800) 854-5000

La Costa is one of our Top 50 resorts.

ACCOMMODATIONS: 300 rooms, some in the main hotel, others along the golf course or near the tennis complex. There are also 75 one- and two-bedroom suites.

AMENITIES: A spa program, widely recognized as one of the finest in the country. Its private, club-like complexes for women and men pamper you with facials, massages, whirlpools, loofah scrubs, pedicures, yoga classes, and exercise sessions. Swiss showers, Roman pools, and herbal wraps are also offered. For the tennis player, there is a 21-court complex under the direction of a tennis professional and staff. If you are not completely exhausted at this point, you might consider a swim in one of the four freshwater pools. Something new is the "Camp La Costa," set up to entertain the small fry while you do... whatever. Each of the five restaurants offers a unique eating adventure. The food and service are excellent. Recently we tried Pisces, located a short distance away. This restaurant must be ranked among the very best for seafood.

GOLF: There are two beautiful courses. The North measures 6,983/6,596/6,263/5,980 yards, with a par of 72/73, while the South layout shows a modest yardage of 6,896/6,534/6,214/5,632, parring at 72/74. There are locker rooms, a snack bar, practice area and a pro shop.

RATES: (EP) Lodging - $325/$365/$365/$550. There are many different packages, including spa plans, golf, and tennis packages. Green fees - $175, including cart.

ARRIVAL: By air - San Diego. By private aircraft - Palomar (three miles). By car - Los Angeles (two hours). Take I-5 to La Costa Avenue exit toward El Camino Real. Entrance is on the left.

La Jolla Hilton Torrey Pines

10950 North Torrey Pines Road, La Jolla, CA 92037

(858) 558-1500; (800) 762-6160

ACCOMMODATIONS: 400 rooms, including 23 suites. Some have balconies or patios, offering a view of either the golf course or the sea.

AMENITIES: Three lighted tennis courts, exercise room, saunas, a heated pool, whirlpool and spa. The sports concierge can arrange many other activities, ranging from scuba diving and fishing to hang gliding or balloon rides. While dining is available within the hotel (The Torreyana Grille or the Alfresco Terrace), there are a number of good restaurants in La Jolla.

GOLF: The South course plays 6,649/6,345 yards, with a par of 72/76; the North layout measures 6,317/6,047, with a par of 72/74. Both courses show extremely long yardage for the ladies.

RATES: (EP) Rooms - $190/$200. Suites - $500/$950. Green fees - $55/$60, carts $28.

ARRIVAL: By air - San Diego International Airport (18 miles). By car - take I-5 north to Genesee Street. Turn north and drive to Torrey Pines Road.

Lake San Marcos Resort

1025 La Bonita Drive, San Marcos, CA 92069

(760) 744-0120; (800) 447-6556

ACCOMMODATIONS: 142 rooms in the lodge as well as cottages equipped with kitchens. There are also some private homes for rent. Guests of the inn (Quails Inn) are really entering a private residential community, with the lodge fronting Lake San Marcos.

AMENITIES: Four tennis courts, three paddle tennis courts, and four pools. Kayot party boats, sailboats or canoes are available for rent. For dining, you have a choice of either the Quails Inn Dinner House, the Country Club, or the Coffee Shop.

GOLF: Available on the championship Lake San Marcos Country Club course or on the Lakeview layout. The San Marcos reaches 6,484/6,260/5,959 yards and pars at 72/73. The Lakeside is an executive 18-hole affair.

RATES: (EP) Lodgings - $99/$149 (weekly rates offered). Green fees - $50, including cart. Golf package (two nights/two days, including lodging, breakfast and lunch each day, two rounds of golf with cart) - $414/$480/$532 per couple.

ARRIVAL: By air - San Diego. By car - I-5, east on Palomar Airport Road. Right on Rancho Santa Fe Road.

Lawrence Welk Resort

8860 Lawrence Welk Drive, Escondido, CA 92026

(760) 749-3000; (800) 932-9355

ACCOMMODATIONS: 132 guest rooms at the inn, plus 256 two-bedroom villas. The villas have living rooms, dining areas, and fully equipped kitchens. All have private balconies.

AMENITIES: Five tennis courts, a spa and five pools. The Lawrence Welk Dinner Theater, seating 300, features professional entertainment Tuesday, Thursday, Friday and Saturday evenings. Within the 1,000-acre complex are gift and beauty shops, a fashion parlor, and even dental offices.

GOLF: The Meadow Lake Country Club course reaches a substantial 6,521/6,312/5,758 yards and pars at 72/74. Also available is The Fountains 18, an executive affair. There are at least 15 championship-caliber courses within a few miles of the village.

RATES: Inn rooms (standard) - $190. Villas - $279. Green fees - $35/$60, carts $24.

ARRIVAL: By air - San Diego (33 miles). By car - eight miles north of Escondido off I-15.

Morgan Run Resort & Club

5690 Cancha De Golf, Rancho Santa Fe, CA 92091

(858) 756-2471; (800) 378-4653

ACCOMMODATIONS: 100 rooms and suites.

AMENITIES: 11 all-weather tennis courts (two lighted), a pool and, of course, golf.

RATES: (EP) Lodgings - $199/$249. Green fees - $80/$100, including cart. Golf package (one night lodging, one round of golf per person with cart) - $318 per couple.

ARRIVAL: By car - Between Oceanside and San Diego. East off I-5, on Via DeValle (2½ miles).

Pala Mesa Resort

2001 South Highway 395, Fallbrook, CA 92028

(858) 728-5881; (800) 722-4700

Pala Mesa has long been considered one of Southern California's better golf resort facilities. Although modest in size, it has a beautiful setting and many amenities.

ACCOMMODATIONS: 133 rooms and several condominiums fully equipped for housekeeping.

AMENITIES: Four tennis courts, a pool and a new fitness center. Alexander's Restaurant presents a variety of outstanding fare and is supported by an excellent lounge.

GOLF: The course is superb. Parring at 72, it plays 6,528/6,194/5,848 yards. While not particularly long, it can test your skill as well as your vocabulary. If your problem is a wild hook, I hope you have been a regular at church – the first three holes might well destroy you. We took the time to come back and play this layout a second time, a luxury we rarely enjoy.

RATES: (EP) Lodgings - $135/$160. Green fees - $65/$80, including cart. Golf packages are available.

ARRIVAL: By air - San Diego. By car - 55 miles north of San Diego on I-15. Exit at Highway 76, go left, then take the first right west of I-15, about two miles.

Rancho Bernardo Inn

17550 Bernardo Oaks Drive, San Diego, CA 92128

(858) 675-8500; (800) 542-6096

Rancho Bernardo is situated in a beautiful valley just 28 minutes from the San Diego Airport. The inn has been recognized as a premier resort for many years. After updating and refurbishing it has really matured, evolving into a lovely destination. The custom of serving afternoon tea with a background of piano music offers a delightful pause to the day.

ACCOMMODATIONS: 287 rooms, including 58 suites.

AMENITIES: 12 tennis courts (four lighted), fitness and spa center with massage, steam, sauna and workout rooms. The inn also offers a Tennis College program. A Kids Camp is offered on major holiday weekends and for three weeks in August, to enable suffering parents a chance to enjoy some of the amenities. You can dine in El Bizcocho, with its three-star gourmet cuisine (jackets required), or in the less formal Veranda Room. Piano music and dancing are offered nightly.

GOLF: This is one of California's most interesting golf complexes. The West, a par-72 layout, plays 6,458/6,182/5,448 yards. With water coming into contention on 14 holes, I would suggest you pay attention to business. An additional 27 holes are offered on the Oaks executive course, with each nine parring at 30.

RATES: (EP) Lodgings - $189/$239/$259 and up. Green fees - $75/$100, including cart. Golf package (two nights/three days, including MAP lodging, unlimited golf, cart, club storage) - $776/$856 per couple. Rates are for January-June.

ARRIVAL: By air - San Diego. By car - from San Diego drive 163 which turns onto I-15 north. Take the Rancho Bernardo Road Exit. Drive to Bernardo Oaks Drive and turn left.

The Ritz-Carlton Laguna Niguel

33533 Shoreline Drive, Laguna Niguel, CA 92677

(949) 240-2000; (800) 241-3333

Situated on a bluff overlooking the Pacific Ocean, the hotel reflects a Mediterranean architectural style.

ACCOMMODATIONS: 393 rooms in the four-story building offer ocean views, oceanfront courtyards, or a poolside lanai location.

AMENITIES: Two miles of beach, four tennis courts, two pools, a fitness center with a steam room, sauna, whirlpool, men's and women's massage, and an exercise room. For nourishment, there is The Dining Room, offering classic and contemporary French cuisine; The Café Terrace; The Club Bar, featuring live entertainment and dancing; The Library Cocktail Lounge, with a fireplace setting; and The Bar, with piano entertainment in the evening.

GOLF: The course, an 18-hole affair, was designed by Robert Trent Jones II. With a yardage of 6,224/5,655/4,984, it pars at 70. It features 88 sand traps, four lakes and three oceanside holes, and is not as easy as the short yardage might indicate.

RATES: (EP) Rooms - $395/$575. Suites - from $495 up. Green fees - $115/$145, including cart.

ARRIVAL: By air - Los Angeles or San Diego. By car - from San Diego on I-5 take Crown Valley Parkway west to Pacific Coast Highway, then south one mile to the hotel.

San Luis Rey Downs

31474 Golf Club Drive, Bonsall, CA 92003

(760) 758-3762; (800) 783-6967

ACCOMMODATIONS: 26 rooms, seven with kitchenettes.

AMENITIES: Four lighted all-weather tennis courts and a pool. For the horse lover they offer a thoroughbred training center, one of the largest in the country. There is a dining room, snack bar and lounge.

GOLF: The course is an interesting one with more than enough trees and water to keep you busy. Parring at 72, it plays 6,610/6,324/5,547 yards.

RATES: (EP) Rooms - $75/$95. Green fees - $38/$55, including cart. Golf package (two nights/two days, including lodging, golf and cart) - $290 per couple (weekends, $310 per couple).

ARRIVAL: By car - Exit I-5 at Oceanside on Mission Avenue. Go east on Highway 76 for 13 miles, then follow signs.

California

San Vincente Inn & Country Club

24157 San Vicente Road, Ramona, CA 92065

(760) 789-8290; (800) 776-1289; condo rentals (760) 789-8678

ACCOMMODATIONS: Rooms in the lodge as well as condominium villas. Each villa has from one to three bedrooms, two baths, fully equipped kitchen and a dining area. Specify whether you prefer to be near the tennis complex or golf course (they are about two miles apart). Stretched over 3,200 acres of California's high desert, this resort has a lovely setting.

AMENITIES: 24 tennis courts at the ranch and horseback riding. There is a dining room in the main lounge just off the first tee.

GOLF: Set on undulating terrain and parring at 72, the golf course plays 6,585/6,180/5,578 yards. There are 12 holes in which water hazards come into play.

RATES: (EP) Lodgings - $71/$76. Green fees - $47/$57, including cart. Golf packages are available.

ARRIVAL: By air - San Diego (38 miles). By car - Highway 67 to Ramona, right on San Vicente Road (seven miles). From Escondido, take Highway 78 (19 miles) to Ramona, then straight ahead for seven miles.

Singing Hills Country Club & Lodge

3007 Dehesa Road, El Cajon, CA 92019

(619) 442-3425; (800) 457-5568

ACCOMMODATIONS: A 102-unit lodge with rooms and suites. The exceptionally large rooms are comprised of a bedroom with large sitting area, a walk-in dressing area, and an oversized bathroom. They would be considered executive suites in most resorts. There is a coin-operated laundry facility. Dollar for dollar, Singing Hills is one of the best buys in the state.

AMENITIES: Two swimming pools and tennis courts. Adjacent to the golf shop is a breakfast/lunch dining area and, on the other side, the lounge and dining room. The location of the resort is ideal. It is 20 minutes from the San Diego Zoo, 25 minutes from Sea World, and 40 minutes from Tijuana, Mexico.

GOLF: The Willow Glen Golf Course reaches 6,605/6,207/5,585 yards and pars at 72. The Oak Glen plays 6,132/5,749/5,308 yards, with a par of 71. They have used raised tees, six lakes, strategically placed bunkers, natural rock outcroppings as well as aged oaks and sycamores to enhance the beauty and character of this course. There is also the Pine Glen, a rather challenging par-54 executive layout. The complex is one of the best in Southern California.

RATES: (EP) Lodgings - $93/$103/$210. Green fees - $37/$45, cart $22. Golf package (two nights/three days, including lodging, three days golf, cart for one round per day, three days tennis fees, taxes) - $450, summer and fall, weekdays only.

ARRIVAL: By air - San Diego (30 minutes). By car - turn off Highway 8 to El Cajon Boulevard, then go to Washington Avenue (which turns into Dehesa Road); travel two miles.

Temecula Creek Inn

Box 129, Temecula, CA 92593

(909) 728-9100; (800) 962-7335

ACCOMMODATIONS: 80 well-appointed rooms with private balconies. Temecula Creek is in the foothills of the beautiful Santa Rosa Mountains.

AMENITIES: A terrace pool with a hydro-spa and two tennis courts. Their dining room, while small, offers a fine menu.

GOLF: There are now 27 holes. When we played the original 18, we found it a bit unusual. It had a front nine that seemed open, offering little challenge. The back nine could do everything but turn you loose. They have toughened up the old front nine: the trees have aged and become a nuisance and a lake has been added. Using a crossover system, the courses play as follows: Creek/Oaks - 6,784/6,375/5,737 yards; Oaks/Stonehouse - 6,693/6,295/5,683; Stonehouse/Creek - 6,605/6,286/5,686 yards. Sharply undulating terrain, narrow fairways, several blind shots, many trees and small greens will keep you fully alert. It is one of the most picturesque golf courses in this part of the country.

RATES: (EP) Lodgings - $145/$165/$185. Green fees - $65/$85, including cart. Golf package (two nights/two days, including MAP lodging, green fees, cart) - $736 per couple.

ARRIVAL: By air - San Diego. By car - from Escondido, take I-15 north to Indio/Highway 79, turn right (east) to Pala Road (about one mile). Turn right and drive to Rainbow Canyon Road. Again turn right and drive to resort.

California

Warner Springs Ranch

31652 Highway 79, Warner Springs, CA 92086

(760) 782-4200

Located in the back country of San Diego County, this 2,500-acre resort is a bit over an hour and a half drive from San Diego. Its history dates back many years to the Butterfield Overland Stage days. More recently, it has seen visits by Bing Crosby, Charlie Chaplin, Clark Gable, John Wayne, and other celebrities.

ACCOMMODATIONS: 234 spacious cottages with fireplace.

AMENITIES: Three swimming pools, horseback riding, tennis, jogging and hiking trails and a spa program, offering massages, facials and body wraps. Located in the main lodge is the Anza Dining Room, with a cantina. The Golf Grille, a snack bar, offers a spot for a quick lunch.

GOLF: The course enjoys a beautiful valley setting with undulating terrain and with water in play on only four holes. There are enough trees and traps coming into play to keep your full attention. Parring at 72/73, the yardage is anything but modest, playing at 7,000/6,701/6,252/5,470 yards.

RATES: Room - $95. Golf package - mid-week (two nights lodging, three days unlimited golf with cart, MAP), $380 per couple. There are many other packages available.

ARRIVAL: East of Lake Henshaw and just off Highway 79. By air - San Diego International Airport (1½ hours).

The Coachella Valley Desert Area

The area known as the Coachella Valley comprises Palm Springs, forming the northwestern boundary, and Coachella on the southeast. There are now several other rapidly growing communities in between: Cathedral City, Palm Desert, Desert Hot Springs, Rancho Mirage, La Quinta, Indian Wells and Indio.

Discovered in the early '20s by Hollywood's elite, it is no longer a group of sleepy little villages. While the area has changed over the years, the one thing that has not is the magnificent clear blue sky and the mild climate. It's a great feeling to be soaking your body in a warm outdoor pool or playing a round of golf on a manicured course while the rest of the country is slipping and sliding behind a snow plow.

The chambers of commerce advise you to bring warmer apparel for evening, stating that "Summer months – June through mid-

September – are warmer." This is one of the most masterful understatements of all time. I have seen the temperature climb well over 125°. I don't care how low the humidity is. When it gets that hot this is no place for a human being, much less a golfer.

Within this area there are over 70 golf courses, 20 or more world-class destination golf resorts, plus a few others a bit farther south in the Borrego Springs region. While not as large, the Coachella Valley is rapidly becoming the West Coast version of Myrtle Beach's golf scene.

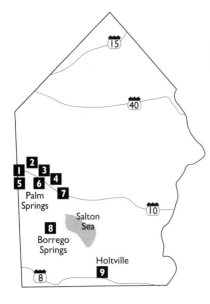

1. Doral Resort
2. Cathedral City
3. Rancho Mirage
   Marriott's Rancho Las Palmas/
   Westin Mission Hills Resort
4. Palm Desert/The Lakes CC/
   Marriott's Desert Springs Resort
   & Villa Rentals/Monterey CC/Palm
   Desert Resort & CC/Palm Valley
   CC/Ironwood CC
5. Indian Wells
   Radisson Resort Indian Wells/
   Hyatt Grand Championship
   Resort/Stouffer's Esmeralda Resort
6. La Quinta
   La Quinta Resort & Club/PGA West
7. Indio
   Indian Palms Resort Club
8. La Casa Del Zorro/Rams Hill/
   Borrego Springs Resort & CC
9. Barbara Worth CC

California

Barbara Worth Country Club

2050 Country Club Drive, Holtville, CA 92250

(760) 356-2806; (800) 356-3806

ACCOMMODATIONS: A 103-room motel overlooking the golf course.

AMENITIES: A heated pool, a lap pool, a whirlpool, driving range, and a dining room and lounge.

GOLF: The course plays at 6,239/5,902 yards, parring at 71/73. There is a pro shop and locker rooms.

RATES: (EP) Lodgings - $70; weekly, $399. Green fees - $30, including cart. Golf packages are available.

ARRIVAL: By air - El Centro-Imperial. By car - eight miles east of El Centro, two miles from Holtville.

Borrego Springs Resort & CC

1112 Tilting T Drive, PO Box 981, Borrego Springs, CA 92004

(760) 767-5700 (888) 826-7734

Borrego Springs enjoys one of the most intriguing desert locations in the United States.

ACCOMMODATIONS: A 100-room hotel., complete with balconies or patios, a small refrigerator and ice makers. Each room has individually controlled air-conditioning.

AMENITIES: Two swimming pools and a spa, six lighted tennis courts, a state-of-the-art fitness center, a guest laundry and a delightful restaurant and lounge. A short distance away are two lovely restaurants: La Casa Del Zorro and Rams Hill Resort. There are also restaurants in the center of Borrego Springs.

GOLF: The course architect was Cary Bickler. Reaching out 6,569/6,502/5,589/4,754 yards, this championship layout pars at 71. Although well-trapped, unlike most desert courses it does not drown you with water. As I recall, water becomes a factor on only four or five holes. The golf facilities are under the supervision of Al Maguire and are supported by an excellent pro shop. There are also several other golf courses available nearby.

RATES: Rooms - $99/$115. Suites - $125/$145. Green fees - $65, including cart. Various golf packages are also available.

ARRIVAL: By air - Borrego Springs Airport. By car - from Palm Springs, drive east on Highway 111 to Highway 86 and continue on through Coachella. At Salton Sea turn right on S-22. Be careful as this turn is not well-marked and is easy to miss. Follow S-22 for approximately 26 miles to first stop sign. Turn left and it's about three miles to resort entrance, which is on the right side of the road.

Doral Resort

Vista Chino & Landau Boulevard, Palm Springs, CA 92263

(760) 322-7000; (800) 637-0577

ACCOMMODATIONS: 289 rooms in a four-story hotel plus a few fully equipped one-and two- bedroom condos. The Doral is on 347 acres less than five miles from the center of Palm Springs.

AMENITIES: Outdoor heated pool, a lap pool, two hydrotherapy pools, men's and women's exercise rooms, a massage center, 10 tennis courts (five lighted), two handball courts, and two handball/racquetball courts. The Promenade Café is available for casual dining. The Oasis Lounge offers entertainment and dancing nightly.

GOLF: The 27-hole Desert Princess Golf Course plays 6,636/6,164/5,719/5,326 yards and pars at 72. While basically flat, it brings water into play on 11 holes.

RATES: (EP) Lodgings - $290/$310/$375. Green fees - $95/$105, including cart. Rates are January through May.

ARRIVAL: By air - Palm Springs International. By car - off I-10 at the Date Palm exit, turn right on Vista Chino. After one mile you have arrived.

California

Hyatt Grand Champions Resort

44-600 Indian Wells Lane, Indian Wells, CA 92210

(760) 341-1000; (800) 233-1234

ACCOMMODATIONS: 340 rooms and suites, along with the Regency Club Level (concierge floor). The sumptuous villa suites have private spas, and a butler is assigned to each villa court.

AMENITIES: Health and fitness center, four pools, 24 whirlpools throughout the hotel property, and walking, hiking and bicycle paths. Tennis can be played on grass, clay or hard surface courts, with a 10,500-seat stadium court. For dining there is Trattoria California restaurant, as well as Charlie's overlooking the clubhouse court.

GOLF: The two 18-hole public golf courses were designed by Ted Robinson. The East layout, with a par of 72, reaches out 6,686/6,259/5,521 yards. The West 18, also parring at 72, measures a fair 6,478/6,115/5,387 yards. The West Course, while shorter, offers undulating terrain and multi-level greens to keep you honest. At first view it looks easy and open. It is neither. Along with waterfalls, the East course has a par-3 island hole, while the West offers a par-4 island green to shoot for. Each of these layouts comes equipped with a tough dogleg finishing hole.

RATES: (EP) Split-level parlor suite - $305/$380/$760. Green fees - $130/$160, including cart.

ARRIVAL: By air - Palm Springs. By car - from the airport, travel south on Highway 111 for 20 minutes. The resort entrance will be on your left.

Indian Palms Resort

48-630 Monroe, Indio, CA 92201

(760) 775-4444; (800) 778-5288

ACCOMMODATIONS: Rooms at the inn or two- to three-bedroom condos. For condo rentals, call (619) 347-7640.

AMENITIES: Nine tennis courts (five lighted) and several pools. There is a lounge and dining in the clubhouse overlooking the 18th green.

GOLF: Available on three nine-hole courses, which you can combine to create three different 18-hole layouts. The yardage from the back tees of each 18 is 6,403/6,284/6,279, and each has a par of 72. Water comes into play on 15 of the 27 holes.

RATES: (EP) Inn - $109; two-bedroom condo (weekly) - $650. Green fees - $65, including cart.

ARRIVAL: From Palm Springs, go east on Highway 111 through Indian Wells. In Indio, turn right on Monroe Street.

Indian Wells Resort Hotel

76-661 Highway 111, Indian Wells, CA 92210

(760) 345-6466; (800) 248-3220

ACCOMMODATIONS: 152 rooms in the inn, each with a balcony, offering a view of either the mountains, the country club or pool.

AMENITIES: A pool, with tennis located nearby. The Loren Room is available for dining; Jake's lounge offers evening entertainment.

GOLF: Played just across Highway 111 at the Indian Wells public courses. For full details on these two excellent championship layouts refer to the Hyatt Grand Champions Resort on page 79. Guests also have playing privileges on the magnificent Indian Wells Country Club's 27 holes, home of the Bob Hope Classic.

RATES: (EP) Lodgings - $200/$259. Green fees - $195. Golf packages are available.

ARRIVAL: By air - Palm Springs Airport (14 miles). By car - from I-10 take Washington to Highway 111, then head west to Club Drive.

Ironwood Country Club

49-200 Mariposa Drive, Palm Desert, CA 92260

(760) 346-0551

ACCOMMODATIONS: Although a private club, rentals of privately owned homes and villas can be arranged through their rental office. A damage deposit of $250 is required. Maid service is provided once each week; additional service can be arranged at the prevailing rate.

AMENITIES: Two fine golf courses, a beautiful clubhouse and dining room, swimming pools, 14 lighted tennis courts, and more.

GOLF: The North Course, 6,238/5,563 yards, pars at 70. The South pars at 72 and stretches 7,286 yards from the masochist tees, or can be played at 6,808/6,518/5,909 yards.

RATES: (EP) Villas - one bedroom, $1,200 per week; monthly, $3,537. Rates are mid-December through April. Green fees - $125, including cart.

ARRIVAL: By air - Palm Springs. By car - from Highway 111 take Portola Drive north. The resort entrance will be on your left.

La Casa del Zorro Desert Resort

Borrego Springs, CA 92004

(760) 767-5323; (800) 824-1884

La Casa del Zorro is located in the Borrego Valley, which is nestled against the 8,000-foot-high Santa Rosa Mountains – a startling and magnificent setting.

ACCOMMODATIONS: Single rooms, suites, deluxe suites, and casitas ranging from one to four bedrooms. Some have a fireplace and all have small refrigerators. Since our first visit here they have added three new buildings (42 guest units), bringing their total to 77.

AMENITIES: Three pools in various secluded spots throughout the resort, six lighted tennis courts, a beauty salon and a gift shop. Recently added is a fitness center, including a lap pool. The dining and lounge areas are very impressive as they showcase beamed ceilings, Spanish tile floors and are furnished with early Spanish-style furniture. The food (continental cuisine) is good, as is the service.

GOLF: The Rams Hill 18-hole championship course is one of the most beautiful we have played. For complete details refer to the Rams Hill listing.

RATES: (EP) Lodgings - $225/$305/$480. Green fees - $95/$105, including cart.

ARRIVAL: By air - Borrego Springs Airport. By car - from Palm Springs, drive south on Highway 111 and branch off onto Highway 86. Drive south to State Road 22. Turn right (west) and continue on to Borrego Springs. At the first stop sign (near school) turn left and drive about four miles. The resort entrance will be on your left.

The Lakes Country Club

75-375 Country Club Drive, Palm Desert, CA 92260

(619) 568-4321; Reservations (619) 345-5695

ACCOMMODATIONS: One- to three-bedroom condos, each fully equipped for housekeeping, with a microwave oven, range, refrigerator (with ice dispenser), washer/dryer, disposal, dishwasher, gas barbecue, and a furnished patio. The resort's name tells all. There are 21 lakes covering 25 acres spread throughout the resort complex. The grounds are further enhanced by the presence of over a thousand towering palm trees.

AMENITIES: 15 tennis courts (eight lighted), a well-equipped tennis shop and clubhouse (overlooking the center stadium court) and three swimming pools.

GOLF: True to its name, water comes into play on at least nine of the 18 holes on the Lakes Course. Measuring a modest 6,502/ 6,130/5,504 yards, the course pars at 72. Architect Ted Robinson did an outstanding job of blending water, trees, Scottish-style grass bunkers, and rolling terrain to produce a fun and challenging course.

RATES: (EP) Lodging - $309/$425. Green fees - $125, including cart. Packages are available, as well as discounts for length of stay. Rates are for mid-December through April.

ARRIVAL: By air - Palm Springs. By car - I-10 to Palm Desert exit.

La Quinta Resort & Club

49-499 Eisenhower Drive, La Quinta, CA 92253

(619) 564-4111; (800) 598-3828

La Quinta Resort & Club has been judged one of the Top 50 resorts. Built in 1926, it qualifies as the area's oldest resort.

ACCOMMODATIONS: 640 units on 900 acres, ranging from rooms and casita suites to a number of privately owned villas. Each of the groupings surrounds a pool. Private homes can also be rented; call (619) 564-6098 for information. The grounds are outstanding, and feature a profusion of plantings.

AMENITIES: 30 tennis courts, supported by a posh clubhouse complete with dining room and bar. There are 25 pools and an excellent spa and fitness center. There are three dining rooms within the hotel, as well as those at the golf courses. The cuisine and manner of presentation are excellent.

GOLF: The Mountain Course is now available for guest play. It features a beautiful layout reaching out 6,758/6,320/5,405/5,010 yards with a par of 72. The Dunes Course plays 6,747/6,230/5,752/5,005 yards, also with a par of 72. It is quite long and open. Play can also be arranged on the TPC Stadium Course as well as the Jack Nicklaus Resort Course.

RATES: (EP) Rooms - $325/$350/$375; Cottage suites - $375/$3,000 per night. Green fees - $130/$205, including cart. Rates are for December-April.

ARRIVAL: By air - Palm Springs. By private aircraft - Thermal (10 minutes). By car - the resort is 19 miles southeast of Palm Springs.

California

Marriott's Desert Springs Resort & Spa

74855 Country Club Drive, Palm Desert, CA 92260

(760) 341-2211; (800) 331-3112

The eight-story indoor atrium entrance is spectacular, with water cascading down to a lower pool containing gondolas and several white swans. The hotel is often crowded on weekends with people who come just to see the atrium area.

ACCOMMODATIONS: 892 units. The 65 suites range from 900 to 3,100 square feet. There is also an assortment of shops; it's almost like being in a department store.

AMENITIES: Two swimming pools, 16 tennis courts (eight lighted), a 27,000-square-foot health spa with jogging paths, a lap pool, therapy pools, sauna and whirlpools, Swiss showers, a luxurious array of salon and beauty treatments. There are five restaurants and at least that many lounges.

GOLF: There are two Ted Robinson courses. The Palms plays 6,761/6,381/6,143/5,492 yards, parring at 72. Situated on gently rolling terrain and well trapped, it has water coming into play on 10 holes. The Valley Course stretches 6,679/6,377/6,063/5,330 yards and also pars at 72.

RATES: (EP) Lodgings - $395/$459 and up. Green fees -$145/ $160, including cart.

ARRIVAL: By air - Palm Springs (13 miles). By car - I-10 from Los Angeles (120 miles).

Marriott's Rancho Las Palmas Resort

41000 Bob Hope Drive, Rancho Mirage, CA 92270

(760) 568-2727; (800) 458-8786

This has been judged one of the Top 50 resorts. The Rancho is impressive, with its early California-style architecture, featuring graceful arches, rough textured stucco, exposed wooden beams, and red tile roofs. The rich Spanish-style furnishings as well as the paintings, tapestries and authentic Mexican tile add to its gentle Southwestern ambiance.

ACCOMMODATIONS: 450 hacienda-style rooms and suites, each with patio or balcony. All are near the golf course or a small lake. There are also a great many condominiums. For condo rentals,call (619) 345-5695. Coin-operated laundry facilities are available.

AMENITIES: 25 tennis courts (eight lighted), two pools with companion hydrotherapy pools, a fitness center, and once-a-week aerobic classes. Dining options include The Cabrillo Room, serving California cuisine; The Fountain Court (a bit less formal); and The Sunrise Terrace, which offers patio dining. Each has good service and a wide menu selection.

GOLF: The North/South nines measure 6,019/5,716/5,421 yards, parring at 71. The West/North combination reaches 5,558/5,295/4,985 yards and pars at 70. The West/South combination weighs in at 5,569/5,219/4,886, again with a par of 70. Winding among six small lakes, 80 sand traps, over 1,500 tall palm trees, and the condominium structures themselves, these are entertaining courses to play.

RATES: (EP) Lodgings - $285/$320/$450. Green fees - $119/$130, including cart. Rates are for December 26-May 30.

ARRIVAL: By air - Palm Springs. By car - I-10 off at Bob Hope Drive. Continue on Bob Hope Drive for five miles, resort entrance will be on your left.

Marriott Villa Rentals

1091 Pinehurst Lane, Palm Desert, CA 92260

(760) 779-1208; (800) 526-3597

While a basic part of the Marriott Desert Springs Hotel, the villas function as a separate operation. They are immediately adjacent to the resort and spa.

ACCOMMODATIONS: Two-bedroom, two-bath villa suites ranging up to 1,650 square feet. Each villa features a whirlpool spa, formal dining area, gas-log fireplace, washer/dryer, fully equipped kitchen with microwave, self-cleaning oven, dishwasher and disposal. The suites are absolutely first class. We have seen very few that come even close to these accommodations. The deli adjacent to the lobby can supply a few basics.

California

AMENITIES: All amenities of Marriott's Desert Springs Resort, including their dining facilities. There are two pools on property.

GOLF: For detail on the golf and other facilities, refer to Marriott's Desert Springs Resort & Spa, above.

RATES: (EP) one Bedroom villa - $350; two-bedroom villa -$475. Weekly and monthly rates available.

Monterey Country Club

41-500 Monterey Avenue, Palm Desert, CA 92260

(760) 568-931; Reservations (619) 345-5695

ACCOMMODATIONS: Condos and homes, most with fireplaces and wet bars, fully equipped for housekeeping.

AMENITIES: 19 tennis courts (10 lighted) and several pools scattered throughout the area. The upper level of the clubhouse houses the dining room.

GOLF: The 27 holes are played using a crossover arrangement. The East/West combination reaches out 6,096/5,798/5,250 yards and pars at 71; the East/South nines measure 6,041/5,780/5,242 yards, also parring at 71; and the West/South combination runs 6,133/5,838/5,346 yards, parring at 72. With water on 15 holes, plus some interesting uphill and downhill fairways, it is an intriguing course to play. For tee times, call (619) 340-3885.

RATES: (EP) Lodgings - $275/$285. Green fees - $95, including cart. There are discounts for weekly or longer stays. Rates are for mid-December through April.

ARRIVAL: By air - Palm Springs.

Palm Desert Resort & Country Club

77-333 Country Club Drive, Palm Desert, CA 92260

(760) 772-3880; Reservations (800) 657-2343

ACCOMMODATIONS: Villas, each with living room, fully equipped kitchen, bedroom, dinette, and private patio. The two-bedroom units have two baths.

AMENITIES: 17 lighted tennis courts with a 1,000-seat amphitheater as the center court. There are also two indoor racquetball courts and 20 pools throughout the property. Papagayo's is available for dining.

GOLF: The course, parring at 72, plays 6,506/6,202/6,026/5,434 yards. With sand, water and rolling terrain, it is one of the most enjoyable desert courses I have played. That is, until I reached the 9th hole. What I said is unprintable. Suffice to say, it is different.

RATES: (EP) Lodgings - $150/$175. Green fees - $60/$75, including cart. Rates are for January-April. There is an additional $75 cleaning fee per unit.

ARRIVAL: By air - Palm Springs. By car - from Los Angeles, I-10 to Washington Street exit, right on Country Club Drive.

Palm Valley Country Club

976-200 Country Club Drive, Palm Desert, CA 62260

(619) 345-2737; Reservations (619) 345-5695

ACCOMMODATIONS: Well-equipped homes and condos either near or on the golf course.

AMENITIES: Spa, racquetball courts, weight room, aerobics room, saunas, massage and steam rooms, whirlpools, tanning rooms, and more. Next to the clubhouse is a pool and an outdoor jogging trail. There are also 19 tennis courts (10 lighted) and a stadium court. The 83,000- square-foot clubhouse, the center of the resort's activities, is a super setting for dining.

GOLF: The South course stretches 6,545/6,105/5,429 yards, parring at 72. With water on 12 holes, palm trees all over the place, as well as part of the Sahara Desert used as sand traps, this layout will keep your attention. Or perhaps I should say it had better keep your attention. The North course is an executive layout. For tee times, call (619) 345-2742.

RATES: (EP) Lodgings - $260/$340. Green fees - $120, including cart. There are discounts for stays of a week or longer. Rates quoted are for mid-December through April.

ARRIVAL: By air - Palm Springs.

California

PGA West

55-900 PGA Boulevard, La Quinta, CA 92253

Reservations (619) 345-5695

ACCOMMODATIONS: Condominiums and homes. Each condo is fully equipped for housekeeping, including washer/dryer, barbecue, patio furniture, and an enclosed garage. Daily maid service can be arranged.

AMENITIES: 19 tennis courts, including an exhibition center court with seating for 3,000. You can choose to play on clay, grass or hard surface.

GOLF: There are now four courses. The TPC "Stadium Resort Course," a par-72 Pete Dye design, reaches out 7,271 yards from the back tees. Anyone playing from these tees is either a masochist or in dire need of a session with a good psychiatrist. The remaining tee settings measure 6,821/6,313/5,228 yards. Mr. Dye used the natural undulation of the desert to create a Scottish links layout. He also introduced water on nine holes. The 17th, a par 3, is aptly named "Alcatraz." While only 128 yards from the regular tees, you will find yourself shooting at a green measuring some 28 by 31 yards.

The Jack Nicklaus Course, available for guest play, measures 7,264/6,671/6,064/5,175 yards, also parring at 72. This entertaining layout brings water into play on seven holes. The ninth and 18th holes share a green, which is reminiscent of many Scottish courses.

The other two layouts are the Arnold Palmer Private Course and the Jack Nicklaus Private Course; both are restricted to member play. For tee times, call the pro shop at (619) 564-7170 or (619) 564-7429.

RATES: (EP) Lodgings - $410/$420. There are discounts for stays of five nights or longer ranging from 15 to 60%. Green fees - $195/$260.

ARRIVAL: By air - Palm Springs or Thermal Airports. By car - from Highway 111, travel west on Jefferson Street about five miles.

Rams Hill

PO Box 664, Borrego Springs, CA 92004

(619) 5595; (800) 732-9200; (800) 524-2800

Few places in the world can match the beauty and grandeur of the Anza-Borrego Desert. The surrounding peaks (sometimes snow-capped) reflecting brilliant blues and greens, the desert with an ever-changing palette of colors, and the stark silence combine to produce a state of profound peace.

ACCOMMODATIONS: Rental homes, fully equipped for housekeeping. Future plans include custom homes, patio homes, and casitas.

AMENITIES: An impressive clubhouse with an excellent restaurant. Tennis courts and swimming pools

GOLF: The course stretches 6,866/6,328/5,694 yards and pars at 72. A few of the hazards include water on six holes, 56 white sand bunkers, and the magnificent views from most of the tees, which really make it difficult to keep your mind on the game. Ted Robinson, architect of Rams Hill, took advantage of the natural terrain, creating rises and falls of more than 100 feet on several holes. We found it a fascinating layout to play. For tee times, call (619) 767-5124.

RATES: (EP) Lodgings - $150/$190. For weekly rates, deduct 10%. Green fees - $75/$105, including cart. Rates are January through April.

ARRIVAL: By air - Borrego Springs. By car - from the Palm Springs area travel south on Highway 111. In Indio, branch off to Highway 86 and travel south to State Road 22. Turn right and drive to Borrego Springs. At the first stop sign (near the school), turn left and go about five miles. The resort entrance is on your left.

The Ritz-Carlton

68-900 Frank Sinatra Drive, Rancho Mirage, CA 92270

(760) 321-8282; (800) 241-3333

The hotel is located about 600 feet above the surrounding Palm Springs area, providing a sweeping view of a good part of the Coachella Valley. As in all Ritz-Carlton Hotels, this one features an interesting assortment of paintings and artifacts.

California

ACCOMMODATIONS: 239 guest rooms, plus 21 suites. All are impeccably furnished with all of the amenities expected of such an establishment. There is also the Club Level (referred to in most hotels as the concierge level). This particular one is very well run. This Ritz does not, however, provide in-room safe deposit boxes.

AMENITIES: A 5,000-square-foot spa, 10 tennis courts (eight lighted), a fitness center and a a swimming pool. Dining options range from The Dining Room, The Café and The Miranda Restaurant for casual poolside dining. A tie is not required during evening hours, but a jacket is. The resort also offers a children's program, the Ritz-Kids, allowing the younger set to enjoy their vacation while the parents sample at least a few of the amenities offered.

GOLF: The Ritz-Carlton is in the process of building its own golf course. In the meantime they have made arrangements for their guests to play a variety of courses (18) in the area and, of course, provide transportation to and from. With any luck at all they will have their own facilities in operation by the time you read this book.

RATES: One bedroom - $325; Club Level - $485; Suites - $585.

ARRIVAL: By air - Palm Springs Airport. By car - take Frank Sinatra Drive, cross Highway 111 and continue up the hill to the resort. The entrance will be on your left.

Stouffer's Esmeraldo Resort

44-400 Indian Wells Lane, Indian Wells, CA 92210

(760) 773-4444; (800) 468-3571

A great deal of attention and planning went into this resort. It consists of eight multi-storied buildings, with an eight-story glass-enclosed atrium entrance. There are several 40-foot palm trees in the lobby.

ACCOMMODATIONS: 560 rooms and suites. Units have French Provincial furnishings and louvered windows. Each has a sitting area, TV in the bedroom and bathroom, and a small balcony. There are also washer/dryer units available for guest use.

AMENITIES: Three pools (one featuring a poolside gazebo bar), seven tennis courts (three lighted), two whirlpools and a health and fitness center. Along with a series of lounges there are two restaurants serving Mediterranean and continental cuisine.

GOLF: The resort is adjacent to two 18-hole public golf courses designed by Ted Robinson. For details, refer to the Hyatt Grand Champions Resort on page 79.

RATES: (EP) Lodgings - $210/$390. Green fees - $110/$120, including cart. Golf packages are available.

ARRIVAL: By air - Palm Springs. By car - the resort is on Highway 111 just a few miles south of Palm Desert. The resort entrance will be on your left.

The Westin Mission Hills Resort

Dinah Shore & Bob Hope Drive, Rancho Mirage, CA 92270

(760) 328-5955; (800) 228-3000

The Mission Hills architecture was adapted from a Moroccan design, using classic stucco, arches, colonnades and formal courtyards.

ACCOMMODATIONS: 16 two-story buildings house the 512 guest rooms, including 40 suites. All units have private patios and separate dressing rooms; many have cathedral ceilings as well as golf course views. The suites feature a living room and wet bar; some have a fireplace, whirlpool, or even a grand piano. There is also a concierge level, offering guests a variety of special services.

AMENITIES: A seven-court tennis center (with a sunken stadium court), a complete health and fitness center, and three pools. The main pool features a 60-foot water slide. Dine either in Bella Vista, serving California cuisine, or La Concha, specializing in fresh seafood and pasta. There are several lounges within the hotel and by the pools.

GOLF: The Mission Hills Course, a Pete Dye design, plays 6,706/6,196/5,629/4,841 yards, with a par of 70. Water is a factor on only five holes. The course has small hard greens and deep pot bunkers. The North Course, Gary Player's first undertaking in the Palm Springs area, is a most unusual, lush desert setting. It uses almost 20 acres of water, four waterfalls, lakes, streams, some 6,000 tons of natural and artificial rock, over 2,500 trees and 25 acres of plantings. Playing to a substantial 7,062/6,643/6,044/4,907 yards, it also pars at 72.

RATES: (EP) Lodgings - $199/$450 and up. Green fees -$140/$160, including cart. Golf packages are available.

ARRIVAL: By air - Palm Springs. By car - from I-10, take the Ramon Road exit and drive two miles to resort.

California

Colorado

1. Sheraton Steamboat Springs
2. Iron Horse Resort Retreat
3. Vail Beaver Creek Area/Beaver Creek Golf Club/Eagle-Vail Golf Club/Singletree Golf Links/Vail Assoc., Inc. /Vail-Beaver Creek Resort Assoc./ Vail Golf Club
4. Copper Mountain Resorts
5. Keystone Resort
6. Inverness Hotel & Golf Club
7. Silvertree Resort Hotel Snowmass Lodge & Club
8. Skyland Resort & Country Club
9. The Broadmoor
10. Best Western at Pueblo West
11. The Sheraton Tamarron Resort
12. Pagosa Lodge
13. The Peaks Resort & Spa

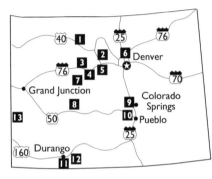

Best Western Inn at Pueblo West

201 S. McCulloch Boulevard, Pueblo West, CO 81007

(719) 547-2111; (800) 448-1972

ACCOMMODATIONS: 80 oversized rooms, some with patios; all have complimentary CNN, ESPN and HBO.

AMENITIES: Two lighted tennis courts, outdoor heated pool, volleyball court, jogging, and bicycling trails. The restaurant and lounge, done in a Spanish motif, presents a varied and excellent menu.

GOLF: The course, next to the resort, reaches out 7,305/6,725/ 5,793 yards and pars at 72. Water challenges on only four holes.

RATES: (EP) Rooms - $74/$89. Green fees - $15/$18, carts $14. Golf package (two nights/two days lodging, green fees for two rounds, breakfast) - $195 per couple. Rates listed are for June through September.

ARRIVAL: By air - Pueblo Airport (15 miles). By car - from I-25 take Highway 50 west for about 10 miles. You will see Best Western signs to guide you. The resort entrance will be on your left.

The Broadmoor

PO Box 1439, Colorado Springs, CO 80901

(719) 634-7711; (800) 634-7711

The Broadmoor has been judged one of our Top 50 resorts. It opened in 1918, and has preserved its glowing past while more than keeping pace with the present.

ACCOMMODATIONS: The original hotel, known as Broadmoor Main, is a unique blend of old world grace and modern convenience. It stands today with its magnificent Italian Renaissance decor largely intact. The Broadmoor has won the Mobil Five Star Award each year since 1960. Keep in mind that only 20 hotel/resorts in the United States out of more than 20,000 earn this award. The recent completion of the 90,000-square-foot Broadmoor Spa, Golf & Tennis Club, with its new restaurant and golf clubhouse, was a substantial undertaking. However, it was almost upstaged by the opening of 150 additional rooms, called the West Tower, which brought the total number of accommodations to 706. At last, after many years of planning, they have constructed a bridge from the east side to the west. It is a beautiful structure and allows immediate access to the newer west side.

The nine-story Broadmoor South, adjacent to the Main, with its Penrose Dining Room and Lounge, offers a spectacular view of the mountains. Broadmoor West and the New West, on the west side of the lake, form a resort hotel complete unto itself. With dining, dancing and entertainment, it also showcases Oriental art dating back to the Ming dynasty.

AMENITIES: 12 Plexipave all-weather tennis courts, including a stadium court; pool; skeet and trap shooting; bicycle rentals; and boating. The new spa has saunas, a plunge pool and whirlpool, a fitness center, 16 massage and six facial rooms, 12 soaking tubs, special showers, and on and on. Horseback riding and tours of this scenic area can also be arranged. The younger set has not been forgotten. From July through August, the hotel provides a supervised program for children ages three through 12; it operates Monday through Friday.

There are nine restaurants and five lounges, not including the Winter House. Several fine restaurants are in the Main: the Tavern, with its original Toulouse-Lautrec lithographs; the Garden Room; the stately Main Dining Room; and the New West.

Colorado

GOLF: There are three courses. The East, designed by Donald Ross in 1918, presents a significant yardage of 7,091/6,551/5,873, with a par set at 72/73. The West, a Robert Trent Jones 1965 design, stretches out 6,937/6,109/5,505 yards and pars at 72/73. Both courses start from the well-stocked pro shop adjacent to the hotel. The Mountain Course reaches out a modest 6,781/6,108/5,609/4,834 yards, with the par set at 72/70. Sounds easy! But this layout is one that can wring your soul and, as a matter of fact, your tail. On the first nine there is only one hole where you are allowed a view of the green from the tee box (the eighth). In fact, from the third tee it is difficult to determine where the fairway is. Ed Seay, of the Arnold Palmer organization, designer of the Mountain layout (1976), found a new way to keep everyone completely alert. On eight of the front nine there are "barrancas" (ravines usually filled with brush). On the second nine there are only two barrancas coming into play. I will not describe the 18th hole, as it should remain a surprise – something each golfer will long remember. The elevation of this layout averages around 6,000 feet. The Director of Golf is Mike Franko.

The Academy of Golf is now available at the Broadmoor. They cover golf fundamentals, as well as simulate every possible type of shot you may encounter. For details, call (800) 832-6235.

RATES: (EP) Lodgings - $295/$345/$375; Suites - $500 and up. Green fees - $150, including cart.

ARRIVAL: By air - Colorado Springs. By car - from the airport take I-25 to Exit #138. Circle Drive becomes Lake Avenue, which heads directly onto the hotel grounds.

Copper Mountain Resorts

PO Box 3001, Copper Mountain, CO 80443

(970) 968-2882; (800) 458-8386

ACCOMMODATIONS: Mountain Plaza and Village Square, are in the heart of the village, with shops and restaurants readily available.

AMENITIES: Horseback riding, swimming, boating on Lake Dillon, two indoor and six outdoor tennis courts, fishing, beginners' fly-fishing clinics, jeep tours, windsurfing, rafting, and bicycling. During winter, skiing takes over. The resort offers over 1,300 feet of vertical drop, 98 trails and 20 lifts.

GOLF: Pete and Perry Dye designed theCopper Creek Golf Club, which measures 6,094/5,742/5,159/4,392 yards with a par of 70. It is an exciting layout. Although three of the holes play along ski runs, it is primarily on gently undulating terrain. The course introduces water on seven of the first nine holes, but only one on the back side. Should your game show unusual power, keep in mind you are playing at about 9,600 feet.

RATES: (EP) Lodgings - $90/$125/$155. Green fees - $75, including cart. Rates are for June-September.

ARRIVAL: By air - Denver. By car - I-70 west, exit at 195, approximately 75 miles.

Inverness Hotel & Golf Club

200 Inverness Drive West, Englewood, CO 80112

(303) 799-5800; (800) 346-4891

ACCOMMODATIONS: 302 guest rooms.

AMENITIES: Indoor and outdoor pools, tennis courts, saunas, whirlpools, an exercise room, and jogging trails nearby. Dining is in the Black Swan (jackets required, ties optional) or, less formal, the Garden Terrace and the Copenhagen Restaurant.

GOLF: The course, designed by Preston Maxwell, reaches out 6,948/6,407/5,681 yards with a par of 70/71.

RATES: (EP) Lodgings - $129/$169/$3. Green fees - $115, including cart.

ARRIVAL: By air - Stapleton International. By car - I-25 to County Line exit. Turn left (east); the second stoplight is Inverness Road. Turn left to resort.

Colorado

Iron Horse Resort Retreat

PO Box 1286, Winter Park, CO 80482

(970) 726-8851; (800) 621-8190

ACCOMMODATIONS: One- , two- or three-bedroom condos, each with balcony, fireplace, living and dining area, microwave and dishwasher. Some have a private Jacuzzi tub, wet bar, and a washer/dryer.

AMENITIES: Indoor and outdoor pools, four outdoor hot tubs, weight and exercise rooms, and a steam room. In the winter, the resort offers 18 lifts, groomed ski runs, sleigh rides, snowmobiling, and virtually every other winter activity. If you decide not to cook for yourself, there is the Rails Bar & Restaurant.

GOLF: Parring at 72, the Pole Creek Golf Club course weighs in at a fair 6,882/6,230/4,956 yards. They did not name this Pole Creek just for kicks. The creek meanders throughout the course, forming four lakes. This layout includes some elevated tees and greens, and is well trapped.

RATES: (EP) Lodgings - $129/$238. Green fees - $85, carts $25. There are several different packages that include golf.

ARRIVAL: By air - Denver (90 minutes). By car - from Denver, take I-70 to Exit 232; follow I- 40 north to the resort.

Keystone Resort

PO Box 38, Keystone, CO 80435

(970) 496-4242; (800) 541-0346

ACCOMMODATIONS: A 152-room lodge, along with 900 condos and homes. All condos have fully equipped kitchens and fireplaces. The resort also offers child-care service and an all- day activities program. Keystone Resort is 75 miles west of Denver in the 9,300-foot-deep Snake River Valley.

AMENITIES: 14 tennis courts (two indoor), bicycling, kayaking, sailing, fishing, raft trips, horseback riding, and several pools. There are four winter ski areas here: Keystone, Outback, North Peak and Arapahoe Basin. The dining facilities include the Bighorn Steak House, the Garden Room (continental), and the Edgewater Café (casual).

GOLF: The Robert Trent Jones, Jr. course is three miles south of the village. Rimmed by towering peaks, it plays 7,090/6,521/5,720 yards and pars at 72. It is an interesting and beautiful layout, traversing woods and meadows. A nine-acre lake and various ponds come into play. It is said to be the highest course in the United States, with portions lying above 9,300 feet.

RATES: (EP) Lodgings - $265/$309. Green fees - $105, including carts.

ARRIVAL: By air - Denver. By car - I-70 west to Exit 205. East on US 6 for six miles.

Pagosa Lodge

PO Box 4400, Pagosa, CO 81157

(970) 731-4141; (800) 523-7704

ACCOMMODATIONS: In the early days, Pagosa meant a teepee or lean-to. There is now a 101-room inn plus condominiums. If you are interested in a condo rather than hotel accommodations, call (800) 365-3149.

AMENITIES: Bicycles, boat and ice skate rentals, a health spa, indoor pool, saunas, hydrotherapy pools, and game rooms. There is a stable offering horseback riding, chuckwagon cookouts, and winter sleigh rides, as well as a racquet club with six courts. Baby-sitting service is also available. Dining is provided in the Great Divide or the Rendezvous Cocktail Lounge.

GOLF: The course has a 27-hole layout. Pine 1/Pine 2 nines weigh in at 6,748/6,282/5,392 yards, parring at 71. Pine 1/Meadows, parring at 72, plays an awesome 7,256/6,524/5,380 yards. Finally, the Pine 2/Meadows combination completes the picture, reaching out 6,956/6,154/5,126 yards, also with a par of 72.

RATES: (EP) Inn - $125/$200. Green fees - $55, including cart. Golf packages are available.

ARRIVAL: By air - Durango. By private aircraft - Pagosa Springs (6,500-foot paved runway). By car - US 160, 3½ miles west of Pagosa Springs.

The Peaks Resort & Spa

136 Country Club Drive, Telluride, CO 81435

(970) 728-6800; (800) 789-2220

The resort is situated at a (breathtaking) elevation of 9,500 feet. It is surrounded by the San Juan Mountain Range reaching up to 14,000 feet. Needless to say, the views from here are spectacular.

ACCOMMODATIONS: 177 rooms, including 28 suites. There are also one- to four-bedroom condominiums completely equipped for housekeeping.

AMENITIES: A 42,000-square-foot spa with steam rooms, a lap pool, racquetball courts, a large swimming pool, mountain biking, horseback riding, five tennis courts with whitewater rafting, fly-fishing, hiking and rock climbing as alternative activities. There is a

Colorado

"Kids Spa" program in place as well as a baby-sitting service. The Legends of The Peaks restaurant seats 130. The resort is also a wonderful winter facility, offering all manner of activities.

GOLF: The Telluride Golf Club reaches out a respectable 6,739/ 6,277/5,724/5,181 yards with a par of 71. The course is a traditional layout in that it is tree-lined and well trapped. Water comes into play on eight holes. There is a driving range, putting green and clubhouse. Remember that you are playing golf at over 9,000 feet. Be prepared for your golf ball to accomplish some unbelievable things.

RATES: (EP) Rooms - $295/$375. Suites - $485/$695. Green fees - $145, including cart. Several different package plans are available.

ARRIVAL: By By air - the resort is about 10 minutes from Telluride regional Airport. By car - from Denver, take I-70 west to Grand Junction, then Highway 50 south (65 miles) to Montrose. Proceed on Highway 550 for approximately 25 miles through Ridgeway. Go west on Highway 62 (40 miles) to Placerville, then take Highway 145 to Telluride and follow the signs.

Sheraton Steamboat Resort

PO Box 774808, Steamboat Springs, CO 80477

(970) 879-2220; (800) 848-8878

ACCOMMODATIONS: The nucleus of this resort complex is the Sheraton Village Hotel (276 guest rooms), along with the Thunderbird Lodge (58 luxurious rooms) and 75 condominium units. For reservations at the Thunderbird, call (800) 525-5502.

AMENITIES: Four lighted tennis courts; whitewater rafting down the Green, Yanpa, or Colorado Rivers; sailing and waterskiing on Steamboat Lake; and excellent fishing in the 900 miles of rivers, streams, or 109 lakes. Four-legged critters are a big part of Steamboat Springs life, with trail rides, Western dinner rides, or hayrack rides available. If you are a ski enthusiast, you already know about this famous winter facility. There are three restaurants: Cipriani's, specializing in Italian cuisine; the Soda Creek Café for lighter dining; or Remington's Restaurant. A nice extra: there is a coin-operated laundry.

GOLF: This Robert Trent Jones, Jr. course measures 6,906/ 6,276/5,647 yards and pars at 72. While you do get some help from the 7,000-foot altitude, the 77 sand traps and seven water holes will bring you quickly back to reality.

RATES: (EP) Lodgings - $119/$149/$175. Green fees - $120, including cart. Golf packages are available. Rates are for late May-September 30.

ARRIVAL: By air - Denver (153 miles) with shuttle flights or private aircraft to Hayden (23 miles from Steamboat Springs). By car - take I-70 to the Silverthorne exit. Travel north to Kremmling, then west on US 40 to resort.

Sheraton Tamarron Resort

PO Drawer 3131, Durango, CO 81302

(970) 259-2000; (800) 678-1000

ACCOMMODATIONS: The great hewn-timber inn offers a wide variety of accommodations, including rooms, suites with living room/kitchen facilities, Loft Inn suites, townhouses with one to three bedrooms, and condominiums.

AMENITIES: Fishing on a private lake (tackle and bait provided, no license required) or fly-fishing the beautiful Animas River with a professional guide (all equipment included). There's also white-water rafting, horseback riding, a hayride and steak cookout, indoor/outdoor pools and indoor and outdoor tennis courts. A complete health club and a supervised children's program complete the picture. For candlelight dining there is Le Canyon. The San Juan Club has a less formal setting. A nice extra: there are washer/dryers available. Another unusual extra: even if you are housed in a condominium you may order up room service.

In the winter this is a ski buff's delight. The slopes of Purgatory average over 200 inches of snow, providing skiing, sleigh rides, tobogganing, ice skating and snowmobile tours.

GOLF: Fairways wind amid tall stands of ponderosa pine, age-old oaks, and aspens. The Tamarron Golf Course, an Arthur Hill design, plays 6,885/6,340/5,380 yards with a par of 72. It offers some of the most interesting golf holes (maybe terrifying would be more appropriate) we have seen. Some of the elevation changes from one part of the fairway to another are spectacular. At this altitude (8,000-plus feet) your golf ball does some rather unexpected things.

RATES: (EP) Lodgings - $179/$209/$309. Green fees - $120, including cart. Golf package (two nights/two days, including lodging, full breakfast, two days golf, cart, club storage, a golf clinic) - $679 per couple. Rates are for July-September.

ARRIVAL: By air - Durango. By car - 18 miles north of Durango on US 550.

The Silvertree Resort Hotel

Box 5009, Snowmass Village, CO 81615

(970) 923-3520; (800) 525-9402

ACCOMMODATIONS: 248 rooms along with 12 suites. There are also a number of one- , two- , and three-bedroom condos and homes equipped for housekeeping. These units have fireplaces; some have pools.

AMENITIES: Two pools, two whirlpools, and a state-of-the-art health club with steam room and sauna. Located nearby are tennis courts, whitewater rafting, and hot air ballooning, Western trail rides, cycling, hiking, and fly-fishing. Three restaurants and a lounge are located within the hotel.

GOLF: For details, refer to The Snowmass Club.

RATES: (EP) Lodgings - $90/$150/$160. Green fees - $95, including cart.

ARRIVAL: By air - Aspen. By car - from Aspen take Highway 82 northwest four miles. Enter Snowmass Village and drive approximately three miles.

The Snowmass Lodge & Club

PO Box G2, Snowmass Village, CO 81615

(970) 923-5600; (800) 525-0710

ACCOMMODATIONS: Villas and condos with fireplaces and fully equipped kitchens.

AMENITIES: 11 tennis courts (two indoor), a heated lap pool and a coed whirlpool, a recreation pool, three racquetball and squash courts, steam rooms, saunas, whirlpools, weight and massage rooms, lockers and showers. During the summer months, guided hiking, horseback riding, and fishing expeditions can also be arranged. While open for all meals, the Four Corners Grill is particularly charming for candlelight dining. Already a mecca for ski enthusiasts, Snowmass is now becoming known for its summer activities.

GOLF: The Links, now playing 6,900/6,055/5,008 yards, pars at 71. It offers an open layout, despite being exceptionally well trapped. The fact that you are at almost 9,000 feet will become apparent after your first tee shot.

RATES: (EP) Lodgings - $229/$259. Green fees - $95, including carts. Golf packages are available. Rates are June-August.

ARRIVAL: By air - Aspen. By car - from Aspen, Highway 82 northwest two miles to enter Snowmass Village. Now on Brush Creek Road, go three miles and turn left onto Highline Road. A club limousine is available from airport.

Vail-Beaver Creek Area

For many years Vail and Beaver Creek have been known for their superb skiing. The area is also renowned for its magnificent mountain and forest settings, which are virtually unmatched in this country. But, alas, winter does come to an end. The beauty is still there and so are the many restaurants, bars, shops, hotels, and condos, all representing a huge dollar investment and earning virtually nothing.

The resorts of Colorado have discovered golf. They did not ease into the field, but went in under a full head of steam, employing such august names as Jack Nicklaus, Arnold Palmer, Pete Dye, Robert Trent Jones, Jr. and Gary Player to produce some of the finest golf courses anywhere. Two such areas are Vail Village Resorts and the Beaver Creek Resort complex, approximately 10 miles apart. Due to their proximity, most of the amenities are available to guests of either resort.

Within a 20-mile radius there are four first-class championship golf courses. Each has a full pro shop, locker rooms and restaurants. The golf season in this area is late June to mid-September.

Due to the great number and diversity of accommodations, it is not possible to list their rates. The majority are posh, expensive winter lodgings that offer vastly reduced summer rates. There are also golf packages, which include play on several courses. Request this information when making reservations. There are also over 50 tennis courts in the area.

Colorado

The Beaver Creek Golf Club

Now semi-private, this course was designed by Robert Trent Jones, Jr. Playing to a par of 70, it measures 6,464/6,026/5,202 yards. This layout stretches along Beaver Creek and into the valley. Native spruce and aspen line the fairways, and some well-bunkered greens are presented. For tee times, call (970) 949-7123.

Eagle-Vail Golf Club

The course plays 6,819/6,142/4,856 yards and pars at 72. Considered one of the most challenging in the valley, its 10th hole, a par 3, plays from 208 to 124 yards. The tee sits 250 feet above the green. Your ball spends so much time in the air you may have to get a permit from NASA. For tee times, call (970) 949-5267.

Singletree Golf Links

Another semi-private course, Singletree lies west of Beaver Creek at the Berry Creek Ranch. The course resembles a Scottish links with its hilly fairways, deep bunkers, and natural grass roughs. Parring at 71, it stretches out 7,024/6,435/5,907/5,293 yards. For tee times, call (970) 949-4240.

Vail Golf Club

This was Vail's first. Just east of Vail Village, it reaches out 7,048/6,282/5,934/5,303 yards, with a par of 71/72. Gore Creek winds throughout this 18-hole layout. For tee times, call (970) 476-1330.

Accommodations

The Vail/Beaver Creek area offers a wide variety of accommodations. For more information, contact:

Vail Associates, Inc.
PO Box 7, Vail, CO 81658
(970) 949-5750; (800) 525-2257

The Vail-Beaver Creek Area Accommodation Association
241 East Meadow Drive, Vail, CO 81657
(303) 476-5677; (800) 525-3875

Florida

Northern Florida

1. Bluewater Bay
2. The Sandestin Beach Resort/Seascape Resort
3. Marriott's Bay Point Resort
4. Killearn CC & Inn
5. Amelia Island Plantation/Summer Beach Resort/The Ritz Carlton Amelia Island
6. Lodge Ponte Vedra/Marriott at Sawgrass Resort/ Ponte Vedra Inn & Club
7. Ponce De Leon Golf Club
8. Palm Coast Golf Resort

Amelia Island Plantation

Highway A1A South, Amelia Island, FL 32034

(904) 261-6161; (800) 874-6878

Amelia Island Plantation is one of our Top 50 resorts.

ACCOMMODATIONS: Guest rooms at the inn, plus over 450 one- to four-bedroom villas. Each villa offers a fully equipped kitchen with dishwasher, microwave, and washer/dryer. Some have a private indoor pool.

AMENITIES: On 1,250 acres, with horseback riding, 25 tennis courts (some lighted) along with a 1,000-seat stadium court. several pools, health & fitness center with steam rooms, sauna, and massage. There is also fishing and sailing. During the summer months, Amelia Island Plantation provides a well-supervised children's program. Dining facilities are excellent, and include The Beach Club, Duneside Club, and the Veranda Restaurant.

GOLF: The original golf facilities consist of three nine-hole courses designed by Pete Dye. Using a crossover system, they play as follows: the Oakmarsh/Osterbay nines measure 6,461/5,767/ 5,451/4,970, with a par of 71; the Oysterbay/Oceanside plays out 5,985/5,361/5,041/4,641 yards and pars at 70; the Oceanside/Oakmarsh combination measures 6,140/5,550/5,186/4,791 yards, also parring at 71. Natural water hazards were used to make these among the better nines to be found anywhere. Three of the holes on the Oceanside front right along the ocean. These short layouts tend to favor a "shotmaker," while punishing a spray hitter.

Should you play the Oysterbay, be careful on the first hole. It is a short par 4 of 280 yards, but neither the water on the right nor a trap on the left just short of the green are visible from the tee. A driver is not recommended on this hole.

The newest course is the Long Point Club championship course. Designed by Tom Fazio, it came into play in late 1987. It reaches out 6,775/6,068/5,539/4,927 yards and pars at 72. This links-type layout is constructed on rolling terrain, with water in play on five of the first nine holes and six on the back side. Two consecutive holes (six and seven, both par 3) run along the ocean and present spectacular views. The Long Point Course has been judged one of the top 12 resort courses in the US and ranks 24th worldwide according to *Golf Digest*. It is one tough layout.

RATES: (EP) Lodgings - $225/$295/$325. Green fees (original 27 holes) - $110/$130, including cart; Long Point Course - $150, including cart. They offer a General Recreation package that may be used for golf, tennis, etc. Rates are for January-May, October-December.

ARRIVAL: By air - Jacksonville (29 miles). By car - I-95 to Fernandina Beach; exit at A1A north of Jacksonville, then go south for 11 miles to Amelia Island Parkway.

Bluewater Bay

PO Box 247, Niceville, FL 32578

(850) 897-3613; (800) 874-2128

Florida

Situated along the waters of the Choctawhatchee Bay near Ft. Walton Beach, this resort was carved from 1,800 acres of natural beauty. If you are not native to this area, I defy you to pronounce the name of the aforementioned bay, at least on the first couple of tries. Even the majority of the locals avoid fooling with this one.

ACCOMMODATIONS: Villas, townhouses, Admiral's Suites and Captain's Suites. The larger units have a living room, fully equipped kitchen, and washer/dryer. Choose from units overlooking the bay, marina, or fairway.

AMENITIES: 21 tennis courts (18 lighted), sailing, private beach, four pools, and excellent fishing. Two restaurants, La Fontana at the marina, featuring gourmet Italian specialties; and the Greenhouse at the golf course. Washer/dryers are also available.

GOLF: The resort's 36 holes play out as follows: the Bay/Lake nines measure 6,808/6,142/5,418 yards; the Bay/Marsh plays 6,726/6,142/5,249; the yardage on the Lake/Marsh is 6,888/6,274/5,401. The new Magnolia nine reaches out 3,290/3,020/2,804 yards. All four combinations par at 72. White sand, water hazards and many trees make these courses a challenge.

RATES: (EP) Lodgings - $80/$125/$205. Green fees - $35, cart $28. Golf package (two nights/two days, including lodging, two rounds of golf, cart, club storage) - $208/$280 per couple. Rates are for March-October.

ARRIVAL: By air - Ft. Walton (15 minutes). By car - Highway 20, four miles east of Niceville.

Killearn Country Club & Inn

100 Tyron Circle, Tallahassee, FL 32308

(805) 893-2186; (800) 476-4101

ACCOMMODATIONS: 40 rooms, four suites, as well as a number of private homes for rent.

AMENITIES: Olympic-sized pool, four lighted Laykold and four Har-Tru tennis courts, racquetball and handball. The Country Club dining room offers Continental and American cuisine; breakfast and lunch are served at the 19th hole.

GOLF: The 27-hole course offers various combinations, as follows: the South/East combination measures 7,006/6,432/6,028/5,661 yards, parring at 72/74; the East/North plays a more modest 6,813/6,360/5,969/5,476 yards, with a par of 72/73; the North/South nines weigh in at 6,899/6,310/5,537 yards, parring at 72/73. It was a challenge even for the PGA Tour players during the Tallahassee Open. These layouts have the normal Florida challenges of oak trees and traps, but only a modest amount of water (just four holes).

RATES: (EP) Lodgings - $72/$89. Green fees - $50, including carts. Golf packages are available.

ARRIVAL: By Air – Tallahassee. By car – From I-10 take Exit #30 to Thomasville Rd Highway 319. Go 1.25 miles to the fourth stop light and make a right onto Killarney Way. Drive to the roundabout, then go right and follow the signs to the resort. Don't be of faint heart, as it is quite a way. Or at least it seems to be.

Lodge at Ponte Vedra

607 Ponte Vedra Boulevard, Ponte Vedra Beach, FL 32082

(904) 273-9500; (800) 243-4304

ACCOMMODATIONS: 66 well-appointed rooms, including 24 suites. The lodge at Ponte Vedra fronts the beach.

AMENITIES: Three pools, biking, jogging, Jet Skiing, windsurfing and fishing. The beach, of course, opens up a great number of water activities. Tennis can be played on the eight tennis courts of the Marsh Landing Country Club, a bit over three miles away. Guests have access to the clubhouse, the golf course, the tennis club and the restaurant. You also will enjoy temporary membership privileges at the Bath Club adjacent to the resort, which offers steam and whirlpool baths, an exercise room and massage facilities. You can dine in the Mediterranean Room, the Oasis Bar & Grill, or order from their 24-hour room service.

GOLF: The Marriott at Sawgrass golf courses are available for play. For details on these courses, refer to the text covering that resort.

RATES: (EP) Lodgings - $295/$365. Rates are for March through October.

ARRIVAL: By air - Jacksonville (45 miles). By car - take I-95 south to J. Turner Butler Road (State Road 202). Travel east on Butler to Highway A1A. Take A1A south approximately four miles, turn left onto Corona Road and you are just a half-mile from the resort.

Marriott at Sawgrass Resort

1000 TPC Boulevard, Ponte Vedra Beach, FL 32082

(904) 285-7777; (800) 457-4653

The Marriott at Sawgrass has been judged one of our Top 50 resorts. This resort along the Atlantic Ocean offers all the amenities you could require.

ACCOMMODATIONS: 326 rooms in a seven-story hotel with a huge atrium area, interior cascading waterfalls, foliage, trees, exterior pools, marshes and lagoons. There are 24 waterview suites, 83 two-bedroom waterfront villas and 35 beach and fairway villas. There are now a total of 550 rooms, suites and condominiums.

AMENITIES: 10 Har-Tru tennis courts (four lighted), 13 courts of grass, clay, and cushion surfaces, 10 courts at Oak Bridge Racquet Club, four pools, health club with weights and rowing machines, and bicycle rentals. Deep-sea and freshwater charter fishing can be arranged. The 2½ miles of white sand beaches let you enjoy swimming, sailing, snorkeling, scuba diving (with licensed instructors), play volleyball, or just relax under a beach umbrella. The Sawgrass Stables can provide Arabians, quarter horses, palominos and appaloosas for daytime or evening trail rides. The resort offers "The Grasshopper Gang" program, designed to provide organized activities for your little darlings (and a furlough for suffering parents).

Restaurants are varied: The Augustine Room, the Cabana Club, the Café On the Green, the 100th Hole, a poolside retreat, three lounges, along with Champs, Cascades and the Cabana Club Lounge. Guests also enjoy dining privileges at each of the four Sawgrass country clubs. There is also the Aw Shucks Restaurant. What they can do with stuffed shrimp - WOW! For reservations, call (904) 285-3017.

GOLF: Golf is served up on a grand scale. There are a total of 99 holes, four clubhouses, four driving ranges and seven practice putting greens. The TPC course at Sawgrass Valley, a Pete Dye/Jerry Pate affair, was built in early 1988. Referred to as the Valley Course, it measures a healthy 6,838/6,491/6,027/5,114 yards and pars at 71. It could also have been named "Big Pond," as water comes into play on every one of the 18 holes. The back tees offer lots of water, but it is not really an overwhelming factor (from the men's tees). Perhaps I wasn't driving it far enough to get into trouble.

The Sawgrass Club has 27 holes. Using a crossover system, the East/West plays 7,073/6,900/6,270/6,080/5,128 yards, bringing water into contention on a total of 12 holes. The West/South nines, reaching out 6,864/6,399/6,031/5118 yards, also bring in the wet stuff on 12 holes. The final combination of the South/East measures 6,916/6,406/6,115/5,176 yards. On this layout you can bring your yacht, as water becomes a bosom companion on 15 holes. Each of the above configurations pars at 72. There is also the Marsh Landing Country Club course, with a yardage of 6,841/6,443/6,001/

4,985, again with a par of 72. The Oak Bridge Club layout plays 6,355/6,019/5,514/4,893 yards, with a par of 70.

And now my favorite golf course: the TPC Stadium layout. Although beautiful, it is frankly a little too much for the average player. My wife offered what I thought was the perfect description: "Playing this course is like giving birth. After it's over, you hope you may soon forget the pain and agony that went with it." Playing 6,857/6,394/5,761/5,034 yards, it pars at 72 and sports water on all 18 holes. Some basic changes have substantially tamed the course, but even so, I'm not sure I want another go.

RATES: (EP) Lodgings - $250 and up. Green fees are $100/$225/$275, depending on the course. Golf packages are available. Rates are for mid-February to May 1st and October-November.

ARRIVAL: By air - Jacksonville (36 miles). By private aircraft - Craig Field (20 minutes). By car - I-95 south to Butler Boulevard, then Highway A1A south to Marriott Sawgrass.

Marriott's Bay Point Resort

100 Delwood Beach Road, Panama City Beach, FL 32411

(850) 234-3307; (800) 874-7105

ACCOMMODATIONS: 200 rooms and suites with Gulf or golf views; 30 cottage villas; and 156 one- and two-bedroom villas, some fronting the lagoon, others on the golf course. In addition, the Bay Point Resort Rental Company has 150 condos. Call (800) 543-3307 (minimum one week stay).

AMENITIES: Tennis complex with 12 Rubico Har-Tru courts (four lighted), six pools (one indoor), children's game room, bicycle rentals, and a 145-slip marina. The Meadows Health Club features a sauna, steam room, Jacuzzi and workout rooms. Sailboats, Waverunners and Hobie Cats can be rented. There are seven restaurants.

GOLF: There are 36 holes. The Club Meadows Course, a Willard Byrd design, reaches out 6,913/6,398/5,784 yards with a par of 72. It can give you fits, with 59 traps, trees, and 12 holes where water becomes a challenge.

The second 18, The Lagoon Legend (aka "The Dragon"), put together by Von Hagge and Devlin, was built in early 1987. It stretches out to 6,942/6,469/6,079/5,614/4,949 yards and pars at 72. Set up as a Scottish links layout, it has water in contention on 16 of the 18 holes, undulating fairways and a number of hummocks. It has been ranked by the USGA as the second most difficult golf course in the United States. If this is number two, I don't ever want to see or experience number one. Two holes are barely playable from the men's tees. The same two (10 and 18) are definitely not playable by the average lady golfer. This course could also turn a saint into a blaspheming sinner very fast.

RATES: (EP) Lodgings - $189/$229/$310 and up. Green fees - $90/$105, including cart. Golf package (two nights/two days, including lodging, breakfast, golf, cart) - $578/$632 per couple. Rates are for March-August.

ARRIVAL: By air - Panama Beach City. By car - Highway 98 to Thomas Drive west of Panama Beach City. Turn left on Magnolia Beach Road and follow signs.

Palm Coast Golf Resort

300 Clubhouse Drive, Palm Coast, FL 32137

(904) 445-3000; (800) 654-6538

ACCOMMODATIONS: 154 guest rooms, including two suites. There are also 68 two-bedroom villas. The new Palm Coast Resort is very modern and offers many amenities not available in the old location.

AMENITIES: 16 tennis courts, racquetball, two pools, an 80-slip marina, and, of course, the beach. There are also spas and exercise facilities. Flagler's Restaurant offers dining.

GOLF: There are five courses. The Palm Harbor layout measures 6,572/6,013/5,346 yards. An Ed Seay/Palmer-designed course, the Pine Lakes Club reaches out a long 7,074/6,122/5,526/5,166 yards. The Matanzas Wood 18 measures 6,985/6,514/5,407 yards. The Hammock Dunes, a Tom Fazio design, plays 6,802/6,317/5,155 yards. The newest addition, a Gary Player design, opened in 1990. Called the Cypress Knoll Course, it weighs in at 6,591/6,261/5,386 yards. Each course pars at 72.

RATES: (EP) Lodgings - $99/$185. Green fees - $65, including cart. Golf packages (one day/one night, including lodging, breakfast, green fees) - $298/$374 per couple. Rates are from February through May.

ARRIVAL: By air - Daytona Beach. By car - I-95 to Exit 91C (Palm Coast Exit). Go east on Palm Coast Parkway. Take a right just prior to the toll bridge. Do NOT go onto the toll bridge. Resort is directly in front of you.

Ponte Vedra Inn & Club

200 Ponte Vedra Blvd., Ponte Vedra Beach, FL 32082

(904) 285-1111; (800) 234-7842

ACCOMMODATIONS: 175 units, some with kitchens and parlors. The 38 newer Sand Dune units have fully equipped kitchens.

AMENITIES: Pools, saunas, Jacuzzi, 15 tennis courts and all types of water sports on the mile-long beach. Dining is available in the Main Inn, at the golf course, and at three locations at the Surf Club.

GOLF: The Ocean course measures 6,484/6,097/5,404 yards, with a par of 72. The West Lagoon course, with a yardage of 5,551/5,254/4,616, has a par of 70. The Ocean course brings water into play on 13 holes, the West on 12. While both are flat, with the water, trees and traps (and, in some cases, trees in the traps), this course will test you.

RATES: (EP) Lodgings - $295/$395. Green fees - $140, including cart. Golf packages are available. Rates are for March-May.

ARRIVAL: By air - Jacksonville. By car - Route A1A, 20 miles south of Jacksonville.

Radisson Ponce de Leon Golf Resort

4000 US Highway 1 North, St. Augustine, FL 32095

(904) 824-2821; (800) 333-3333

ACCOMMODATIONS: 194 rooms and suites, each featuring its own veranda. They have recently added 20 one-bedroom condos.

AMENITIES: Tennis courts and one of the largest cloverleaf pools in Florida. Dining is offered at Michael's restaurant.

GOLF: The course, a Donald Ross design first built in 1907, is a most interesting layout; the fairways wander through coastal salt marshes, bringing a fair number of traps as well as water into play. Stretching out 6,878/6,472/5,936/5,315 yards, it pars at 72.

RATES: (EP) Lodgings - $129/$159. Green fees - $50, including cart. Golf packages are available.

ARRIVAL: By air - Jacksonville (45 miles). By car - US 1, north of St. Augustine.

The Ritz-Carlton

4750 Amelia Island Parkway, Amelia Island, FL 32034

(904) 277-1100; (800) 241-3333

In the Ritz-Carlton tradition, this outstanding resort offers every amenity you could wish for.

ACCOMMODATIONS: 449 rooms, including 43 suites (many beachfront or with beach views). As with all Ritz hotels, this one features crystal chandeliers, antiques, as well as 18th- and 19th-century oil paintings. They also have a "Club Level," the equivalent of most hotels' concierge level.

AMENITIES: Access to a wonderful beach and swimming area (1½ miles of beachfront), water-related activities (Jet Skiing - sailing), nine tennis courts, a pool and outdoor whirlpool, a fitness and exercise center with an indoor pool, steam and saunas along with massage rooms. Dining options include The Grill & Bar, with spectacular ocean views; The Café, for more casual dining; the Lobby Lounge; and poolside food service. The hotel has a children's program, "The Ritz Kids."

GOLF: The Golf Club of Amelia Island plays to a substantial yardage of 6,681/6,119/5,741/5,039, parring at 72. If you can find a ball that floats it would surely help as water comes into play on 16 of the 18 holes. The phone number for tee times is (904) 277-8015 (or just dial 65 from your room).

RATES: (EP) Lodgings - $309/$399/$425/$499. Green fees - $145, including cart. Golf packages are available. Rates are for peak season of March through May.

ARRIVAL: By car - from I-95, take Exit 129 (Fernandina Beach). East on Highway A1A to Amelia Island. Turn right at the first traffic light and drive 2.3 miles to entrance.

The Sandestin Beach Resort

Highway 98 East, Destin, FL 32541

(850) 267-8000; (800) 622-1623

We underestimated the size and quality of this resort. It is a very large complex, consisting of 2,400 acres and physically located on both sides of the highway. There are so many things to do and partake of, it is difficult to cover it all. There is Grand Harbour (three-bedroom townhouses), Harbour Point (one- and two-bedroom units), North Shore units, Vantage Point, Players Club, The Inn, Baypine Cottages, Heron Walk, Turnberry Villas, Beachside Towers (a high rise), Westwinds (a higher high rise), Southwinds and several more. Each consists of groupings of accommodations.

ACCOMMODATIONS: One- to four-bedroom villas with fully equipped kitchen, washer/dryer. On the Gulf side are two high-rise condominiums, with lodgings ranging from efficiencies to three-bedroom units with fully equipped kitchens. There are also patio homes and villas bordering the golf course.

AMENITIES: 14 tennis courts (five lighted), sailing, fishing with a 98-slip marina, a health club, saunas, swimming pools, bicycle rentals and wonderful beaches. The Bayview and the Elephant Walk Restaurants provide both food and cocktail service. Adjacent to the resort entrance is the Market Place - with some 30 shops offering a great variety as well as additional restaurants.

GOLF: There are 63 holes available for play. The Links course stretches out 6,710/6,265/5,777/4,969 yards and pars at 72. Bounded by the bay and generously laced with lakes (water comes into play on 12 holes), it is a challenging course. The Dunes/Harbor combination measures a substantial 6,890/6,270/5,729/4,862 yards, with a par of 72. The Troon/Dunes stretches out an awesome 7,185/6,537/5,969/5,158; the par remains at 72. The final link-up is the Harbor/Troon, weighing in at 6,891/6,417/5,780/4,884 yards, also with a par of 72. The new Burnt Pine Course, designed by Rees Jones, is now in play. Parring at 72 it plays a substantial 6,996/6,524/6,000/5,096 yards. Flirting with Choctawhatchee Bay and bringing water into contention on 12 holes it could well have been named "burning or flaming water." This course can be a zinger.

RATES: (EP) Lodgings - $170/$420. Weekly rates are also available. Green fees - $78, including cart. (Surcharge of $40 to play Burnt Pine Course). There are so many different golf packages we suggest you ask for what you would like when making reservations. Rates are for late- May to August.

ARRIVAL: By air - Ft. Walton Beach or Panama City. By car - eight miles east of Destin on Highway 98.

Seascape Resort

100 Seascape Drive, Destin, FL 32541

(850) 837-9181; (800) 874-9141

ACCOMMODATIONS: Garden villas or lakefront townhouses, ranging in size from one to three bedrooms and featuring full kitchens and living rooms. Seascape Resort is directly on the Gulf of Mexico and has over 1,600 feet of dazzling white sand beach.

AMENITIES: Four tennis courts, five pools, four lakes and deepsea fishing. For dining and entertainment there is the Whale's Tail.

GOLF: The course measures 6,455/6,074/5,250 yards, with a par of 72/71. It is well-trapped, bringing water into play on nine holes.

RATES: (EP) Lodgings - $125/$265. Green fees - $45/$60, including cart. Golf packages are available. Rates are for June-September.

ARRIVAL: By air - Ft. Walton Beach. By car - Highway 98, six miles east of Destin.

Summer Beach Resort

5000 Amelia Island Parkway, Amelia Island, FL 32034

(904) 277-0905; (800) 862-9297

ACCOMMODATIONS: Two- and three-bedroom condos.

AMENITIES: Two tennis courts, horseback riding, fishing, windsurfing, ocean as well as pool swimming, bicycling and golf. The clubhouse restaurant is now open for breakfast, lunch and dinner.

GOLF: For details on the Golf Club of Amelia Island, refer to the entry for The Ritz-Carlton, Amelia Island.

RATES: (EP) Lodgings - $145/$185/$245. Green fees - $108, including cart and bag storage. Golf packages are available. March-September.

ARRIVAL: By air - Jacksonville International. By car - north on I-95, Exit #129 to A1A. Proceed on A1A to Amelia Island Parkway south. The resort will be on your left.

Central Florida

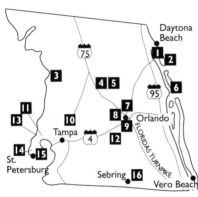

1. The Indigo Lakes Holiday Inn
2. Sugar Mill CC
3. Plantation Inn & Golf Resort
4. Mission Inn Golf & Tennis Resort
5. Errol Estate
6. Royal Oak CC Resort
7. The Bay Hill Club & Lounge/Disney Caribbean Resort/Hyatt Regency Grand Cypress/Walt Disney World/ Buena Vista/Disney Beach Club/ Disney Contemporary Resort/Disney Floridian Resort/Disney Ft. Wilderness/ Disney Polynesian Resort/ Disney Village Resort/Disney Yacht Club/Grosvenor Resort/Guest Quarters Resort/The Hilton Disney World/Hotel Royal Plaza/Walt Disney Dolphin Hotel/Walt Disney Swan Hotel
8. Marriott's Orlando World Center
9. Orlando Lake CC/Poinciana Golf Resort
10. Saddlebrook
11. Westin Innisbrook
12. Grenelefe Resort
13. The Belleview Biltmore
14. Don Cesar Resort
15. Renaissance Vinoy Resort
16. The Ridge Resort at Sun 'N Lake

The Bay Hill Club & Lodge

9000 Bay Hill Boulevard, Orlando, FL 32819

(407) 876-2429; (800) 422-9445

Florida

ACCOMMODATIONS: 65 rooms and one guest house.

AMENITIES: A pool and six tennis courts (two lighted). Fishing is reported to be excellent in this area. The Club complex houses the dining room (The Bay Window), open on Friday and Saturday evening, the lounge and the Grill Room. Jackets are required after 6 PM. Although Bay Hill is a private club, all amenities are available to guests of the Lodge.

GOLF: A crossover system utilizes 27 holes. The Challenger/Champion nines play 7,014/6,547/6,184/5,214 yards; the Challenger/Charger stretches 6,670/6,224/5,879/5,087 yards; the combination of the Champion/Charger measures 6,624/6,237/5,879/ 5,079 yards. No matter how you mix them, the par remains at 72. This is not a run-of-the-mill resort course. It will present you with some of the most challenging holes in the country and has been the scene of several extremely prestigious tournaments. The course is considered one of the top 50 in the US by *Golf Digest*. As a matter of interest, Arnold Palmer maintains a home within the complex and has contributed a great deal of time, money and effort to make Bay Hill one of the best facilities.

RATES: (EP) Lodgings - $175 and up. Green fees - $175, including cart. Golf package (one night/one day, including lodging, club breakfast, green fees, cart, club storage) - $380 per couple, per night. Rates are for January through April.

ARRIVAL: By air - Orlando (15 miles). By car - Florida Turnpike to Exit 75, then I-4 Tampa west. Take 528A west, then turn right on Apopka-Vineland Road.

The Belleview Biltmore

25 Belleview Boulevard, Clearwater, FL 34616

(727) 442-6171; (800) 237-8947

ACCOMMODATIONS: The large rambling hotel (325 rooms and 40 suites) takes you back to a bygone era, with Victorian architecture accented by green gables, white wicker furniture and verandas.

AMENITIES: One indoor and two outdoor pools, four tennis courts, the beach area and a marina. There are three dining rooms: the Candlelight, the Tiffany Dining Room and the Beach Cabana Club.

GOLF: The Belleview Country Club course was originally put together by Donald Ross in 1926. Parring at 72/74, it reaches out 6,498/6,173/5,620 yards. With slightly undulating terrain and elevated greens, it brings water into play on 10 of the 18 holes.

RATES: (EP) Lodgings - $230/$290/$370. Green fees -$70, including cart. Golf packages are available. Rates are for January-April.

ARRIVAL: By air - Tampa (20 miles). By car - follow State Route 60 west to Clearwater, then turn left on Ft. Harrison (Alt 19 South). Go 1.1 miles. Take a right onto Belleview Boulevard at the traffic light. Bear left at Bellair Country Club, proceed through the guard gate and follow signs to the hotel.

Don CeSar Resort

3400 Gulf Boulevard, St. Petersburg Beach, FL 33706

(727) 360-1881; (800) 282-1116

Modern where it should be modern and grand where it should be grand, this flamboyant palace of pink commands its own crescent beach.

ACCOMMODATIONS: 277 rooms, including 49 suites. It also has the "Beach House," with additional rooms.

AMENITIES: Kayaking, sailing, water-skiing, a health club, exercise rooms, saunas and two tennis courts. Their "Kids LTD" program is set up to handle the five- to 12-year-olds. The resort provides a variety of dining options. Zelda's Café and the magnificent King Charles Restaurant are both repeat winners of Mobil Four Star Awards. Lighter fare can be enjoyed at the Beachcomber Bar and the Poolside Grill.

GOLF: There are several championship golf courses in the immediate area, the closest of which is the Isla-Del-Sol, a half-mile away. Measuring 6,266/6,004/5,090 yards, it pars at 72.

RATES: (EP) Lodgings - $334/$389/$524. Green fees - $90/$100, including cart. Rates are for December-April.

ARRIVAL: By air - Tampa. By car - get off Highway 275 at 22nd Avenue south. Take a left on Highway 19 and cross the toll bridge.

Errol Estate

1355 Errol Parkway, Apopka, FL 32712

(407) 886-5000

ACCOMMODATIONS: Golf villas with two bedrooms, two baths, kitchen, washer/dryer and private patio.

AMENITIES: Six lighted all-weather tennis courts and a restaurant.

GOLF: The 27 holes combine as follows: The par-72 Lake/Highland combined nines reach out a fair 6,689/6,402/6,125/5,782 yards. Parring at 72/73, the Highland/Grove combination reaches out 6,566/6,631/6,129/5,748 yards. The Grove/Lake measures 6,643/6,369/6,158/5,654 yards and also pars at 72/73. Each layout gives plenty of challenge, with water, bunkers, towering trees and many interesting side-hill lies.

RATES: (EP) Lodgings - $90/$125 and up. Rates are for January-April. Green fees - $60, carts $25.

ARRIVAL: By air - Orlando (15 miles). By car - off US 441.

Grenelefe Resort

State Road 546, Haines City, FL 33844

(863) 422-7511; (800) 237-9549

ACCOMMODATIONS: 865 fairway condo apartments and hotel rooms. Washer/dryer facilities are available in each villa cluster.

AMENITIES: 13 tennis courts (10 lighted) and a 1,700-seat center court. The 6,400-acre lake provides fishing and boating. There are also four pools. The two restaurants are the Green Heron and the Camelot. We do not, however, recommend the Camelot.

GOLF: The West course, unlike so many Florida layouts which depend on water to spice up the action, has only three holes featuring water. Instead, this course provides lush green fairways with trees and bunkers. This layout, parring at 72, stretches an awesome 7,325/6,898/6,199/5,398 yards. Should you elect to play from the 7,325-yard Green tee settings, you may also turn green. The par-72 East course weighs in at 6,802/6,356/6,168/5,114 yards. The South 18, parring at 71 from all tees, reaches 6,869/6,333/5,939/5,174 yards.

RATES: (EP) Lodgings - $190/$420 (January-April 14); $140/$310 (January 1-20, April 17-May 14, October 1-December 31); $99/$208 (summer season. Green fees - South and East courses, $110, including cart; West course $130. Golf packages are available.

ARRIVAL: By air - Orlando. By car - from the north, I-75 to the Florida Turnpike, then south to US 27 and to Highway 544. Head east six miles.

Hyatt Regency Grand Cypress

One Grand Cypress Boulevard, Orlando, FL 32836

(407) 239-1234; (800) 233-1234

ACCOMMODATIONS: The Hyatt Regency is an 18-story structure showcasing a magnificent 200-foot-high atrium lobby entrance. It has 750 rooms, including 74 suites. There are also 146 Mediterranean-style, fully equipped two- to four-bedroom villas; for details and reservations on these units, call (800) 835-7377 or (407) 239-4700.

AMENITIES: A half-acre pool; three Jacuzzis; 45-foot water slide; 21-acre lake with 1,000 feet of sand beach; marina with sailboats, canoes, and paddleboats; bicycles, 12 tennis courts (six lighted); two racquetball courts; complete health club with saunas, massage, and weights; and a fitness and jogging trail. The Cypress also has its own equestrian center, which offers both English and Western saddles. Dining is provided in Hemingway's; La Coquina, a gourmet restaurant; and Cascades, for informal dining.

GOLF: The golf complex now totals 45 holes. Designed by Jack Nicklaus, they play as follows. North/South nines combined reach out a solid 7,024/6,349/5,854/5,360 yards. The South/East layouts weigh in at 6,937/6,357/5,820/5,158 yards. Finally, the East/North nines stretch 6,955/6,294/5,790/5,056 yards. No matter how you mix them, the par comes out to 72. The new course is more modest in length and plays 6,773/6,181/5,314 yards, with a par of 72/71.

To overcome the flat terrain so characteristic of Florida, the fairways have been constructed with a "ledged" effect, placing certain portions on different levels. With sand bunkers and water in play on many holes, plus the natural wild growth of the roughs, this certainly is not a boring golf complex. There is also a nine-hole pitch and putt layout.

RATES: (EP) Lodgings - $335/$465. Green fees (including bag storage and cart) - $150. Golf packages are available. Rates are for March-April.

ARRIVAL: By air - Orlando International. By car - 20 miles south of Orlando on I-4. Take State Route 535 north (Lake Buena Vista exit). Turn left at the second traffic light.

Florida

Indigo Lakes Holiday Inn

2620 International Speedway Blvd., Daytona Beach, FL 32120

(904) 258-6333; (800) 465-4329

ACCOMMODATIONS: 150 rooms and suites, along with 63 condos equipped for housekeeping.

AMENITIES: Ten lighted tennis courts, a racquetball court, six-lane Olympic-size pool, and Parcourse Fitness Trail for jogging.

GOLF: As many say, "Nature made the course at Indigo beautiful, Lloyd Clifton made it tough." Playing 7,168/6,601/6,176/5,450 yards, it pars at 72. With 87 sand traps, 50 acres of water, three miles of lush, tropical rough and not a single parallel fairway, it offers a challenge. If the sand does not get your ball, the alligators surely will. The greens are huge. Depending on pin placement, the size of the greens can make as much as a three-club difference.

RATES: (EP) Lodgings - $75/$125/$225. Green fees - $75, including carts.

ARRIVAL: By air - Daytona Beach. By car - US 92 at I-95.

Marriott's Orlando World Center

8701 World Center Drive, Lake Buena Vista, FL 32821

(407) 239-4200; (800) 228-9290

The 27-story tower overlooks lagoons, woods and the golf course. There are close to 200 acres of waterfalls, lagoons and palm trees.

ACCOMMODATIONS: 1,500 rooms and 101 suites.

AMENITIES: 12 lighted tennis courts, four pools, 10 restaurants and parking space for over 2,000 cars.

GOLF: Designed by Joe Lee (architect of Disney World's three courses), the course plays 6,265/5,956/5,048 yards with a par of 71. They have used many trees, about 85 bunkers and water to spice up the action. When I say water, I mean lots of water. There are 16 holes where water either comes into play or threatens to.

RATES: (EP) Lodgings - $249/$289. Green fees, including cart - $105/$115. Golf packages are available. Rates are for February-March.

ARRIVAL: By air - Orlando International. By car - Exit I-4 at the entrance to Disney World's Epcot Center.

Mission Inn Golf & Tennis Resort

10400 County Road 48, Howey-In-The-Hills, FL 34737

(352) 324-3101; (800) 874-9053

ACCOMMODATIONS: 189 hotel rooms, plus suites and golf patio homes. The homes are completely equipped for housekeeping and include a washer/dryer.

AMENITIES: Six tennis courts (four lighted) and a large heated pool. The 52-slip marina on the shores of Lake Harris provides access to boating and fishing. Dining is provided in the El Conquistador room.

GOLF: The Mission Inn Golf Club Course stretches out 6,770/6,224/5,021 yards and pars at 72/73. The fairways rise and fall as they wend their way through the pines. On several holes there are elevation changes of 85 feet between tee and green, which is a welcome change for Florida. A new course came into play in 1992. Parring at 71/70 and reaching 6,814/6,202/5,578/4,500 yards, it brings water into the picture on seven holes.

RATES: (EP) Lodgings - $205/$225/. Green fees - $95, including cart. Golf packages are available. Rates are for January-March.

ARRIVAL: By air - Orlando. By car - from Florida Turnpike, take Exit 285. At light (Highway 27), take a left, go one block and turn left onto State Road 19 north. Drive approximately six miles.

Orange Lake Country Club

8505 West Irlo Bronson Highway, Kissimmee, FL 34746

(407) 239-0000; (800) 877-6522

ACCOMMODATIONS: Villas, fully equipped for housekeeping with washer/dryers and microwaves. There is a restaurant, lounge and snack bar.

AMENITIES: 16 Tru-Flex tennis courts, including a 5,000-seat stadium court; Olympic-size pool; spas and saunas. Water-skiing, boating, fishing and just plain loafing on their 300-foot white sand beach are but a few of the activities available.

GOLF: There are 54 holes. The Orange/Cypress combination is 6,667/6,294/5,539 yards, while the Orange/Lake nines measure

6,551/6,176/5,322 yards. The Lake/Cypress course weighs in at 6,548/6,190/5,495 yards. All three layouts par at 72. These courses all feature a substantial amount of water. A new Palmer-designed course has joined the grouping.

RATES: (EP) Lodgings - $120/$225. Green fees - $65/$90, including cart. Various packages, including golf and Disney World visits, are available. Rates are for January-March.

ARRIVAL: By air - Orlando. By car - from I-4, take Exit 25B. Go to the corner of Route 182 and Route 27.

Plantation Jnn & Golf Resort

9301 Kings Bay Road, Crystal River, FL 32629

(352) 795-4211; (800) 632-6262

ACCOMMODATIONS: A two-story, 142-room structure features custom decorating and individual room climate control.

AMENITIES: Fishing, both saltwater and freshwater. The hotel can also arrange charter excursions. Tennis can be played on four lighted courts.

GOLF: There are 27 holes of golf. The Championship Course plays 6,644/6,320/5,385 yards with a par of 72. The Lagoon nine is an executive affair, measuring a very short 2,511/2,338/2,032 yards. Although the terrain is flat, it can produce surprises, with water in play on 12 holes.

RATES: (EP) Lodgings - $89/$95/$120. Green fees - $50, including carts.

ARRIVAL: By air - Tampa or Orlando. By private aircraft - Crystal River (3,600-foot, paved, lighted runway). By car - I-75 to Wildwood, west on Highway 44 (34 miles) to Crystal River. The resort is just south of the city.

Poinciana Golf Resort

500 East Cypress Parkway, Kissimmee, FL 34759

(407) 933-0700; (800) 331-7743

ACCOMMODATIONS: One- , two- and three-bedroom condos, most with private patio.

AMENITIES: Four lighted tennis courts (two clay surface), an Olympic-size pool, a kiddie pool, outdoor racquetball courts and jogging paths. The clubhouse dining room serves all three meals and is supported by a lounge.

GOLF: Designed by architects Devlin/Van Hagge, the course pars at 72 and reaches out 6,701/6,171/5,664/4,988 yards. There is plenty of water here. The many cypress trees lining the fairways and substantial number of sand traps are a navigational nuisance.

RATES: (EP) Lodgings - $80/$160. Green fees - $35, including cart. Weekly and monthly rates are also available. Golf packages are offered.

ARRIVAL: By air - Orlando. By car - from I-4, exit to Highway 192 east. Drive three miles to Poinciana Blvd. Turn right, drive 13½ miles and turn right onto Pleasant Hills Road. Proceed to Cypress Parkway and turn right. The resort is on the right.

Renaissance Vinoy Resort

501 Fifth Avenue NE, St. Petersburg, FL 33701

(727) 894-1000; (800) 468-3571

ACCOMMODATIONS: 360 rooms and 28 suites.

AMENITIES: Two heated swimming pools, three outdoor spas, a fully equipped fitness center featuring saunas, steam, spa massage and Nautilus equipment, a 16-court tennis complex (nine lighted), along with two croquet courts and a 74-slip marina. For dining there is Marchand's Grille; the Terrace Room with its view of Tampa Bay; and Alfresco, a glass-walled restaurant overlooking the tennis complex.

GOLF: The course, formerly Sunset Golf & Country Club, was redesigned and restored by Ron Carl. With new tees and greens, nine lakes, narrow fairways, two double greens and a signature "island" green, it has a Scottish feel to it. Reaching out a modest 6,378/6,022/5,691/4,828 yards, it pars at 71.

RATES: (EP) Lodgings - $289/$309. Green fees - $105, including cart. Golf packages are available.

ARRIVAL: By air - St. Petersburg/Clearwater International (12 miles). By car - from I-275, take Exit 10. Follow 4th Avenue north to Beach Drive and make a left turn to resort.

Florida

Ridge Resort at Sun 'n Lake

4245 Sun 'n Lake Boulevard, Sebring, FL 33872

(863) 385-2561; (800) 237-2165

ACCOMMODATIONS: One- and two-bedroom villas, each with semi-private pool, full kitchen, living room and washer/dryer.

AMENITIES: Six tennis courts (two lighted). The new clubhouse features the Candlelight Restaurant and Lounge.

GOLF: The course, with its four tee settings, reaches out a strong 7,024/6,731/6,430/5,760 yards, parring at 72/74. It features tree-lined fairways with water coming in play on nine holes.

RATES: (EP) Lodgings - $1,300/$1,500 monthly, with a three month minimum. Green fees are included in rates; carts are $35.

ARRIVAL: By air - Tampa or Orlando (60 miles). By car - on US 27, three miles north of Sebring, two miles south of Avon Park.

Royal Oak Country Club Resort

2150 Country Club Drive, Titusville, FL 32780

(321) 269-4500; (800) 884-2150

ACCOMMODATIONS: Well-appointed, motel-type rooms.

AMENITIES: Olympic-size pool and tennis courts. Dining is provided in Bogey's Bistro and the Royal Oak.

GOLF: The course, designed by Robert Von Hagge and the late Dick Wilson, plays 6,709/6,257/5,908/5,473 yards and pars at 71/72. Eight lakes, large greens, 55 traps and many palm trees add to the challenge.

RATES: (EP) Lodgings - $75. Green fees - $43, including cart. Golf package (seven nights/seven days, including lodging, green fees and cart, bag storage) - $994 per couple. Rates are January 1-April 3rd.

ARRIVAL: By air - Orlando. By car - from Orlando, take the Bee-line Expressway to I-95 north. Go five miles to Highway 50 and take a left at the first stoplight onto Route 405. After three-quarters of a mile, turn right and follow signs.

Saddlebrook Golf & Tennis Resort

100 Saddlebrook Way, Wesley Chapel, FL 33543

(813) 973-1111; (800) 729-8383

Saddlebrook has been judged one of the Top 50 resorts. It enjoys a truly picturesque setting. A tree-lined drive leads to the Walking Village, where you find yourself surrounded by 480 acres laden with cypress, pine and palm trees. No cars are allowed within this area. What a nice arrangement.

ACCOMMODATIONS: 500 lodging units, which can be converted from one- to three-bedroom suites, each with fully equipped kitchen, living room, dining room, and private bath for each bedroom.

AMENITIES: The main pool is 270 feet long, and features sundecks, a cocktail lounge and two poolside whirlpools. It forms the focal point of the Walking Village. There are 45 tennis courts (five lighted). Saddlebrook also has a complete fitness center, plus bicycle and jogging trails. This resort offers a wide selection of restaurants: the Cypress Room, the Gourmet Room and, for more casual dining, the Little Club. The food and service are outstanding at all of them.

GOLF: The Saddlebrook Course weighs in at 6,603/6,144/5,183 yards, parring at 70. The Palmer layout measures 6,469/6,044/5,212 yards and pars at 71. With undulating terrain, lots of water (each course brings water into play on 17 holes), trees and traps, these will more than test your game. The Director of Golf is Jerry Couzynse.

RATES: (EP) Lodgings - $370/$394. Green fees - $130, including cart. Golf package (three nights/three days, including lodging, breakfast each day, dinner for one night, green fees, cart, bag storage) - $1,068/$1,404 per couple. Rates are for January-April.

ARRIVAL: By air - Tampa (45 minutes). By car - I-75, exit at Highway 54 (Zephyrhills). Drive east for one mile.

Sugar Mill Country Club

100 Clubhouse Circle, New Smyrna Beach, FL 32168

(904) 426-5200; (800) 352-5942

ACCOMMODATIONS: Golf villas and cluster homes, available for no less than one week and no longer than one month. All are fully equipped, including washer/dryer. Sugar Mill is a private resort community of 850 acres; it is located in a gently rolling, heavily wooded area seven miles from New Smyrna Beach.

AMENITIES: Health spa, steam rooms, dining facilities and lounge. Tennis courts and swimming pools are on the grounds, with nearby New Smyrna Beach and the Intracoastal Waterway providing beach, boating, fishing and swimming activities.

GOLF: The 27 hole courses, Joe Lee designs, play Red/White 6,766/6,449/6,027/5,428 yards; the White/Blue reach out 6,725/6,444/6,045/5,435 with the final combination of the Blue/Red nines playing 6,671/6,385/6,050/5,381 yards. No matter how you mix them the par is 72. With over 100 traps and water in play on many holes, it will test you.

RATES: (EP) Lodgings - town house $950 (for two weeks, two-week minimum); villas from $1,100/$1,750/$1,950. Green fees - $55, including cart.

ARRIVAL: By air - Daytona Beach. By car - junction of I-95 and Route 44.

Westin Innisbrook Resort

US Highway 19 South, Tarpon Springs, FL 34689

(727) 942-2000; (800) 456-2000

ACCOMMODATIONS: Lodges that can be divided into any configuration you may require. Each suite is equipped for housekeeping.

AMENITIES: 18 tennis courts (seven lighted), and acres of lakes for fishing or for the simple pleasure of watching the great number of black swans, peacocks and mallards. There are three restaurants: the Island, the Sandpiper and the Copperhead.

GOLF: How about 72 holes? The Island Course, stretching out a long 6,999/6,625/6,150/5,578 yards with a par of 72, brings into play water, traps and fast greens. The par-71 Copperhead, playing 7,087/6,536/6,126/5,537 yards, offers rolling hills and small streams. It requires great accuracy. The Hawk's Run layout reaches out a more modest 6,405/5,920/5,530/4,955 yards, parring at 71. The Eagle's Watch measures 6,635/6,145/5,690/4,975 yards, parring at 71. Unlike the eastern part of the state, which has only slightly rolling hills, this area has much more pronounced elevation changes.

Note: Unless you are on a golf package (available at an additional charge), you are not allowed to reserve tee times more than 48 hours in advance.

RATES: (EP) Lodgings - $160/$235. Green fees - $140, including cart. Golf package (four nights/five days, including lodging in a club suite, breakfast each day, five days green fees with cart, bag storage, daily golf clinic, advanced tee-time selection, gratuities) - $1,720 per couple. Rates are for February to mid-April.

ARRIVAL: By air - Tampa (39 minutes). By car - US 19, five milessouth of Tarpon Springs.

Walt Disney World

So much has been written about Walt Disney World that it is difficult to add anything of significance. There literally is something for everyone, especially in accommodations. There are excellent camping facilities, beautiful high-rise hotels, well-equipped villa townhouses, individual treehouse villas, multi-level Club Fairway Villas and Club Lake Villas. There are some 20,000 hotel rooms. Listed on the next few pages are some of the various resorts, hotels and motels. There are others. For information, contact PO Box 10000, Lake Buena Vista, FL 32830; (407) 934-7639; www.disney.go.com/disneyworld. Request the *Walt Disney World Vacation Guide*, a magazine that lists every facility available; things to do, eat, and see; where to stay; baby-sitting services; how to get there and how much it will cost.

GOLF: The golf facilities are impressive. The Palm Golf Course, a Joe Lee design, is regarded as one of this country's top 100 layouts. It reaches out 6,957/6,461/6,029/5,311 yards, parring at 72/74. Small greens, narrow fairways, and water on 10 holes can leave you talking to yourself. The Magnolia layout, again a Joe Lee design, stretches out an awesome 7,190/6,642/6,091/5,232 yards and also pars at 72/74. The 17th hole here is a real zinger: a 400-yard par 4, with water on both sides of the fairway almost from tee to green and with the added challenge of a sharp dogleg left.

The Eagle Pines course, a Pete Dye layout, measures 6,772/6,309/5,520/4,838 yards, parring at 72. The only portion that does not have a water hazard is the parking lot. The Osprey Ridge, a Tom Fazio course, shows a massive yardage of 7,101/6,680/6,103/5,402, parring at 72. Water comes into play on 10 holes.

Florida

The Lake Buena Vista Club is a bit more modest, with a yardage of 6,829/6,268/5,917/5,176, parring at 72/73. While quite open, it does introduce water on six holes.

RATES: Green fees - $110/$130, including cart. For tee times on all of the above courses call (407) 824-2270. There are also two other golf courses: the Oak Trail (nine holes) and an executive nine-hole course.

ARRIVAL: By air - Orlando. By car - take I-4 west to Exit 26B, then follow the signs.

Buena Vista Wyndham Palace

1900 Buena Vista Drive, Lake Buena Vista, FL 32830

(407) 827-2727; (800) 327-2990

ACCOMMODATIONS: 1,028 rooms and suites. The newest addition offers one- and two-bedroom Island suites.

AMENITIES: Three tennis courts, three pools, a sauna and ahealth club. There are several restaurants and lounges.

GOLF: See *Walt Disney World*, above.

RATES: (EP) Lodgings - $159/$179/$229.

Disney's Beach Club Resort

1800 Epcot Resorts Blvd., Lake Buena Vista, FL 32830

(407) 934-8000

ACCOMMODATIONS: 580 rooms accompanied by the adjacent 634-room Yacht Club Resort. The two share amenities and recreation facilities, including restaurants.

AMENITIES: A three-acre pool, complete with a water slide; health club; child care center; and game arcade.

GOLF: See *Walt Disney World*, listed above.

RATES: (EP) Lodgings - $329/$485.

Disney's Caribbean Beach Resort

900 Cayman Way, Lake Buena Vista, FL 32830

(407) 934-3400

ACCOMMODATIONS: 2,112 rooms in several two-story buildings.

AMENITIES: Six counter-service restaurants, lounge, poolside snack bar, seven pools, marina with boat and bicycle rentals, jogging paths and game room.

GOLF: See *Walt Disney World* on the foregoing pages.

RATES: (EP) Lodgings - $159/$179.

Disney's Contemporary Resort

4600 N. World Drive, Lake Buena Vista, FL 32830

(407) 824-1000

ACCOMMODATIONS: 360 rooms in the main tower with an additional 693 in the three-story Garden Wings. The monorail stops on the fourth floor of this huge layout and transports you 21st-century-style to Disney World.

AMENITIES: Swimming pool, tennis courts, a marina and beach.

GOLF: See *Walt Disney World*, above.

RATES: (EP) Lodgings - $269/$600.

Disney's Grand Floridian Resort & Spa

4401 Grand Floridian Way, Lake Buena Vista, FL 32830

(407) 824-3000

ACCOMMODATIONS: 900 rooms and suites.

AMENITIES: Swimming pools, a marina, a health club and several restaurants.

GOLF: See *Walt Disney World* on the foregoing pages.

RATES: Lodgings - $365/$500.

Disney's Fort Wilderness Resort & Campground

3520 N. Ft. Wilderness Trail, Lake Buena Vista, FL 32830

(407) 824-2900

ACCOMMODATIONS: 785 campsites and 407 trailer homes. The trailer homes feature fully equipped kitchens, full-size baths and daily maid service. There are also laundry facilities.

AMENITIES: Two heated pools, two lighted tennis courts, biking and jogging paths, horseback riding, two game rooms, and a marina with rental boats and fishing. There are several restaurants.

GOLF: See *Walt Disney World*, above.

RATES: (EP) Trailer homes - $185. Campsites - $75. Inn - $254/ $400.

Disney's Polynesian Resort

Seven Seas Drive, Lake Buena Vista, FL 32830

(407) 824-2000

ACCOMMODATIONS: 841 rooms, including 14 suites spread over several two- and three-story longhouses.

AMENITIES: Pool, marina and beach, and several restaurants.

GOLF: See *Walt Disney World*.

RATES: (EP) Lodgings - $275/$355 and up.

Disney Village Resort

1901 Buena Vista Drive, Lake Buena Vista, FL 32830

(407) 827-1100; (800) 647-7900

ACCOMMODATIONS: 39 one-bedroom and 152 two-bedroom villas, along with 316 club suites. The villas feature fully equipped kitchens.

AMENITIES: This layout sits on top of a golf course. It also sports three lighted tennis courts, five pools and bicycle rentals. There is the Pompano Grill for casual dining; many additional restaurants and places of entertainment are nearby.

GOLF: For details on golf refer to *Walt Disney World*, above.
RATES: Lodgings - $190/$270/$300/$345.

Disney's Yacht Club Resort

1700 Epcot Resorts Blvd., Lake Buena Vista, FL 32830

(407) 934-7000

For complete details on this 634-room resort, refer to the above text on *Disney's Beach Club Resort*. These two hotels share facilities. The rates are also the same at each location.

Doubletree Guest Quarters Resort

2305 Hotel Plaza Blvd., Lake Buena Vista,FL 32830

(407) 934-1000; (800) 424-2900

ACCOMMODATIONS: All suites. Each unit is equipped with a mini-bar, refrigerator, living room and bedroom.
AMENITIES: Heated pool, hot tub, two tennis courts, exercise room and a poolside snack bar. The Parrot Patch Restaurant is available for dining and also provides room service.
GOLF: See *Walt Disney World* on the foregoing pages.
RATES: Lodgings - $179/$259.

Grosvenor Resort

1850 Hotel Plaza Blvd., Lake Buena Vista, FL 32830

(407) 828-4444; (800) 624-4109

ACCOMMODATIONS: 628 rooms and suites equipped with video cassette players and mini- bars.
AMENITIES: Two heated pools, children's pool, two lighted tennis courts and two racquetball courts. The Baskerville is the main dining room, while The Café is less formal.
GOLF: Refer to *Walt Disney World*, above.
RATES: (EP) Lodgings - $145/$165.

The Hilton at Disney World Village

1751 Hotel Plaza Blvd., Lake Buena Vista, FL 32830

(407) 827-4000; (800) 782-4414

ACCOMMODATIONS: This 10-story hotel consists of 814 rooms, including 26 suites and a concierge level.

AMENITIES: Two heated pools, a health club and two tennis courts. They offer a "Youth Hotel" program designed to keep the four- to 12-year-olds occupied. Restaurants include American Vineyards along with the more casual setting of County Fair and the outdoor County Fair Terrace. Benihana Japanese restaurant is also here.

GOLF: See *Walt Disney World*, above.

RATES: (EP) Lodgings - $295/$365 and up.

Hotel Royal Plaza

PO Box 22203, Lake Buena Vista, FL 32830

(407) 828-2828; (800) 248-7890

ACCOMMODATIONS: 396 rooms in a 17-story hotel.

AMENITIES: Four tennis courts, a pool, a hot tub and saunas. Dining is available at Memory Lane and the Plaza Diner (casual).

GOLF: Refer to *Walt Disney World*, above.

RATES: (EP) Lodgings - $239/$318/$438 and up.

Walt Disney World Dolphin Resort

1500 Epcot Resort Boulevard, Lake Buena Vista, FL 32830

(407) 934-4000; (800) 227-1500

ACCOMMODATIONS: 1,509 rooms in a 27-story structure.

AMENITIES: Eight lighted tennis courts, a health club, three pools and various shops. There are a total of seven restaurants on premises.

GOLF: See *Walt Disney World.*
RATES: Lodgings - $335/$465.

Walt Disney World Swan Resort

1200 Epcot Resort Boulevard, Lake Buena Vista, FL 32830

(407) 934-3000; (800) 248-7926

ACCOMMODATIONS: 758 rooms, including 64 suites, in a 12-story hotel.

AMENITIES: Eight tennis courts, a fully equipped health club, a grotto swimming pool, an outdoor pool, a children's pool, and outdoor Jacuzzis. There is the "Camp Swan" program, at an additional charge, for four to 12 year group. There are three restaurants: Palio (Italian), the Garden Grove Café and the Splash Grill, a poolside café serving lighter fare.

GOLF: For details, refer to *Walt Disney World*, above.
RATES: (EP) Lodgings - $335/$380/$425 and up.

Southern Florida

1. The Resort at Longboat Key Club
2. The Plantation Golf & CC
3. Gasparilla Inn & Cottages
4. Port LaBelle Inn
5. South Seas Plantation
6. Admiral Lehigh Golf Resort
7. Naples Beach Hotel/Quality Inn Golf & CC
8. Marriott's Marco Beach Resort
9. Harbour Ridge
10. PGA National Resort & Spa
11. The Breakers
12. Boca Raton Resort & Club/ Boca Teeca CC & Inn/ Boca West Club
13. Palm-Aire Spa Resort
14. Bonaventure Resort & Spa/ Inverrary Plaza Golf Resort
15. Grand Palms Golf & CC
16. RainTree Golf Resort/Rolling Hills Golf Resort/The Wyndham Resort & Spa
17. Turnberry Isle Resort Club
18. Don Shula's Resort
19. The Doral CC

Admiral Lehigh Golf Resort

225 East Joel Boulevard, Lehigh, FL 33936

(941) 369-2121; (800) 843-0971

ACCOMMODATIONS: 121 rooms in a motel-type layout, plus 154 efficiency units.

AMENITIES: Four lighted tennis courts and a pool. The dining rooms are the Master Tavern and the 225 East Dining Room and Lounge.

GOLF: The North Course plays 6,459/6,115/5,316 yards and pars at 71/72. A pesky creek runs throughout, eventually emptying into a lake adjacent to the inn. It comes into play on 12 holes. The course has small, well-bunkered greens and narrow, tree-lined fairways. The South Course stretches out a hefty 6,949/6,490/5,840 yards, with a par of 72. Two miles south of the resort, it serves up large traps, gently rolling fairways and contoured greens to keep your attention. An extra, not often found, is a practice sand trap. There is also a pro shop, clubhouse and a practice driving range.

RATES: (EP) Lodgings - $96/$103. Green fees - $46, including carts. Golf packages are available. Rates are for mid-December to mid-April.

ARRIVAL: By air - Fort Myers (15 miles). By car - I-4 to US 27 south. Turn west on Route 29, right on Route 80, follow signs.

Boca Raton Resort & Club

501 E. Camino Real, Boca Raton, FL 33432

(561) 395-3000; (800) 327-0101

ACCOMMODATIONS: 912 guest rooms and suites, available in the Cloisters, the Tower, the Golf Villas and the Boca Beach Club. As you enter the grounds at the Camino Real entrance, you will see the magnificent Cloisters, truly a living museum. Done in a Mediterranean style with fountains and formal gardens, it is most impressive.

AMENITIES: This is one very busy complex. There are 22 clay-topped tennis courts (four lighted), a full-service marina, swimming pools and beach activities. Several dining options are available: the

Cathedral Room, the Top of the Tower, Patio Royale, Court of the Four Lions, the Boca Beach Club, the Shell and the Cabana.

GOLF: The course measures 6,682/6,154/5,518 yards and pars at 71. Wind, sand and water (not in long roughs) are the major concerns here. A pretty layout, with little or no rough to fight, it is a delightful course to play. A short distance away is a second course. Playing 6,654/6,175/5,565, it pars at 72.

RATES: (EP) Lodgings - $240/$310/$415. Green fees - $150, including carts. Golf packages are available. Rates are for January-April.

ARRIVAL: Boca Raton is 22 miles south of Palm Beach and 45 miles north of Miami on A1A. From I-95 take the Glades Road exit east to US 1, then head south (one mile). Make a left at Camino Real.

Boca Teeca Country Club & Inn

5800 Northwest 2nd Avenue, Boca Raton, FL 33487

(561) 994-0400; (800) 344-6995

ACCOMMODATIONS: 46 rooms in the inn and many one- to three-bedroom condos.

AMENITIES: Six lighted tennis courts, large pool and three dining areas.

GOLF: The 27-hole course offers several configurations. The South/North plays 6,483/6,144/5,557 yards, parring at 72/73. The North/East nines reach out 6,609/6,312/5,551 yards, parring at 73. The East/South combination measures 6,072/5,816/5,262 yards, with a par of 71/72. The clubhouse facility has steam rooms, saunas and a pro shop.

RATES: (EP) Lodgings - $125/$135. Green fees - $60, including cart. Rates are for mid-December through April.

ARRIVAL: By air - West Palm Beach. By car - I-95, exit Yamato Road eastbound. This road becomes 51st Street. Proceed to 2nd traffic light (Northwest 2nd), turn left.

Florida

Boca West Club

Rental Office: Suite 101, 7763 W. Glades Road, Boca Raton, FL 33434

(561) 479-5900

ACCOMMODATIONS: Fully equipped private villas tucked away among the trees, with living rooms, kitchens and private verandas. The 1,436-acre Boca West has golf, tennis, canoeing and an awe-inspiring 700-year-old cypress tree. Boca West was purchased by its members in 1988, but still offers rental villas.

AMENITIES: 34 tennis courts. The Boca West Clubhouse and the Village Store (a gourmet snack shop), offer a varied and outstanding selection of food.

GOLF: The four courses, each parring at 72, play 6,400/5,520 yards; 6,153/5,298 yards; 6,169/5,068, and 6,578/5,334 yards.

RATES: (EP) one-bedroom villa - $2,700 per month; two-bedroom villa - $3,500 per month. Rates are for mid-December through April. A temporary membership fee allows you to pay green fees on a day-by-day basis.

ARRIVAL: By air - Palm Beach (30 minutes); Miami (50 minutes). By car - from I-95, exit Glades Road (Route 808), travel west. From Florida Turnpike, Exit 28.

The Breakers

1 South County Road, Palm Beach, FL 33480

(561) 655-6611; (800) 833-3141

The architectural design of the exterior, with its twin towers and graceful arches, was inspired by the famous Villa Medici in Rome. In fact, the resort claims its magnificent design represents the greatest bit of architectural thievery and mental ransacking of Rome to have ever taken place. It is a Mobil Five Star and AAA Five Diamond resort.

ACCOMMODATIONS: 569 guest rooms, including 45 suites.

AMENITIES: 17 tennis courts (including Breakers West), a private beach, Olympic-size pool, cabanas, a patio bar, snorkeling, a dance studio, movies and a supervised children's program. There are several dining rooms: the Circle Room, the Florentine for fine dining, the Pasta House, the Beach Club, Flagler's Stweak House, as well as several pubs. If that's not enough, there is 24-hour in-room dining service.

GOLF: The West Course, some 10 miles from the resort, plays 6,905/6,340/5,690/5,420 yards, parring at 71/72. The Ocean layout, recently redone and supported by a new 32,000-square-foot golf and tennis clubhouse, features 18 new greens, added bunkers (88 total) and new cart paths. It plays 6,146/5,730/5,149 yards, with a par of 70. Water becomes a factor on seven or eight holes.

RATES: (EP) Lodgings - $465/$500/$600. Green fees - $150, including cart. Golf packages are available. Rates are for mid-December through mid-April.

ARRIVAL: By air - Palm Beach International Airport. By car - from the airport, take a left onto Australian Avenue. Exit onto Okeechobee Blvd. (Do not take Old Okeechobee Road). Go east 1½ miles over the Intracoastal bridge. Take a left at the second light after the bridge, onto A1A. Resort is about a half-mile north from there on the right side.

The Doral Golf Resort & Spa

4400 NW 87th Avenue, Miami, FL 33178

(305) 592-2000; (800) 713-6725

ACCOMMODATIONS: Over the last few years Doral has invested millions in a complete renovation, and it shows.

AMENITIES: 15-court tennis complex, a 24-stable equestrian center, lake fishing, jogging on their measured three-mile cross-country trail, several swimming pools, and the multi-million-dollar International Spa and Health Club. For dining there is Provare, the Sandpiper Restaurant, the new Champions Restaurant & Bar and the outdoor Staggerbush Bar & Lawn Grill.

GOLF: There are five championship golf courses along with a par-3 executive layout. Doral's Blue Course is often referred to as "The Blue Monster," and for good reason. The wind really comes into play on this layout. With its length, scattered traps and water on virtually every hole, the wind can turn this from a monster into a nightmare. Stretching out 6,939/6,597/5,786 yards, it pars at 72. The White Course plays 6,208/5,913/5,286 yards and also pars at 72; The Red Course measures 6,120/5,681/5,204, parring at 71; and the Gold reaches 6,279/5,876/5,422 yards and pars at 70. The Blue Monster was designed by Dick Wilson; the others were done by

Robert Von Hagge. There is a good amount of water on all four courses.

RATES: (EP) Lodgings - $325/$355/$395. Green fees - $190/$210, including cart. Blue Monster Course - $250, including cart. Golf package (two nights/two days, including lodging, breakfast, green fees, cart, club storage), $980/$1,230 per couple. Rates are for January-April.

ARRIVAL: By air - Miami International Airport. By car - from the airport, take State Road 836 West; exit on State Road 826 North. Drive three miles to exit on NW 36th St. (West). Proceed one mile to a right on NW 87th Ave. Drive one block to entrance on left.

Gasparilla Jnn & Cottages

Gasparilla Island, Boca Grande, FL 33921

(941) 964-2201

ACCOMMODATIONS: 64 rooms and 16 adjacent cottages. It is an old hotel that works hard and is successful in offering old-fashioned hospitality and warmth. Although there are many things to see and do here, this is not a high-powered nightlife resort. Rather, it is a place to relax and unwind. The inn is a delightful structure. Still showing its graceful white columns, it has changed little since it was built in 1912.

AMENITIES: Three hard and six Har-Tru tennis courts, a large heated pool with a thatched-roof sundeck enclosure.

GOLF: The course is reserved for guest play, so you do not need tee times. The 18 holes are bound by the seawall of the Gulf, the boat channel on two sides and Charlotte Harbor on the other. With slightly rolling terrain, traps and palm trees, and water in play on 10 holes, it is an interesting layout. The course plays 6,392/5,763 yards, parring at 72/74.

RATES: (FAP) Lodgings - $416/$462. Rates are per couple and include all three meals. Green fees - $45, carts $36.

ARRIVAL: By air - Fort Myers; air taxi to Rotunda (10 minutes). By car - Route 771 from Charlotte to Boca Grande Causeway at Placida.

Grand Palms Golf & Country Club

14800 Pines Blvd., Pembroke Pines, FL 33027

(954) 431-8800; (800) 327-9246

ACCOMMODATIONS: 137 rooms and suites.

AMENITIES: An Olympic-size pool, three tennis courts, sauna, men's and women's locker rooms, laundry facilities and a new health spa. The clubhouse has a dining room, snack bar, lounge, and pro shop.

GOLF: A few recent changes include installation of a new drainage system, improved greens and tees, adding height variations in the fairways and creating lakes in some of the rough areas. The new layout plays 6,373/5,915/5,464 yards and pars at 72. An additional nine holes have just been added.

RATES: (EP) Lodgings - $138/$158. Green fees - $75, including cart. Golf packages are available. Rates are for December 22-April 15.

ARRIVAL: By air - Miami or Ft. Lauderdale.

Harbour Ridge

PO Box 2451, Stuart, FL 33495

(561) 336-1800; (877) 336-1801

ACCOMMODATIONS: 20 three-bedroom villas; 27 cottages; Harbour Village (38 homesites); two- and three-bedroom apartments; single family villas.

AMENITIES: Four tennis courts, a pool, a café lounge and a very complete tennis pro shop. The yacht club has 196 slips and a ship's store. There is a waterfront boardwalk along the St. Lucie River and several miles of winding trails for jogging and biking.

GOLF: The Golden Marsh Golf Course, a Joe Lee design, plays 6,607/6,297/5,366 yards with a par of 72. This layout requires placement and finesse. Not only are the trees and rolling terrain a factor, but water plays on all but four holes. A second course, a Pete Dye design, is very different from the Golden Marsh layout. The River Ridge 18 plays 6,626/6,212/5,613/5,104/4,509 yards and also pars at 72.

RATES: (EP) Lodgings - $3,500/$4,500 monthly. Green fees - $85, including cart. Rates are for mid-December through April.

ARRIVAL: By air - Palm Beach International (45 minutes). By car - north on the Florida Turnpike, Exit #52 at Stuart. Straight ahead for one mile to High Meadows Avenue. Turn left and travel one mile to intersection of Murphy Road (blinking light). Turn left and go three more miles.

Inverrary Plaza Golf Resort

3501 Inverrary Boulevard, Fort Lauderdale, FL 33319

(954) 485-0500; (800) 241-0363

ACCOMMODATIONS: 204 rooms and suites.

AMENITIES: 30 tennis courts, swimming pools, a fitness center along with the Cypress Garden and the Oak Room Restaurants.

GOLF: The Inverrary Country Club Course West plays 6,621/6,331/5,930/5,414 yards, parring at 71. With water featured on 12 holes, this layout will keep your attention. The East Course, reaching out a massive 7,124/6,693/6,220/5,623 yards, pars at 72. It uses water on 13 holes. The Sunrise Country Club is another option. Measuring 6,668/6,632/5,962/5,311 yards, it pars at 72/73.

RATES: (EP) Lodgings - $159/$169 per couple. Green fees - $99, including cart. Golf packages are available.

ARRIVAL: By air - Ft. Lauderdale/Hollywood Int. Airport. By car - take I-95 to Oakland Park Blvd. Go west to 56th Avenue and turn right at the Inverrary waterfall.

Marriott's Marco Beach Resort

400 S. Collier Boulevard, Marco Island, FL 33937

(941) 394-2511; (800) 438-4373

ACCOMMODATIONS: 736 rooms, including 86 suites and eight villas, most housed in an 11-story hotel. This is one extremely busy place, and it is frequented by families with children.

AMENITIES: Three pools, a 16-court tennis complex (13 clay and three hard), bicycle rentals, sailing, and fishing charters. There are five restaurants: the Marco Dining Room, Quinns on the Beach Restaurant, the Voyager, the Café del Sol and the Tiki Terrace.

GOLF: The Golf Club at Marco, located some distance away, pars at 72 and reaches out a substantial 6,898/6,471/5,416 yards. The course has about 45 acres of water, which comes into play on 15 holes. The combination of water, trees and traps will more than keep your attention.

RATES: (EP) Lodgings - $275/$325/$385 and up. Green fees - $150, including cart. Golf packages are available. Rates given are for mid-December through May 31.

ARRIVAL: By air - Fort Myers (50 miles). By car - from Fort Myers take I-75 south to Exit 15. Bear right onto 951 south. Continue to Marco Island. Pass over bridge. From the fourth traffic light the resort will be approximately 1,000 yards on your right side.

Naples Beach Hotel

851 Gulf Shore Blvd., North, Naples, FL 33940

(941) 261-2222; (800) 237-7600

ACCOMMODATIONS: 315 well-furnished rooms, including 42 suites, as well as several apartments and efficiencies. Most have balconies overlooking either the Gulf or the golf course.

AMENITIES: Four tennis courts and an Olympic-size pool. Guests may also enjoy swimming in the Gulf. Boating, sailing or deep-sea fishing can be arranged at the nearby marina. The Everglades Restaurant, HB's or the Deli is available for dining.

GOLF: The course, with a par of 72, reaches out a respectable 6,462/6,101/5,315 yards. A few of the challenges include water on 11 holes, undulating greens, fairway bunkers and trees.

RATES: (EP) Lodgings - $215/$245/$350. Green fees - $105, including cart. Golf package (two nights/two days, including lodging, breakfast, green fees, cart, club storage) - $840/$980 per couple. Rates are for January-April.

ARRIVAL: By air - Fort Myers Airport or Naples Airport (10 minutes). By car - southbound on I-75, take Exit 16 to Naples. Travel US 41 south to Golf Drive, then to Gulf Boulevard North.

Florida

Palm-Aire Spa Resort

2501 Palm-Aire Drive North, Pompano Beach, FL 33069

(954) 972-3300

ACCOMMODATIONS: 118 rooms and suites, all fully equipped for housekeeping. Palm-Aire is a delightful resort, providing an almost endless variety of activities.

AMENITIES: A world famous health spa (rated among the top 10 in the US by *Golf* magazine), 37 tennis courts, several swimming pools, a beach club and racquetball courts. Dining is provided in three restaurants and lounges.

GOLF: There are four championship courses. The Cypress, without doubt the most difficult of all, plays 6,910/6,147/5,447 yards. The Oaks reaches out 6,782/6,075/5,481 yards; The Palms measures 6,932/6,371/5,434 yards; and The Pines reaches out 6,610/6,279/5,212 yards. All four par at 72. The Sables, an executive course parring at 60, plays 3,401 yards. All of the courses, with the exception of The Pines, offer plenty of water. Be sure to bring a ball retriever, as they request you do not feed the alligators by hand!

RATES: (EP) Lodgings - $169/$249 and up. Green fees - $60, including carts. Rates are mid-December through April.

ARRIVAL: By air - Ft. Lauderdale. By car - Florida Turnpike, Exit 24, Pompano Parkway to resort.

PGA National Resort & Spa

400 Avenue of the Champions, Palm Beach Gardens, FL 33418

(561) 627-2000; (800) 633-9150

ACCOMMODATIONS: 335 guest rooms and suites as well as 90 housekeeping cottage suites. The resort property extends over 2,340 acres; the hotel is situated on a slight knoll.

AMENITIES: 26-acre lake with private beach, European-style spa, Waters of the World mineral pools, fitness training, Nautilus equipment, jogging paths, full-service salon, lap pool, saunas, whirlpools, two racquet ball courts, 19 Har-Tru tennis courts (12 lighted), croquet facility. For dining, choose from the Citrus Tree, Oasis Bar & Grille, Bear Trap Bar & Grill, Arezzo (Italian), Shula's Steak House, the 19th Hole, the Health Bar, the Oasis Bar & Grill, or the Citrus Tree. The Hall of Fame Lounge offers live entertainment.

GOLF: There are four championship layouts now in play: the Champion, reaching out a monstrous 7,022/6,742/6,373/6,023/5,377 yards; the Haig, stretching 6,806/6,352/5,648 yards; the Squire, at 6,478/6,025/5,114; and the General, playing 6,768/6,270/5,324 yards. Each course pars at 72. There is a fifth course approximately six miles away.

RATES: (EP) Lodgings - $319 and up. Green fees - $130, the Championship Course - $285, carts $130. Golf packages - (one night/one day, including lodging, two rounds of golf with cart, bag storage, breakfast) - from $630 a person.

ARRIVAL: By air - Palm Beach Airport (15 miles). By car - go north from Palm Beach Airport on I-95 to PGA Boulevard. Go west two miles. The entrance will be on your left.

The Plantation Golf & Country Club

490 Rockley Boulevard, Venice, FL 34293

(941) 493-2146; (800) 826-4060

ACCOMMODATIONS: Fully equipped one- and two-bedroom condos, villas and single family estate homes.

AMENITIES: Swimming pools, 13 tennis courts and 27 acres of inter-connected lakes providing excellent freshwater fishing. Arrangements for deep-sea fishing excursions can also be made. The Manor offers lunch and dinner; The Bermuda Grill serves breakfast and lunch.

GOLF: The resort boasts 36 holes of golf. The Bobcat, playing 6,862/6,526/6,128/5,418 yards, pars at 72. A Scottish-style layout, complete with pot bunkers, undulating hills, and water on 16 holes, it will give you all you can handle. In fact, water is prominent on both courses. The newest course, The Panther, measures 6,307/5,941/5,133 yards and also pars at 72.

RATES: (EP) Lodgings - Weekly rates - $1,075. Monthly, $3,150. Green fees - $46, carts $28. Rates are for February-March.

ARRIVAL: By air - Sarasota (45 minutes). By car - I-75 to Venice. Resort is on US 41, four miles south of Venice.

Florida

Port LaBelle Inn

One Oxbow Drive, Port LaBelle, FL 33935

(863) 675-4411; (800) 282-3375

While it is somewhat off the beaten tourist trail and not well known outside the area, this 3,200-acre resort has a great deal to offer.

ACCOMMODATIONS: A 50-room, four-story inn and country club.

AMENITIES: Access to a marina adjacent to the Caloosahatchee River, horseback riding, swimming, fishing and two lighted tennis courts. There is an excellent restaurant.

GOLF: The setting of slightly rolling hills and tree-lined fairways is unusual for southern Florida. Playing 7,043/6,688/5,794 yards, the course pars at 72. Water either threatens you or comes into play on 16 holes.

RATES: (EP) Lodgings - $89/$139. Green fees - $55, including cart. Golf packages are available.

ARRIVAL: By air - Palm Beach or Fort Myers. There is also a private airport three miles southwest in LaBelle. By car - on highway 80 between Lake Okeechobee and Fort Myers.

Quality Inn Suites & Golf Resort

4100 Golden Gate Parkway, Naples, FL 33116

(941) 455-1010; (800) 277-0017

ACCOMMODATIONS: A 204-room hotel/motel.

AMENITIES: A pool and two tennis courts. The clubhouse offers a lounge and restaurant. A second restaurant, T. A. Fitzgerald's, is at the inn.

GOLF: The Golden Gate Country Club course plays 6,570/6,210/5,374 yards and pars at 72. There are a great number of traps, trees, and lots of water coming into contention on the second nine. They have a lighted driving range.

RATES: (EP) Lodgings - $119/$288. Green fees -$65,including cart. Golf packages are available. Rates are for February-April.

ARRIVAL: By air - Naples. By car - off US 41, near the intersection of the Golden Gate Parkway.

Raintree Golf Resort

1600 South Hiatus Road (Box 8699), Pembroke Pines, FL 33084

(954) 432-1500; (800) 346-5332

ACCOMMODATIONS: 12 one-bedroom and 12 two-bedroom condos adjacent to the clubhouse.

AMENITIES: A swimming pool, a spa and cabana, along with a whirlpool tub in each master bath. The clubhouse has a restaurant.

GOLF: The course, parring at 72, stretches out 6,461/6,201/5,308 yards. While it is relatively flat, water either comes directly into play or intimidates you on 12 holes. With plenty of palm trees, the course is also well-trapped. Worthy of note and a bit unusual is the fact that this layout has six par threes, six par fours and six par fives.

RATES: (EP) Lodgings - $160/$195. Green fees - $45/$55, including cart. Golf package (four nights/five days, including lodging, golf with cart, full American breakfast, club storage) - $1,000 per couple.

ARRIVAL: By air - Ft. Lauderdale or Miami International (30 minutes). By car - from I-95, take Hollywood Pines Blvd. west to Hiatus Road and turn left (south).

The Resort at Longboat Key Club

301 Gulf of Mexico Drive, Longboat Key, FL 34228

(941) 383-8821; (800) 237-8821

The Longboat Key Club has been judged one of the Top 50 resorts. This 1,000-acre complex is actually a group of privately owned vacation suites. Situated along a stretch of white sand beach on an island off Longboat Key. It is also one of the few world-class resorts located within a wildlife sanctuary.

ACCOMMODATIONS: 227 suites, ranging from guest room studios to two-bedroom family suites. All are impeccably furnished. The structures consist of several four- to 10-story buildings fronting the beach. There are also garden apartments, townhouse condos and family homes.

AMENITIES: 18 Har-Tru tennis courts (six lighted), sailing and boating from the Longboat Moorings Marina (277 slips), fishing for sea bass, silver, king or tarpon, and swimming in both the pool and the Gulf of Mexico. The variety of birds on display along this private beach is something to behold. The resort's three restaurants are Orchids, Spike'n Tees and the Island House. Lighter dining is available poolside at the Barefoot Bar & Grille.

GOLF: There are two outstanding championship layouts. The Islandside 18 plays 6,890/6,158/5,368 yards and pars at 72. Bring hip boots, as there is water in play on every hole! This Billy Mitchell layout has a tropical setting with many palm trees. The Harbourside layout (27 holes) presents some interesting combinations. The Red/White duo plays 6,783/6,223/5,425 yards; the White/Blue reaches out 6,871/6,358/5,282 yards; the Blue/Red crossover weighs in at 6,752/6,243/5,141 yards. All three par at 72. Any of these combinations will give you a much different golfing experience than the Islandside. Bordering Sarasota Bay, the fairways wind their way through virgin stands of live oak and sable palms.

RATES (EP) Lodgings - $245/$295/$380. Green fees - $130, including cart. No packages during peak season. Rates are for January-April.

ARRIVAL: By air - Tampa (65 miles) or Sarasota, just across the bay (eight miles), for commercial or private aircraft. By car - from Sarasota, travel south on 41 to Ringling Causeway (SR 789) to St. Armands, then north to the resort. The entrance is on your left.

Rolling Hills Golf Resort

3501 West Rolling Hills Circle, Ft. Lauderdale, FL 33328

(954) 475-0400; (800) 327-7735

ACCOMMODATIONS: 222 rooms.

AMENITIES: Four tennis courts and large freeform pool with surrounding decks. Breakfast, lunch and dinner are served in the Waterfall Café.

GOLF: This course is somewhat unusual for Florida, as there is not one palm tree on the entire 27-hole layout. Designed by William Mitchell, it features rolling terrain, contoured greens, fairways lined with giant Spanish oaks, towering Australian pines and 43 lakes and canals. There is at least one hole where water does not threaten you. The course uses a crossover system, as follows: the East/Middle course plays 6,905/6,306/5,630 yards; the Middle/West, 6,763/6,230/5,582 yards; and the East/West, 6,856/6,298/5,636 yards. Each combination has a par of 72.

RATES: (EP) Lodgings - $120/$145/$180. Green fees - $50/$55, including cart.

ARRIVAL: By air - Ft. Lauderdale. By car - Florida Turnpike, exit Route 84; west to University Drive; south to Rolling Hills Circle, turn right.

Don Shula's Resort

Miami Lakes Drive & Palmetto Expressway, Miami Lakes, FL 33014

(305) 821-1150; (800) 247-4852

ACCOMMODATIONS: 310 rooms and suites.

AMENITIES: Ten lighted tennis courts, nine indoor racquetball courts, a Nautilus fitness center, saunas and whirlpools. Dining and evening dancing are offered in the Main Street Restaurant and at the Country Club.

GOLF: The course reaches out 7,055/6,512/5,639 yards and pars at 72. It is well maintained with trees everywhere and water coming into play on all but three holes. There is also a par-54 executive course available.

RATES: (EP) Lodgings - $149/$179/$209. Green fees - $90/$125, including cart. Golf packages are available. Rates are for December-April.

ARRIVAL: By air - Miami. By car - Florida Turnpike to Golden Glades Interchange, then west on Palmetto Expressway.

South Seas Plantation

PO Box 194, Captiva Island, FL 33924

(941) 472-5111; (800) 227-8482

ACCOMMODATIONS: 500 rooms and suites, located on 330 acres in Harbourside Village, Gulf Cottages (three bedrooms), Land's End Village (two and three bedrooms), Beach Homes, Marina Villas, Beach Villas, Tennis Villas and others. Located on the northern tip of Captiva Island, three miles out into the Gulf of Mexico, this resort is a perfect place to relax.

AMENITIES: 22 tennis courts, 18 swimming pools, deep-water marina with full-service facilities, water-skiing, windsurfing, kayaks, and a two-mile stretch of white sand beach. The fishing in this area is great; catch ranges from tarpon and snook to redfish and groupers. For dining there is Chadwick's, Cap'n Al's, The Kings Crown, Mama Rosa's for pizza; and Uncle Bob's for ice cream treats.

GOLF: The nine-hole course measures (if played twice) 5,892/5,558/4,308 yards with a par of 72. Guests of The Plantation also have playing privileges on nearby Sanibel Island (about a 15- minute drive). The Dunes, a private course, is a regulation 18. Parring at 70, it plays 5,715/5,426/5,093 yards.

RATES: (EP) Lodgings - $185/$410; beach homes (minimum seven days rental) - $780 per night. Green fees - $95, including carts.

ARRIVAL: By air - Fort Myers. By car - I-75 to Exit 21, west to State Route 869, south to Sanibel Causeway. Follow to the tip of Captiva Island.

Turnberry Isle Resort Club

19999 W. Country Club Drive, Aventura, FL 33180

(305) 932-6200; (800) 327-7028

Turnberry is a private island set in the Intracostal Waterway. For several years it has been a getaway place for many of the world's great stars of sports, entertainment and the arts.

ACCOMMODATIONS: Rooms and suites (240 at the Country Club and 70 at the Marina Hotel). Recent additions bring the total to 350 rooms.

AMENITIES: 24 tennis courts (16 lighted), an exhibition court, an internationally acclaimed health spa and a magnificent marina with a capacity for berthing craft up to 150 feet long. There are two dining rooms and two lounges at the Country Club and a lounge, dining room and café at the Marina Hotel.

GOLF: Both courses, designed by Robert Trent Jones, have been in play for over 15 years. The North layout measures 6,323/5,970/5,589/4,991 yards, with a par of 70. The South Course, playing considerably longer, weighs in at 7,003/6,458/6,078/5,581 yards and pars at 72. They offer what is reputed to be the world's largest triple green, measuring some 150 yards in length and serving three different holes. You could, if you came in short, have the delightful prospect of a putt over 100 yards.

RATES: (EP) Lodgings - $375/$425/$465. Green fees - $120, carts $40. Golf packages are available. Rates are for January-April.

ARRIVAL: By air - Miami or Ft. Lauderdale. By car - Turnberry is at the intersection of 199th Street and Biscayne Boulevard.

The Wyndham Resort & Spa

250 Racquet Club Road, Ft. Lauderdale, FL 33326

(954) 389-3300; (800) 327-8090

ACCOMMODATIONS: 600 well-appointed guest rooms and suites with view of either the golf course or the lake.

AMENITIES: 18 lighted Har-Tru clay tennis courts. There is a nearby racquetball building with four courts, a pro shop and three pools. A short shuttle ride away is the Equestrian Center, boasting a 51-stall stable, bunkhouse, and blacksmith shop, with a restaurant and lounge overlooking the show rings. The world-class hotel spa is equipped to provide the finest in health, fitness, nutrition and beauty care available. Dining facilities include the Renaissance Restaurant, the Gardens, the Pool Snack Bar, the Terrace Lounge, the Bonaventure Country Club and the Saddle Club.

GOLF: Played on two courses. The East measures 7,011/6,557/5,345 yards, with a par of 72/73. The West is somewhat shorter at 6,189/4,993 yards, parring at 70. You will enjoy the courses if you can stay out of the 24 lakes and creeks, the 86 diabolically placed traps and the many trees. Both are excellent layouts. Bonaventure features a clubhouse, pro shop, locker rooms, saunas and a lounge.

RATES: (EP) Lodgings - $215/$245/$290. Green fees - $90, including cart. Golf package (two nights/two days, including lodging, breakfast, two rounds of golf, cart, club storage) - $572/$672 per couple. Rates are for mid-December to April 30th.

ARRIVAL: By air - Ft. Lauderdale. By car - due west of airport on Route 84 (25 miles).

Florida

Georgia

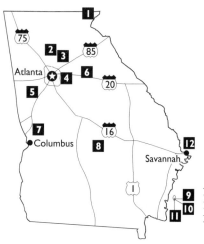

1. Sky Valley Resort
2. Lake Arrowhead Resort
3. Stouffer's Pineisle Resort/
   The Inn at Chateau Elan/
   Lake Lanier Islands Hilton Resort/
   Brasstowne Valley Resort
4. Marriott's Evergreen Resort/
   Stone Mountain Resort
5. Fairfield Plantation
6. Hard Labor Creek State Park
7. Callaway Gardens
8. Little Ocmulgee State Park
9. The Cloister
10. Sea Pines Golf & Tennis Resort
11. The Jekyll Island Club Hotel
12. The Westin Savannah Harbor Resort

The Golden Isles

The "Golden Isles," some 12 in total, are off Georgia's southern coast. The favorable year-round climate, protected waterways and lush vegetation have been well known for many years. First settled in the days of pirates and slave trading, they were finally developed as a summer residence by some of America's more affluent: the Rockefellers, Bakers, Goodyears and Pulitzers, to name a few. Although a few resorts were developed prior to World War II, the majority were established and began to flourish after that time.

We will cover three of these islands: Sea Island, the smallest, but with an outstanding resort; St. Simon's Island, with two major resorts; and Jekyll Island, where for 56 years no uninvited person set foot without permission of the area's notables, who included the above named families along with the Astors, Morgans and Vanderbilts. They knew a good thing, for this is a magnificent area.

The Cloister

100 First Street, Sea Island, GA 31561

(912) 638-3611; (800) 732-4752

The Cloister has been judged one of the Top 50 resorts. The beautiful Mediterranean-style main lodge, built in 1927, has been kept in impeccable condition. Surrounded by moss-draped oaks and gardens of magnolias, it is truly outstanding. The Cloister has repeatedly won the Mobil Five Star Award (given to only a few resorts and hotels out of 21,000 in the United States each year).

ACCOMMODATIONS: 262 rooms in several buildings (the Cloister, River House, Beach Houses and Guest Houses), all within a short walk of the main lodge. There are also privately owned homes, locally referred to as "cottages," that may be rented. Ask for the Sea Island Cottage Rentals when calling the reservation number.

AMENITIES: Horseback riding, swimming, shooting school (skeet or trap shooting), tennis on 17 fast-dry courts, fishing, various surf craft available from the dock, and a Spa & Fitness Center at the beach club. The spa offers facials, massages, Swiss showers, hydrotherapy and esthetics treatments. Dining is available in the Main Dining Room, the Beach Club or either of the two golf clubhouses. There is only one way to describe the food – superb. Dinner dancing is provided each evening except Sunday (jacket and tie required). Special events are often planned, such as Big Band Time at the Cloister with "Music From Yesterday," annual bridge tournaments, food & wine festivals and many more events.

GOLF: The road leading into the Sea Island Golf Club is a picture-postcard setting, lined with massive, venerable oaks; azaleas and snapdragons are in full display. Soon to be added is a new clubhouse. The plan is to keep the old affair for special functions and as a golf museum.

For many years the Cloister courses formed four nine-hole layouts and played under a crossover system. The Seaside and the Marshside nines have been joined to form an 18-hole course. The Retreat nine and the Plantation were also joined as an 18-hole layout. The Plantation Course reaches out a modest 6,549/6,068/5,194 yards with a par of 72. A portion of this layout winds past the ruins of an old plantation, with water coming into play on six holes. The newest 18, designed by Tom Fazio in 1999, measures 6,550/6,006/5,048 and pars at 70.

A few years ago the Cloister acquired The St. Simons Island Golf Club. Playing 6,490/6,114/5,206 yards and parring at 72, it comes complete with tight, tree-lined fairways and well-trapped greens. Water becomes a factor on only eight holes. The clubhouse, built in the old plantation style, is impressive and also provides a dining room.

Built in 1991, the "Golf Learning Center" offers private as well as group lessons. They have the most sophisticated teaching arrangement we have seen.

RATES: (FAP) Lodgings - $380/$434/$546/$640 and up per couple. Green fees - $145/$195, including cart. Golf package (three nights/four days, including FAP, lodging, golf and cart) - $1,956/$2,118 per couple. Rates are for March 15-May 31st.

Note: The Cloister accepts personal checks, but will not take credit cards. No tipping is allowed at this resort. You are assessed a fixed amount to cover all tips, including check-in and check-out bell service.

ARRIVAL: By air - Jacksonville (70 miles); Brunswick/Glynco Jet-Port (15 miles). By private aircraft - McKinnon Airport. Pickup can be arranged from all three airports. Check when making reservations. By car - I-95/US 17, enter the causeway off US 17 at Brunswick; then 10 miles to Sea Island.

Jekyll Island

Jekyll Island has held onto its sense of history while melding it with a new and exciting resort atmosphere. With the construction of new convention facilities, it has become one of the South's major meeting and conference centers.

There are three championship 18-hole golf courses and a full-size nine-hole layout on this island. The Oceanside nine, built in 1917 by Scotch golf architect Walter Davis (at the direction of such influential names as J. P. Morgan, Astor, Rockefeller and Goodyear), plays 3,289 yards and pars at 36. The Oleander plays 6,602/6,151 yards and pars at 72. The Pine Lakes course stretches out 6,698/6,265 yards, parring at 72. Finally, the Indian Mound layout measures 6,601/6,206 yards, also parring at 72.

Bring extra ball retrievers with you, as these layouts delight in water hazards. (Also useful when confronting alligators, in which case you leave it for him to pick his teeth with while you move rapidly in the opposite direction!)

All of the above-mentioned golf courses are owned and operated by the state and are available for play by guests of the various resorts on Jekyll Island. The golf courses on Sea Island, St. Simons Island and Brunswick are also available for play on a space-available basis.

You will also find tennis, swimming, tours, the Jekyll Island Music Theater, fishing trips, boat tours and an art gallery on the island.

For information on the many accommodations and facilities, contact the Jekyll Island Welcome Center at (912) 635-3636; in Georgia, (800) 342-1042; nationwide, (800) 841-6586.

The Jekyll Island Club Hotel

371 Riverview Drive, Jekyll Island, GA 31520

(912) 635-2600; (800) 535-9547

The Jekyll Island Club dates back to the period of the Morgans, Rockefellers and Vanderbilts. Now restored, it once again offers the comfort and amenities that made it a favorite of long ago.

ACCOMMODATIONS: 134 rooms and suites.

AMENITIES: An outdoor heated pool, one indoor and five outdoor tennis courts, a marina, a variety of elegant boutiques and 63 holes of golf. The Grand Dining Room serves outstanding cuisine.

GOLF: For detail on the golf facilities, refer to Jekyll Island, above.

RATES: (EP) Lodgings - $139/$289. Green fees - $32, carts $28. Golf packages are available. MAP as well as FAP plans are also offered.

ARRIVAL: By air - Jacksonville International Airport (60 miles). Glynco Jet Port (15 miles). By private aircraft - Jekyll Island's 3,700-foot runway. By car - 10 miles from I-95 at Exit 6. Take Georgia Route 50 and follow signs.

St. Simons Island

Georgia

True not only on St. Simons, but on the other islands in this area as well: the natives do not feed their mosquitoes. They depend on visiting northern golfers. Bring repellent spray or risk being devoured.

Sea Palms Golf & Tennis Resort

5445 Frederica Road, St. Simons Island, GA 31522

(912) 638-3351; (800) 841-6268

ACCOMMODATIONS: A hotel and nearby villas. The villas range from one to three bedrooms, and feature living rooms and fully equipped kitchens. The deep beauty of this island, with its century-old oaks and sweeping salt marshes, may well entice you to make more than one visit.

AMENITIES: 12 tennis courts (three lighted), a pool, a health spa with exercise equipment, whirlpools and saunas. Bicycle rentals or horseback riding can be arranged. Dining is at the Country Club with food service also available at the Beach Club.

GOLF: There are 27 holes to negotiate. Using a crossover system, you wind up with the following: The par-72 Tall Pines/Great Oak layout stretches 6,658/6,214/5,325 yards. The Great Oaks/Sea Palms West course plays 6,350/5,901/5,110 yards, parring at 72/73. The Sea Palms West/Tall Pines combination measures 6,198/5,825/5,249 yards and again carries a par of 72/73. Out of a total of 27 holes, water comes either into action or threatens you on 19.

RATES: (EP) Lodgings - $144/$154/$175/$275. Green fees - $60, including cart. Golf package (two nights/two days, including lodging, breakfast, green fees, cart, club storage) - $440/$460/$500 per couple (hotel). Rates are February through May.

ARRIVAL: By air - Jacksonville (75 minutes). By private aircraft - Malcolm McKinnon Airport. By car - I-95 south, take Exit 8. If going north, take Exit 6 and follow the signs for 15 miles.

Mainland Georgia

Brasstown Valley Resort

6321 U.S. Highway 76, Young Harris, GA 30582

(706) 379-9900; (800) 201-3205

ACCOMMODATIONS: 102 rooms in the main lodge with an additional 32 in eight spit level cottages.

AMENITIES: Indoor/outdoor swimming pool, four lighted tennis courts, steam, sauna, whirlpool, massage, horseback riding, fishing, boating on Lake Chatuge, with whitewater rafting nearby. There is also a Mountaineer's Kids Club. There are two dining rooms, including the golf grill and a lounge.

GOLF: A links-style affair, this layout reaches out a substantial 6,957/6,553/5,962/5,028 with a par of 72. The course is well bunkered with water coming into play on 10 holes.

RATES: (EP) Rooms - $164/$204. One-bedroom suite - $300 per couple. Green fees - $65/$75. Golf package - one day/one night (includes lodging, breakfast, unlimited golf, cart for 18 holes), $338 per couple. Rates are for April-December.

ARRIVAL: By air - Atlanta (two hours). By car - take Highway 19 north to Highway 76 and Young Harris.

Callaway Gardens

US Highway 27, Pine Mountain, GA 31822

(706) 663-2281; (800) 282-8181

ACCOMMODATIONS: 350 rooms at the inn, plus 155 two-bedroom, two-bath cottages featuring fully equipped kitchens. The Gardens' 2,500 acres are in the foothills of western Georgia's Appalachian Mountains.

AMENITIES: Fishing, water-skiing, trap shooting, riding, bicycle and jogging trails, tennis on 17 lighted courts. There are several dining possibilities to choose from: the Plantation Room at the Inn, the Gardens Restaurant, the Country Kitchen, the Veranda, the Flower Mill and the Georgia Room.

GOLF: There are three courses. The Mountain View, stretching out 7,040/6,605/5,834 yards, pars at 72/74. Parring at 72, the Garden View course plays 6,392/6,108/5,848 yards. The Lakeview layout measures 6,006/5,452 yards, parring at 70/71.

RATES: (EP) Lodgings - $115/$205/$333. Green fees -$75/$110, including cart. Golf packages are available. Rates are for March-November.

ARRIVAL: By air - Columbus (35 miles). By private aircraft - Callaway Gardens/Harris County Airport (five minutes). By car - from Atlanta, head southwest on Highway 85 to 185 south, Exit 14. Drive south to 27, then southeast to Pine Mountain.

Fairfield Plantation

1602 Lakeview Parkway, Villa Rica, GA 30180

(770) 834-7781

ACCOMMODATIONS: Range from inn rooms or suites to beach-view villas or condos fully equipped for housekeeping.

AMENITIES: Water-skiing, fishing, a 102-slip marina, a sandy white beach, six tennis courts (four lighted) and a pool. The 15,000-square-foot Country Club offers Southern food.

GOLF: The Plantation layout, measuring 6,612/6,193/5,358 yards, pars at 72. With the challenge of 46 traps, water, tree-lined fairways, along with rolling hills and doglegs, this layout will more than keep your full attention.

RATES: (EP) Lodgings - $100/$300. Green fees - $33/$45, including cart. Golf packages are available. There is a minimum stay of two nights.

ARRIVAL: By air - Atlanta. By car - I-20 to Exit 5 at Carrollton. South on Route 61 (6½ miles). Left at Fairfield Plantation sign.

The Inn at Chateau Elan

100 Rue Charlemagne, Braselton, GA 30517

(678) 425-0900; (800) 233-9463

ACCOMMODATIONS: 144 rooms and suites. The resort is about 25 miles from Lake Lanier.

AMENITIES: Health spa, equestrian center, six lighted tennis courts, bicycle rentals, pool, fitness center and golf. There are several dining locations, including the Spa Restaurant and the Golf Clubhouse Restaurant.

GOLF: The Legends Golf Course architect was Dennis Griffiths, with design guidance from such notables as Sam Snead and Gene Sarazen. Playing to a substantial 7,030/6,484/5,900/5,092 yards, it pars at 71. This is a well-bunkered course with water on 11 holes. **Note:** The course is private and is not always available. The Chateau Elan Golf Course pars at 72 and reaches a modest 6,781/6,144/5,555 yards. It takes advantage of the north Georgia foothills and spectacular scenery. There is also a par-3 pitch and putt course.

RATES: Lodgings - $169/$225. Green fees (including cart) - Elan Course, $65/$77; Legends Course, $135.

ARRIVAL: By air - Atlanta International Airport (60 miles). By car - take I-85 north to Exit 48. Drive one mile past the winery.

Lake Arrowhead Resort & Country Club

PO Station 20, Waleska, GA 30183

(770) 479-5505

The resort is set in the rugged and beautiful mountain area of northern Georgia. Perched on the shores of Lake Arrowhead, it occupies 8,100 acres.

ACCOMMODATIONS: Cluster homes with one to three bedrooms, fireplaces and decks, or townhouse condos.

AMENITIES: Six tennis courts (two lighted) and a swimming complex. The 540-acre Lake Arrowhead offers all types of water activity. Lake Chicaway (12 acres) is restricted to electric trolling motors so the outstanding bass fishing will not be disturbed. The Country Club, a beautiful structure of 40,000 square feet, features towering chimneys, blooming atriums and an outstanding main dining room. **Note:** This is a dry county, so bring your own liquor. They do, however, serve beer and wine.

GOLF: The course weighs in at 6,400/5,988/4,468, with a par of 72/70. It is an interesting layout with five of the 18 holes wandering along the lakefront and the remainder meandering into the hills.

RATES: (EP) Lodgings - $155/$185. Green fees - $75, including cart. Golf and tennis packages are available.

ARRIVAL: By air - Atlanta. By car - I-75 north from Atlanta to I-575, north to Canton. In Canton, take Highway 140 (12 miles).

Lake Lanier Islands Hilton Resort

7000 Holiday Road, Lake Lanier Islands, GA 30518

(770) 945-8787; (800) 768-5253

ACCOMMODATIONS: Set on a knoll overlooking the lake, the four-story hotel has 224 guest rooms and suites.

Georgia

AMENITIES: A pool, three lighted tennis courts, a fitness center complete with saunas, whirlpools, and massage therapy, horseback riding, bicycling and a jogging trail. Adjacent to the hotel is the Beach & Water Park with water slides and wave pools. You may water-ski or rent canoes, power boats, sailboats and paddleboats. There are two restaurants: Sylvan's and the clubhouse restaurant.

GOLF: Designed by Joe Lee, the course plays to a modest 6,341/6,104/5,659/4,935 yards with a par of 72. This layout skirts along the edge of the lake with 13 out of the 18 holes flirting with the wet stuff. While there are some trees, the main challenge comes from water and the large number of traps.

RATES: (EP) Lodgings - $149/$169. Green fees - $60/$70, including cart. Golf packages are available.

ARRIVAL: By air - Atlanta (one hour). By private aircraft - Gainesville (15 minutes). By car - from Atlanta, take I-85 north to I-985. From there, take either Exit 1 or 2 and follow the signs.

Marriott's Evergreen Resort

One Lakeview Drive, Stone Mountain, GA 30086

(770) 879-9900; (800) 228-9290

ACCOMMODATIONS: 250 rooms, including 29 suites.

AMENITIES: A lighted tennis court, indoor and outdoor pools, a fitness center, jogging paths and, of course, golf. The Waterside Restaurant, located within the hotel, is available for breakfast, lunch and dinner.

GOLF: The course is a Robert Trent Jones 27-hole layout. Using a crossover system, the Lake/Stone nines play 6,588/6,065/5,099 yards, the Stone/Wood is 6,875/6,232/5,492 yards and the Wood/Lake is 6,595/6,093/5,231 yards. No matter how you mix them, the par is 72.

RATES: (EP) Lodgings - $159/$189. Green fees - $45, including cart. Golf package (two nights/two days, including lodging, green fees, breakfast, cart) - $504 per couple.

ARRIVAL: By air - Atlanta International (30 miles). By car - from I-85 or I-75 take 1-285 east.

Renaissance PineIsle Resort

9000 Holiday Road, Lake Lanier Island, GA 30518

(770) 945-8921; (800) 468-3571

ACCOMMODATIONS: 250 guest rooms plus penthouse suites.
AMENITIES: Sailing, water-skiing, swimming, a beautiful beach
and excellent fishing, seven lighted indoor and outdoor tennis
courts. They also provide horseback riding facilities and a large
heated indoor/outdoor pool. A variety of dining facilities are available: the Grille Room, the Gazebo (less formal), the Marina Grill
and the Clubhouse.
GOLF: The course, a Kirby/Player design parring at 72, measures
6,527/6,154/6,025/5,297 yards. Tree-lined fairways, traps and water coming into play on at least eight holes make this a fun but very
demanding layout. For tee times call (770) 945-8921.
RATES: (EP) Lodgings - $129/$475. Green fees - $75/$105, including cart. Golf packages are available. Rates are for March-November.
ARRIVAL: By air - Atlanta (one hour). By private aircraft -
Gainesville (15 minutes). By car - I-85 to Route 365 then north to
Route 20 (Exit 1). Then west and follow signs for Lake Lanier.

Sky Valley Resort

PO Box 1, Dillard, GA 30537

(706) 746-5301; (800) 262-8259

This resort straddles the North Carolina-Georgia border. It sits on
2,400 acres in the Blue Ridge Mountains of northeastern Georgia.
ACCOMMODATIONS: Privately owned homes, condos or chalets. All units are fully equipped for housekeeping.
AMENITIES: Six tennis courts (two clay, four all-weather), a new
equestrian center, a junior- size Olympic pool and many miles of
hiking trails. There are also two dining rooms.
GOLF: The course has been expanded to 27 holes. The Blue Valley/Estatoah Falls nines play 7,003/6,688/5,926/5,066. The combination of Estatoah Falls/Rabun Bald reaches 6,534/5,980/5,604/
4,939 yards. The Blue Robin/Rabun Bald has a yardage of 6,765/
6,200/5,773/4,961. All three combinations par at 72. The Valley
nine offers the prospect of two waterfalls, four lakes and five brooks.

The Estatoah Falls nine requires a great deal of accuracy and placement with its large lake, a pond and eight small streams that wander all over the place. The Rabun nine is literally carved out of the forest. While shorter, it can give you all you want, with its six waterfalls, three ponds and five streams. The number six hole is spectacular, requiring a shot over the waterfall.

RATES: (EP) Lodgings - $100/$135 per couple; weekly $500/$700. Green fees - $45, including cart. Golf packages are available. Rates are for May-October.

ARRIVAL: By air - Atlanta. By car - from Atlanta (105 miles). Take I-85 to SR 985 to Cornelia. Take US 441 north to Dillard.

Stone Mountain Park Inn

PO Box 775, Stone Mountain, GA 30086

(770) 469-3311; (800) 317-2006

ACCOMMODATIONS: 92 rooms.

AMENITIES: Eight lighted courts and a pool. You can ride to the mountaintop in a Swiss-made cable car to see the awesome Confederate Memorial carvings. These reliefs, carved across the face of the mountain, have some figures as tall as a nine-story building. The dining room is noted for its excellent Southern cuisine.

GOLF: A Robert Trent Jones, Sr. 27-hole layout. The Lake/Stone plays 6,588/6,065/5,099 yards; Stone/Wood reaches out 6,875/6,232/5,492 yards; and the Woods/Lake combination weighs in at 6,595/6,093/5,231 yards. All three combinations par at 72. These are beautiful courses, with the bordering lake and the mountains as a backdrop. It is a well-trapped complex with many trees adding to the challenge.

RATES: (EP) Lodgings - $149/$169. Green fees - $48/$55, including cart. Peak season is June-August.

ARRIVAL: By air - Atlanta (30 minutes). By car - from I-85 or I-75, take I-285 east.

The Westin Savannah Harbor Resort

410 E. Bay Street, Savannah, GA 31401s

(912) 201-2000; (800) 937-8461

Opened in late 1999, The Savannah Harbor Resort is one of the better locations in the country. If you have not had the opportunity to visit this lovely area, by all means, take the time to explore Savannah. You might well consider a carriage ride through the historic district.

ACCOMMODATIONS: On an island overlooking Savannah's downtown historic River Street, this 16-story hotel offers 403 guest rooms, including 55 club level rooms and 19 suites.

AMENITIES: Four lighted tennis courts, two swimming pools, and a marina on the Savannah River offering docking facilities. A water taxi service to the historic district is available. There is a 180-seat dining room, AquaStar, plus a bar. Of course, there is always the 24-hour room service menu. Additional dining is available at the Golf Club. The club house is also the location of the Greenbrier Spa.

GOLF: Designed by Sam Snead and Robert Cupp, this affair reaches out a monstrous 7,288/6,627/6,048 yards and, from the ladies tees, a substantial 5,261 yards, with a par of 72. Water is not much of a factor on the front side but watch it on the second nine. The course is also the location of the "Greenbrier" Spa.

RATES: Rooms - $189/$299. Suites - $500 and up. Green fees - $180, including cart.

ARRIVAL: By air - Savannah International (20 minutes). By car - take I-95 to I-16, then proceed to 17 north. Cross the Talmadge Bridge. Exit to Hutchinson Island. You are now on Harbor Drive; follow the signs to the resort.

Georgia

Georgia State Parks

While there are a formidable number of state parks in Georgia, only two have lodgings, a restaurant and a golf course – Hard Labor Creek and Little Ocmulgee. For information on any of the parks, call (404) 656-2770, or write Georgia Department of Natural Resources, 205 Butler Street SE, Suite 1258, Atlanta, GA 30334. For reservations, call (800) 864-7275.

Hard Labor Creek State Park

Fairplay Road, Rutledge, GA 30663

(706) 557-2863

ACCOMMODATIONS: Cottages plus tent and trailer sites.

AMENITIES: Horseback riding, swimming beaches (there are two lakes), boat rentals, bicycling, 17 miles of hiking trails and a golf course.

GOLF: Reputed to be one of the finest public golf facilities in the Southeast, the Hard Labor Golf Course plays 6,343/5,687 yards, with a par of 72/75. They claim the park derived its name from a stream that runs throughout the course and brings water into play on eight holes.

RATES: (EP) Lodgings - $75/$85. Green fees - $23/$28, carts $24.

ARRIVAL: By car - from I-20 take Exit 49 into Rutledge and proceed two miles on Fairplay Road to the park.

Little Ocmulgee State Park

PO Box 97, McRae, GA 31055

(912) 868-2832

ACCOMMODATIONS: Some cottages and a 30-room lodge.

AMENITIES: A pool, two tennis courts and a 265-acre lake, all manner of rental boats and canoes as well as fishing. There is a restaurant.

GOLF: The Wallace Adams Golf Course. Measuring 6,625/6,312/6,053 yards, it pars at 72/78. That's a pretty good par for the ladies, but the yardage set for them is something else. While a flat course, it is well-trapped and lined by trees.

RATES: (EP) Lodgings - $70/$85. Green fees - $23/$28, carts $24.

ARRIVAL: By car - from I-16 take Exit 14 onto State Route 319/441 and drive due south. The resort is two miles north of McRae.

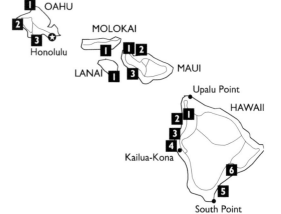

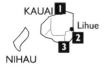

KAUAI
1. Princeville
   Hanalei Bay Resort & Embassy Suites/Princeville Hotel/The Cliffs/
   Hawaiian Islands Resorts, Inc./Princeville Travel Service
2. Marriott Kauai Resort & Villas
3. Poipu Beach Area/Hyatt Regency Kauai/Kiahuna Plantation/Stouffer
   Waiohai Beach Resort

OAHU
1. Turtle Bay Hilton Golf & Tennis Resort/Marriott's Ihilani Resort & Spa

MOLOKAI
1. Kaluakoi Hotel & Golf Club/Kaluakoi Villas/Panoiolo Hale Resort Condos

LANAI
1. The Lodge at Koele/Manele Bay Hotel

MAUI
1. Kapalua Bay Hotel & Villas/Ritz-Carlton Kapalua
2. Hyatt Regency Maui/Maui Marriott Resort/Royal Lahaina Resort/Westin
   Maui
   Condos: Kaanapali Alii/The Whaler at Kaanapali Beach
3. The Wailea Area
   Four Seasons Resort/Grand Wailea Resort & Spa/Kea Lani Hotel/
   Outrigger Wailea Resort/Maui Prince Hotel/Renaissance Wailea Beach
   Resort/Wailea Elua Village

HAWAII
1. Mauna Kea Beach Hotel/Hapuna Beach Prince Hotel
2. Islands at Mauna Lani/Ritz-Carlton Manau Lani/Mauna Lani Bay Hotel/
   Mauna Lani Point Condos
3. Hilton Waikola Village/Royal Waikoloan/The Shores at Waikoloa
4. Keauhou Beach Hotel/Keauhou Resort Condos/Kona Surf Resort/
   Four Seasons Resort Hualalai
5. Sea Mountain at Punalu'u
6. Volcano House Inn

Hawaii

The Island of Oahu

While one of the smaller Islands in the chain, Oahu is the population center, the hub of commercial activities and still the location of most restaurants and night spots. You will also find many wonderful hotels and a few golf resorts. While crowded with people and heavily congested with traffic, it remains beautiful.

Marriott's Jhilani Resort & Spa

Ko Olina Resort, 92-1001 Olani Street, Kapolei, HI 96707

(808) 679-0079; (800) 626-4446

ACCOMMODATIONS: 387 rooms, some with ocean/beach views. There are 42 Executive, Junior, and Ihilani suites. "Ihilani" means "Heavenly Splendor," though that may be a slight exaggeration here.

AMENITIES: A white sand lagoon, nearby beach area, two pools and a spa program. There is an arcade with various shops and four dining areas, including the golf club.

GOLF: The Ko Olina Golf Course was designed by Ted Robinson in 1990. It reaches 6,867/6,324/5,358 yards with a par of 72 and brings water into the picture on eight holes.

RATES: (EP) Lodgings - $340/$390/$495. Suites - $800 and up. Green fees -$120, including cart.

ARRIVAL: By air - Honolulu International Airport. By car - travel west on H-1 to the Ko Olina exit.

Turtle Bay Hilton Golf & Tennis Resort

57-091 Kamehameha Hwy, PO Box 187, Kahuku, Oahu, HI 96731

(808) 293-8811; (800) 445-8667

The resort is on the northern part of Oahu (locally referred to as the country, and removed from the congestion). Driving from Honolulu you will pass near some of the most famous surfing beaches in the world: Sunset Beach, the Banzai Pipeline and Waimea Bay. Waves of up to 30 feet high have been observed during the winter.

ACCOMMODATIONS: 485 guest rooms.

AMENITIES: 10 Plexipave tennis courts (four lighted), a completely equipped exercise room, and two pools. There's also surfing, boogie boarding, scuba diving and horseback riding; fishing, including overnight charters, can be arranged. The hotel provides a children's program, available seven days a week, for a modest fee. There is a coin-operated washer/dryer for guest use. Fine dining is offered in The Cove, while the Palm Terrace presents a more casual setting.

GOLF: There are now 27 holes of golf to enjoy. The newest, an Arnold Palmer layout, reaches out an awesome 7,199/6,795/6,225/5,574 yards and pars at 72. The Country Club nine (if played twice), measures 6,050/5,165 with a par of 71. While beautiful, it caused me a few problems. The course has small greens, lots of sand, and what they refer to as an "ocean breeze." I refer to it as WIND.

RATES: (EP) Lodgings - $165/$185/$205/$525. Green fees - $75, including cart. Country Club Course - $50, including cart. Golf packages are available.

ARRIVAL: By air - Honolulu (one hour). By car - Kamehameha Highway north. Travel H-1 north to H-2, then take Route 83.

The Island of Hawaii

The "Big Island" is one of sharp contrasts, with Hilo on the eastern "wet side" and the warm and drier Kona and Kohala coast areas on the other. There are about 96 road miles between the two, separated by the volcanic mountains of Mauna Loa, at 13,680 feet, Mauna Kea, at 13,796, and Mt. Hualalai, at 8,271 feet. Although the volcanoes are an obvious attraction, the island is also rich in history, for this was once home to the kings of Hawaii.

Kailua-Kona Resort Area

At the heart of the Big Island's famed Kona Coast, the Keauhou Beach/Kailua-Kona area is an open door to Hawaii's history, heritage, and hospitality. There are multitudes of things to do and see, including visiting century-old churches and tiny villages along the coast, tennis, golf, marlin fishing or just daydreaming and relaxing.

Although the various resorts offer good food, if you are visiting for any period of time or are staying in a condominium, you may want a change of pace. I suggest Jamison's By The Sea. Formerly named Dorians, its name may have changed but the food is still magnificent. The address is 77-6452 Alii Drive, Kona. For reservations, phone (808) 329-3195.

Guest of several resorts in this area may use the Kona Country Club Course. This Bell layout plays 6,589/6,165/5,499 and pars at 72/73. Lava-bordered fairways, a profusion of sand traps and flowering shrubs, along with the wind, make this a tester. The Alii course, the newest addition, is on the hillside above the pro shop area. Measuring 6,451/5,823/4,886 yards and parring at 72, it offers some of the most spectacular views we have seen.

Keauhou Beach Hotel

78-6740 Alii Drive, Kailua-Kona, Hawaii, HI 96740

(808) 322-3441; (800) 321-2558

ACCOMMODATIONS: 350 rooms, each with a refrigerator.
AMENITIES: Six tennis courts, a pool and a small sand beach. (There are not many sand beaches on this side of the island.) The

Kuakini Terrace is available for casual dining; the Makai Bar offers nightly Hawaiian entertainment.

GOLF: Guests can play the Kona Country Club golf courses described above.

RATES: (EP) Lodgings - $175/$190/$270. Green fees - $75, including cart. When making reservations, ask about their package arrangements, which include golf, cart rentals, tennis and more.

The Keauhou Resort Condominiums

78-7039 Kam II Road, Kailua-Kona, Hawaii, HI 96740

(808) 322-9122; (800) 367-5286

ACCOMMODATIONS: A 48-unit cluster of one- and two-level townhouses is set in a five- acre tropical garden setting. Each unit has a fully equipped all-electric kitchen with icemaker, dishwasher, washer/dryer, and TV. Most units have an ocean view and all have either one or two lanais.

AMENITIES: Swimming pool. You are a short distance from the waters of the Kona Coast and world-class fishing, snorkeling, and scuba diving.

GOLF: The property is right alongside the Kona Country Club Course. For details on golf refer to the Keahou Beach/Kailua-Kona Resort Area above.

RATES: (EP) Lodgings (five-night minimum) - $97/$145, weekly $679/$1,015. There is a 10% discount on stays of over four weeks. The management of the resort has access to tee times at special rates.

Kona Surf Resort

Keauhou Bay, Hawaii, HI 96740

(808) 322-3411; (800) 367-8011

Rising some six stories, the resort sits like a castle at the entrance to Keauhou Bay. With the bay on one side, the ocean and golf course on the other, it is a spectacular setting.

ACCOMMODATIONS: 535 rooms, including suites, with the majority of the rooms offering a view of the Pacific Ocean. All rooms are air-conditioned and each has a private lanai. They are also equipped with cable TV, refrigerators, and individual coffee makers.

AMENITIES: Fresh and saltwater pools, deep-sea fishing, snorkeling, three lighted tennis courts and, of course, golf. Restaurants include the elegant S.S. James Makee or the more casual Pele's Court.

GOLF: Guests can play on the Kona Country Club course, which overlooks the hotel. For details and a description of the courses refer to Keauhou Beach/Kailua-Kona Resort Area, above.

RATES: (EP) Lodgings - $109/$185/$375/$550. Green fees - $85, including cart.

The Kohala Coast Area

The Kohala Coast area, stretching north of Kona, is experiencing rapid growth. With little rainfall, a number of wonderful golf courses and magnificent hotels, this area has a great deal to offer.

No matter how good a resort's food, if you stay for more than a day or two you will probably want to try other places to eat. In the small town of Kamuela, a few miles from The Mauna Kea Beach Resort, is the Edelweiss Restaurant. I promise you won't be disappointed.

Four Seasons Resort Hualalai

PO Box 1269, Kailua-Kona, HI 96745

(808) 325-8000; (888) 336-5662

A real plus with this location: you can arrange a direct flight to Kona from the Mainland, avoiding the mess and delay of transferring flights in Oahu.

ACCOMMODATIONS: 243 rooms (including 30 suites), housed in 36 low-rise bungalows. Each unit has a private lanai (or garden if on the ground floor).

AMENITIES: Eight tennis courts (four lighted), three oceanfront pools, plus a half-mile stretch of beach. Although beautiful, much of the water is underlined with lava rock and is not very user-friendly. Snorkeling and scuba lessons can be arranged. There is also the Sports Club and Spa for those who wish to pamper or destroy themselves exercising. Dining facilities include: the elegant beachfront restaurant (Pahui'a) set up for indoor and outdoor dining. For lighter fare the poolside Beach Tree Bar & Grill and the Haulalai Club Grill, overlooking the 18th green, are available. There are washer/dryer facilities for guests.

GOLF: Designed by Jack Nicklaus/Associates, the Haulalai Golf Club course reaches out a monstrous 7,117/6,632/6,032/5,374 yards with a par of 72. With several holes right along the ocean and lava rock much in evidence, this layout will give you all you can handle. It is a beautiful, well-bunkered course. Water becomes a factor on only two holes. The course is supported by a 14,000-square-foot clubhouse with dining facilities for luncheon and dinner.

RATES: (EP) Rooms - $475/$600/$675. Suites - $800/$950 and up. Green fees: $160, including cart. Several package plans are available, excluding December 19th through January 3rd.

ARRIVAL: By air - Kona. By car - the turn off to the resort is seven miles north of the airport and will be on your left.

Hapuna Beach Prince Hotel

62-100 Kauna'oa Drive, Kohala Coast, Hawaii, HI 96743

(808) 880-1111; (800) 882-6060

Many years ago, due to the occasional appearance of bubbling springs in this otherwise dry and barren coastal area, the native people named it "Hapuna," meaning "spring."

ACCOMMODATIONS: 350 rooms, including 36 suites, each with a private lanai.

AMENITIES: 13 tennis courts, a fitness center with state-of-the-art equipment, steam rooms, sauna, massage and locker rooms, a freshwater pool, snorkeling, scuba diving, sailing, catamaran rides, deep-sea fishing and, during the season, whale watching. You may also enjoy jogging, horseback riding (nearby) and, of course, the wonderful white sands of Hapuna Beach. Dining facilities consist of five areas, ranging from seafood and regional contemporary to authentic Japanese cuisine. There is, in addition, the golf course clubhouse and the garden restaurant for a more casual setting.

GOLF: Completed by Arnold Palmer & Ed Seay in late 1992, the Hapuna Golf Course has some of the most scenic holes on the islands. Attaining an elevation of some 700 feet, the views are startling. Watch the 12th hole – it's short and the problems are over the hill and out of view from the tee. While you look at the beautiful ocean below you, water only becomes a factor on four holes. Reaching out 6,875/6,534/6,029/5,067 yards, it pars at 72.

RATES: (EP) Lodgings - $345/$415/$520. Green fees - $105, including cart. Golf packages are not available during peak season. Rates quoted are for the peak season.

ARRIVAL: By air - Keahole Airport (27 miles). By car - drive north from the airport; resort entrance is on your right.

Hilton Waikoloa Village

69-425 Waikoloa Beach Drive, Kohala Coast, Hawaii, HI 96743

(808) 885-1234; (800) 445-8667

ACCOMMODATIONS: With its 1,240 guest rooms, this is a massive complex. The locals refer to it as the "Disneyland of Hawaii."

AMENITIES: Eight tennis courts with an exhibition court, a racquetball court, a 25,000-square-foot health spa, and two pools. The main pool features waterfalls, slides, and a grotto bar. Adjacent to the clubhouse is one of the better eating facilities on this island – The Waikoloa Beach Grill, (808) 885-6131. What they can do to a prime rib of beef is something else (provided you like garlic). Reservations are highly recommended.

GOLF: Designed by Robert Trent Jones, Jr., the Waikoloa Beach Golf Course opened in 1981. Parring at 70 and reaching out 6,566/5,958/5,094 yards, it spreads over 150 acres. Built over a solid lava flow, the course is now lush with palm trees, bougainvillea, oleander and plumeria. The newest course, the Kings Golf Club layout, was designed by Weiskopf-Morrish. While the Beach Course is a fun affair and not terribly demanding, the Kings layout requires far more attention. Reaching out 7,074/6,594/6,010/5,459 yards, it pars at 72. A Scottish style, featuring six lakes (a total of nine acres of water) and 83 traps, it is no pussycat. Some of the traps are extremely deep.

RATES: (EP) Lodgings - $300/$405. Green fees - $120, including cart.

 ## Mauna Kea Beach Hotel

One Mauna Kea Beach Drive, Kohala Coast, Hawaii, HI 96743

(808) 882-7222; (800) 882-6060

Mauna Kea Beach Hotel has been judged one of our Top 50 resorts.

Surrounded by lush green fairways, tropical gardens and beautiful crescent white sand beaches, this hotel is something very special.

ACCOMMODATIONS: 310 rooms, including 10 suites, each with stunning decor.

AMENITIES: A beautiful pool; ocean swimming from one of the finest beaches on the island; scuba diving from the 32-foot powerboat, *The Island Voyager*; a complete fitness center with state-of-the-art equipment; horseback riding; a two-mile cinder jogging trail; and 13 Plexipave tennis courts. While there is dancing at the Pavilion, our favorite entertainment was watching the giant Pacific manta rays. From a lighted viewing area overlooking the ocean you can watch them do their swirling dance. It is a spectacular sight. You should also make time to view the priceless collection of over 1,600 works of art gathered from Asia and the Pacific.

Dining here is an experience you will remember. You may start with breakfast at the Terrace, or have room service bring it to you to enjoy on your private lanai. The Batik Dining Room offers an elegant evening (jackets required) or you can have a spectacular candlelight dinner on your private lanai (and believe me, they handle this just right).

GOLF: This Robert Trent Jones, Sr. design, acclaimed as one of the best courses in the nation, is perched on top of a lava flow. Much of the topsoil had to be brought in. Stretching out 7,114 yards (masochist tees)/6,737 yards (championship)/6,365 (regular tees), it pars at 72. From the ladies' tees the par remains at 72, and the yardage is set at 5,277. With 120 traps, lava-bound fairways and an occasional gusting wind, you may find par rather elusive. Golf on the Hapuna Prince Golf Course is also available. (For details, refer to the text on the Hapuna Prince Resort.)

RATES: (EP) Lodgings - $345/$375/$575. Green fees - $105, including cart. Golf packages are not available during peak season.

Mauna Lani Bay Resorts

Within the area known as Mauna Lani Resorts are two outstanding golf courses and many tennis courts. It has one of the finest hotels to be found anywhere, The Mauna Lani Bay Hotel (which has exquisite bungalows). The area also offers two of the most posh groupings of condominiums: the Islands at Mauna Lani and the Mauna Lani Point Condominiums.

Guests have playing privileges on both courses and may use the various restaurants. No matter where you decide to stay here, you will have made a very good choice.

The South Course opened in late 1991. It encompasses a new nine, joined with the front nine of the older layout. Weighing in at a strong 7,015/6,370/5,331 yards, it pars at 72. The North Course reaches out 6,968/6,335/5,398 yards and also pars at 72. The South Course sports a par five of 601 yards with water along the entire side stretching from tee to green. The North has a couple of interesting challenges, notably number 10 with an "island tee box," and the ninth hole, a par 4 reaching out a monstrous 459 yards.

Virtually sculpted from lava with some "over the ocean" holes you will not soon forget, these courses will test not only your skill but your nerve as well. They can also test your vocabulary should you tangle with the many lava outcroppings.

The Mauna Lani Bay Hotel

One Mauna Lani Drive, Kohala Coast, Hawaii, HI 96743

(808) 885-6622; (800) 367-2323

The Mauna Lani Bay Hotel has been judged as one of our Top 50.

ACCOMMODATIONS: The uniquely designed 350-room structure provides virtually every room with an ocean view. The air-conditioned rooms are equipped with refrigerators and ceiling fans. Five magnificent bungalows have recently been added. Each of these 4,000-square-foot freestanding units features two master bedrooms, 2½ bathrooms, fully equipped serving kitchen, private pool, steam bath, whirlpool and spa. Each has a butler assigned, and a private chef to prepare lunch or dinner.

AMENITIES: 10 variable-speed tennis courts and a supervised health, sports, aerobic, and physical fitness center. Other activities include deep-sea fishing trips, glass-bottom boat cruises, helicopter sightseeing trips, horseback riding, sailing, bicycling, jogging, scuba diving, snorkeling, windsurfing and, of course, swimming. There are several lounges, and dining is offered in the Bay Terrace, the award-winning Le Soleil Restaurant, the golf club restaurant, and the poolside Ocean Grill.

GOLF: For details on the golf facilities, refer to The Mauna Lani Bay Resorts, above.

RATES: (EP) Lodgings - $350/$435/$490/$620. Bungalows - $4,750. Green fees - $110, including cart.

Mauna Lani Point Condominiums

Kohala Coast, Hawaii, HI 96743

(808) 885-5022; (800) 642-6284

The Mauna Lani Point Condominiums has been judged as one of our top 50 resorts.

ACCOMMODATIONS: 116 condominiums, ranging from one to two bedrooms (with 1½ to 2½ baths). They rank among the best we have seen. Beautifully appointed, they have the latest appliances, including microwave ovens and washer/dryers. Daily maid service is also provided. You have a choice of either an ocean or golf course view.

AMENITIES: See the facilities listed under Mauna Lani Bay Resorts.

GOLF: See Mauna Lani Bay Resorts, above.

RATES: (EP) Lodgings - $290/$370. Green fees - $110, including cart.

The Islands at Mauna Lani

2 Kaniku Drive, Kohala Coast, Hawaii, HI 96743

(808) 885-5022; (800) 642-6284

The Islands at Maunai Lani has been judged as one of our top 50 resorts.

ACCOMMODATIONS: 45 townhouse units; each cluster has its own beautifully planted private courtyard. The large two- and three-bedroom units feature three or four baths, large living room, dining room, and a two-car garage with automatic door opener. Each kitchen has a dishwasher, huge built-in refrigerator with icemaker, full-size washer/dryer, and microwave; the patio has a built-in gas barbecue grill and wet bar. They are impeccably furnished. Surrounded by seven man-made lagoons and waterfalls, the units are adjacent to the golf course.

AMENITIES: Each cluster has a recreational center with a pool. The entire grouping is adjacent to the Mauna Lani Racquet Club.

GOLF: The multitude of activities indicated in the text for Mauna Lani Resorts is also available to guests of the Islands.

RATES: Two-bedroom units, $450.

The Orchid at Mauna Lani

One North Kaniku Drive, Kohala Coast, Hawaii, HI 96743

(808) 885-2000; (800) 845-9905

ACCOMMODATIONS: 485 rooms and 54 suites, all of which are outstanding.

AMENITIES: A fitness center offers massage therapy, body treatments, exercise schedules, 10 outdoor tennis courts (seven lighted), and catamaran snorkeling. The resort also has romantic sunset cocktail cruises, a 10,000-square-foot pool (with a 20,000-square-foot surrounding deck), and a white sand beach. There are several interesting shops to peruse. The excellent dining facilities include The Grill (offering soft jazz), The Orchid Court, and Brown's Beach House. There are several cocktail lounges. They also have a children's program.

GOLF: For details on the golf facilities, refer to The Mauna Lani Bay Resorts text on the preceding pages.

RATES: Lodgings - $385/$425/$495/$695. Suites - $1,500 and up. Green fees - $110. There are many different package plans that feature tennis or golf. Rates shown are for the peak season late December through May.

Royal Waikoloan Resort

69-275 Waikoloa Beach Drive, Kohala Coast, Hawaii, HI 96743

(808) 885-6789; (800) 462-6262

ACCOMMODATIONS: 546 rooms, including 18 lagoon cabanas.

AMENITIES: Six tennis courts, a freshwater pool, horseback riding at nearby Waikoloa stables, a fitness center, fishing, catamaran sailing, scuba, snorkeling, kayaking and canoeing. Restaurants include the Cafe Tiare and the Royal Terrace. The clubhouse offers some of the better food, value, and service on the Island. Their prime rib of beef is spectacular (if you like garlic). Make reservations as The Waikoloa Beach Grill is popular with the locals. Phone (808) 885-6131.

GOLF: For details on the golf facilities, see the description under the Hilton Waikoloa Village in the Kohala Coast area.

RATES: (EP) Lodgings - $186/$210/$230. Cabana - $275. Green fees - $95, including cart. An all-inclusive package plan is also available.

Waikoloa Village Resort

1035 Keana Place, Waikoloa Village, Hawaii, HI 96743

(808) 885-5001; (800) 922-7866

These suites are on a Robert Trent Jones, Jr. golf course, approximately six miles from the water.

ACCOMMODATIONS: Well-furnished one- or two-bedroom suites. Each unit has a fully equipped kitchen and a private lanai. The resort provides daily housekeeping service.

AMENITIES: Tennis courts, a pool and barbecue facilities.

GOLF: Details on the Waikoloa Village Golf Course are given in the text for Waikoloa Villas.

RATES: (EP) Lodgings - $290/$345. Green fees - $99. The resort offers some packages, including car rental.

The Ka'u Coast

While still on the Big Island, we now have shifted to the east side, where the startling black sand beaches are found. This is home to one of the most active volcanoes in the world, Kilauea Crater, and of "Madame Pélé," the Hawaiian goddess of volcanoes. It is also where you will find two resorts, SeaMountain at Panulu'u and the Volcano House Inn.

SeaMountain at Punalu'u

PO Box 70, Pahala, Hawaii, HI 96777

(808) 928-8301; (800) 488-8301; (808) 928-6200; (800) 344-7675

This resort captures the essence of Hawaii. On the southeastern side of the Big Island, a few miles north of the southern tip, the setting is most unusual, with lush green sugarcane fields behind it, the Pacific Ocean fronting the entire property, and black lava rock and palm-fringed lagoons all about.

ACCOMMODATIONS: Studios plus one- and two-bedroom cottage apartments fully equipped for housekeeping, including washer/dryers.

AMENITIES: Black sand beaches to swim from, a pool, and nearby tennis courts. The Panalu'u Black Sands Restaurant is open seven days a week. Something relatively new is the Sea-Mountain clubhouse restaurant.

GOLF: Parring at 72 the course reaches out 6,492/6,106/5,663 yards. A Jack Snyder design, with water hazards, traps, pine trees, lava outcroppings, black sand beaches and wind, this can be a tough and challenging layout. It is the southernmost golf resort layout in the United States.

RATES: (EP) Lodgings - $95/$115/$130/$146. Green fees - $35, including cart. Rates are for mid-December through March. Minimum stay is two nights.

The Volcano House

Kilauea Crater, Hawaii, HI 96718

(808) 967-7321

The Volcano House is one of the few tropical hotels in the world where you will enjoy sitting in front of the lounge's roaring fire. The walls of the lounge are lined with the works of world famous artists, drawn here to paint the enchanting view of the volcano or their vision of Madam Pélé, the Hawaiian goddess of volcanoes.

ACCOMMODATIONS: This is an old inn and rather small (41 guest rooms). Though comfortable, the rooms are not elaborate.

GOLF: The Volcano Golf Course is bordered by dark forests of pine and scarlet-blossomed ohia trees. In the background rise the towering slopes of 13,680-foot Mauna Loa. The course plays 6,119 yards and pars at 72.

RATES: (EP) Rooms: $85/$185. Green fees - $55, carts $24.

ARRIVAL: By air - Hilo (29 miles). You are on the opposite side of the island from Kona.

The Island of Kauai

Justifiably referred to as the Garden Island, Kauai presents a mixture of scenery: ferns and grottoes to the north, deserts to the west, flowers everywhere and, in the middle, towering mountains, with a spectacular "Grand Canyon." The canyon, some 4,000 feet deep, is certainly one of the least accessible places in the world. The northernmost island in the Hawaiian chain, Kauai was populated between 200 and 300 A.D., some 500 years prior to any of the other islands. It is rich in history and legends.

On the east side of the island is the Kauai Marriott; at the northern end is Princeville, home to Hanalei Bay Resort and The Princeville Hotel. On the south side, in the Poipu Beach area, is the Kiahuna Plantation and the Hyatt Regency Kauai.

The Princeville Resort Area

Within the 9,000-acre resort community of Princeville can be found golf, the new and huge 60,000-square-foot Princeville Clubhouse, a shopping center, 10 restaurants, and approximately 700 homes and condominiums. The resort area has 20 outdoor tennis courts, two fully equipped pro shops, a health club, helicopter tours, boat tours, scuba diving, snorkeling, kayaking and horseback riding.

Princeville now offers 45 holes of golf. The Ocean/Woods combination stretches 6,912/6,365/5,631 yards; the Woods/Lake combination plays 6,878/6,357/5,543 yards; and the Lake/Ocean nines weigh in at 6,900/6,306/5,516. All three combinations par at 72. Each of the nines lives up to its name, bringing ocean, woods, and a fair amount of lake into play.

The newest layout is the Prince Course, also a Robert Trent Jones, Jr. design. It has been judged one of the finest in the islands and also the most difficult in the state of Hawaii – a statement with which I fully agree. The holes were originally named in the traditional Scottish fashion. Some of the names are Burma Road, Hazard, Waterfall, and Dunkirk. If you can clear the two ravines, stay right of the O.B. stakes, avoid the six deep bunkers, and land on the postage-stamp-size green, Dunkirk will be a piece of cake. I will not attempt to describe the par-5, 597-yard Burma Road, or the Eagles Nest, a par 4 featuring a 150-foot drop from tee to fairway. From its five tee settings the course plays to an awesome 7,309/6,960/6,521/6,005/5,338 yards with a par of 72. Play from the back tees is limited to handicaps of five or less.

Hanalei Bay Resort & Embassy Suites

5380 Hanalei Road, Princeville, Kauai, HI 96722

(808) 826-6522; (800) 827-4427

ACCOMMODATIONS: 189 hotel rooms with mountain, garden or ocean views. The Embassy Suite condominiums are one-, two-and three-bedroom units with living room, fully equipped kitchen, washer/dryer, cable TV, and daily maid service.

AMENITIES: Eight tennis courts (two lighted), swimming pool, and a swimming lagoon complete with a sand beach. Sailing, trolling for game fish, and horseback riding over the beautiful Princeville ranchland are popular activities. Dining is provided in the Bali Hai Restaurant with cocktails in the Happy Talk Lounge.

GOLF: For a detailed description of the golf facilities refer to "The Princeville Resort Area."

RATES: (EP) Lodgings - $170/$190/$200/$320/$350. Green fees - $95, including cart. Prince course - $120. Hanalei Bay Resort offers golf packages.

Princeville Hotel

Princeville, Kauai, HI 96714

(808) 826-9644; (800) 826-4400

The Princeville Hotel is one of our Top 50 Resorts. The film *South Pacific* was shot on these magnificent white beaches, which should give you some idea of its beauty. A real plus here is that they have not lost sight of Hawaii. The decor is muted and quiet, matching the soft ambiance that makes this area so alluring.

ACCOMMODATIONS: 252 rooms, including suites, many offering a view of beautiful Hanalei Bay.

AMENITIES: Swimming in both the pool and the ocean (there is an excellent beach), deep-sea fishing, horseback riding, and tennis. A new addition is the Princeville Health Club & Spa. There are three restaurants: the Café Hanalei with its open-air setting overlooking the bay; the Mediterranean restaurant La

Cascata, serving authentic southern Italian cuisine; and the Beach Restaurant & Bar for lighter fare served poolside.

GOLF: For details on the courses refer to "The Princeville Resort Area."

RATES: (EP) Lodgings - $380/$430/$535. Jr, Suite - $625. Green fees - Makai Course $115, Prince Course $150, including cart. There are many different packages available. Ask when making reservations.

ARRIVAL: By air - Lihue Airport. Commuter flights also run to and from the Princeville Airport.

Condominium Lodgings – Princeville Area

For condominium-type lodgings and reservations in the Princeville Resort complex, contact the following:

The Cliffs
PO Box 1005
Hanalei, HI 96714
(808) 826-6219; (800) 367-6046

Hawaiian Islands Resorts Inc.
PO Box 212
Honolulu, HI 96810
(808) 531-7595; (800) 367-7042

Princeville Travel Service
PO Box 990
Hanalei Kauai, HI 96714
(808) 826-9661; (800) 445-6253

The East Side Of Kauai

This part of Kauai, the location of the Marriott Kauai Resort & Villas, is less than two miles from the major airport of Kauai and the town of Lihue.

The Marriott Kauai Resort & Villas

Kalapaki Beach, Kauai, HI 96754

(808) 245-5050; (800) 220-2925

ACCOMMODATIONS: 356 guest rooms and 232 one- and two-bedroom vacation beach villas.

AMENITIES: Eight tennis courts, and a complete European health spa, including Jacuzzi, massages, body buffs, herbal wraps, facials, saunas, and steam baths. There is also a regulation-size swimming pool along with over 1,400 feet of beach along Kalapaki inlet. There are now four restaurants and lounges scattered throughout the new resort ranging from informal (swimwear acceptable) to one where shoes and slacks are required (in Hawaii that is formal).

GOLF: Although both courses are Jack Nicklaus-designed layouts, the Kauai Lagoons, spreading over 190 acres, is principally intended for the recreational golfer. It shows a yardage of 6,942/6,545/6,108/5,607 with a par of 72. The 262-acre Kiele Lagoons layout is a tournament-class affair, complete with substantial gallery areas. This course weighs in at 7,070/6,637/6,164/5,417 yards and also pars at 72.

RATES: (EP) Lodgings - $270/$625. Green fees - Kauai Lagoons Course, $120, including cart; Kiele Championship Course, $135, including cart.

The Southeast "Poipu Beach" Area

Stay with us. We are still on Kauai. This area of the island is conceded to be the "dry" side. There are two top resorts, the Hyatt Regency Kauai and the Kiahuna Plantation. The Hyatt provides hotel rooms, while lodgings at the Kiahuna Plantation consist of fully equipped condominiums.

Hyatt Regency Kauai

1571 Poipu Drive, Poipu Beach, Kauai, HI

(808) 742-1234; (800) 233-1234

Extensive gardens, open-air courtyards, and the fact that none of the structures are higher than a coconut tree create a relaxing Hawaiian atmosphere. All in all, it is one of the more beautiful resorts in Hawaii.

ACCOMMODATIONS: 600 guest rooms, including 41 suites and 38 Regency Club rooms.

AMENITIES: 500-yard sand beach and an action pool with waterfalls and slides. They also have a saltwater lagoon system complete with islands. There are four tennis courts. Nearby activities include horseback riding, sailing, scuba diving, and deep-sea fishing. The 25,000-square-foot fitness center has massage rooms; hydro, facial and loofah rooms; sauna; steam rooms; whirlpools; and a lap pool. The Hyatt has three restaurants, ranging from Italian or seafood to continental cuisine.

GOLF: A Robert Trent Jones Jr. layout, the course plays to a yardage of 6,959/6,499/6,023/5,241 with a par of 72. It is definitely an ocean/links style layout. With wind, a generous sprinkling of bunkers (80 or more) and four lakes, it will offer up all the challenge you might desire. The PGA "Grand Slam of Golf" was held here in 1994.

RATES: (EP) Lodgings - $350/$370/$415/$590. Green fees - $85, including cart.

ARRIVAL: By air - Lihue Airport (25 minutes). By car - follow signs to the Poipu Beach area.

Kiahuna Plantation

RR #1, Box 73, Koloa, Kauai, HI 96756

(808) 742-6411; (800) 367-5004

ACCOMMODATIONS: 333 well-equipped condominiums. Ranging from one-to two-bedroom units, they feature a separate living and dining area, lanais, and fully equipped kitchens, ceiling fans, rattan furniture, and cable TV. Although there are no washer/dryers in the units, coin- operated machines are available.

At one time this 35-acre site was part of the oldest sugarcane plantation in Hawaii.

AMENITIES: Swimming from one of the best beaches in the islands or in the pool, snorkeling, surfing, sailing, tennis on 10 courts, deep-sea fishing, helicopter tours and trips to the Waimea Canyon (some 4,000 feet deep), historic Hanalei and, of course, golf. Dining ranges from casual lagoon-side barbecue pits and picnic tables to the Courtside Bar & Grill and the Clubhouse Restaurant.

GOLF: A Robert Trent Jones, Jr. design, the Kiahuna Golf Club stretches out 6,380/5,669/4,901 yards with a par of 70. While only a modest amount of water comes into play (on six holes) it seems to be just where it should not be. Carts are mandatory and must keep on the cart paths at all times.

RATES: (EP) Lodgings - $200/$440. Rates are for high season, mid-December to mid-April. Lower at other times. Green fees - $75, including cart. Golf packages are available.

ARRIVAL: By air - Lihue Airport (15 miles). By car - from the airport take Highway 50 west (signs will say Poipu Beach). Turn off onto Highway 520 and follow signs to Poipu Beach.

The Island Of Maui

Many years ago, when the only method of reaching the Hawaiian Islands was by ship, Oahu was the ultimate destination. Then along came aircraft and some of the heartier souls ventured to the outer islands. Not too many, however. Rather than drone along for 2,600 miles from the West Coast in a piston-driven aircraft, most people settled for the beauty and relaxation of Waikiki. But the advent of the jet turned the islands into a reachable destination. And, with the sudden flood of new *Haoles*, the islanders felt they had been overrun. Seeking to rediscover the "Old Hawaii," they began a retreat to the outlying areas.

The rest is history. The development of Maui has been rapid and, it is nearly as congested as Oahu. It is still, however, a place of beautiful beaches, magnificent hotels, condominiums, and golf courses by the ton. It is also the location of Lahaina, the first capital of the islands, and of Mt. Haleakala, a dormant volcano rising to almost 10,000 feet.

The Wailea Area
Of Maui

Dominating the area from the southeast is Haleakala (House of the Sun), the world's largest dormant volcanic crater. Its slopes embrace 500 square miles of tropical rain forest, arid deserts, lush cattle ranches and some of the most spectacular scenery anywhere on this planet.

Golf is available to guests of the various hotels or condominiums of Wailea on three 18-hole layouts. Each of these courses will provide not only a real test of your skill, but views that make it difficult to keep your mind on the game.

The Wailea Blue Course reaches out 6,758/6,152/5,291 yards and pars at 72. While this layout brings water into contention on four holes, it is more open and forgiving than the Gold Course. The Gold Course, also with a par of 72, measures a very healthy 7,070/6,653/6,152/5,317 yards. Both operate from the same pro shop. A third course, The Emerald, opened in early 1995. Parring at 72, it plays to a yardage of 6,824/6,395/5,887/5/444.

Now back to Wailea. In addition to golf, there is a picturesque hillside tennis complex offering 14 courts (11 hard and three grass), a pro shop, and an exhibition stadium seating 1,200.

Hotel accommodations are offered at the Maui Prince Hotel, Stouffer Wailea, the superb Four Seasons Resort Wailea, the lovely Kea Lani Hotel, the massive Grand Wailea, Outrigger Wailea, Renaissance Wailea Beach Resort, and Wailea Elua Village.

Although the restaurants at the various resorts are excellent, we also suggest The Chart House Restaurant, adjacent to the Blue Course at Wailea, at 100 Wailea Ike Drive. You will find it very good indeed. For reservations call (808) 879-2875. Another great place is the Sea Watch Restaurant, located in the clubhouse of the Wailea Gold/Emerald Courses. The food, service and realistic pricing is very welcome, and they are open for breakfast, lunch and dinner.

Four Seasons Resort Wailea

3900 Wailea Alanui, Wailea, Maui, HI 96753

(808) 874-8000; (800) 334-6284

This world-class Four Seasons Resort is on a particularly beautiful 15-acre site on the southwest coast of Maui. It happens to have one of the best beaches in the islands. Like all Four Seasons, they do things right.

ACCOMMODATIONS: 380 rooms and suites, most with an ocean view. The eighth floor gives you access to the private club level (concierge floor). One of the more delightful aspects of this hotel is brought about by its structure. The various wings form an enclosed U shape, facing out to the pool and using the beach and ocean as a backdrop.

AMENITIES: Two lighted tennis courts, a 40x80-foot swimming pool, whirlpools and, of course, the magnificent beach. The resort offers a variety of complimentary services: valet parking, a library lounge with a wide selection of books and periodicals, programs for children and teens, a health club, bicycles and much more. For dining, there is the main dining room, the Pacific Grill, a casual restaurant, the poolside Cabana Cafe, the Games Bar, and the Lobby Lounge.

GOLF: You have access to all of the offerings described under the section titled "The Wailea Area of Maui." This includes additional tennis courts as well as the three golf courses.

RATES: (EP) Lodgings - $310/$390/$455/$615. There are no golf packages during peak season. Green fees - $110/$120/$125, including cart.

Grand Wailea Resort & Spa

3850 Wailea Alanui Drive, Wailea, Maui, HI 96753

(808) 875-1234; (800) 888-6100

ACCOMMODATIONS: 760 rooms, including 53 suites, within a massive eight-story resort.

AMENITIES: A 50,000 square-foot spa, 2,000-foot-long river pool, a 15,000 square-foot pool and deck area, hot tubs, swim-in caves, a bubbling spring, and a swim-up bar. There are several dining possibilities, including the Grand Dining Room; Bistro Molokini; Kincha, a Japanese restaurant; and a coffee shop.

GOLF: For details refer to "The Wailea Area of Maui."

RATES: (EP) Lodgings - $395/$495/$595 and up. Green fees - $105/$115/$125, including cart.

Kea Lani Hotel

4100 Wailea Alanui Drive, Wailea, Maui, HI 96753

(808) 875-4100; (800) 659-4100

ACCOMMODATIONS: 413 one-bedroom suites, 24 two-bedroom suites, and 13 three-bedroom suites. Each of the one-bedroom units has a living room, separate bedroom, mini-kitchen (refrigerator, microwave, wet bar, dinnerware, coffee maker) along with a private lanai. Each also has two TV sets (one in the bedroom) along with a VCR, and stereo system. The hotel has, by the way, an excellent video library. There are also coin-operated washer/dryer units on every other floor. Located across from the Wailea golf and tennis facilities, this all-suite hotel is a super location.

AMENITIES: Tennis, a 22,000-square-foot lagoon-style swimming pool featuring a 140-foot water slide, beautiful Polo Beach and a health spa, complete with an exercise fitness room. The hotel dining options are the Kea Lani Restaurant, Cafe Ciao, and the Polo Beach Grille & Bar. They also offer a Keiki Lani (children's program), which operates seven days a week. It can turn your Hawaiian vacation into a delight and also let the kids enjoy their trip.

GOLF: Available at the three Wailea courses. For details on the golf and tennis facilities, refer to "The Wailea Area of Maui."

RATES: (EP) Lodgings - $295/$395/$495. Green fees - $105/$115, including cart.

Maui Prince Hotel

5400 Makena Alanui, Kihei, Maui, HI 96753

(808) 874-1111; (800) 321-6284

ACCOMMODATIONS: 310 rooms. The resort is on 1,800 acres and offers almost every Hawaiian amenity and recreation facility you could wish for.

AMENITIES: Six tennis courts (two lighted), two swimming pools, a beautiful beach, sailing, or perhaps just loafing and sunning. During the winter months, a favorite pastime is watching the humpback whales as they cavort along the coast of Maui. A complimentary children's program is offered each day from 9 AM until noon. There are three restaurants: the Prince Court, for American Cuisine; the Cafe Kiowai, with its lovely garden setting; and the Hakone, an authentic Japanese restaurant.

GOLF: Both courses were designed by Robert Trent Jones, Jr. The South reaches out an awesome 7,017/6,629/6,168/5,529 yards. The North layout is not far behind with a yardage of 6,914/6,567/6,151/5,303. Each pars at 72. The South Course has been selected as the site of the Hawaii State Open Tournament.

Be sure to bring a camera, as the ocean and mountain views (particularly of Haleakala Crater) from each course are such that you will be angry with yourself if you don't get a few pictures. The golf facilities include a driving range, putting green and locker rooms.

RATES: (EP) Lodgings - $300/$340/$390. Green fees - $140, including cart. Golf packages are available. Rates are for the resort's peak season.

ARRIVAL: By air - Maui's Kahului Airport. By car - from Kahului Airport drive south to Wailea. Continue on for three more miles. The entrance is on the right.

Outrigger Wailea Resort

PO Box 779 Wailea, Maui, HI 96753

(808) 879-1922; (800) 367-2960

ACCOMMODATIONS: Formerly the Aston Wailea, the Outrigger offers 550 rooms and suites.

AMENITIES: Snorkeling, sailing, surfing, catamaran sailing, deep-sea fishing, two swimming pools, ocean swimming, 11 tennis courts (three lighted). There are six restaurants, including the two swimming pool areas. Try a visit to the Inu Inu Piano Bar & Lounge to watch the sun go down as it can only be seen in Hawaii. I love some of the Hawaiian names – Inu Inu means "Drink Drink."

GOLF: For details, refer to "The Wailea Area of Maui," page 185.

RATES: (EP) Lodgings - $295/$345/$455. Golf packages are not available during peak season. Green fees - $125, including cart.

Renaissance Wailea Beach Resort

3550 Wailea Alanui Drive, Wailea, Maui, HI 96753

(808) 879-4900; (800) 992-4532

ACCOMMODATIONS: In addition to 347 rooms in the main buildings, there are lodgings in the Makapu Beach Club, offering seclusion and luxury. A nice extra that we wish all hotels offered: laundry facilities in each wing.

AMENITIES: Two large swimming pools, a lovely beach area offering windsurfing, scuba and snorkel charters and sunset sails. There is horseback riding (located nearby). The dining options include the Raffles Restaurant, the Palm Court for less formal dining, or the Maui Onion for cocktails and/or a light repast by the pool.

GOLF: For details on golf and tennis refer to "The Wailea Area of Maui," page 185.

RATES: (EP) Rooms - $279/$299/$329/$389. Green fees - $125, including cart. Golf packages are available. Rates are for December-April.

Wailea Elua Village

3600 Alanui Drive, Wailea, Maui, HI 96753

(808) 879-4055; (800) 367-5246

ACCOMMODATIONS: Approximately 150 individually owned furnished condominiums, ranging in size from one to three bedrooms. Each well-equipped unit has a private lanai, living room, and kitchen. They are across from the Wailea Blue Course and front directly on the ocean.

AMENITIES: Two swimming pools, one of the better beaches on the island, a paddle tennis court, and a barbecue adjacent to each of the swimming pools. Maid service is provided once a week.

GOLF: For detailed information on the courses, refer to the Wailea Area of Maui.

RATES: Lodgings - $270/$325/$475. Rates are for peak season. Green fees - $125.

The Lahaina-Kaanapali Area

This large stretch of beach on the northwest side of Maui offers many world-class hotels, several luxury condominium complexes, over 150 shops, 60 restaurants, and an outdoor whaling museum. In addition, there are a dozen dinner and lounge shows, 28 tennis courts, 36 holes of golf and all the beach activities you expect in the islands: snorkeling, surfing, outriggers, deep-sea fishing, etc.

The Royal Kaanapali courses are available for guests of the various hotels and condominiums. The South plays 6,555/6,067/5,485 yards and pars at 71. The North, reaching out 6,994/6,136/5,417 yards, pars at 71/72. The older of the two, the North, a Robert Trent Jones design developed in 1961, starts at the ocean and winds its way up the lower reaches of the mountain. It provides some beautiful views en route.

The South was originally an executive layout and has been re-designed by A.J. Snyder. Although flat, it brings into play palms, monkey pod trees, banyans, and brilliant bougainvillea. There are a few places on the back nine of the South course where, if you were to hook just right, you could easily find yourself in the lobby of one of the hotels. Green fees - $110, including cart.

Hyatt Regency Maui

200 Nohea Kai Drive, Lahaina, Maui, HI 96761

(808) 661-1234; (800) 233-1234

ACCOMMODATIONS: 815 rooms offering views of either the ocean, mountains, or the Royal Kaanapali golf course. The Regency is on 18-plus acres of tropical forest complete with lagoons, waterfalls, and grottoes.

AMENITIES: All activities indicated under The Lahaina-Kaanapali Area are available to guests of this resort. For dining, there is the Swan Court, Spats and the Lahaina Provision Company. Whatever your favorite libation may be, you will find it at any of the three lounges, including the Weeping Banyan. One of the island's favorite drinks is a "Fog Cutter." Should you dive too deeply into a "Fog Cutter" you may well wind up emulating a "Weeping Banyan."

RATES: (EP) Lodgings - $300/$355/$460/$495 and up.

Maui Marriott Resort

100 Nohea Kai Drive, Lahaina, Maui, HI 96761

(808) 667-1200; (800) 763-1333

ACCOMMODATIONS: 720 rooms in two nine-story towers, with a four-story lobby between. The Maui Marriott is directly across from the Royal Kaanapali golf course.

AMENITIES: Five lighted tennis courts, two swimming pools and spas as well as beach activities. They have a variety of dining areas, ranging from a Japanese steak house to the rustic atmosphere of old Lahaina Town.

GOLF: See course descriptions under The Lahaina-Kaanapali Area.

RATES: (EP) Rooms - $200/$278/$328. Suites - $475 and up.

Royal Lahaina Resort

2780 Kekass Drive, Lahaina, Maui, HI 96761

(808) 661-3611; (800) 447-6925

ACCOMMODATIONS: Range from luxurious private cottages to guest rooms. Each of the 514 lodgings includes air-conditioning and refrigerators.

AMENITIES: Three swimming pools and three restaurants. This resort happens to be the location of the Royal Lahaina Tennis Ranch, which has 11 courts.

GOLF: all the attractions described under The Lahaina-Kaanapali Area.

RATES: (EP) Rooms: $270/$385. Suites - $790.

The Westin Maui

2365 Kaanapali Parkway, Lahaina, Maui, HI 96761

(808) 667-2525; (800) 228-3000

ACCOMMODATIONS: Two 11-story towers, "the Ocean Tower and the Beach Tower," have air-conditioned rooms equipped with remote control TVs, mini-bars and small private balconies. There are also 37 posh rooms available at the Royal Beach Club (concierge level), bringing the total of guest rooms to 854.

AMENITIES: Swimming, snorkeling, surfing and sunning. The resort virtually revolves around 55,000 square feet of pools, waterfalls, and meandering streams. There are five freeform swimming pools on various levels, three of which are joined by two waterslides ranging in length from 20 to 150 feet. There are eight restaurants and lounges.

GOLF: For detailed information on tennis and the golf courses, refer to The Lahaina-Kaanapali Area.

RATES: (EP) Lodgings - $295/$335/$495. Suites - $850 and up. Green fees - $110, including cart.

Lahaina-Kaanapali Area Condominiums

Kaanapali Alii

50 Nohea Kai Drive, Lahaina, Maui, HI 96761

(808) 667-1400; (800) 642-6284

ACCOMMODATIONS: One- to three-bedroom condominiums. Each unit has a full kitchen, two baths, living room, and washer/dryer. This 11-story resort is on the beach across from the Royal Kaanapali golf complex.

AMENITIES: Three tennis courts, swimming pool, and beach. While the resort does not have a restaurant of its own, specialized room service menus are available from several nearby restaurants.

GOLF: For details on the courses, refer to The Lahaina-Kaanapali Area.

RATES: Lodgings - $300/$315/$360. Rates are for January 5th through mid-April.

The Whaler at Kaanapali Beach

2481 Kaanapali Parkway Lahaina, Maui, HI 96761

(808) 661-4861; (800) 367-7052

ACCOMMODATIONS: Two large condominium complexes with 360 one- and two-bedroom oceanfront suites, equipped for housekeeping.

AMENITIES: Mini-market, underground parking, an oceanside pool, paddle tennis, four tennis courts, saunas, and exercise rooms.

GOLF: See description under Lahaina-Kaanapali Area.

RATES: Lodgings - $195/$250/$380. Rates are for peak season.

Kapalua Resort Area

A bit north of Lahaina (approximately 10 miles), the 23,000-acre Kapalua Plantation property is the site of several destination resorts. Possible accommodations consist of the lovely Kapalua Bay Hotel & Villas and the magnificent Ritz-Carlton Kapalua.

Two of the three golf courses are Arnold Palmer designs. The Bay layout, parring at 72, stretches 6,600/6,051/5,124 yards. The Village Links reaches out 6,632/6,001/5,134 yards with a par of 71. Both courses take full advantage of the natural terrain, rolling hills, lava outcroppings and the spectacular views offered from elevations up to 750 feet above the sea. Water only comes into play on four holes of the Village layout and on six of the Bay Course.

The Plantation Course is high on slopes of the old pineapple plantation, affording panoramic views of the ocean. Designed by the team of Bill Coore and Ben Crenshaw, it opened in mid-1991. They may call Mr. Crenshaw "Gentle Ben," but his course is anything but gentle. Parring at 73 (the ladies' par is 75), it reaches out a monstrous 7,263/6,547/5,627 yards. The opening hole will more than get your attention. A par 4, this gem measures 473 yards – but what the heck, the 18th is a 663-yard par 5.

There is a restaurant adjacent to the main pro shop of the Bay Course called The Grill & Bar. Not only are the food and the service outstanding, but it's a wonderful place for people watching. Make reservations early, as it is one busy place.

Kapalua Bay Hotel & Villas

One Bay Drive, Maui, HI 96761

(808) 669-5656; (800) 367-8000

The Kapalua Bay Hotel is situated on 18 acres within the 23,000-acre Kapalua Plantation property, and is nestled between the coastline and the rolling hills of a lush pineapple plantation.

ACCOMMODATIONS: 194 guest rooms in the hotel, plus approximately 90 villas. Some offer bay exposure, others a golf course view. Each room is equipped with a refrigerator and cable TV and has a separate sitting area and private terrace. The villas include fully equipped kitchens, washer/dryers, and daily maid service. There is also a year-round, supervised children's program.

AMENITIES: Swimming in several freshwater pools (between the hotel and the villas there are about 10), tennis on 10 private courts (four lighted), and an exercise facility with stair climber, treadmill, multicisor and two ergometers. It is a few minutes by shuttle to three sand beaches offering up snorkeling, scuba, surfing, sailing, or deep-sea fishing – so much to do that sometimes doing nothing becomes an attractive alternative. For dining you may choose from the Pool Terrace for casual dining and cocktails, the Garden Restaurant and Lounge, or, for gourmet dining, the Bay Club (jackets suggested).

GOLF: For details of the golf facilities refer to The Kapalua Resort Area.

RATES: (EP) Lodgings - $380/$430/$490/$570; suites - $1,400/$2,000; villas - $430/$570. Green fees - $110/$120, including cart. Golf package - two nights/two days (includes lodging, green fees, cart), $790 per couple. Rates are for peak season.

The Ritz-Carlton Kapalua

One Ritz-Carlton Drive, Kapalua, Maui 96761

(808) 669-6200; (800) 262-8440

The Ritz-Carlton Kapalua has been judged one of our Top 50 resorts. It has also recently received the AAA Five Diamond Award.

Ten miles north of Lahaina, this is one of the better choices on the island of Maui. Visible throughout the public areas is the hotel's magnificent collection of original paintings and ceramics created by local artists, which has been blended with 18th- and 19th-century works of art.

ACCOMMODATIONS: 490 rooms plus 58 suites. Included in this mix are the concierge level Ritz-Carlton Club Rooms.

AMENITIES: A white sand beach fronts the hotel, and there is a 10,000 square foot swimming pool surrounded by a 20,000-square-foot sunning deck. There are also 10 tennis courts (five lighted), fitness center, a men's/women's steam & sauna, along with a spa treatment and massage facility. Ocean activities include snorkeling, scuba, sunset sailing, windsurfing and deep-sea fishing. There are three excellent dining facilities, The Grill and

The Terrace Restaurants, and the poolside indoor/outdoor Banyan Tree. The hotel now has a children's program in place.

GOLF: For details on the 54 holes of golf directly adjacent to the hotel, refer to "The Kapalua Resort Area."

RATES: Lodgings - $325/$425/$500/$625. Green fees - $110/$125, including cart. There are many different package plans available: golf, tennis, with or without car rental, etc.

The Island Of Lanai

Lanai is the sixth largest of the major islands in the Hawaiian group, and is located between Maui and Molokai. Triangular in shape (18 miles long and up to 13 miles wide), it has remained generally unspoiled. Its culture is based on farming, ranching, and fishing, and it has a population of only 2,600. Two resorts are here, The Lodge at Koele and the Manele Bay Hotel.

Shopping on the island is extremely limited. There are only a handful of stores, including three old-time general stores. There are, however, gift shops at the two resorts, along with the golf shops. As a possible alternative, the bustling seaport of Lahaina (on the island of Maui) offers a profusion of shops and boutiques and is only a nine-mile ferry ride away. The ferry has four scheduled round-trips daily.

The Lodge at Koele

PO Box 774, Lanai City, Lanai, HI 96763

(808) 565-7300; (800) 321-4666

The Lodge at Koele has been judged one of our Top 50 resorts. Blending high-beamed ceilings, natural stone fireplaces, artifacts gathered from throughout the world, the tropical setting of huge banyan trees, and an overwhelming garden fragrance, this beautiful and unusual lodge has been described as reminiscent of a worldly plantation owner's residence or perhaps a country estate.

ACCOMMODATIONS: 102 guest rooms and suites. A few of the more unusual features in the rooms include four-poster beds, ceiling fans, and beautiful oil paintings. You can choose from Garden, Koele, or Plantation rooms.

AMENITIES: Tennis, horseback riding from the Lanai Ranch stables, and swimming in the hotel pool. Just behind the hotel is an 18-hole putting course – more than a practice area, it is a miniature golf course. It's not only a great way to sharpen up your putting, but also fun. One activity I recommend: a dawn ride followed by a hearty ranch-style breakfast. Hunting on the island is a big thing, as it is overrun by deer, quail, wild turkeys, partridges, pheasants, and sheep. Guided tours can be arranged by the hotel. The dining rooms serve a mixture of Hawaiian cuisine and traditional continental dishes. Jackets are required in the evening in the gourmet dining room.

GOLF: The Greg Norman/Ted Robinson-designed championship golf course opened for play in 1991. It takes full advantage of the natural terrain. They placed the first nine on a high plateau, providing a spectacular view of the Pacific Ocean (a few miles distant), while the back nine was built in the valley surrounded by those towering pines. Reaching out 7,014/6,628/6,217/5,425 yards, it pars at 72. Guests of the lodge also have golfing privileges at the new Nicklaus course at the Manele Bay Hotel. The names of the two courses may give some indication of what you might expect. The Challenge at Manele is okay, but "The Experience" at Koele can raise the hair on the back of your head. While there are several synonyms for the word experience, two quickly come to mind – "to suffer" and "to undergo a religious conversion." I'm not sure which was in the architect's mind when this course was named. One of the most spectacular golf holes I have seen is #8 – a par four, reaching out 444 yards, with a drop of some 250 feet from tee to fairway. In order to provide additional frustration, the approach shot to the green is guarded by a 70-foot sentinel eucalyptus – reminiscent of #18 on the world-renowned Cypress Golf Course in California.

RATES: (EP) Lodgings - $400/$450/$575. Green fees - $150, including carts. There are golf packages available that include play on both courses.

ARRIVAL: By air - Lanai Airport (recently renovated at a cost of $50 million dollars). When making reservations advise the resort of your flight number and time of arrival. They will meet and transport you to the lodge.

The Manele Bay Hotel

PO Box 774, Lanai City, Lanai, HI 96763

(808) 565-7300; (800) 321-4666

Judged one of our Top 50 resorts, the Manele Bay Hotel overlooks the sand beaches and water of Hulopoe Bay.

ACCOMMODATIONS: 250 rooms and suites, each with a private lanai.

AMENITIES: Swimming pool, tennis courts, a beautiful clubhouse, full-service spa, a massage treatment program, beach and many water sports. For more details covering horseback riding, hunting, and water sports, refer to The Lodge at Koele. Dining ranges from the Main Dining Room (Hulopu'e Court), to the Ihilani Dining Room (gourmet), or the Pool Grille for lighter fare. The food and service level is among the best you will find.

GOLF: The Challenge at Manele golf course, a Jack Nicklaus design, opened in December of 1993. Parring at 72, it reaches out a monstrous 7,039/6,684/6,310/5,847/5,024 yards. It plays at sea level, unlike the Experience, which is not only a mountain course but more traditional, with bordering trees, etc. The Challenge might also be referred to as a European links affair or a desert type "target" layout with over-the-water (Pacific Ocean) holes and the added distraction of the magnificent views.

RATES: (EP) Lodgings - $405/$550/$650/$695 and up. Green fees - $150. Package plans are available.

ARRIVAL: By air - Lanai Airport. There are 90 or more flights each week to this island. When making your reservations be sure to advise them as to the flight number and time of arrival. Arrangements will be made to pick you up and transport you to the resort.

The Island Of Molokai

The fifth-largest island in the Hawaiian group, with a population of only 6,000, Molokai has long been referred to as "The Lonely Isle." Although lovely, it has suffered more than its share of privation. In 1860, a Missionary priest, Father Damien, established a leper colony on the remote northernmost end of the island. Although leprosy (Hansen's disease) has been completely eradicated, the stigma remains. The location of the colony is now, by the way, a National Historic Park.

One of the reasons this island is gaining popularity is that it is about 50 years behind in development. In other words, this is old Hawaii – friendly and still not crowded. In fact, it has yet to get its first traffic light.

There is one hotel and two condominium destination resorts, all adjacent to a championship golf course. Each of these units is described on the following pages.

It is almost mandatory that you rent a car, as it is approximately 18 miles to the small town. From the airport it is eight miles to the turn off to "KaluaKoi," then about four miles from that point to the various resorts.

The KaluaKoi course is available for play by guests of all four resorts. Reaching out 6,564/6,187/5,461 yards and parring at 72, it was designed by Ted Robinson. Featuring some water along with ingeniously placed trees and traps, it is a fun layout to navigate. Holes 10 through 12 are some of the most interesting you may ever find. Be advised that this layout is no pushover.

KaluaKoi Hotel & Golf Club

PO Box 1977, Molokai, HI 96770

(808) 552-2555; (888) 552-2550

ACCOMMODATIONS: 130 rooms and suites with high-beamed ceilings, tropical fans, and rattan furnishings.

AMENITIES: Swimming pool or complimentary tennis. Dining is provided in the Ohia Lodge.

GOLF: For details on the golf course refer to The Island of Molokai.

RATES: (EP) Lodgings - $105/$155/$170/$185. Green fees -$55, including cart.

ARRIVAL: Shuttle service is available from the airport.

KaluaKoi Villas

1131 KaluaKoi Road, Molokai, HI 96770

(808) 552-2721; (800) 367-5004

The KaluaKoi Villas, set along a lovely white sand beach, are adjacent to the Kaluakoi Hotel.

ACCOMMODATIONS: 90 units in about 21 two-story buildings. Most units feature mini- kitchens with small range, microwave, small refrigerator, color TV with VCR and a private lanai.

AMENITIES: See KaluaKoi Hotel.

GOLF: For details on the golf course, directions for arrival, etc., refer to the description of the Island of Molokai, above.

RATES: (EP) Lodgings - $135/$145/$155. Green fees - $55, including cart. Golf packages are available.

Paniolo Hale Resort Condominiums

PO Box 190, Molokai, HI 96770

(808) 552-2731; (800) 367-2984

Directly adjacent to the golf course, the Paniolo Hale Resort represents a delightful change of pace. You can experience a taste of "old Hawaii," the soft quiet tranquility so treasured, but not often found.

ACCOMMODATIONS: One- and two-bedroom condominiums. Each unit has two baths and a fully equipped kitchen including dishwasher, refrigerator/freezer, icemaker, range, oven, microwave and washer/dryer. The two-bedroom units also have a Jacuzzi. All units have extremely large screened-in lanais. Maid service is provided once a week. These are the finest condominiums on Molokai.

AMENITIES: Swimming pool, two gas barbecue grills and picnic tables. You need only stroll a short distance to experience miles of untouched private beaches. The Kaluakoi Hotel dining room and six tennis courts are available at the adjacent Kaluakoi Resort.

GOLF: For details on the golf facilities, refer to the Island of Molokai, above

RATES: (EP) Lodgings - $115/$155/$/$265. Green fees -$60, including carts. Excellent packages plans are available, some including car rental. Monthly rates are also available.

ARRIVAL: By air - Molokai Airport (about 12 miles). Drive eight miles from the airport to the turnoff to KaluaKoi Resort, then four miles to a very small sign bearing the name of the resort.

Idaho

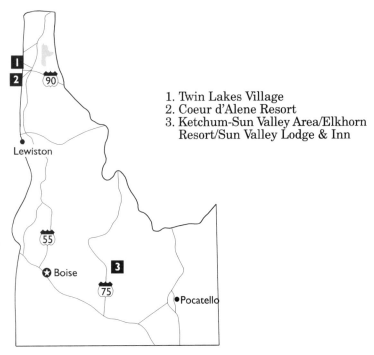

1. Twin Lakes Village
2. Coeur d'Alene Resort
3. Ketchum-Sun Valley Area/Elkhorn
   Resort/Sun Valley Lodge & Inn

Ketchum–Sun Valley Area

Sun Valley, the first complete ski resort in the United States, opened in December of 1935. The idea was that a visit to this resort area was to be "roughing it." That is, roughing it Hollywood style – glass-enclosed swimming pools, exquisite food, impeccable service, and orchestras performing nightly.

Today, of course, it is a large, self-contained village, with an opera house (movies), its own lake (rowing and paddleboat rentals), swimming pools, horseback riding, skeet and trap shooting, whitewater raft trips on the Salmon River, and fishing. Additional services include a drug store, barber and beauty shop, post office, several clothing stores, florist, bank, hospital, taxi service, excellent meeting and convention facilities, and so many restaurants I could not name them all. The summer months feature a jazz festival, motorcycle and bicycle races, flower and musical festivals, a back-country run, a Mexican Fiesta Grande, ballet performances, parades, a rodeo, and much more.

There are two major golf resorts in Sun Valley – The Elkhorn Lodge & Condominiums and The Sun Valley Lodge Inn & Condominiums. For a wide selection of additional accommodations, call the Sun Valley-Ketchum Chamber of Commerce's toll-free reservations number, (800) 634-3347.

Elkhorn Resort

PO Box 6009, Sun Valley, ID 83354

(208) 622-4511; (800) 355-4676

ACCOMMODATIONS: 132 guest rooms in the lodge and 80 condominiums fully equipped for housekeeping.

AMENITIES: Tennis on 16 Laykold courts, a spa program, five swimming pools (two Olympic size), horseback riding, hayrides, biking, balloon and glider flights. Ski season moves into high gear during the winter months. The resort has 16 lifts and 64 runs ranging from gentle to hair-raising. There are several good restaurants: Tequila Joe's featuring Mexican food; Jesse's for fish and beef; and, during the summer for breakfast and lunch, the Clubhouse Café.

GOLF: The Elkhorn layout, like the Sun Valley course, is a Robert Trent Jones, Jr. design. Stretching out 7,101/6,524/5,424 yards, the course pars at 72. With elevation changes from 6,150 feet to 5,750 feet on the front nine, and Willow Creek becoming a nuisance on the back side, it is a tester. One caution: you are playing golf at 6,000 feet above sea level. If you play from the blue tees you will feel as if you are playing about 6,400 yards, not 7,100. Your ball gets that much extra carry. Don't, however, try to make the same shots when you return to the beach area or you are going to be embarrassed.

RATES: (EP) Lodgings - $128/$178/$299. Green fees - $89, including cart. Rates quoted are for the summer season.

ARRIVAL: By air - Salt Lake City or Boise, Idaho with flight connections to Sun Valley. By car - State Highway 75, approximately 80 miles from Twin Falls, Idaho.

Sun Valley Lodge & Inn

Sun Valley, ID 83353

(208) 622-4111; (800) 786-8259

ACCOMMODATIONS: Provided in the Lodge and the Inn; there are also eight large groupings of condominiums.

AMENITIES: 18 tennis courts, three swimming pools, fishing, horseback riding, archery, indoor and outdoor ice skating (available year-round), sailing, kayaking, hayrides, and hiking. A children's program is also offered. Dining choices include The Lodge and Gretchen's Restaurant. The Duchin Lounge, with dancing to music from a few years back, has become a favorite gathering place in the evening. During the winter months, Sun Valley Lodge becomes a skier's paradise.

GOLF: The Sun Valley Resort course was designed by Robert Trent Jones, Jr. It stretches out 6,565/6,057/5,241 yards, with the men's par set at 72 and the ladies' at 73. Trail Creek wanders all over the place and the tight fairways and trees make this no run-of-the-mill resort layout. There are a couple of par 3s that may well produce a hard swallow. Not only is the course well-bunkered, but its beauty has been further enhanced by the use of brilliant "Petersburg White" sand.

RATES: (EP) Lodgings - $124/$399. Green fees - $80, carts $32. Golf packages are available. Rates are for June-September.

ARRIVAL: By air - Salt Lake City or Boise with flight connections to Hailey Airport (14 miles). By car - State Highway 75 (Twin Falls is 81 miles).

The Coeur d'Alene Resort

Second & Front Streets, Coeur d'Alene, ID 83814

(208) 765-4000; (800) 688-5253

ACCOMMODATIONS: This 18-story hotel has 337 guest rooms, ranging from the Parks Wing to the Lake Tower. There are also 20 condominiums, fully equipped for housekeeping.

AMENITIES: Indoor and outdoor swimming pools, racquetball court, complete fitness center, and four tennis courts at the golf club. Huge Lake Coeur d'Alene (10 miles wide at its midpoint and 25 miles long) opens up a host of activities, including excellent fishing. Horseback riding (20 miles of trails) and whitewater rafting (75 miles of rivers) are also available. Dining is available in Beverly's, which is on the seventh floor and offers a beautiful view of the lake. Less formal is the Dockside, a family restaurant on the boardwalk. New is Tito Macaroni's restaurant located across the street.

GOLF: Designed by golf architect Scott Miller, The Coeur d'Alene Resort Golf Course plays to a modest 6,309/5,899/5,490/4,446 yards and pars at 71. They are quite proud of the 14th hole, a "floating green." It is, at least so far, unique – the green can be floated to a new location and the yardage changed from 100 to 175 yards.

RATES: (EP) Lodgings - $179/$259/$269/$339 and up. Green fees - $200, including cart. Golf package - one night/one day (includes lodging, one round of golf with cart, and caddy), $438/$690 per couple. Rates are for April through September.

ARRIVAL: By air - Spokane Washington International Airport (40 miles). By car - take I-90 east to Exit 11. Resort is at the intersection of Sherman Avenue and Northwest Boulevard.

Twin Lakes Village

Route 4, Box P-551, Rathdrum, ID 83858

(208) 687-1311; (888) 836-7949

ACCOMMODATIONS: One- to three-bedroom condominiums with living rooms, fireplaces and completely equipped kitchens. Twin Lakes, an intimate village-type complex, is situated on 160 acres.

AMENITIES: The proximity of the lake provides immediate access to fishing, boating, and sandy beaches, with several swimming pools and tennis courts at various locations within the grounds. The hub of activity is the clubhouse, site of the dining room and lounge.

GOLF: There is a full-size, 18-hole course. Measuring 6,158/5,836/5,362 yards, it pars at 71/72. It is a beautiful layout, taking advantage of the lush terrain and magnificent trees that surround the entire area.

RATES: (EP) Lodgings - $120/$145. Rates are for June-August. Green fees - $30, carts $25.

ARRIVAL: By air - Spokane (30 miles) or Coeur d'Alene (20 miles). By car - from Rathdrum, five miles north on 41.

Jllinois

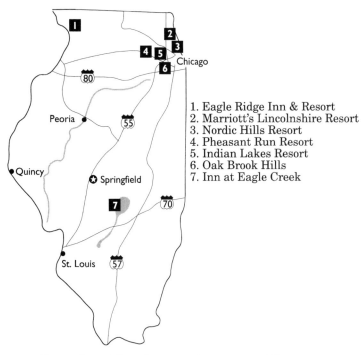

1. Eagle Ridge Inn & Resort
2. Marriott's Lincolnshire Resort
3. Nordic Hills Resort
4. Pheasant Run Resort
5. Indian Lakes Resort
6. Oak Brook Hills
7. Inn at Eagle Creek

Eagle Ridge Jnn & Resort

Box 777 Highway 20 West, Galena, IL 61036

(815) 777-2444; (800) 892-2269

Eagle Ridge Inn has been judged one of our Top 50 resorts. It also is one of the best kept secrets in the United States. We expected to find a modest little resort, but instead encountered a world-class destination. The 6,800-acre resort is located in the northwest corner of Illinois, on a ridge overlooking Lake Galena. By all means, take the time to visit the quaint town of Galena – you will find it enchanting.

ACCOMMODATIONS: 80 rooms in the charming inn, and over 300 one- to four-bedroom resort homes, condominiums, and townhouses, some on the fairway, others by the lake. These first-rate lodgings have excellent equipment and furnishings.

Take the time to visit the quaint, enchanting town of Galena, just six miles from Eagle Ridge.

AMENITIES: Indoor swimming pool (it is actually convertible, with a roof that can be opened in summer), sauna, whirlpool, four tennis courts, sailing, fishing, horseback riding, and a fitness center offering many types of exercise equipment. Bike rentals are also available.

During the winter months, the South Course golf shop turns into an indoor golf school, and outdoor activities include cross-country skiing, ice skating, sleigh rides, tobogganing, and snow-shoeing.

If you are not accustomed to it, snowshoeing is one of the greatest ways to disable yourself that has ever been devised.

During the summer season, Eagle Ridge offers a supervised children's recreational program from Monday through Saturday. The Woodlands Restaurant is outstanding.

GOLF: The Eagle Ridge North course reaches out a hefty 6,836/6,386/5,578 yards and pars at 72. The well-trapped terrain is hilly with small creeks running throughout. While bringing water into contention on only one hole on the front side, it makes up for that with the second nine showing water on seven holes. The second 18, the South course, plays 6,762/6,361/5,609 yards, also with a par of 72. You will find its undulating terrain and water in play on 10 holes all you can handle.

Now a third layout has been added. Designed by Andy North/Roger Packard, The General plays 6,820/6,434/6,006/5,335 yards with a par of 72. Extremely hilly with elevation changes of up to 200 feet, water becoming a challenge on five holes, modestly trapped, tree lined and with large greens - it will give you all you can handle.

RATES: (EP) Lodgings - $199/$229/$259; townhouses - $219/$279. Green fees - $88/$103, including cart. For the General Course, green fees are $125, including cart. There are many different plans available, including golf packages.

ARRIVAL: By air - Dubuque (25 miles) or Chicago, a bit over 150 miles. By car - Route 20, six miles east of Galena, Illinois. Resort entrance will be on your left at the very top of the hill.

Indian Lakes Resort

250 West Schick Road, Bloomingdale, IL 60108

(630) 529-0200; (800) 334-3417

ACCOMMODATIONS: 308 guest rooms and 23 suites. The resort is about an hour from downtown Chicago.

AMENITIES: Health club, indoor and outdoor swimming pools, six tennis courts, two 18-hole golf courses and three restaurants.

GOLF: The Iroquois Trail 18 has 6,580/6,239 yards with a par of 72, and the Sioux Trail layout measures 6,564/6,225 yards, also with a par 72. With only two tee settings, the yardage can be difficult for some ladies.

RATES: (EP) Lodgings - $129/$250. Green fees - $55/$65, including cart.

ARRIVAL: By air - O'Hare Airport (30 minutes). By car - between Bloomingdale Road and Gary Avenue on Schick Road.

The Inn at Eagle Creek

Eagle Creek State Park, Findlay, IL 62534

(217) 756-3456; (800) 876-3245

ACCOMMODATIONS: 138 rooms, each with a patio or balcony. There are also 10 suites with fireplaces. The majority of the paintings, furnishings, and quilts on display at the inn are the work of the local Amish community. The inn, on 11,000-acre Lake Shelbyville, is within Eagle Creek State Park.

AMENITIES: Four tennis courts, indoor and an outdoor swimming pool, sauna, whirlpool. Archery, hunting, fishing, hiking, and bicycling are at your disposal as well. There are two dining rooms, the Wildflowers Room and, on the lower level, Roomers Lounge & Grill.

GOLF: Reaching out a respectable 6,908/6,559/5,901/4,978 yards, the course pars at 72. While water comes into play on only four holes (and only then if you are having a dismal day), the undulating ravine-laced terrain more than makes up for the lack of water. Tight, tree-lined fairways and very large greens also add to the excitement. Though definitely challenging, it is also entertaining.

RATES: (EP) Lodgings - $119/$165. Green fees - $65, including cart. Golf packages are available. Rates shown are for April through October.

ARRIVAL: By air - Mattoon or Decatur. By car - from SR 51, I-57, or I-70 to Findlay. Resort is on the west side of Lake Shelbyville just east of Findlay.

Marriott's Lincolnshire Resort

Marriott Lane, Lincolnshire, IL 60015

(847) 634-0100; (800) 228-9290

ACCOMMODATIONS: 393 rooms

AMENITIES: Legitimate theater presentations, game rooms, the use of canoes or paddleboats on the private resort lake, tennis on five indoor courts, four racquetball courts, and a health spa. They also have two outstanding restaurants.

GOLF: Parring at 71, the course measures 6,600/6,6315/5,795 yards. The typical Fazio design has greens that are raised and often small. While the general terrain is flat, the course is made interesting by water on five or six holes.

RATES: (EP) Lodgings - $190/$225. Green fees - $75, including cart. Golf packages are available.

ARRIVAL: By air - Chicago. By car - on Route 21.

Nordic Hills Resort

Nordic Road, Itasca, IL 60143

(630) 773-2750; (800) 487-1969

ACCOMMODATIONS: 220 guest rooms and six luxurious penthouse suites.

AMENITIES: Eight indoor racquetball courts, six bowling lanes, five outdoor tennis courts (three lighted), indoor and outdoor swimming pools, and a full health club with exercise equipment. Dining is offered in the Montclair Chop House or the less formal Mulligans.

GOLF: The resort has its own 18-hole, 5,897-yard, par-71/73 course. Playing privileges are also extended at the nearby Indian Lakes Resort and its two championship layouts.

RATES: (EP) Lodgings - $145/$295. Green fees - $65, including cart.

ARRIVAL: By air - Chicago. By car - the resort is on Old 53 Rohlwing Road and Nordic Road, off Highway 20.

Oak Brook Hills Hotel & Resort

3500 Midwest Road, Oak Brook, IL 60522

(630) 850-5555; (800) 445-3315

ACCOMMODATIONS: The 11-story structure has 382 rooms, including 38 suites.

AMENITIES: Large swimming pool with sundeck, five lighted tennis courts, exercise/weight room, lap pool, sauna, whirlpool, and massage facilities. Ascots, the main dining room, offers a golf course view and wide range of cuisine. The Waterford provides more intimate dining.

GOLF: The Oak Brook Hills course is a Dick Nugent design. Parring at 70, it plays 6,409/6,019/5,339 yards. Its gently rolling terrain features beach-type bunkers, water on 12 holes, and trees.

RATES: (EP) Lodgings - $189/$209. Green fees - $75, including cart. Golf package: one night/one day, $278 per couple (includes lodging, breakfast, one round of golf with cart, $50 dinner coupon, bag storage – available weekends only).

ARRIVAL: By air - O'Hare or Midway Airports. By car - from O'Hare take 1-294 south to 1-88 west. Exit at Route 83 south. Go one mile to 31st street. Turn left onto 31st and travel to Midwest (one mile). At this point turn left and travel to resort.

Pheasant Run Resort

PO Box 64, St. Charles, IL 60174

(630) 584-6300; (800) 426-8700

ACCOMMODATIONS: 550 rooms. The resort is located on 200 acres in the Fox River Valley.

AMENITIES: Health spa, nine outdoor tennis courts, indoor and outdoor pools. Dining rooms include Smuggler's Cove, Baker's Wife Steak House, and the dinner-theater, showing Broadway hits.

GOLF: The Challenge course has five lakes, sloping greens and what seem to be too many traps. It plays at 6,315/5,955/5,472 yards and pars at 71/73.

RATES: (EP) Lodgings - $130. Green fees - $45, carts $25. Golf package: two nights/two days (includes lodging, MAP, with one night a dinner show, green fees), $406 per couple.

ARRIVAL: By air - Chicago. By private aircraft - DuPage County, paralleling the golf course. By car - on Route 64, three miles east of St. Charles.

Indiana

Fourwinds, A Clarion Resort

Lake Monroe, PO Box 160, Bloomington, IN 47402

(812) 824-9904; (800) 252-7466

ACCOMMODATIONS: 126 rooms, all with private steam baths. The Fourwinds Resort is on the shores of Indiana's Lake Monroe.

AMENITIES: Tennis, indoor/outdoor pool, Jacuzzi and saunas. They claim their marina is the largest one of its type in the United States. You can bring your own craft or, if you prefer, rent a pontoon boat for a tour of the lake or a little fishing. Classic French and American dishes are served in the Tradewinds.

GOLF: The Pointe championship course reaches out 6,639/6,131/5,252 yards and pars at 71.

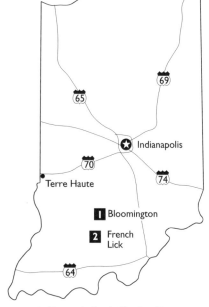

1. Fourwinds: A Clarion Resort
2. French Lick Springs

RATES: (EP) Lodgings - $130/$145/$160 and up. Green fees - $65, including cart. Golf packages are available.

ARRIVAL: By air - Bloomington (10 miles). By car - from Bloomington, take Highway 37 south to the Harrodsburg exit, go east to Fairfax Road, then south to the resort.

French Lick Springs

French Lick, IN 47432

(812) 936-9300; (800) 457-4042

ACCOMMODATIONS: 480 rooms, including suites; there are also approximately 120 two-bedroom condominiums, fully equipped for housekeeping. For condo information, call (812) 936-5000.

AMENITIES: Eight indoor and 10 lighted outdoor tennis courts, indoor and outdoor pools, six bowling lanes, health spa, and horseback riding from the resort's own stables. For dining, choose from Chez James, Le Bistro (for a quick breakfast), and the Hoosier Dining Room.

GOLF: The course, adjacent to the hotel and called the Valley Course, plays 6,003/5,687 yards and pars at 70/71. The Country Club course measures 6,629/6,291/5,781 yards, parring at 71/73. The architect, Donald Ross, used hilly terrain, trees along holes six, seven, and eight, a little water on three holes, and traps to keep you alert. I will not describe the 18th green, other than to say one look at it will hold your full attention.

RATES: (EP) Lodgings - $119/$225. Green fees - Valley course $35; Country Club course - $55/$66, including cart. Golf package - one night/two days (includes MAP, lodging, green fees and cart), $318/$358 per couple. Rates are April-October.

ARRIVAL: By air - Louisville (75 minutes). By car - Highway 150 to 145.

Kansas

Terradyne Resort Hotel & Country Club

1400 Terradyne, Andover, KS 67002

(316) 733-2582; (800) 892-4613

ACCOMMODATIONS: 42 guest rooms (including suites). Suites have a sitting and dining area, wet-bar, and refrigerator. The hotel entrance is impressive, with Italian marble used throughout.

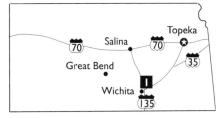

1. Terradyne Resort Hotel & CC

AMENITIES: Two indoor racquetball courts, a fully equipped weight and exercise room, sauna and whirlpool, three lighted tennis courts and an outdoor pool. Dining is provided in the Greens Dining Room and the Blairemore Room.

GOLF: Designed by Donald R. Sechrest, Terradyne Golf Club plays 6,704/6,215/5048 yards, with a par of 71. For tee times, call 733-5851. The Scottish-style peaks, rolling fairways, bunkers and high rough are a welcome change from many courses in this area.

RATES: (EP) Lodgings - $84/$125/$154/$250. Green fees - $50, carts $24. Golf packages are available.

ARRIVAL: By air - Wichita International Airport (40 minutes). By car - from Wichita, take Highway 54 east to Greenwich. Take a left (north) to Central Street. Go right (east) to 159th. Turn left and drive a quarter-mile.

Kentucky

1. Marriott's Griffin Gate Resort
2. Kentucky Dam State Park Lodge
3. Lake Barkley State Park Lodge
4. Woodson Bend Resort
5. Barren River State Park Lodge

Marriott's Griffin Gate Resort

1800 Newtown Pike, Lexington, KY 40511

(606) 231-5100; (800) 228-9290

ACCOMMODATIONS: 409 guest rooms, including 17 suites. This is a very impressive complex.

AMENITIES: Three lighted tennis courts, indoor and outdoor pools, a health club with exercise rooms, saunas and whirlpools. Dining facilities include the Griffin Gate Gardens; the Pegasus Restaurant and Lounge; and the Mansion Restaurant. A beautiful structure, this resort has much to offer.

GOLF: The Griffin Gate course measures a substantial 6,801/6,296/5,948/4,979 yards and pars at 72. A Rees Jones design, it has large, undulating greens, variation in tee heights, 64 traps and water coming into play on 10 holes. It will offer all the challenge you want.

RATES: (EP) Lodgings - $175/$295. Green fees - $42/$52, including cart. Golf package - one night/one day, available weekdays only (includes lodging, green fees, cart, breakfast, bag storage), $249 per couple.

ARRIVAL: By air - Lexington. By car - off I-64, south on Newton Pike (922).

Woodson Bend Resort

14 Woodson Bend Road, Burnside, KY 42518

(606) 561-5311; (800) 872-9825

ACCOMMODATIONS: Well-designed one- and two-bedroom air-conditioned condominiums, each with fully equipped kitchen and fireplace. Several patio homes have now been added. The resort is on a magnificent limestone peninsula jutting out into Lake Cumberland.

AMENITIES: Swimming pool; lighted tennis courts; recreation building with saunas, locker rooms and showers; fishing; and water-skiing. The multi-purpose clubhouse includes a delightful restaurant and lounge.

 Warning: This is a dry county. Bring your own or suffer.

GOLF: With the second nine put into play, the golf course has finally become a full 18-hole layout. Designed by Lee Trevino/Dave Bennet, it plays 6,036/5,752/5,446 yards and pars at 71.

RATES: (EP) Lodgings - $185/$350. Green fees - $27/$35, carts $24.

ARRIVAL: By air - Lexington. By car - Highway 27, south of Somerset.

Kentucky State Parks

There are 15 resorts spanning the state, from the lake area of western Kentucky to the mountains in the eastern highlands. Of these, 11 have golf courses but only three are open year-round, have lodges and sport a full 18-hole course. Each of the three have dining rooms, tennis courts, golf, horseback riding, a lake and boating activities.

None of the state parks is allowed to serve alcoholic beverages. It just so happens that the majority of the counties are also dry, so I would suggest you bring a supply. If you don't, you either go without or you may be in for a long drive.

For additional information write **Kentucky State Parks**, Frankfort, KY 40601, or call each resort toll-free at (800) 255-7275.

Barren River Lake State Park Lodge

1149 State Park Road, Lucas, KY 42156

(502) 646-2151; (800) 325-0057

ACCOMMODATIONS: 51 air-conditioned lodge rooms as well as 22 cottages. There are also camping facilities. The lodge has a 198-seat dining room.

GOLF: The Barren River Golf Course, with a par of 72, measures 6,376/5,942/4,919 yards.

RATES: Lodgings - $69/$75. Green fees -$20/$25, carts $20.

ARRIVAL: From Bowling Green, take I-65 northeast to Cumberland Parkway east. Then US 31E south to the park.

Kentucky Dam State Park Lodge

PO Box 69, Gilbertsville, KY 42044

(502) 362-4271; (800) 325-0146

ACCOMMODATIONS: 48 rooms in the lodge, plus 34 cottages fully equipped for housekeeping. Dam State Park is one of the larger resorts in Kentucky, occupying 1,352 acres at the northern tip of Kentucky Lake.

GOLF: The 18-hole course is a short walk from the 72-room Henry Ward Lodge and 225 campsites. Playing to a par of 72/79, the course reaches out 6,745/6,255 yards.

RATES: (EP) Lodgings - $65/$75. Green fees - $20/$25, carts $20.

ARRIVAL: By private aircraft - 4,000-foot paved and lighted runway. Rental cars available. Free pickup for guests. By car - 21 miles east of Paducah on US 641.

Lake Barkley State Park Lodge

PO Box 790, Cadiz, KY 42211

(502) 924-1131; (800) 325-1708

ACCOMMODATIONS: The lodge has 124 rooms, including suites; 80 camping sites; and nine two-bedroom executive cottages, each with a kitchen and living and dining area. Barkley is the largest in the chain of state parks, covering 3,700 acres and resting on the eastern shore of 57,920-acre Lake Barkley.

GOLF: The 18-hole, par-72 layout measures 6,751/6,448/5,659/5,409 yards.

RATES: (EP) Lodgings - $72/$140. Green fees - $20/$25, carts $20.

ARRIVAL: By private aircraft - 4,800-foot paved, lighted runway. Courtesy car to lodge. By car - seven miles west of Cadiz on US 68 and Route 80.

Kentucky

Louisiana

The Bluffs on Thompson Creek

1. Emerald Hills Resort/
   Cypress Bend Resort
2. The Bluffs on Thompson Creek

PO Box 1220,

St. Francisville, LA 70775

(504) 634-3410; (888) 634-3410

ACCOMMODATIONS:
39 one- and two-bedroom suites. These beautifully furnished and decorated units are lovely.

AMENITIES: Two lighted tennis courts, swimming pool and, of course, golf. The 200-seat Bluffs Dining Room presents a mixed cuisine of Cajun, continental, seafood and steak. The dress code is casual. There is also a snack bar at the course. The area surrounding St. Francisville is rich in history (dating back to the late 1700s) with many places to visit.

GOLF: Designed by the Palmer Course Design Company, The Bluffs Course enjoys one of the more beautiful settings. Reaching out a substantial 7,151/6,533/5,980/4,781 yards, it pars at 72. Trees, bunkers, water coming into play on 16 holes and undulating terrain will keep your full attention.

RATES: (EP) Lodgings - $119/$139. Green fees - $50/$60, carts $24. Golf packages are available.

ARRIVAL: By air - Baton Rouge. By car - take I-110 north until it ends. Bear right onto US Highway 61, and continue for approximately 20 miles. Turn right onto LA Highway 965 and drive six miles to resort.

Cypress Bend Golf Resort

2000 Cypress Bend Parkway, Maney, LA 71449

(318) 590-1500; (877) 519-1500

Cypress Bend Golf Resort is situated next to Toledo Bend Lake, the liquid line dividing Louisiana from Texas. The setting is pastoral, with the lake, a profusion of flowers, wildlife and the rolling terrain.

ACCOMMODATIONS: A very new hotel with 70 rooms and suites, featuring spacious sitting areas.

AMENITIES: Include an indoor/outdoor swimming pool, a spa program and fitness center. Guided fishing trips are also an option. Canoeing, lake swimming and hiking also join the list of activities. Future plans call for tennis courts. There is the Cypress Dining Room, by day a casual affair and by night a delightful dining facility, along with the Sabrina Social Room and Lounge. The Cypress Café, at the clubhouse, is also available for breakfast and lunch.

GOLF: Designed by Dave Bennett, The Cypress Bend Golf Course reaches out a very respectable 6,707/6,248/5,784/5,091 yards, with a par of 72. The area is one of undulating terrain. Unusual for Louisiana is the fact that it offers hills lined with a hardwood tree forest, along with 72 bunkers and water in action on 10 or 11 holes. The course actually wraps itself around the edge of Toledo Bend Lake. Or perhaps I should say the Lake wraps itself around the course.

RATES: (EP) Lodgings - $149/$250 per couple. Green fees - $37/$50, including cart. Golf packages are also available. Rates are for February-May and September-November.

ARRIVAL: By air - Shreveport, LA (approximately 90 miles). Private aircraft - Many Airport, with a 4,000-thousand-foot paved runway. By car - from Shreveport, take I-49 south to State Route 6, just south of Natchitoches. Turn southwest and drive through the town of Many to State Route 191 (12 miles). Go south approximately three miles on Route 191 to the resort entrance. From Dallas, take I-20 (approximately 195 miles) to Shreveport, then follow above instructions.

Louisiana

Emerald Hills Golf Resort

PO Box 460, Florien, LA 71429

(318) 586-4661; (800) 533-5031

ACCOMMODATIONS: 107 guest rooms, plus 23 fully equipped condominiums.

AMENITIES: Two swimming pools, a children's pool, and lighted tennis courts. There is also a new restaurant, lounge, and office.

GOLF: The par-72 Emerald Hills course virtually surrounds the property, and measures 6,548/6,307/5,329 yards. The lush, tree-lined fairways and water coming into play on five holes make it an entertaining layout.

RATES: (EP) Lodgings - $75/$138. Green fees - $25/$37, including cart. Golf package - two nights/three days (includes lodging, green fees, cart, taxes), $230 per couple; weekends $310 per couple. Rates are March-September.

ARRIVAL: By air - Shreveport (2½ hours). By private aircraft - Hodges Garden, a 2,200-foot strip. By car - US 171 between Many and Leesville.

Maine

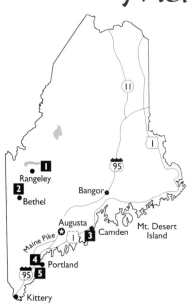

1. Sugarloaf Mountain Hotel
2. Bethel Inn & CC
3. Samoset Resort
4. Portland Marriott Resort
5. Black Point Inn

Bethel Inn & Country Club

One Broad Street, Bethel, ME 04217

(207) 824-2175; (800) 654-0125

ACCOMMODATIONS: 65 guest rooms plus accommodations in the main building. The resort also has 40 fairway townhouses. The Bethel Inn features elegant colonial architecture.

AMENITIES: Tennis, sailing, canoeing, lake swimming, swimming in the heated pool, and use of a fitness room. In the winter you can add cross-country and downhill skiing. Meals are served in an elegant dining room overlooking the golf course.

GOLF: Until recently, golf was played on the Country Club's nine-hole, par-36 layout. Now a second nine has been brought into play. A Geoffrey Cornish design, it now reaches out 6,663/6,330/6,209/5,340 yards, with a par of 72.

RATES: (MAP) Lodgings - $258/$418 per couple. Green fees are included in the room rates. Carts: $30.

ARRIVAL: By air - Portland (70 miles). By private aircraft - Bethel. By car - on Route 2 and 26, 70 miles northwest of Portland, Maine.

Black Point Inn

510 Black Point Road, Scarborough, ME 04074

(207) 883-4126; (800) 258-0003

The Black Point Inn is over 120 years old. Although it has been improved, enlarged and modernized over the succeeding years, care was taken to preserve the Inn's original style and ambiance.

ACCOMMODATIONS: The main building has 80 rooms, and there are six suites in the adjacent Colonial-style guest houses.

AMENITIES: 14 tennis courts, bathing beach, fishing, sailing, large outdoor swimming pool, billiards, ping-pong, and complimentary bicycles. You may arrange boat rentals at the Prouts Neck Yacht Club. In addition to the indoor pool and Jacuzzi, there is exercise equipment, including a treadmill, stationary bikes and rowing machine. The food and service here are outstanding.

GOLF: The adjoining Prouts Neck Country Club, an 18-hole par-70 course, plays 6,005/5,822/5,271 yards. This is a fun layout. Be careful, however, as it is not as easy as it would first appear. Two additional courses, a few miles away, are also at your disposal – the newer and more difficult Sable Oaks or the older Willowdale layout.

RATES: (MAP) Lodgings - $345/$385/$520 per couple. Minimum stay three nights. Green fees - $50, including carts. Rates are for July 1-September 5.

ARRIVAL: By air - Portland (eight miles). By car - from the Maine Turnpike, take Exit 7, then turn right for Scarborough and Old Orchard Beach (Route 1). At the second traffic light, go left on Route 207 (4.3 miles).

Portland Marriott Resort

21 Running Hill Road, South Portland, ME 04106

(207) 871-8000; (800) 228-9290

ACCOMMODATIONS: A six-story hotel with 227 rooms, including five suites.

AMENITIES: Executive fitness center, indoor swimming pool and whirlpool. At the country club you can add two tennis courts. Dining is provided in the Garden Court Restaurant and also at the Grill Room and lounge.

GOLF: The Sable Oaks golf course was designed by Geoffrey Cornish and Brian Silva. Water comes into the picture on 12 holes. Jackson Brook, seemingly without a home, becomes a nuisance on eight or nine holes, and there are a couple of ponds to contend with. With tree-lined fairways and some unexpected and spectacular drops (100 feet from one part of the fairway to another), this layout is both beautiful and challenging. Playing to a par of 70/72, it reaches out a modest 6,359/6,056/4,786 yards. Don't let the yardage fool you – this is a placement golf course.

RATES: (EP) Lodgings - $190/$300. Green fees - $70, including carts. Golf packages are available. A real plus: you can reserve tee times up to 30 days in advance.

ARRIVAL: By air - Portland International Jetport (three miles).

Samoset Resort

Warrenton Road, Rockport, ME 04856

(207) 594-2511; (800) 341-1650

On the mid-coast of Maine, Samoset is set on 230 acres of oceanfront, overlooking Penobscot Bay.

ACCOMMODATIONS: 150 rooms and suites, each with balconies offering a view of the bay. There are also 72 one- or two-bedroom condominiums.

AMENITIES: Indoor and outdoor swimming pools and tennis courts, boating, fishing, health club, saunas, a poolside hot tub and golf. In the winter, you can add ice skating, tobogganing, sleigh rides and cross-country skiing. Dining is at Marcel's Restaurant.

GOLF: The Samoset Resort Course has been described as the "Pebble Beach" of the east; it has eight holes running along the ocean. I suspect the comparison to Pebble Beach is due to the fact that it is very open and gets lots of wind. It plays 6,362/6,008/5,529 yards, with a par of 70. Unlike Pebble Beach, however, it has several holes that share greens, in the older Scottish tradition. Shared greens can make you a bit nervous when you are putting and other golfers are attempting to approach a portion of the green you are standing on.

RATES: (EP) Lodgings - $259/$289. Green fees - $95, including cart. Golf package: two night/two days (includes lodging, golf, cart), $730 per couple.

ARRIVAL: By air - Knox County Airport. By car - take US Highway 1 north to Rockport.

Sugarloaf Mountain Hotel

On The Mountain, Carrabassett Valley, ME 04947

(207) 237-2222; (800) 527-9879

The location of this resort, within the Carrabassett Valley, is something to behold. The heavily timbered, rolling, mountainous terrain lends itself to outstanding ski facilities as well as one of the most picturesque and unique golf settings you could envision.

ACCOMMODATIONS: 119 guest rooms in the hotel and 125 condominiums located throughout the property. The condos are fully equipped for housekeeping.

AMENITIES: Indoor and outdoor swimming pools, fly-fishing, a health club, mountain biking or whitewater rafting on the nearby Kennebec River. There is also a 12-person hot tub, a plunge pool, sauna, steam rooms and a fitness center. The skiing facilities are recognized as among the best in the New England area. They have an excellent dining room called Arabella's. It is supported by Arabella's Pub, a congenial meeting place at the end of a hard day on either the golf course or the ski slopes.

GOLF: The Sugarloaf Golf Club is a Robert Trent Jones, Jr. design. I will not attempt to describe the beauty of this magnificent layout, but *Golf Digest* rated it the most beautiful golf course in the country. The desk in the hotel offers "second-time-around" golf balls for sale. I suggest you tuck your pride in your pocket and avail yourself of the offer. You are going to need them.

From its various tee settings the course reaches out 6,922/6,400/5,324 yards and pars at 72. While it is extremely well-trapped, the major challenge is in the tree-lined fairways that wind their way through the undulating terrain. Another contribution to the excitement is the Carrabassett River. This devil parallels holes 2, 10, 11, 12, 13, 14 and 15. In total, water either threatens or becomes involved on nine holes. The signature hole, number 11, a spectacular par 3, gives you a drop of approximately 130 feet from tee to green, with traps on the right and the river running along the left side.

RATES: (EP) Lodgings - $95/$135/$360. Green fees - $96, including cart. Golf package: one night/one day (includes lodgings, breakfast, one round of golf with cart), $280 per couple.

ARRIVAL: By air - Farmington. By car - 36 miles north of Farmington on Route 27.

Maine

Maryland

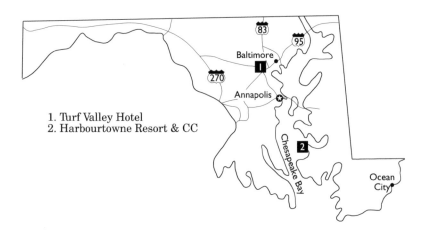

1. Turf Valley Hotel
2. Harbourtowne Resort & CC

Harbourtowne Resort & Country Club

Box 126, St. Michaels, MD 21663

(410) 745-9066; (800) 446-9066

ACCOMMODATIONS: 111 rooms and suites fronting on Chesapeake Bay.

AMENITIES: Bicycle rentals, three tennis courts, and swimming pool. Fishing and hunting can be arranged with advance booking. There are two dining rooms.

GOLF: The unusual and interesting course was designed by Pete Dye, and plays 6,320/6,128/5,597/5,036 yards with a par of 70/71. Its many lakes, tree-lined fairways (on the back side) and typical Pete Dye small, firm greens will keep you occupied. The first few holes are relatively easy, but it gets more and more difficult and demanding as you play on.

RATES: (EP) Lodgings - $179/$259. Green fees - $55, including cart. Golf package - two nights/three days (includes lodging, three rounds of golf, cart, club storage, range balls, daily continental breakfast), $458/$578 per couple.

ARRIVAL: By air - Washington DC or Baltimore. By car - from Washington/Baltimore area, take 301 to Route 50, then 322 to Easton. Turn right on Route 33 to St. Michaels. The resort is one mile west of St. Michaels.

Turf Valley Hotel

2700 Turf Valley Road

Ellicott City, MD 21043

(410) 465-1500; (800) 666-8873

ACCOMMODATIONS: 173 rooms and suites.

AMENITIES: Two lighted tennis courts, outdoor swimming pool, and complete fitness center, along with 36 holes of golf. The centerpiece of the hotel is Alexander's Restaurant. Flanked by a four-story atrium, it is most impressive.

GOLF: The South Course, parring at 70/72, plays a modest 6,323/5,596/5,572 yards, bringing water into the picture on 11 holes. The North Course reaches out a bit farther, with a yardage of 6,825/6,361/5,994 and a par of 70/74.

RATES: (EP) Lodgings - $149/$159/$240. Green fees - $40/$60, carts $29. Golf packages are available.

ARRIVAL: By air - Washington, DC National Airport (45 minutes), the Baltimore/Washington International airport (25 minutes), or Dulles Airport (one hour). By car - take I-70 toward Frederick. Follow I-70 to Marriottsville Road exit. Turn left on Marriottsville Road to first stop sign. Turn left and go to Turf Valley Country Club entrance, which will be on your left.

Maryland

Massachusetts

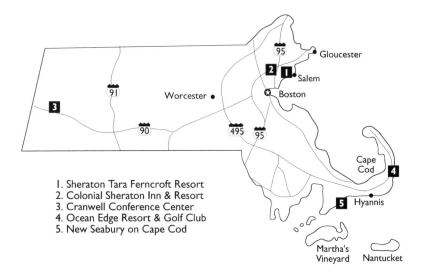

1. Sheraton Tara Ferncroft Resort
2. Colonial Sheraton Inn & Resort
3. Cranwell Conference Center
4. Ocean Edge Resort & Golf Club
5. New Seabury on Cape Cod

The Colonial Sheraton Inn & Resort

427 Walnut, Wakefield, MA 01880

(781) 245-9300; (800) 325-3535

ACCOMMODATIONS: 300 guest rooms, including suites.

AMENITIES: Their $2 million racquet and fitness center offers eight racquetball courts, four indoor and three outdoor tennis courts, fully equipped gym, saunas, steam, massage, and a pool. Page's Restaurant presents dining in a wine-and-candlelight atmosphere. The Gaslight Tavern provides entertainment and music.

GOLF: The 18-hole layout has a par of 70, and weighs in at 6,635/6,328/5,625 yards.

RATES: (EP) Lodgings - $119/$129 and up. Green fees - $75, including carts. Golf packages are available.

ARRIVAL: By air - Boston. By car - Exit 31 or 32, Route 128/I-95.

Cranwell Conference Center & Golf Club

55 Lee Road, Lenox, MA 01240

(413) 637-1364; (800) 272-6935

ACCOMMODATIONS: 65 rooms and suites, some located in the "Mansion" (the main building, a massive Tudor-style structure); there are a few cottage suites.

AMENITIES: Heated outdoor pool, two tennis courts, fitness center, and dining room.

GOLF: Originally put together in 1926, the course plays a modest 6,387/6,157 yards with a par of 71. While the terrain is generally flat and open, the back nine is heavily tree-lined.

RATES: (EP) Lodgings - $259/$449. Green fees - $68/$80, including cart. Golf packages are available (three-night minimum, weekends only).

ARRIVAL: By air - Bradford International Airport (Hartford CT). By car - take 91 north into Massachusetts and go to the Mass Turnpike exit. Take the turnpike west to Exit 2. Turn right onto Route 20 west and follow it for 3½ miles. The resort is on Route 20 and will be on your right.

New Seabury on Cape Cod

PO Box 549, New Seabury, MA 02649

(508) 477-9111; (800) 999-9033

ACCOMMODATIONS: Varied. The Tidewatch and Colony Villas provide lodgings in one- and three-bedroom suites with panoramic views of the ocean. Maushop Village, which looks like a 19th-century fishing village, has one- and two-bedroom villas. Popponesset Inn and its cottages overlook the waters of Nantucket Sound. On 2,000 acres, with almost four miles of secluded beaches, New Seabury has much to offer its guests.

AMENITIES: 16 lighted tennis courts, swimming at the beautiful sandy beaches, sailing, fishing, jogging and walking paths or bicycling. Day camp arrangements for children are provided during the season. Dining is at the Country Club and, during the summer season, at the Popponesset Inn.

GOLF: There are two exceptionally well-groomed courses to be enjoyed. The championship Blue Course, referred to as the Challenger, stretches out 7,200/6,909/6,508/5,764 yards with a par of 72. The Green Course is a par-70 affair measuring 5,930/5,105 yards. The Blue layout, also referred to as the "Pebble Beach of the East," can become a tiger for the same reason Pebble Beach in California does: the prevailing and whimsical wind. Water also becomes a factor on 11 holes. The Green Course, while shorter and more sheltered from winds, can also be difficult. With its narrow fairways, it places more emphasis on accuracy than distance. A nice plus – there is no water coming into play on this layout.

RATES: (EP) Lodgings - $210/$270/$400. Green fees - Blue Course $115, Green Course $75, including carts. Rates are for June-August.

ARRIVAL: By air - Barnstable-Hyannis Airport. By car - halfway between Falmouth and Hyannis, via Route 28. The resort is approximately an hour and a half drive from New York's LaGuardia airport and 70 miles from Boston.

Ocean Edge Resort & Golf Club

Route 6A, Brewster, MA 02631

(508) 896-9000; (800) 343-6074

ACCOMMODATIONS: 300 one- , two- , and three-bedroom villas, fully equipped for housekeeping, are only a short walk from either the hotel or the tennis facilities. There are also 90 hotel rooms.

AMENITIES: Two indoor and four outdoor swimming pools; five Har-Tru clay and six all-weather tennis courts; two tennis shops; basketball court; saunas; Jacuzzis; jogging paths; bicycle rentals; and a private beach. The resort is justly proud of the Ocean Grille Dining Room, along with Bayzo's Pub for lighter fare. There are also two restaurants at the clubhouse: Mulligan's and The Reef.

GOLF: The Ocean Edge Golf Club was designed by the renowned Geoffrey Cornish and Brian Silva. Reaching out 6,665/6,127/5,098 yards, it pars at 72. Although the general area is flat, the course enjoys slightly undulating terrain. It is heavily wooded and brings water into play on only one hole (a welcome change of pace).

RATES: (EP) Lodgings - $300/$365/$625. Green fees - $64, carts $30. Golf packages are available.

ARRIVAL: By air - Boston Logan International Airport (95 miles). From the airport, take Route 3 south. Pick up Route 6 (Mid Cape Highway) at the end of the Sagamore Bridge. Follow Route 6 to Brewster/Harwich Exit 10. Turn left onto Route 124 and right onto Route 6A. From there, it is 1.6 miles to resort.

Sheraton Tara Ferncroft Resort

Ferncroft Drive, Danvers, MA 01923

(978) 777-2500; (800) 325-3535

ACCOMMODATIONS: 300 rooms.

AMENITIES: Indoor pool and tennis courts; horseback riding, boating and fishing are available nearby. Dining is in the Ferncroft Grill and the Bogey's Lounge.

GOLF: The 18-hole Robert Trent Jones course reaches out 6,536/6,112/5,488 yards and pars at 72.

RATES: (EP) Lodgings - $129/$149/$350. Golf packages are available. Green fees - $95, including cart.

ARRIVAL: By air - Boston. By car - I-95 to Highway 1, then take the Ferncroft Road exit.

Michigan

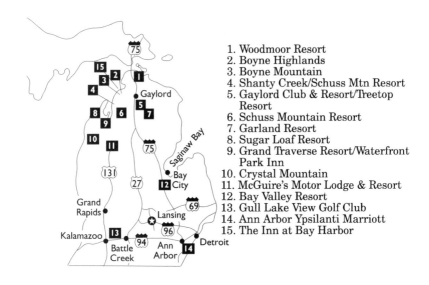

1. Woodmoor Resort
2. Boyne Highlands
3. Boyne Mountain
4. Shanty Creek/Schuss Mtn Resort
5. Gaylord Club & Resort/Treetop Resort
6. Schuss Mountain Resort
7. Garland Resort
8. Sugar Loaf Resort
9. Grand Traverse Resort/Waterfront Park Inn
10. Crystal Mountain
11. McGuire's Motor Lodge & Resort
12. Bay Valley Resort
13. Gull Lake View Golf Club
14. Ann Arbor Ypsilanti Marriott
15. The Inn at Bay Harbor

Ann Arbor Ypsilanti Marriott

1275 Huron Street, Ypsilanti, MI 48197

(739) 487-2000; (800) 228 9290

ACCOMMODATIONS: 236 rooms, along with seven suites and a concierge level.

AMENITIES: Health club with indoor swimming pool, whirlpool, weight room, and sauna bath, jogging and bicycling trails, tennis courts, and boating facilities. In the winter they offer ice skating and cross-country skiing. Dining is in the Fairways, with evening entertainment in Players sports lounge.

GOLF: Since the terrain is generally flat, the architect of the Huron Golf Club (Karl Litten) decided to introduce a bit of spice in the form of water. In fact, he must have loved the stuff. It's bad enough that the front nine is virtually surrounded by Ford Lake, but there are six or seven ponds getting into the act on nine holes.

Parring at 72, this affair reaches out 6,755/6,470/6,150/5,185 yards.

RATES: (EP) Lodgings - $140/$209 and up. Green fees - $28/$39, carts $24. Golf packages are available. Rates are for the period of April through October.

ARRIVAL: By air - Detroit Metro Airport (15 minutes away). By car - take I-94 to Huron Street.

Bay Valley Resort

2470 Old Bridge Road, Bay City, MI 48706

(517) 686-3500; (800) 292-5028

ACCOMMODATIONS: 150 guest rooms in a comfortable country-inn atmosphere.

AMENITIES: Six indoor and six outdoor tennis courts, swimming pool, sauna, and a Jacuzzi/whirlpool. Dining is provided in the Heatherfield Restaurant overlooking the golf course, or in the intimate English Room.

GOLF: Designed by Desmond Muirhead/Jack Nicklaus, the resort's course is reminiscent of many Scottish layouts. This beautiful, challenging course plays 6,610/6,113/5,587/5,151 yards and pars at 71. Apparently the Scots liked water, as the course has over 60 acres of the stuff – not in just one place, but seemingly wherever you look.

RATES: (EP) Inn - $79/$89/$150. Green fees - $45/$55, including cart. Golf packages are available. Rates are for June to mid-October.

ARRIVAL: By air - Tri-City Airport. By car - I-75, take M-84 Saginaw Road exit. Turn right, go one block, then turn right at the Standard Station.

Boyne Highlands

The Springs, Harbor Springs, MI 49740

(231) 526-2171; (800) 462-6963

ACCOMMODATIONS: 165 rooms in The Highland Inn, and 72 units in the new Heather Highlands Inn Condo Hotel. There are also many privately owned condominiums. Situated in northern Michigan, Boyne Highlands is just four miles from Lake Michigan.

AMENITIES: Two swimming pools, saunas, fishing, and four tennis courts. Horseback riding is available nearby. They also have a children's program and babysitting service. There are several dining rooms.

GOLF: The Moor Course, parring at 72, plays a monstrous 7,179/6,521/6,032/5,459 yards. The Heather links weighs in at an even more generous 7,218/6,554/6,090/5,263 yards, also parring at 72. Heavily wooded hills and an abundance of water provide a wide variety of possible shots and a great deal of challenge. The Donald Ross Memorial Course came into play in the mid-1990s. This course duplicates 18 of the most memorable holes designed by Mr. Ross, who was one of the world's finest golf architects. Examples include Pinehurst Course #2, Oakland Hills, Royal Dornoch, Seminole, and many others. This unique and intriguing golf adventure plays 6,840/6,308/4,977 yards and has a par of 72.

RATES: (EP) Lodgings - $115/$160/$185. Green fees - $75/$105, including cart. Golf package - two nights/two days (includes MAP, lodging, green fees, cart), $616/$916 per couple.

ARRIVAL: By air - Emmett County Airport (11 miles from Boyne Highlands).

Boyne Mountain

Highway 131, Boyne Falls, MI 49713

(231) 549-6000; (800) 462-6963

ACCOMMODATIONS: 400 rooms, including the Deer Lake Beach Villas, each with private suite and full kitchen; the Mountain Villa condominium complex; the Edelweiss Lodge; the Boynehof Lodge; the Cliff Dweller; and the Main Lodges.

AMENITIES: Three swimming pools, saunas, fishing, sailing, the Beach Club, and a tennis complex with 14 courts. There are also several restaurants on the property.

GOLF: The par-72 Alpine Links course plays 7,017/6,546/6,014/4,986 yards. The Boyne Monument Championship Course, which opened in early 1986, stretches out 7,086/6,377/5,744/4,904 yards, also parring at 72.

RATES: (EP) Lodgings - $89/$375. Green fees - $65/$110, including cart. Golf package - two nights/two days (includes lodging, MAP, green fees, and cart), $576/$736 per couple.

ARRIVAL: By air - Traverse City. By private aircraft - Boyne Mountain, 4,200-foot lighted runway. By car - off US 131, one mile south of Boyne Falls.

Crystal Mountain

12500 Crystal Mountain Drive, Thompsonville, MI 49683

(231) 378-2000; (800) 968-7686

ACCOMMODATIONS: Varied, including one- or two-bedroom condominiums, 38 poolside rooms and The Colony rooms, with private Jacuzzi/whirlpool baths. There are also the Village Chalets and Resort Homes – each fully equipped for housekeeping.

AMENITIES: Indoor and outdoor swimming pools, two tennis courts, fitness center, jogging, and biking trails; boating, charter fishing, and canoeing are available on the nearby Betsie and Platte Rivers. During the summer months they offer "Camp Crystal," a children's program. The main dining room offers dancing and entertainment.

GOLF: The 27-hole course offers the following combinations: the Mountain Meadows/Ridge nines configuration measures 6,689/5,955/4,983 yards, parring at 72; Creek/Meadows has 6,320/5,657/4,859 yards, with a par of 71; the Ridge/Creek plays 6,450/5,698/4,784 yards, also parring at 71. There is plenty of undulating terrain, with trees, well-trapped greens, and water coming into play. A new nine is under development, which will turn this into a 36-hole layout.

RATES: (EP) Lodgings - $79/$269. Condos - $139/$399. Green fees - $45/$70, including cart. Golf packages are available.

ARRIVAL: By air - Traverse City or Cadillac (36 miles). By car - north on US 31, turn east on County Road 602, six miles north of Bearlake.

Garland Resort

Country Road 489, Lewiston, MI 49756

(517) 786-2211; (800) 968-0042

ACCOMMODATIONS: 25 guest rooms in the inn and 32 rooms, including four suites, in the south wing; most with either balcony or patio. There are also 28 one-bedroom and 16 two-bedroom, two-bath villas. Some lodgings feature a shower/spa; others have Jacuzzis. A hotel with 32 units has been added.

AMENITIES: Practice putting green and driving range, lighted tennis courts, bicycle trails, outdoor swimming pool, indoor lap pool, Jacuzzi, sauna, whirlpool, and exercise and weight rooms. Winter sports include 50 kilometers of cross-country skiing and a lighted ice skating rink. Herman's Restaurant has a wide selection ranging from casual snacks to fine dining

GOLF: The Swampfire course weighs in with a yardage of 6,868/6,419/5,937/4,812 and a par of 72. Water comes into play on 15 of the 18 holes. The Reflections course, the newest addition, measures a more modest 6,464/5,966/4,767 yards, also parring at 72. Don't let the yardage fool you. While this gem does not have much water (in play on only seven holes), sand traps are sprinkled all over the place. Its tree-lined, tight fairways will keep you honest. The Reflections layout has six par 5s, six par 4s and six par 3s. I can't recall another course with this configuration.

The Monarch course is relatively open, with water a factor on 13 holes. It measures an outrageous 7,101/6,585/6,056/4,861, with a par of 72. Last, but by no means least, is Herman's Nine, parring at 36.

RATES: (EP) Lodgings - $189/$209/$306. Green fees - $60/$80/$100, including cart. Golf package - one night/one day (includes lodging, MAP, golf with cart, club storage, tax), $389/$439 per couple – available weekdays only. Rates are for the peak summer season.

ARRIVAL: By air - Detroit. By private aircraft - Garland (5,000-foot paved runway on the property). By car - from I-75, take Exit 254. After the exit turn right at the first light and take M-72 east to Luzerne (16 miles). Turn left (north) at the blinking light on County Road 489, then travel 14 miles to the resort.

Grand Traverse Resort

6300 North US 31, Acme, MI 49610

(231) 938-2100; (800) 748-0303

ACCOMMODATIONS: The 17-story, 186-room Tower is the centerpiece of the resort; it has one floor with over 20,000 square feet of shopping space. The six-story Resort Hotel offers 238 rooms, while The Beach Club on East Grand Traverse Bay provides additional accommodations, with 236 studio and one-bedroom condominiums.

AMENITIES: Weight rooms, aerobic classes, tennis on indoor and outdoor courts, racquetball, indoor and outdoor pools, saunas, and whirlpools. Deep-water charter fishing, canoeing, sailing, hunting, and water-skiing are also available. There are a variety of restaurants and lounges: the Trillium, Paparazzi, and the Sandtrap Restaurant to name a few. One restaurant is designed with the kitchen in full display of the guests; you will be able to watch them prepare and cook your meal.

GOLF: The Spruce Run course designed by Bill Newcomb, a par-71/72, reaches out 6,579/5,885/4,973 yards. The Bear Course, home of the Michigan State Open, measures 7,065/6,176/5,281 yards. A Jack Nicklaus-designed layout, it pars at 72. The Bear presents several different challenges, including multi-level fairways, many extremely deep bunkers, four lakes, and water hazards on 10 holes. All in all it is one tough golf course. The scorecard says, "Attention golfers, beware of deep bunkers and terraced fairways." I suggest you pay attention to those words.

Two new layouts will be added: The Northern Knight, a Gary Player layout and, later, a Lee Trevino signature course. The CompuSport Golf School is available at Grand Traverse.

RATES: (EP) Lodgings - $235/$265/$275. Green fees - Bear Course, $110, including cart; Resort Course, $80. Golf package - two nights/two days (includes lodging, two rounds of golf with cart), $726/$774 per couple. There is an additional charge of $30 per person to play the Bear Course. Rates are for June through August.

ARRIVAL: By air - Traverse City. By car - US 31, six miles north of Traverse City.

Gull Lake View Golf Club

7417 M-89, Richland, MI 49083

(616) 731-5013; (800) 432-7971

ACCOMMODATIONS: 40 Fairway Villas and 40 two-bedroom, two-bath units with kitchen and living room.

GOLF: There are four golf courses here. The West measures 6,300/6,058/5,216 yards and pars at 71/72. The East Course, while shorter, plays 6,002/5,546/4,918 yards and pars at 70. It provides its own stimulation with water on 10 holes, tree-lined fairways, and small greens. The Bedford course, parring at 72, also gets a little exciting with its rather long yardage of 6,890/6,554/6,076/5,106. The newest of the group is the par-72 Stonehenge course. On rolling, wooded terrain, it reaches out 6,656/6,234/5,775/5,191 yards.

RATES: (EP) Villas - $264. Green fees - $31/$34, carts $25. Golf packages are available.

ARRIVAL: By air - Kalamazoo. By car - I-94, Exit 85.

The Inn at Bay Harbor

3600 Village Drive

Bay Harbor, MI 49770

(231) 439-4000; (800) 462-6963

This resort lies on a very large development property that includes approximately 1,000 feet of frontage along Lake Michigan.

ACCOMMODATIONS: The Inn at Bay Harbor is a magnificent six-story structure with 130 rooms, including 80 suites.

AMENITIES: Five tennis courts, a pool and hot tub, plus a total of six restaurants in the area, including the Inn and one located at the golf course. There is a very large (115 slips) marina that is part of this resort complex.

GOLF: The present layout includes 27 holes, much of it running along the shores of the lake. The Preserve plays 3,378 yards, The Quarry Nine measures 3,348 yards and The Links nine measures 3,342 yards. Each nine pars at 36, and each offers a variety of golfing experiences – from 160-foot bluffs to traditional woodland holes. Some are even routed through a former shale quarry.

RATES: Rooms - $280. Suites - $395 and up. Green fees - $105/$125, including cart.

ARRIVAL: By air - Pelleston Airport. By car - take 31 south to Petoskey, then continue approximately two miles to Bay Harbor.

McGuire's Motor Lodge & Resort

Mackinaw Trail, Cadillac, MI 49601

(231) 775-9947; (800) 632-7302

ACCOMMODATIONS: 123 well-appointed guest rooms.

AMENITIES: Heated indoor pool, sauna, whirlpool spa, two game rooms, and tennis on two outdoor courts with additional courts available in Cadillac. Across the street are 14 racquetball courts and a complete athletic club, including weight rooms. Dining is in the Terrace Room.

GOLF: There are 27 holes. The Spruce course stretches out 6,601/6,202/5,217 yards, with a par of 71; the Norway, a nine-hole affair playing 2,792 yards, pars at 36.

RATES: (EP) Lodgings - $99/$109/$139/$199. Green fees - $44, including cart. Golf package - two nights/three days (includes lodging, two breakfasts, one dinner, unlimited green fees), $598 per couple.

ARRIVAL: By air - Cadillac. By car - one mile south of Cadillac on Highway 131.

Otsego Club & Resort

PO Box 556, Gaylord, MI 49735

(517) 732-5181; (800) 752-5510

ACCOMMODATIONS: 142 guest rooms plus two condominiums. Gaylord is in the northern region of the Michigan peninsula.

Michigan

AMENITIES: Hiking trails, a heated swimming pool, four tennis courts. Both dining rooms in the Main Lodge offer views and a menu selection.

GOLF: The Hidden Valley Club Course, a William H. Diddle design, plays 6,386/6,123/5,591 yards, with a par of 71/73. The resort also offers golf on two additional courses – the Lake and the newer Loon layouts.

RATES: (EP) Rooms - $99/$109. Green fees - $55/$50, including cart. Golf package - two nights/three days (includes lodging, golf with cart), $249 per couple.

ARRIVAL: By air - Detroit. By private aircraft - Otsego Airport. By car - one mile east of Gaylord on M-32.

Schuss Mountain Resort

Schuss Mountain Road, Mancelona, MI 49659

(231) 533-8621; (800) 678-4111

ACCOMMODATIONS: The Village Square has fully equipped condominiums. The Sudendorf Condos and Schuss Mountain Chalets are located a short distance away, and offer sleeping arrangements for two to six people.

AMENITIES: Outdoor swimming pool, six tennis courts, bicycling, volleyball and, on nearby Torch Lake, sailing, canoeing, snorkeling, and wind-surfing. Dining is provided in the Ivanhof. In the evening it transforms itself into the Supper Club, featuring the "Schussycats," 11 collegiate waiters and waitresses singing the hits of the 40s through the 80s.

GOLF: Schuss Mountain Golf Club stretches out a rather substantial 6,922/6,394/5,383 yards and pars at 72. It's an interesting affair, with large greens, tree-lined fairways, strategic water holes, and traps that blend with the terrain.

RATES: (EP) Lodgings - $138/$185/$340. Green fees - $65/$125, including cart. Golf package: two nights/two days (includes lodging, MAP, two rounds of golf, club storage), $578/$720 per couple. Rates are for mid-June through August.

ARRIVAL: By air - Traverse City. By private aircraft - Bellaire. By car - six miles west of Mancelona, on Highway 88.

Shanty Creek/Schuss Mountain Resort

Shanty Creek Road, Bellaire, MI 49615

(231) 533-8621; (800) 678-4111

ACCOMMODATIONS: Guest rooms and suites in the Main Lodge, the Trapper Lodge, the Timberline Studio Apartments, and many one- to three-bedroom condominiums. Some accommodations are equipped with whirlpool baths; all are well-appointed.

AMENITIES: Fishing, tennis, golf, bicycling, bowling, horseback riding, water-skiing on Torch Lake, canoeing, indoor and outdoor swimming pools or lake swimming, racquetball, skeet shooting, and a one-mile exercise course. For dining, there are numerous choices: the Main Dining Room, the pro shop Snack Bar, the Cafeteria, or La Bodega Deli, which is located in the village.

GOLF: The resort's Shanty Creek Course is a Bill Diddle design; it weighs in at 6,559/6,197/5,285 yards with a par of 72/74. This layout has undulating fairways, 35 traps, and tough greens to keep your attention. Fairly wide open, it has water on only one hole.

The Legend, an Arnold Palmer design, is the newest addition. Also parring at 72, it measures 6,764/6,269/5,801/4,953 yards. Many say this is Palmer's best effort. The first hole is, in my opinion, the most beautiful opening golf hole I have ever played. A tree-lined par 5, it has a 175-foot drop from the tee area to the green. The fourth, a par 3 playing 135 yards, gives you a drop of 180 feet to the green.

RATES: (EP) Lodgings - $138/$185/$340. Green fees - $65/$125, including cart. Golf package - two nights/three days (includes lodging, golf, cart, club storage), $578/$720 per couple. Rates are for mid-June through August.

ARRIVAL: By air - Cherry Capital. By private aircraft - Antrim County Airport (5,000-foot surfaced and lighted runway, two miles). By car - from Mancelona take Route 88 west.

Michigan

Sugar Loaf Resort

4500 Sugar Loaf Mountain Road, Cedar, MI 49621

(231) 228-1808; (800) 952-6390

ACCOMMODATIONS: 150 rooms in the lodge, with additional lodging offered in two- to four-bedroom townhouses.

AMENITIES: Five outdoor tennis courts, three swimming pools (one indoor, two outdoor), weight room and Jacuzzi. Nearby Lake Michigan provides many water-oriented activities. The Four Seasons Dining Room provides a spectacular view of the mountains and Lake Michigan beyond.

GOLF: The Sugar Loaf Golf Club course stretches out 6,813/ 6,124/5,134 yards. The men's par is 72, while the ladies' is set at 74. Their 8th hole will make a believer out of you: it's a 360-yard par 4, running between two ponds, with five traps between the ponds and the green. It calls for a fast exit to the 19th hole. There is also a newer 18, designed by Arnold Palmer & Associates. Called the Lakeview Golf Club Course, it reaches out a substantial 6,671 yards, with a par of 71.

RATES: (EP) Lodgings - $109/$129. Green fees - $45, including cart. Golf packages are available. Rates are for July-August.

ARRIVAL: By air - Traverse City. Private aircraft - 3,700 foot paved runway on property. By car - 18 miles northwest of Traverse City on Route 651.

Treetop Resort

3962 Wilkinson Road, Gaylord, MI 49735

(517) 732-6711; (800) 444-6711

ACCOMMODATIONS: 172 hotel rooms and suites, and individual chalets with kitchenettes. This year-round resort is centrally located in the upper part of Michigan's lower peninsula.

AMENITIES: Indoor and outdoor swimming pools, indoor and outdoor whirlpool spas, two saunas, exercise rooms, tennis courts, hiking trails, volleyball, putting greens and, of course, golf. During the winter months there is cross-country skiing (offered at night as well), ice skating, and downhill skiing. Dining and nightly entertainment are offered in the Ale House Dining Room and Lounge.

GOLF: The Treetop Links is a Robert Trent Jones, Sr. layout. It is considered by many, including Mr. Jones, to be a masterpiece. After having played this course I would have to agree. The par-71 course reaches out 7,060/6,399/5,817/4,972 yards. Built on undulating terrain, it has tree-lined fairways and some of the most interesting water hazards we have seen. While the wet stuff comes into play on only five holes, the eighth green will get your attention. It is a beautiful layout and, though not a backbreaker, will require your attention and patience.

Theother course, designed by Tom Fazio, was the first Fazio course to be built in Michigan. Parring at 72, it plays 6,871/6,280/5,821/5,045 yards. While generally open, the well- bunkered course has a variety of settings, ranging from spectacular views to park-like surroundings. Mr. Fazio felt that, because of the general topography, there was no need to introduce a great deal of water. Although certainly challenging, the course is "user friendly" and playable.

RATES: (EP) Lodgings - $115/$175. Green fees - $74/$84, including cart. Golf package: one night/one day (includes lodgings, one round of golf, carts, taxes), $258 per couple.

ARRIVAL: By air - Mackinaw City (55 miles). By car - from Lansing, travel State 27 intersecting I-75 approximately 170 miles north.

Waterfront Park Inn

2061 US 31 North, Traverse City, MI 49685

(616) 938-1100; (800) 551-9283

ACCOMMODATIONS: 128 guest rooms, including suites. Eight of the rooms have a two-person whirlpool tub, living room, and wet bar. All have remote-controlled cable TV. The Inn is set along a 750-foot stretch of beach on east Grand Traverse Bay.

AMENITIES: Indoor heated swimming pool, whirlpools, spa, tanning booth, exercise room, and beach. Rental equipment includes wave runners, paddleboats, windsurfers and Hobie Cats; there is also a boat launch ramp. The Reflections Restaurant specializes in seafood.

GOLF: The High Point Golf Course, a Tom Doales design, is a bit over two miles away. It offers rolling terrain, trees, and water on only two holes. Parring at 71/72, the course measures 6,819/ 6,140/5,258 yards.

RATES: (EP) Lodgings - $163/$173/$225. Green fees - $62/ $64, including cart. Golf package: two nights/two days (includes lodging, golf and cart), $623/$753 per couple.

ARRIVAL: By air - Traverse City Airport. By car - the resort is on US Highway North at Four Mile Road, two miles east of Traverse City.

Woodmoor Resort

26 Maxton Road, Drummond Island, MI 49726

(906) 493-1000; (800) 999-6343

ACCOMMODATIONS: 40-room lodge and 25 waterfront or woodside fully equipped homes, ranging from one-bedroom/one-bath units to five-bedroom/five-bath units.

AMENITIES: Tennis, platform tennis, outdoor pool and whirlpool, sauna, weight room, sailboat rentals, horseback riding, mountain biking, bowling and fishing. For dining, you may choose from the Bayside, The Waterfront or Pins Bar & Grille.

GOLF: The Rock Golf Course, designed by Harry Bowers, is a traditional layout with tree-lined fairways, traps, and water in play on eight holes. Reaching out a substantial 6,837/6,190/ 6,679/4,992 yards, it pars at 71. For tee times call (800) 999-6343.

RATES: Lodgings - $89/$140. Homes - $130/$575. Green fees - $65, including cart. Golf package - one day/one night (includes lodging, one round of golf with cart), midweek $290, weekends $314 per couple.

ARRIVAL: By air - commercial flights (Pellston, MI). By car - from I-75 travel east on M-134 to the village of DeTour. Take the ferry to Drummond Island and follow signs to the resort.

Minnesota

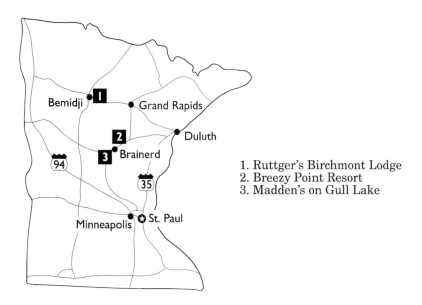

1. Ruttger's Birchmont Lodge
2. Breezy Point Resort
3. Madden's on Gull Lake

Breezy Point Resort

HCR 2 Box 70, Breezy Point, MN 56472

(218) 562-7811; (800) 432-3777

ACCOMMODATIONS: 250 guest accommodations in the Lodge Apartments on Pelican Lake, Pinewood Cabanas, Executive Beach Houses, and Beachside Apartments. Recently added to this mix are 32 Point Place one- and two-bedroom condominiums, each with fully equipped kitchen, dishwasher, microwave, and washer/dryer. Breezy Point is 140 miles north of the Minneapolis- St. Paul Airport.

AMENITIES: Tennis on four Laykold courts, indoor and outdoor swimming pools, horseback riding at nearby stables, and bicycling. At the marina, there is fishing, canoeing, powerboating, and sailing. Dining facilities include the Marina Restaurant overlooking Breezy Bay, and the Captain's Cove at the Breezy Center.

GOLF: The Breezy Point course, named "Traditional," plays 5,192/5,127 with a par of 68/72. The second course, "Excellence," has a yardage of 6,601/6,602/5,718 with a par of 72/76.

RATES: (EP) Lodgings - $115/$145/$300. Green fees - $38/$48, carts $32. Rates are for the summer season. Many different package plans are available.

ARRIVAL: By air - Minneapolis-St. Paul, or Brainerd Airport. By car - take I-94 north to Monticello, then go right to Highway 371. Turn left (north) on 371 going beyond Brainerd to Pequot Lakes. At this point take a right (east) and continue on to resort.

Madden's on Gull Lake

8001 Pine Beach Peninsula, Brainerd, MN 56401

(218) 829-2811; (800) 233-2934

ACCOMMODATIONS: In Madden Lodge, Madden Inn & Golf Club and Madden Pine Portage.

AMENITIES: Six Laykold tennis courts, badminton courts, official USA croquet facilities, indoor and outdoor swimming pools (six in total), saunas, whirlpools, game rooms and, in season, a children's program. The lake offers opportunities for sailing, water-skiing, and fishing, or you can just relax on one of the three beaches. Restaurants include the main dining room of Madden Inn and Golf Club, the Coffee Shop, and the O'Madden Pub.

GOLF: There are two 18-hole courses and a par-3, nine-hole affair. The par-72 Pine Beach East layout plays 5,920/5,498 yards. The Pine Beach West course measures 5,086/4,725 with a par of 67/69.

RATES: (EP) Lodgings - $105/$153/$250. Package plans are available. Green fees - $25, carts $30. Rates are for July-August.

ARRIVAL: By air - Brainerd. By private aircraft - East Gull Lake. By car - from Brainerd, 4½ miles on 371, left on 77 for 7½ miles.

Ruttger's Birchmont Lodge

530 Birchmont Beach Road, Bemidji, MN 56601

(218) 751-1630; (888) 788-8437

ACCOMMODATIONS: Rooms and suites in the main lodge, or one-to four-bedroom cottages with living room and fireplace. This family-style resort is on the northern shore of Lake Bemidji.

AMENITIES: Two heated pools, four tennis courts, 1,600 feet of sandy beach, playground, recreation rooms, paddle-boats, kayaks, canoes, sailboats, water-skiing, and a supervised recreational program for the younger set. The Lakefront dining room prepares its own pastries daily. (I defy you to pass on these.)

GOLF: The Bemidji Town & Country Club, site of the annual Birchmont International Golf Tournament, reaches out 6,385/6,198/5,489 yards; it pars at 72/74.

RATES: (EP) Lodgings - $108/$279. Cottages - $136/$165/$212. Green fees - $40/$45, carts $26.

ARRIVAL: By air - Bemidji. By car - five miles north of Bemidji on old US 71.

Mississippi

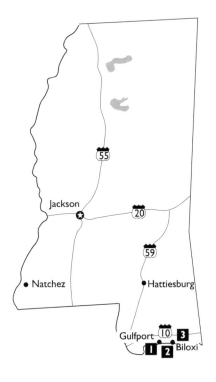

1. Diamondhead Resort
2. Hickory Hill Resort
3. Gulf Hills Resort/St. Andrews on the Gulf

Diamondhead Resort

100 NW Interchange, Bay St. Louis, MS 39520

(601) 255-3550; (800) 221-2423

ACCOMMODATIONS: One- to three-bedroom townhouses adjacent to the golf course, fully equipped for housekeeping.

AMENITIES: Eight tennis courts, and fishing and boating from Diamondhead's marina. Restaurant and lounge facilities are at the Country Club and the less formal Yacht Club.

GOLF: The par-72 Cardinal has a healthy yardage of 6,730/6,086/5,378/5,033. The Pine Course, also parring at 72, plays 6,832/6,358/5,890/5,280 yards. Both layouts can test you with their long tees, tree-lined fairways and undulating greens.

RATES: (EP) Lodgings - $79/$84. Green fees - $62, including cart. Golf packages are available. Peak golf season is March-April.

ARRIVAL: By air - New Orleans. By private aircraft - Diamondhead (3,800-foot lighted runway). By car - I-90, 58 miles east of New Orleans. Take the Diamondhead exit.

Gulf Hills Resort

13701 Paso Road, Ocean Springs, MS 39564

(228) 875-4211; (800) 875-4211

ACCOMMODATIONS: 65 rooms.

AMENITIES: Fishing, swimming pool, and children's playground. Good food is a tradition at the Gulf Hills, with meals served both buffet and menu style.

GOLF: The course, now more than 65 years old, takes advantage of its Bayou country location, with towering oaks, pines, magnolia trees and water. Playing 6,376/6,200/5,438 yards, it pars at 71/72.

RATES: (EP) Lodgings - $60. Green fees - $45, including cart. Golf package (includes lodging, breakfast, green fees) - $116 per couple per night.

ARRIVAL: By air - Gulfport-Biloxi (17 miles) By car - from I-10 south, at Ocean Springs take Exit 50.

Hickory Hill Resort

7900 Martin Bluff Road, Gautier, MS 39553

(228) 497-5150; (800) 568-3155

ACCOMMODATIONS: 80 two-bedroom/two-bath villas, each with fully equipped kitchen, fireplace and balcony.

AMENITIES: Boat rentals, scheduled fishing trips, fitness center, racquetball courts, swimming pool, Jacuzzi, sauna, two tennis courts, miniature golf and a full 18-hole championship course. Weather permitting, you can enjoy outdoor dining and a spectacular view of the Singing River.

GOLF: The course, rated among the top 10 public layouts in Mississippi, reaches out a substantial 7,003/6,517/5,229 yards and carries a par of 72. Water in play on 10 holes and bordering pine trees make it a real tester. For tee times, call (601) 497-2372. There are several additional golf courses within a 10-minute drive.

RATES: (EP) Lodgings - $125. Green fees - $42, including cart. Golf package (two-night minimum; two days/two nights, includes lodging, two rounds of golf, including cart), $398 per couple. Rates quoted are for the peak season of February-April.

ARRIVAL: By air - Biloxi/Gulfport Airport. By car - from I-10 take Exit #61 (Gautier/Vancleave exit). Go north and turn right onto Frontage Road. Drive one mile and take a left onto Martin Bluff Road. From there it's a mile to Hickory Hill.

St. Andrews on The Gulf

Golfing Green Drive, Ocean Springs, MS 39564

(228) 872-1000; (888) 872-4961

ACCOMMODATIONS: There are fully equipped townhouses, apartments and condominiums, ranging from one to three bedrooms, all with 1½ baths, kitchen, living room, and dining room.

AMENITIES: Three lighted tennis courts and an Olympic-size swimming pool. There is also a restaurant.

GOLF: St. Andrews Golf Course, parring at 72, plays 6,460/6,037/4,960 yards. With water coming into play on 15 or 16 holes, liberal use of bunkers and several dogleg fairways, this becomes an interesting layout.

RATES: (EP) Lodgings - $79/$99. Green fees - $45, including cart.

ARRIVAL: By air - Biloxi. By car - US 90; turn south at the intersection with State Highway 57. Follow signs for 3½ miles.

Missouri

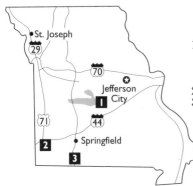

1. Lake of the Ozarks
   Dogwood Hills Golf Club & Resort
   The Lodge of Four Seasons
   Marriott's Tan-Tar-A Resort
2. Loma Linda Country Club
3. Pointe Royale Condominium Resort/
   Thousand Hills Golf Resort

The Branson Area

We had heard of Branson prior to our arrival but where not pre-pared for what we found. At first we had chuckled at the idea that Branson, Missouri could have as many, let alone more, shows and entertainment than New York City. After visiting the area, I stopped snickering, and started to pay attention.

Space will not allow a listing of all shows, but perhaps a short reference will do. They offer everything from Music Hall presentations to Andy Williams Theater, to Will Rogers Theater. In total there are some 70 shows going on day and night.

Within the area are several golf courses; two are golf resorts. Pointe Royale Condominiums with its championship golf course, and Thousand Hills Golf Resort. Although Thousand Hills has a par 64 executive layout, it is one that has embarrassed more than a few low-handicap players looking for any easy score. For reservations and tee times, call (800) 864-4145.

The area has one problem: traffic. At times it is difficult to get around this small town.

Pointe Royale
Condominium Resort

158-A Ponte Royale Drive, Branson, MO 65616

(417) 334-5614; (800) 962-4710; for show tickets (800) 233-7469

Pointe Royale is five minutes from Branson's Music Boulevard and offers a view of Lake Taneycomo.

ACCOMMODATIONS: 255 one- , two- and three-bedroom condominiums, situated along the fairways or greens. All feature living room, dining area and fully equipped kitchen.

AMENITIES: Two outdoor swimming pools, tennis courts, fishing and boating. There are also two dining rooms as well as cocktail lounges. There are a great many different restaurants within easy driving distance of the resort.

GOLF: The Pointe Royale Golf Course was built in 1986 and designed by Ault-Clark and Associates. Playing to a par of 70 it reaches out a modest 6,067/5,629/4,388 yards. The terrain is undulating with water coming into play on eight holes. Trees, sand and grass bunkers add to the challenge.

RATES: Lodgings - one-bedroom $119; on fairway - $139. There are several package plans. Green fees - $45. Rates are for June-October.

ARRIVAL: By air - Springfield-Branson Regional Airport (45 miles). By car - from Highway 65 traveling north, turn east onto Road 165. Drive approximately 7.3 miles and the resort will be on your right. The resort's entrance is directly across from the Welk Champagne Village.

The Lake Of
The Ozarks

Developed with the construction of Bagnell Dam on the Osage River in 1933, the 140-mile-long Lake of the Ozarks has 1,400 miles of shoreline. Three resorts in this area, Dogwood Hills, the

Lodge of the Four Seasons, and Marriott's Tan-Tar-A, are described on the following pages.

Dogwood Hills Golf Club

Route 4, Box 1300 State Road KK, Osage Beach, MO 65065

(573) 348-1735; (800) 220-6571

ACCOMMODATIONS: 45 rooms overlooking the golf course. There are also Fairway Villas with one to four bedrooms, featuring fully equipped kitchens, fireplaces, living and dining rooms.

AMENITIES: Fishing, boating, swimming in the lake or in their own heated pool. Mitch & Duff's Restaurant & Bar is in the clubhouse.

GOLF: The Dogwood Hills course shows a yardage of 6,105/ 5,893/5,262, parring at 71/73. They not only have a driving range, but a practice sand trap as well – something not found on many courses.

RATES: (EP) Lodgings - $72/$86/$97/$125. Green fees - $34/ $40, carts $28. Golf packages are available.

ARRIVAL: By air - Lee C. Fine Airport (25 minutes). By car - the resort is just off Highway 54 on State Route KK.

The Lodge Of Four Seasons

Lake Road HH, Lake Ozark, MO 65049

(573) 365-3000; (800) 843-5253

The Lodge of Four Seasons has been judged one of our Top 50 resorts. It is tucked away in a unique showcase of Japanese gardens and cascading waterfalls – truly a beautiful setting.

ACCOMMODATIONS: 311 rooms, ranging from lakeside rooms and suites to fully equipped condominiums and villas.

AMENITIES: 23 tennis courts, complete health spa program, five indoor and outdoor swimming pools, water-skiing, horseback riding, fishing (from their own 200-slip marina), trap shooting and bowling. Another option: the resort has two cruise boats, the 150-passenger *Seasons Queen* and the 42-seat *Four Seasons Two.*

Dining at the Four Seasons is a treat you will long remember. There is the Toledo Room (a four-star dining room), and HK's Steakhouse, which has a relaxed country-club atmosphere overlooking the golf course. In addition, family-style dining is offered in Roseberry's Restaurant. Combined, they can destroy your will to stay trim.

GOLF: Robert Trent Jones, Sr., who designed the Four Seasons RTJ course, made it a thing of beauty and challenge. With a par of 71, it plays 6,404/5,772/5,198 yards. Shortly after its opening in 1974, the 13th hole was recognized as the apex of the course. It is bisected by an inlet of the lake. You will need all the cunning (or skill) you possess to avoid the water and the five hungry traps guarding the green. There is also the Seasons Ridge Golf Club. Designed by Ken Kavanaugh, it reaches out 6,416/6,020/5,461/4,657 yards, with a par of 72. There are elevation changes of some 180 feet. We played this layout and found it a most delightful golfing experience. Occasionally it looks much more difficult from the tee box than it really is. What a wonderful surprise that becomes.

RATES: (EP) Lodgings - $189/$275/$299. Green fees - $53/$85, including cart. Golf package - two nights/two days (includes standard room, green fees, cart), weekdays $259, weekends $299 per couple. Rates are for June-August.

ARRIVAL: By air - Jefferson City. By car - US 54 to Bagnell Dam, turn left onto Business Highway 54. Drive approximately one mile, exit left to Lake Road HH, and follow it to the resort.

Loma Linda Country Club

Route 5, Box 1000, Joplin, MO 64804

(417) 623-2901; (800) 633-3542

ACCOMMODATIONS: 100 one- and two-bedroom villas as well as some private homes. Set on 2,350 acres, this resort/residential community has a great deal to offer.

AMENITIES: Three tennis and racquetball courts, a 25-meter lighted swimming pool, five miles of equestrian trails (located nearby and with riding instructions available), and excellent fishing facilities. There is also a dining room, lounge, and pro shop.

GOLF: The course, situated on slightly rolling terrain, comes complete with contoured, elevated greens, several natural water hazards (water on nine holes), and tree-lined fairways. The North Course plays 6,628/6,086/5,333 yards and pars at 71/73. The newer South Course reaches out a modest 6,397/5,674/4,706 yards with a par of 71.

RATES: (EP) Lodging $60/$80/$135. Green fees - $24/$29. Golf package - two nights/three days (includes lodging, green fees, dinner each night), $220/$300 per couple.

ARRIVAL: By air - Joplin (10 miles). By car - take 43 south to US 44 west. Continue to the Baxter Springs exit and follow signs to the resort.

Missouri

Marriott's Tan-Tar-A Resort

State Road KK, Osage Beach, MO 65065

(573) 348-3131; (800) 826-8272

ACCOMMODATIONS: Rooms or suites in the hotel, as well as villas or "estate-style" homes. Several washer/dryer units are available for guest use.

AMENITIES: Six outdoor and two indoor tennis courts, four indoor racquetball courts, five pools, bowling, and the new Windjammer Spa, offering a wide spectrum of programs. Several types of watercraft can be rented, ranging from water-ski and trolling boats to canoes. For dining, there is the Black Bear Lodge, the Windrose, and, at the golf course, the Oaks Restaurant, open for breakfast and lunch.

GOLF: The Oaks golf course was designed by Van Hagge and Bruce Devlin. It plays a respectable 6,442/6,002/5,329/3,943 yards and pars at 71/70. Accuracy, rather than distance, is the prime requirement on this layout. Watch the 16th hole, a par 3 with an elevated tee. Looking down, you will see water almost everywhere, and the green is guarded by two sand traps. Water, by the way, becomes a factor on 10 holes. A third nine, Hidden Lakes, plays 3,015/2,705 yards with a par of 35 from the men's tees and 2,232 yards parring at 36 for the ladies. The John Jacobs' Practical Golf School is available at this resort.

RATES: (EP) Lodgings - $175/$203/$346. Green fees - $69/$79, including cart. Golf package - two nights/two days (includes lodging, green fees, breakfast, club storage), $416/$482. Rates are for the summer season.

ARRIVAL: By air - Springfield (90 minutes). By car - take I-70 to Route 5, to Camdenton. Go east on Highway 54 for 10 miles to Lake Road KK, then take a left and drive two miles.

Montana

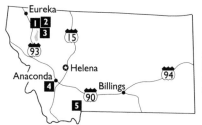

1. Grouse Mountain Lodge
2. Meadow Lakes Golf & Ski Resort
3. Marina Cay Resort
4. Fairmont Hot Springs Resort
5. Big Sky

Big Sky

PO Box 160001, Big Sky, MT 59716

(406) 995-4211; (800) 548-4486

The drive to this area is something you will long recall. The highway winds its way along the Gallatin River as it tumbles down from Lone Mountain (11,166 feet) and the high country. You can occasionally spot elk or moose, along with pools that cry to be fished.

ACCOMMODATIONS: 204 guest rooms in the main lodge, plus over 194 condominiums equipped with all-electric kitchens and fireplaces, many with private Jacuzzis.

AMENITIES: Swimming pools, saunas, Jacuzzis, health club,live entertainment, tennis courts, hayrides, and horseback riding. The Lodge has two restaurants and a saloon (Chet's Bar). During the winter there are 35 miles of ski slopes, four-passenger gondola lifts and double and triple chairlifts. At the base of the ski area are seven restaurants and two ski rental and repair shops.

GOLF: The Arnold Palmer-designed 18-hole course in the Meadow Village area stretches 6,748/6,115/5,374 yards; it has a par of 72. The elevation (some 6,500 feet above sea level) creates some interesting conditions for play. While relatively flat and open, it has mountain streams and ponds coming into contention on six holes.

RATES: (EP) Lodgings - $138/$191 and up. Green fees - $42/$55, carts $30. Golf packages are available. Rates are for summer.

ARRIVAL: By air - Bozeman (44 miles). By car - Route 191. South from Bozeman (44 miles), then turn right at the Conoco station.

Fairmont Hot Springs Resort

1500 Fairmont, Anaconda, MT 59711

(406) 797-3241; (800) 443-2381

ACCOMMODATIONS: 151 guest rooms, equipped with saunas.

AMENITIES: Trail riding (with experienced guides) and fishing for some of the most belligerent brook, brown, rainbow, and native cutthroat trout found anywhere. There are two indoor and two larger-than-Olympic-size swimming pools. Dining is available in either the main dining room or in the coffee shop.

GOLF: The resort has a 6,732-yard, par-72 course. The women's tees are set at a long 6,193 yards, parring at 74 – a long reach for most ladies.

RATES: (EP) Lodgings - $109/$229. Rates include use of mineral water pools and saunas. Green fees - $27/$35, carts $26.

ARRIVAL: By air - Butte (15 miles). By car - I-90 Exit 211, then south approximately three miles.

Grouse Mountain Lodge

1205 Highway 93W, Whitefish, MT 59937

(406) 862-3000; (800) 321-8822

ACCOMMODATIONS: 145 guest rooms, including 10 loft rooms with kitchenettes. Grouse Mountain Lodge opened in 1984, and is located just 27 miles from Glacier National Park.

AMENITIES: Indoor swimming pool, sauna, one indoor and two outdoor spas. Tennis is available across the road. Only eight miles from the fabulous ski area of Big Mountain, and with transportation provided by the Lodge, Grouse Mountain becomes a base for many other activities during the winter months. Dining is available in the 100-seat Logan's Bar and Grill.

GOLF: Whitefish Lake Golf Club has 27 holes. The Woods/Mountain nines par at 72/73 and reach out for a total of 6,548/6,322/5,593 yards. The Mountain/Lake combination weighs in at 6,458/6,200/5,489 yards, also parring at 72/73, while the Woods/Lake plays 6,460/6,302/5,590 yards and pars at 72. Though the fairways are not particularly narrow or tight, these tree-lined layouts bring water into play on a total of six holes.

RATES: (EP) Lodgings - $179/$239. Green fees - $39, carts $30. There are golf packages available. Rates are for May-September.

ARRIVAL: By air - Glacier International (20 minutes with pickup by Lodge). By car - one mile west of Whitefish on Highway 93W.

Marina Cay Resort

PO Box 663, Bigfork, MT 59911

(406) 837-5861; (800) 433-6516

ACCOMMODATIONS: One- to three-bedroom condominium suites, each fully equipped for housekeeping.

AMENITIES: A few steps from the lodging is Quincy's, offering a smorgasbord of amenities: lounge, restaurant, swimming pool and nearby marina. Boating activities range from water-skiing and windsurfing to sunset cruises. In addition, trips can be arranged on the *Questa*, a world-class 51-foot racing sloop. During the winter months, some of the best downhill skiing to be found anywhere is on nearby Big Mountain. There are also many miles of cross-country ski trails.

GOLF: Less than two miles away is the Eagle Bend Golf Club. Designed by William Hull & Associates, this beautifully manicured layout plays 6,758/6,237/5,398 yards and pars at 72. A well-trapped layout, with aspen, birch, and pine trees becoming an occasional nuisance, it brings water into play on eight holes.

RATES: (EP) Lodgings - $109/$185. Green fees - $64, carts $28. Rates are mid-July to late August.

ARRIVAL: By air - Kalispell (15 miles). By car - US 93 south to the intersection of State Road 82. Turn east to Bigfork.

Meadow Lake Golf & Ski Resort

1415 Tamarack Lane, Columbia Falls, MT 59912

(406) 892-7601; (800) 321-4653

You could easily get carried away attempting to describe the magnificent beauty of this area. It is also one of the few places in the world where your golf cart could get bashed by a moose.

ACCOMMODATIONS: 40 one- and two-bedroom condominiums, as well as villa homes – all of which border Meadow Lake's first and 18th fairways. Fully equipped, each unit features such amenities as a woodburning fireplace, all-electric kitchen with dishwasher, microwave oven, blender, and toaster oven, washer/dryer, barbecue, TV in both living room and master bedroom, and VCR.

AMENITIES: Tennis and outdoor heated swimming pool and Jacuzzi (even though it is heated 12 months a year, remember you have to get out). In addition, there is excellent trout fishing on the Meadow's private lake and horseback riding five miles away. During winter there is cross-country skiing, ice skating, and daily transportation to one of the finest downhill ski areas in the country – nearby Big Mountain. Should you choose not to cook for yourself, try Tracy's Restaurant and Lounge.

GOLF: The Meadow Lake Course, reaching out 6,574/6,321/5,890/5,488 yards, has a par of 71/72. This beautiful layout is surrounded by towering pines and gently rolling terrain. It is well trapped, with water coming into contention on seven holes. Early in the morning, it is not at all unusual to see elk, moose, or deer.

RATES: (EP) Lodgings - $139/$189/$249/$299. Green fees - $34, carts $26. Golf packages are available. Rates quoted are for mid-June through Labor Day.

ARRIVAL: By air - Kalispell Glacier Park Airport (seven miles). By car - travel north on Highway 2 to the intersection of Highway 40, then turn east to Meadow Lake Blvd. Travel north for one mile.

Nevada

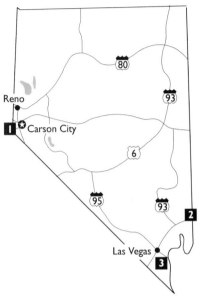

1. Hyatt Regency Lake Tahoe
   Incline Village
2. Oasis Resort Hotel & Casino
3. Showboat Hotel & CC

Hyatt Regency Lake Tahoe

Country Club Dr. & Lakeshore Rd., Incline Village, NV 89450

(702) 832-1234; (800) 233-1234

ACCOMMODATIONS: 460 guest rooms and suites; some suites are equipped with fireplaces.

AMENITIES: Water-skiing, boating, and use of the beach (no swimming, unless you have polar bear blood; Lake Tahoe is deep and very cold), three tennis courts (a total of 42 nearby), indoor health spa, outdoor heated pool, and, not far away, horseback riding. Dining choices include Hugo's Rotisserie and the Sierra Café.

GOLF: Two Robert Trent Jones courses are located at Incline Village. For a more complete description of these courses, refer to "Incline Village" below.

RATES: (EP) Lodgings - $195/$270/$320/$370. Suites - $600/$650. Green fees - $115, including cart. Executive course - $65, including cart.

ARRIVAL: By air - Reno. By car - US 395, south of Reno, turn off southwest on Highway 431.

Incline Village

PO Box 7107, Incline Village, NV 89451

(775) 831-3318; (800) 468-2463

ACCOMMODATIONS: Incline Village has a number of homes,condominiums and several casino/hotel complexes.

AMENITIES: Horseback riding, backpacking, tennis, and the full gamut of water sports on Lake Tahoe.

GOLF: The two courses near Incline Village are well worth playing. Surprisingly enough, one is an executive par 58, 3,513/3,002-yard course. It is absolutely not a pushover. The rugged terrain of this Robert Trent Jones design has embarrassed some fine golfers who were looking for an easy conquest. It has been referred to by more than one golfer as a "little stinker." The Championship golf course, also a Jones design, plays 6,910/6,446/5,350 yards and pars at 72. With mean fairway traps, a wandering stream, ponds, and towering pines, this is a fun but difficult layout.

RATES: There are so many different accommodations that it is not possible to quote exact rates. Contact the above address for reservations. When using the toll-free number you must ask for the BRAT Realty extension. Green fees - Incline Championship Course, $115, including cart; Executive Course, $50, including cart.

ARRIVAL: By air - Reno. By car - US 395, south of Reno, turn off southwest on Highway 431.

Oasis Resort Hotel Casino

PO Box 360, Mesquite, NV 89024

(702) 346-5232; (800) 621-0187

ACCOMMODATIONS: 720 guest rooms, including suites; 20 time-share units.

AMENITIES: Six swimming pools, three spas, horseback riding and a health club. There are four restaurants and a large casino.

GOLF: The Palms Golf Course was designed by William Hull. With 26 acres of lakes and several large, deep bunkers, this layout plays 7,022/6,284/5,162 yards and pars at 72. Water comes into the picture on eight holes. The front side is open and offers up curving, undulating terrain. The second nine is a canyon layout, featuring some definite elevation changes. Although the course is just a bit over three miles from the resort, it is in the state of Arizona. A second course came into play in late 1995. Reaching out 6,878 yards, with a par of 72, it has the same delightful challenges that the layout shows – undulating terrain, water and deep bunkers.

RATES: (EP) Lodgings - $55/$75. Green fees - $45/$55, including cart. Golf packages are available.

ARRIVAL: By air - Las Vegas (86 miles). By private aircraft - Mesquite (paved runway). By car - from Las Vegas travel north on I-15 exit at the first Mesquite/Bunkerville (Exit 120).

Showboat Hotel & Country Club

2800 East Fremont Street, Las Vegas, NV 89104

(702) 385-9123; (800) 826-2800

ACCOMMODATIONS: 500 guest rooms.

AMENITIES: 106-lane bowling facility and casino gambling. The various dining areas and the coffee shop offer a wide selection of dishes, ranging from foreign to American cuisine.

GOLF: The Desert Rose Golf course measures 6,511/6,135/ 5,458 yards and pars at 71. For tee times call (702) 431-4653.

RATES: (EP) Lodgings - $39/$59/$89.

ARRIVAL: By air - Las Vegas.

New Hampshire

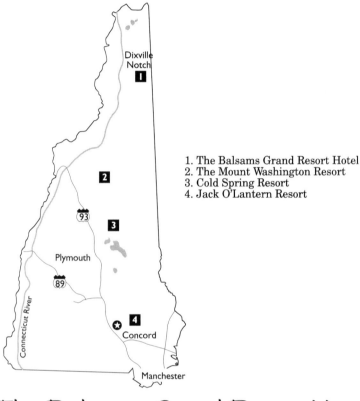

1. The Balsams Grand Resort Hotel
2. The Mount Washington Resort
3. Cold Spring Resort
4. Jack O'Lantern Resort

The Balsams Grand Resort Hotel

Route 26, Dixville Notch, NH 03576

(603) 255-3400; (800) 255-0600

The Balsams Grand Resort has been judged one of our Top 50 resorts. The magnificent scenery here is something you must experience. If you can imagine an area the size of Manhattan Island, with mountains and towering trees in place of tall buildings, and only 30 or so voting residents instead of millions, then you have a clear vision of this destination resort.

ACCOMMODATIONS: 332 rooms, including suites.

AMENITIES: Olympic-size heated pool, six tennis courts, and fishing (they can provide tackle, and no license is required). Rowboats, canoes and paddleboats are available for use on their private lake, and there are many walking, hiking and beautiful bicycling trails. In addition, the 250-seat theater presents different full-length films each evening. They also offer a fully organized and supervised children's program. The supervisors are, in most instances, local school teachers and are obviously well qualified. He programs are named "Wind Whistle" (ages five to 13) and "Wee Whistle" (ages three to four). The resort also provides the service of a wildlife biologist, Mr. Charles Willey, who will acquaint you and the children with the overwhelming amount of wildlife here.

During the winter the Balsams/Wilderness offers alpine and cross-country skiing. The menu in the 500-seat dining room changes daily and goes from one gastronomical pinnacle to another. Their staff is exceptionally well-trained and the service level reflects that. The orchestra plays nightly for dancing. I'm sure you will agree after dining here that the Mobil Four Star Award is richly deserved.

GOLF: The Panorama Golf Club course, built in 1912, was designed by architect Donald Ross. Parring at 72, it plays 6,804/6,097/5,069 yards. It is one tough layout. The slope rating of 136, from the blue and 130 from the white tees, may give you some clue as to the degree of difficulty. At least a portion of the challenge is formed by fact that it was built along the side of Keyser Mountain and that water comes into the picture on 11 holes. Putting these small, mounded and sometimes multi-level greens can be an experience to remember. You will swear that your ball occasionally takes an "uphill" break. The setting offers a magnificent view of two states and a portion of Canada. The Coashaukee course, a par-32, nine-hole, 1,917-yard layout, is also available. A great way to sharpen up your iron play.

RATES: (FAP) Lodgings - $410/$440/$470 per couple (based on double occupancy). Unlimited green fees, all meals, and tennis are included in the basic rates. Golf carts - $32.

ARRIVAL: By air - Portland, Maine (130 miles). By private aircraft - Berlin Airport (35 miles). By car - I-95 to Route 26, northeast to Dixville Notch.

New Hampshire

Cold Spring Resort

RR 3, PO Box 40, Plymouth, NH 03264

(603) 536-4600

ACCOMMODATIONS: Townhouses or homes, each with two bedrooms, kitchen, living room, fireplace and deck, are fully equipped for housekeeping.

AMENITIES: Heated outdoor pool, tennis, boating, canoeing, water-skiing, sailing and fishing at nearby Squam Lake. Dining is available at the Terrace on the Green Restaurant and Lounge.

GOLF: The White Mountain Country Club course, home of several New England tournaments, was designed by well-known golf course architect Geoffrey Cornish. This layout plays 6,600 yards and pars at 72.

RATES: (EP) Lodgings $91/$130. Green fees - $36, carts $22.

ARRIVAL: By air - Boston or Manchester. By car - I-93 to Exit 24 at Ashland. At bottom of ramp turn left onto Route 3. Go north for one mile until you see a Cold Spring sign. Turn right (before crossing bridge) and proceed for 2½ miles down North Ashland Road.

Jack O'Lantern Resort

PO Box A, Woodstock, NH 03293

(603) 745-8121; (800) 227-4454

ACCOMMODATIONS: Cottages, motel units and vacation homes. Jack O'Lantern rests in a quiet valley in the heart of the White Mountains, miles from even the thought of a traffic light.

AMENITIES: Two tennis courts, indoor and outdoor swimming pools, saunas, Jacuzzi, shuffleboard and ping-pong. The resort has two restaurants plus a poolside snack bar.

GOLF: This layout has a modest yardage of 5,829/4,725 and a par of 70. The Pemigewasset River makes a nuisance of itself, and that, along with the slightly undulating terrain and several dog-leg holes, turns this course into a tester.

RATES: (EP) Lodgings - $102/$116/$132/$396. Green fees - $35/$38, carts $26. Golf package - one night/one day (includes lodging, dinner & breakfast, one round of golf), from $204 to $234 per couple. Rates are for July-September.

ARRIVAL: By car - take I-93 north to New Hampshire Exit 30, and you are there.

The Mount Washington Resort

Box D Route 302, Bretton Woods, NH 03575

(603) 278-1000; (800) 258-0330

ACCOMMODATIONS: 225 hotel rooms and six suites; the Lodge at Bretton Woods; and the Rosebrook Townhouses and condominiums.

AMENITIES: 12 tennis courts, two indoor and one outdoor swimming pool, saunas, bicycling, horseback riding and fishing. There are several dining rooms: Bretton Arms Inn, Darby's at the Lodge and the Mount Washington Room.

GOLF: The Donald Ross-designed course, parring at 71, reaches out a respectable 6,543/6,054/5,156 yards. Somewhat flat on the front nine, rolling terrain comes into play on the back side. The Ammonoosuc River wanders all over this 2,800-acre layout. The newer Mount Pleasant nine plays 3,096/3,292/2,631 yards, with a par of 35.

RATES: (MAP) Lodgings - $219/$479 per couple. Green fees - $48, carts $30. Golf package - two nights/two days (includes lodging, MAP, golf with cart), $758/$958 per couple.

ARRIVAL: By air - Commuter flights to Berlin or Manchester. By car - take I-93 to US 3 north to Twin Mountain, then US 302 east.

New Hampshire

New Jersey

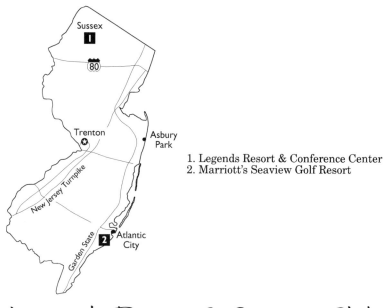

Sussex
1

80

Trenton

Asbury
Park

New Jersey Turnpike

Garden State

2 Atlantic
City

1. Legends Resort & Conference Center
2. Marriott's Seaview Golf Resort

Legends Resort & Country Club

PO Box 637, Route 517, McAfee, NJ 07428

(973) 827-6000; (800) 835-2555

ACCOMMODATIONS: 544 rooms and suites.

AMENITIES: Outdoor and indoor heated pools, fully equipped health club, sauna, steam bath, whirlpools, horseback riding, game rooms, shuffleboard, and indoor and outdoor tennis courts. Dining facilities are at the Café in the Park, the Deli and Seasons Grille.

GOLF: Great Gorge Country Club's 27-hole layout was designed by George Fazio. The courses are interesting, with undulating terrain, trees and water (always, it seems, in the wrong place). As for water – the Lake Side nine is appropriately named. Using a crossover system, you wind up with the Lake Side/Quarry Side combination stretching out 6,819/6,250/5,474 yards; the Rail Side/Lake Side layout measures 6,802/6,325/5,586 yards; and the combination of the Quarry Side/Rail Side nines plays

6,707/6,061/5,486 yards. No matter how you mix them, the par stays at 72.

RATES: (EP) Lodgings - $120/$159. Suites - $149/$199. Green fees - $59/$89, including cart.

ARRIVAL: By air - Newark, NJ or Stewart International, Newburgh, NY. By car - on 517 just outside Vernon, New Jersey.

Marriott's Seaview Golf Resort

US Route 9, Absecon, NJ 0820

(609) 652-1800; (800) 228-9290

ACCOMMODATIONS: The original 157 rooms have been refurbished using rich woods and textures reminiscent of the colonial period. A four-story wing was completed in mid-1986 and provides 149 additional guest rooms, including 12 suites.

AMENITIES: Eight outdoor tennis courts (four lighted), indoor and outdoor swimming pools, paddle tennis courts, saunas, and a steam room. The main dining room features a traditional menu. Jacket and tie are no longer required, but you might feel more comfortable with a jacket here.

GOLF: There are two distinctively different 18-hole layouts. The Bay Course, a seaside links affair designed by Donald Ross in 1912, offers play on broad fairways with fresh bay breezes to contend with. With a yardage of 6,263/5,981/5,586, it pars at 71/74. The 1942 PGA championship was held here. Such legendary names as Sam Snead, Byron Nelson, Ben Hogan, Walter Hagan, Gene Sarazen and many others played in that event.

The Pines Course, designed by Howard Toomey/William Flynn and later reworked by William Gordon, relies on narrow fairways, trees and very fast greens to present the challenge. Parring at 71/75, it reaches out a substantial 6,885/6,394/5,837 yards. Seaview is an elaborate golf facility, with a state-of-the-art "Learning Center" (driving range), featuring four chipping, putting and bunker practice greens, as well as over 60,000 square feet of hitting area.

RATES: (EP) Lodgings - $370/$600. Green fees - $129, including cart. Golf package - two nights/two days (includes lodging, two rounds of golf with cart, club storage and breakfast each day), $610/$798 per couple.

New Jersey

ARRIVAL: By air - limousine service is available from Philadelphia International or Atlantic City International Airports. By car - on Route 9, just south of Jimmie Leeds Road.

New Mexico

Angel Fire

PO Drawer B, Angel Fire, NM 87710

(505) 377-6401; (800) 633-7463

ACCOMMODATIONS: 163 rooms in the Legend Hotel. There are also approximately 200 fully equipped condominiums, with living rooms and kitchens.

AMENITIES: Tennis, indoor pool, sailing, paddleboating, trout fishing and horseback riding.

GOLF: The resort's own layout reaches out 6,624/6,349/5,356 yards. Parring at 72, the course introduces you to water on 10 holes,

1. Angel Fire
2. Inn of the Mountain Gods

hilly terrain, and trees. And then more trees. Should you be an early morning golfer, you might well run across the added distraction of elk watching your swing. Keep in mind that, at 8,000 feet, you have not gotten better; the ball just flies farther at that altitude.

RATES: (EP) Lodgings - $85/$125/$135. Green fees - $55, carts $25. Golf packages available. Rates are for the summer season, July-September.

ARRIVAL: By air - Albuquerque (150 miles). By private aircraft - Angel Fire, 8,900-foot paved runway. By car - Route 64 to New Mexico State Highway 434.

Inn Of The Mountain Gods

PO Box 269, Mescalero, NM 88340

(505) 257-5141; (800) 545-9011

This resort was the dream of Tribal Chief Wendell Chino of the Mescalero Apache Tribe, who chose the site so that it viewed the sacred Indian grounds. After many years of political and administrative maneuvering, The Inn of The Mountain Gods became a reality in 1975. The tribe's primary objective was for the resort to function as a training ground and job center for their people. Located within the heavily forested 463,000-acre Apache Indian Reservation, it is owned and operated by the Mescalero Apache Tribe.

ACCOMMODATIONS: 134 spacious rooms and suites, all with sweeping views of the lakes and mountains. A five-story complex with an additional 116 rooms is also available.

AMENITIES: Hunting for mule deer and elk, trap and skeet shooting, fishing, archery, bicycling, canoeing, and two indoor and six outdoor tennis courts. Horseback riding is available, and trail horses are provided for all ages and riding abilities. Now the resort has added a casino featuring poker, slots and craps.

A few years back the Tribe purchased Ski Apache ski area, which is 17 miles away. It has become one of the most popular winter sports centers in New Mexico. There are three restaurants and four cocktail lounges, providing dancing, entertainment, and excellent food.

GOLF: The Ted Robinson-designed golf course has many holes with elevated tees or greens; most enjoy a panoramic view of the Sierra Blanca Mountains. Parring at 72, it stretches out a substantial 6,834/6,478/5,478 yards. It plays at an elevation of 7,000 feet, and is one heck of a course.

RATES: (EP) Lodgings - $135/$165. Green fees - $40, carts $24. Golf package - three nights/three days and available on weekdays only (includes lodging, three rounds of golf with cart, breakfast each day, all taxes), $678 per couple.

ARRIVAL: By air - El Paso (124 miles); Alamagordo (45 miles). By private and commercial aircraft - Sierra Blanca Regional Airport (21 miles). By car - 3½ miles out of Ruidoso.

New York

1. Whiteface Resort
2. The Sagamore
3. Gideon Putman Hotel
4. Holiday Inn Resort
5. The Otesaga Hotel & Cooper Inn
6. Hanah Country Inn
7. Villa Roma Resort
8. Concord Resort Hotel
9. The Nevele CC
10. Kutsher's CC
11. Wyndham Wind Watch Hotel

Concord Resort Hotel

Route 42, Kiamesha Lake, NY 12751

(914) 794-4000; (888) 448-9686

ACCOMMODATIONS: 1,225 guest rooms.

AMENITIES: 16 indoor and 24 outdoor tennis courts, horse-back riding, boating, fishing and swimming in the indoor or the two-tiered, 280-foot-long outdoor pool. There is also a new 8,000- square-foot fitness center, and separate health clubs for men and women (sauna, steam, massage, facials). There are six dining rooms with the combined capacity to feed approximately 3,500 people at one seating

GOLF: The aptly named Monster Course can be stretched out to 7,672 yards (enjoyed only by the masochist) or 7,471/6,989/ 6,548 yards. This beautiful par-72 layout requires accuracy and patience; the fairways appear to narrow as you approach the green and water often crosses where you would rather it did not. With 6,548 yards from the front red (ladies) tees, this is the most difficult red tee setting of any golf course in the US. The International Course plays a more modest 6,619/5,968/5,554 yards and pars at 71. Don't let the shorter yardage lull you; this layout calls for careful placement. There is also a par-31, 2,200-yard nine.

RATES: (FAP) Lodgings - $120 per couple. Green fees - International, $45/$55, including cart; Monster, $65/$95, including cart. Golf packages available.

ARRIVAL: By air - New York (approximately 90 miles), or Newburgh's Stewart Airport (45 minutes). Several major airlines have recently added Stewart Airport to their schedule. By private aircraft - Sullivan Airport (eight miles). By car - Route 17 to Exit 105-B, on 42, and follow signs to The Concord.

Gideon Putnam Hotel

PO Box 476, Saratoga Springs, NY 12866

(518) 584-3000; (800) 732-1560

ACCOMMODATIONS: 132 rooms, including suites.

AMENITIES: Eight outdoor tennis courts (four indoor courts nearby), horseback riding, and swimming. There is a restaurant.

GOLF: An 18-hole public course is adjacent to the property. Parring at 72, it plays 7,100/6,320/5,355 yards. There is also a par-30, nine-hole layout.

RATES: (EP) Lodgings - $139/$159/$205. FAP plan is available. Rates during racing season (August) are considerably higher. Green fees - $27/$32, carts $26.

ARRIVAL: By air - Albany (22 miles). By private aircraft - Saratoga (three miles). By car - go north on I-87 to Exit 13N, then drive approximately three miles.

Hanah Country Inn

Route 30, Margaretville, NY 12455

(914) 586-2100; (800) 752-6494

ACCOMMODATIONS: 62 motel-type rooms plus three private homes.

AMENITIES: Swimming pool, two tennis courts, and fishing; horseback riding and bowling alleys are located nearby.

GOLF: The Terminator course, with a par of 70/72, plays 6,370/6,146/5,597 yards. There is nothing hidden about the water on this layout. The eastside branch of the Delaware River seems to run everywhere.

RATES: (MAP) Lodgings - $138/$158. Green fees - $45/$60, including carts. Various packages are available. Rates are for late June through August.

ARRIVAL: By air - Albany (72 miles). By car - New York Thruway to Exit 19, then northwest on Route 28. Prior to the railroad tracks turn right, go one mile to intersection with Route 30, then right again for ½ mile on Route 30.

Holiday Inn Resort

100 Whitehaven Road, Grand Island, NY

(716) 773-1111; (800) 465-4329

ACCOMMODATIONS: 262 rooms, including suites.

AMENITIES: Indoor and outdoor swimming pools, outdoor tennis courts, sauna, boat docks and fishing.

GOLF: The River Oaks Club course, adjacent to the inn, has a par of 72 and reaches out 7,389/6,588/5,630 yards. A few of the challenges include: trees, water, many traps and gently undulating terrain. The course is located on the Niagara River, and the scenery is outstanding.

RATES: (EP) Lodgings - $89/$129. Green fees - $45, carts $30. Golf packages are available.

ARRIVAL: By air - Buffalo. By car - New York Thruway 324 to Grand Island, Exit 19.

New York

Kutsher's Country Club

Kutsher's Road, Monticello, NY 12701

(845) 794-6000; (800) 431-1273

ACCOMMODATIONS: Over 500 guest rooms.

AMENITIES: Beauty shop, apparel, sundries and gift shops, cosmetic counter, men's and women's health spas, indoor and outdoor pools, indoor ice skating, a private lake with fishing and boating, tennis on 12 outdoor and four indoor courts, and four racquetball courts. There are excellent dining facilities. If your vacation plans call for lots of entertainment (four bands and all-night dancing), this may well be the place for you. A very important extra: their children's program has a nursery and day camp, with activities for toddlers, pre-teens and teens.

GOLF: The William Mitchell-designed golf course has been rated among the top 10 in the state. It reaches out a substantial 7,001/6,510/5,676 yards, and pars at 71. While obviously long, it also sports some extremely large traps, too many trees (or so it seemed) and very large greens.

RATES: (FAP) Lodgings - $182/$208/$252 per couple. Green fees - $37/$45, including carts. Golf package are available weekdays only. Rates are for June-September.

ARRIVAL: By air - New York or Stewart Airport, service by several major airlines (45-minute drive). By car - from New York (two hours), thruway to Exit 16, then proceed to Route 17W. Take Exit 105B, turn left at the first traffic light and follow signs.

The Nevele Country Club

Route 209, Ellenville, NY 12428

(845) 647-6000; (800) 647-6000

ACCOMMODATIONS: 500 guest rooms within a large hotel complex.

AMENITIES: Horseback riding, tennis (five indoor, 10 outdoor courts), platform tennis, complete health spa, swimming (indoor and outdoor) and boating. There are several dining rooms.

GOLF: The course, while flat, has trees, streams and two lakes that add a bit of spice to the play. Parring at 70/72, it reaches out

6,500/5,737/4,570 yards. The course was redesigned by Tom Fazio in 1987.

RATES: (EP) Lodgings - $170/$240 per couple. Green fees - $42/$55 including cart.

ARRIVAL: By air - New York. By car - New York Thruway Exit 16, then Route 17 (Quickway) to Exit 113. From there, take Route 209 north.

The Otesaga Hotel & Cooper Inn

PO Box 311, Cooperstown, NY 13326

(607) 547-9931; (800) 348-6222

ACCOMMODATIONS: 137 hotel rooms.

AMENITIES: Swimming (lake or pool), boating, tennis. The dining room is outstanding.

GOLF: The Leatherstocking Golf Course, adjacent to the hotel, is beautifully situated alongside the lake. Parring at 72, it shows a yardage of 6,388/6,006/5,175. An excellent professional staff is available for lessons. They might even supply a crying towel for your game, should you feel the need.

RATES: (MAP) Lodgings - $310/$450/$470 per couple. Green fees - $55/$65, carts $34. Rates are for July through Labor Day.

ARRIVAL: By air - New York. By car - I-88, Exit at 28 and head northeast.

New York

The Sagamore

100 Sagamore Road, Bolton Landing, NY 12814

(518) 644-9400; (800) 358-3585

Situated on its own private 70-acre island in the rugged majesty of the Adirondacks, Sagamore is surrounded by the shimmering beauty of Lake George.

ACCOMMODATIONS: A combination of 350 suites, rooms and lodges.

AMENITIES: Sailing, para-sailing, six tennis courts (two indoor), indoor swimming pool, and men's and ladies' health spa.

Horseback riding can be arranged nearby. For dining, you can select the Trillium Room (a gourmet restaurant), the Sagamore Dining Room, Mr. Brown's All Day Cafe or the Clubhouse Grill. You can also elect to take a dinner cruise on *The Morgan*, the resort's own luxury yacht.

GOLF: The beautiful Donald Ross-designed course is set on its own 200 acres. Recently restored, it plays 6,706/6,410/5,265 yards, parring at 70/71. With its excellent use of traps, water and tree-lined fairways, you will find this layout well worth the time to play.

RATES: (EP) Lodgings - $240/$359/$465. Green fees - $95, including cart. Golf packages are available. Rates are for July-August.

ARRIVAL: By air - New York, Boston or Albany. By car - from Albany take Northway (Route 87N) to Exit 24, Bolton Landing. Follow signs (approximately six miles) to Bolton Landing and The Sagamore.

Villa Roma Resort

Villa Roma Road, Callicoon, NY 12723

(845) 887-4880; (800) 533-6767

ACCOMMODATIONS: 216 guest rooms and 198 time-share suites. The suites have a bedroom, sitting area and pullman kitchen.

AMENITIES: Indoor and outdoor swimming pools, four racquetball courts, three indoor and two outdoor tennis courts, complete fitness center, saunas, Jacuzzi, hot tub and a miniature golf layout. Horseback riding, trout fishing, rafting or canoeing on the Delaware River are available nearby.

GOLF: The Villa Roma Country Club course, traversing rolling terrain and parring at 71, reaches out a modest 6,237/5,416/4,813 yards.

RATES: (MAP) Lodgings - $218/$518 per couple. Green fees - $49, including cart. Golf package - two nights/three days (includes lodging, breakfast, dinner, unlimited green fees, bag storage and cart), $608/$680 per couple. Rates are for late June through August.

ARRIVAL: By air - Newburg, NY (Stewart International Airport). By car - from Newburg, take I-84 west to Middletown (Exit

4), then Route 17 west to Exit 104. On Route 17B (Raceway Road), go west to Fosterdale (17 miles). At the blinking light turn right (the intersection of 17B and 52A) and follow signs to the resort.

Whiteface Resort

PO Box 231, Whiteface Inn Road, Lake Placid, NY 12946

(518) 523-2551; (800) 422-6757

ACCOMMODATIONS: Cabins are situated along the 1,200-foot lakefront beach; some have kitchens.

AMENITIES: Tennis courts, Olympic-size heated pool, a boathouse with canoes, sailing, and paddleboats. Lake Placid offers great fishing.

GOLF: The Whiteface Resort course, with its super view of the lake, measures a respectable 6,490/6293/5,635 yards. It pars at 72/74. Although water only becomes a factor on one hole, the tree-lined fairways will keep you honest.

RATES: (EP) Lodgings - $120/$375. Green fees - $36, carts $28. Golf package - two nights/three days (includes lodging, MAP, golf and gratuities), $480 per couple.

ARRIVAL: By air - Saranac (11 miles). By car - turn off Route 86 at Whiteface Inn Road and continue to end.

Wyndham Wind Watch Hotel

1717 Vanderbilt Motor Parkway, Hauppauge, NY 11788

(631) 232-9800; (800) 996-3426

On Long Island 10 minutes from Islip's MacArthur Airport, the Wind Watch is a bit over an hour from either JFK or LaGuardia Airports.

ACCOMMODATIONS: 10-story hotel with 362 guest rooms.

AMENITIES: Indoor and outdoor swimming pools, whirlpools, saunas, two tennis courts, and a health club featuring standard weights, Stairmaster and Lifecycle. Horseback riding and deep-sea fishing facilities are located nearby. Dining is in either the Terrace Café or the Atrium Lounge.

GOLF: The Wind Watch course, a Joe Lee design, reaches out 6,405/6,138/5,135 yards. Parring at 71, it introduces you to water on 12 holes and offers the opportunity to enjoy 62 sand bunkers. There are about 15 acres of water ready to dunk your ball. It is a fun layout, situated on slightly undulating terrain. While not easy (these greens will keep you fully awake), it was designed to be enjoyed, not beat you to death. There is a practice putting green and an extremely large driving range.

RATES: (EP) Lodgings - $214/$234/$350 per couple. Green fees - $90, including cart.

ARRIVAL: By air - JFK International Airport. By private and commercial aircraft - Islip MacArthur Airport (10 minutes). By car - Go east on the Long Island Expressway (495) to Exit 57. Turn left at the first traffic light onto Motor Parkway. Continue on Motor Parkway for 1½ miles. The hotel will be on the left side.

North Carolina

1. Green Park Inn/Hound Ears Club
2. Eseeola Lodge/Grandfather Golf & CC
3. Tanglewood Park
4. Washington Duke Inn & Golf Club
5. Alpine Village
6. Wolf Laurel Resort
7. Maggie Valley CC Resort
8. Waynesville CC Inn
9. Springdale CC
10. Holiday Inn Great Smokies/Grove Park Inn & Resort
11. Carolina Trace
12. CC at Whispering Pines
13. Woodlake CC
14. Foxfire Inn & CC
15. Fairfield Mountains/Pine Needles Resort/Sand Hills Golf Lodge/
    Beacon Ridge Golf & CC/Pinehurst Hotel & CC/Mid-Pines Resort
16. Etowah Valley CC Lodge
17. Fairfield Sapphire Valley
18. Cherokee Hills CC/High Hampton Inn CC
19. The Village at Nags Head
20. Fairfield Harbour
21. Belvedere Plantation
22. Sea Trail Golf Resort

Alpine Village

200 Overlook Drive, Burnsville, NC 28714

(704) 675-4103

ACCOMMODATIONS: Homes bordering the fairways or townhouses adjacent to the 18th hole. They are available for prospective buyers. This is a small resort, located in one of the most beautiful parts of North Carolina.

AMENITIES: Heated pool, tennis, ice skating at a nearby indoor rink, art and craft shops, an excellent summer stock theater, and hiking in the beautiful mountains. The hub of activity is the clubhouse, which offers candlelight dining.

This is a dry county – there is no way to secure liquor. The nearest supply is about 45 minutes away.

GOLF: The lush and very exclusive Mount Mitchell Golf Club stretches out 6,475/6,110/5,455 yards and pars at 72. With tree-lined fairways, this layout brings water into play on 13 holes and is very well-trapped. Even though you are in mountain country at about 3,000 feet, the course is fairly flat, with only gentle elevation changes.

RATES: (EP) Lodgings - $95/$135. Green fees - $38, including cart. As these condominiums are time-share units, maid service is not included but can be arranged.

ARRIVAL: By air - Asheville (50 miles). By car - Blue Ridge Parkway, off on North Carolina 80, then travel two miles west.

Beacon Ridge Golf & Country Club

PO Box 525, West End, NC 27376

(910) 673-2950; (800) 416-5204

ACCOMMODATIONS: Available in the second homes of the resort's property owners. Located in the Sandhills of North Carolina, the resort is eight miles west of the village of Pinehurst.

AMENITIES: Fishing, boating, water-skiing, and three lighted tennis courts.

GOLF: The Beacon Ridge course plays 6,414/6,143/5,354/4,730 yards, with a par of 72. With trees and a liberal use of water, this well-manicured, lush layout will offer you all you handle.

RATES: Lodgings - $145. Green fees - Beacon Ridge, $54, carts $32; Seven Lakes, $75, including carts.

ARRIVAL: By air - Fayetteville. By private aircraft - Southern Pines or a 3,000-foot sod strip on premises. By car - 10 miles west-northwest of Pinehurst.

Belvedere Plantation

PO Box 4000, Hampstead, NC 28443

(910) 270-4444; (800) 334-8318

The Belvedere Plantation Golf & Yacht Club, a retirement community, is on the scenic North Carolina Intracoastal Waterway and the Atlantic Ocean. Situated on over 1,000 acres, it is removed from the hustle and bustle of the area.

ACCOMMODATIONS: Condominiums of one to three bedrooms or townhouses, all completely furnished and equipped for housekeeping.

AMENITIES: Tennis courts, swimming pool, lockers, showers and saunas. There is also a full- service marina and a restaurant.

GOLF: The Belvedere Plantation Course, parring at 71/72, reaches out 6,393/6,0495/4,982 yards. As it wanders throughout the resort, this layout brings more than a little water into play. In fact, there are only four holes where water is not a factor. Other courses nearby and available for guest play include Olde Point and Top Sail Greens. For tee times, call (910) 270-2703.

RATES: (EP) Lodgings - $85. Golf packages are available.

ARRIVAL: By air - Wilmington Airport. By car - the resort is 17 miles north of Wilmington on US Highway 17.

Carolina Trace

PO Box 2665, Sanford, NC 27330

(919) 499-5103; (800) 227-2699

Keep in mind Carolina Trace is a privately owned resort development. When making reservations, it is imperative that you secure a unit belonging to a golfing member. Thus you will be able to play.

ACCOMMODATIONS: Range from villas to condominiums or rustic contemporary homes. Each unit has from one to three bedrooms, dining area, kitchen and daily maid service.

AMENITIES: Ten swimming pools and 16 lighted tennis courts. Boating or sunbathing on Lake Trace are other options.

GOLF: The 36-hole Carolina Trace courses were designed by Robert Trent Jones, Sr. Using the natural undulating terrain, trees and water, Jones was able to create two of the better golf

North Carolina

courses in North Carolina. The Lakeside Golf Course reaches out a very respectable 6,870/6,315/5,789/4,986 yards, with a par of 72. The Creekside layout weighs in at 6,792/6,270/5,635/5,113 yards, and also pars at 72. You can also play the Carolina Lakes, a shorter par-70 affair, with a yardage of 6,377/5,940/5,010.

RATES: (EP) Lodgings - $85/$125. Green fees - $75, including cart.

ARRIVAL: By air - Raleigh-Durham Airport (50 miles). Fayetteville (30 miles). By car - US 1 to Sanford, then State 87 south 3½ miles.

Cherokee Hills Country Club

PO Box 647, Murphy, NC 28906

(828) 837-5853; (800) 334-3905

ACCOMMODATIONS: 12-unit motel with efficiencies, along with 36 two-bedroom, 1½-bath townhouses. Most units also have a washer/dryer. Once the hunting grounds of the Cherokee Indians, the area has rolling terrain and a laid-back atmosphere.

AMENITIES: Two tennis courts, swimming pool, croquet, shuffleboard and a fitness trail. Fishing in this area, particularly along the Hiwassee River, is outstanding. There is a dining room adjacent to the pro shop.

 This is a dry county. You either "brown bag" it or go without.

GOLF: The country club course reaches out 6,324/5,172 yards and pars at 72. It is a well-trapped affair with enough water coming into play (nine holes) to keep you fully alert.

RATES: (EP) Lodgings - $75/$290. Golf package - one night/one day (includes lodging, green fees with cart for one round), $150 per couple. Rates shown are for April-October.

ARRIVAL: By air - Chattanooga, TN (1½ hours). By private aircraft - the county airport (a 5,000-foot paved and lighted runway), 10 miles from the resort. By car - resort is on Harshaw Road, three miles east of Murphy.

The Country Club Of Whispering Pines

263-B Pine Ridge Drive, Whispering Pines, NC 28327

(910) 949-3777; (800) 334-9536

ACCOMMODATIONS: 32 guest rooms, and nine one- to two-bedroom villa suites.

AMENITIES: Lake swimming, swimming pool, and the clubhouse bar and grill. Jackets are requested in the evening for the Terrace Dining Room; ties are optional.

GOLF: There are three 18-hole golf courses. The East Course, referred to as "The Long One," stretches 7,138/6,406/5,441 yards, with a par of 72. The West Course, known as the "Wet One," has a more modest yardage of 6,358/5,860/5,135 yards and pars at 71. The South Course, very aptly named "The Tight One," weighs in with an even shorter yardage of 6,037/5,460/4,879 and pars at 72. Do not allow the yardage on the West course to fool you. The course's 12 water holes will keep you awake. Well-trapped, elevated greens will also hold your attention. The resort has a working arrangement with 14 other golf courses in the area, which opens up a great selection for their golfing guests.

RATES: (EP) Lodgings - $75/$149. Green fees - $38, carts $34. Golf package - two nights/three days (includes lodging, green fees, continental breakfast), $598 per couple. Rates are for March-May and September-November.

ARRIVAL: By air - Fayetteville (50 miles), Raleigh-Durham (65 miles). By car - US 1, off on Vass-Carthage Road (there will be a sign for Whispering Pines), then on to the resort.

Eseeola Lodge

Highway 221, Linville, NC 28646

(704) 733-4311; (800) 742-6717

ACCOMMODATIONS: 28 rooms, plus a few private home rentals.

AMENITIES: Eight tennis courts, swimming pool, horseback riding (with an instructor) and fishing. They offer an organized children's recreation program during July and August. The resort has a lovely dining room. (Jacket and tie are required in the evenings).

 This resort is in a dry county, so bring your own or learn to do without.

GOLF: The Linville Golf Club (adjacent to the inn) dates back to 1928. This par-72 layout can be played from three tee settings: 6,780/6,286/5,086 yards. The altitude is 3,800 feet, so remember your shots will carry a little farther than usual.

RATES: (MAP) Lodgings - $325/$425 per person. Green fees - $75, including cart. Resort is open mid-May to mid-October.

ARRIVAL: By air - Asheville (70 miles). By car - on Highway 221, 17 miles from Blowing Rock.

Etowah Valley Country Club Lodge

PO Box 2150, Hendersonville, NC 28793

(704) 891-7022; (800) 451-8174

The country club is in a rolling valley between the rugged Smokies and the magnificent Blue Ridge Mountains.

ACCOMMODATIONS: Their "Golf Lodges" provide views of the 10th fairway as well as the mountains.

AMENITIES: Three putting greens, driving range, heated swimming pool, clubhouse and pro shop. There is also a dining room.

 The resort is in a dry county, so bring your own or suffer.

GOLF: Designed by Edmund B. Ault, the course features some of the largest greens in the south (some up to 9,000 square feet). There are three nines to choose from. The South/West combination plays a healthy 7,108/6,880/6,394/5,707 yards, parring at 72/75. The West/North nines weigh in at 7,005/6,700/6,227/5,498 yards, again with a par of 72/75. The South/West combo reaches out 6,911/6,604/6,251/5,435 yards, this time with a par of 72/74.

RATES: Golf package - (includes balcony room, MAP, green fees, club storage), $182 per couple per day. Golf carts - $30.

ARRIVAL: By air - Asheville (25 miles). By car - Etowah Valley is off Highway 64 W between Hendersonville and Brevard.

Fairfield Harbour

750 Broadcreek Road, New Bern, NC 28560

(919) 638-8011, Ext 228

ACCOMMODATIONS: One- to two-bedroom suites with kitchen and living room, or the Waterwood Villas.

AMENITIES: Swimming pool, 12 tennis courts (four lighted), a miniature 18-hole golf course, and dining facilities. They also have a marina with 216 slips, which can accommodate boats up to 60 feet in length.

GOLF: The Fairfield Harbour Course is available for play by members and resort guests. Parring at 72, it reaches out 6,654/6,310/5,832 yards. The newest addition, the Harbour Point nine, is a Rees Jones course. It measures 6,554/5,998/5,078, also with a par of 72.

RATES: (EP) Lodgings - $75/$85/$100/$155. Green fees - $55, including cart.

ARRIVAL: By air - Raleigh. By car - eight miles from New Bern. Take Highway 17, cross the Neuse River, right at first traffic light onto Highway 55 east and follow signs.

Fairfield Mountains

Route 1, Lake Lure, NC 28746

(704) 625-9111; (800) 829-3149

ACCOMMODATIONS: One-bedroom suites, or master suites with kitchen, dining area and living room.

AMENITIES: 50-slip marina on Lake Lure (27 miles of shoreline), water-skiing, fishing, sailing and beachside swimming, indoor heated pool, and six tennis courts. Horseback riding is available at their new stable. The Country Club's dining room serves three meals daily; for more casual dining, try Uncle Adam's family restaurant.

North Carolina

GOLF: The Bald Mountain Course, playing 6,689/6,125/5,312/4,838 yards, pars at 72. The front side starts out with few problems, but watch out on the back nine. With a generous use of water, hills, traps, trees and more water, it can burn you. The Apple Valley Course, also parring at 72, reaches out 6,726/6,297/5,662/4,661 yards. Featuring rolling hills and water in the form of a creek coming into play on 11 or 12 holes, this one is entertaining.

RATES: (EP) Lodgings - $89/$125/$225. Green fees - $49, including cart. Rates are April-October.

ARRIVAL: By air - Asheville (38 miles southeast). By car - four miles off Highway 74 on the north shore of Lake Lure.

Fairfield Sapphire Valley

4000 Highway 64 West, Sapphire, NC 28774

(828) 743-3441; (800) 533-8268

This resort is located in a particularly beautiful part of North Carolina, high in the Blue Ridge Mountains, where there are many lakes and lush forests.

ACCOMMODATIONS: Mountain and lake villas, each with from one to three bedrooms, and kitchens; many with fireplaces.

This is a dry area, so bring your own liquor or suffer. It's a long way (14 miles) to a source of supply.

AMENITIES: Swimming (lake or pool), outstanding fishing, boating, riding (Fairfield stables) and tennis on eight courts. The Mountain Mica's Restaurant serves three meals daily and will prepare a box lunch for picnics on request. The resort also offers a children's program.

GOLF: The Holly Forest Golf Course offers some of the most spectacular golf holes we have seen. Set at 3,400 feet above sea level, it includes a par 4 playing 187 yards (from the regular men's tees), with a drop from tee to green of well over 150 feet. You either hit this green or spend the remainder of the day looking for your ball. The most scenic hole, however, is number 13 – a par 4 curving down from an elevated tee to the fairway. As you set up your shot to the green, you will find trees guarding the left side and a waterfall cascading on the right side. The water is so close to the green that it sprays onto the putting surface. Playing 6,147/5,690/4,515 yards and parring at 70, this gem brings hazards into play in the form of lakes, streams, bunkers and huge hardwood trees. While the scenery of the entire area is magnificent, the course itself has such a spectacular setting that you may not even notice the rest of the area.

RATES: (EP) Lodgings - $90/$245. Green fees - $55, including cart. Rates are for May-October.

ARRIVAL: By air - Asheville (60 miles). By car - Highway 64, three miles east of Cashiers.

Foxfire Inn & Country Club

PO Box 711, Pinehurst, NC 28374

(910) 295-5555; (800) 736-9347

ACCOMMODATIONS: Villas, townhouses and condominium.

AMENITIES: Two tennis courts and a new 25-meter swimming pool. The clubhouse houses a dining room, pro shop and lounge.

GOLF: The West Course reaches out 6,742/6,333/5,273 yards, with a par 72. This layout brings water into contention on six holes. The East Course, also parring at 72, plays 6,851/6,286/5,256 yards, with water becoming a problem (challenge) on five holes. With the combination of large greens, ponds, a great many traps and lots of towering pine trees, you may indeed require some help.

RATES: (EP) Lodgings - $126/$190. Green fees - $84, carts included. Golf package - one night/one day (includes lodging, golf and cart), $228. Rates are for March 15th to June 15th and September 8th to November 12th.

ARRIVAL: By air - Charlotte, Raleigh-Durham, Southern Pines. By car - just off US 1, six miles west of Pinehurst.

North Carolina

Grandfather Golf & Country Club

PO Box 368, Linville, NC 28646

(828) 898-4531

ACCOMMODATIONS: There are two- to four-bedroom condominiums, and private homes with three to five bedrooms. All feature a fully equipped kitchen, fireplace, laundry facilities, and daily maid service. The setting of this very private club is one of the loveliest we have seen in North Carolina.

AMENITIES: Three indoor and six outdoor tennis courts, horseback riding nearby, and two beaches – one for swimming and one for boating, Dining facilities are located in the clubhouse.

GOLF: The well-manicured, wooded valley layout reaches out 6,850/6,290/5,805/5,215 yards, with a par of 72. It has extremely tight fairways with streams, lakes, boulders, huge sand traps and trees all posing a challenge. The Mountain Springs Course, a 3,226-yard, par-59 executive affair, should be approached with due respect. Situated at the base of Grandfather Mountain, it requires accurate shotmaking. More than one golfer, expecting an easy conquest, has come away from this layout very badly embarrassed.

Provided you have been sponsored by a member (the person from whom you rent can sponsor you), you can purchase a privilege card which allows full use of the clubhouse and the various facilities. Tee times for guests are restricted to early morning or late afternoon on the Grandfather Course.

RATES: (EP) Lodgings - (during June-August minimum stay is three nights) $1,500. Green fees - $125, carts $30.

ARRIVAL: By air - Asheville (75 miles). By car - Highway 105, two miles north of Linville.

Green Park Inn

PO Box 7, Blowing Rock, NC, 28605

(828) 295-3141; (800) 852-2462

ACCOMMODATIONS: 86 guest rooms.

AMENITIES: The Blowing Rock Country Club, adjacent to the Inn, is the location of the tennis courts, swimming pool and the golf course. There are excellent dining facilities. This county used to be dry. All that has changed and the resort now has a full-fledged lounge, offering cocktails, beer and wine.

GOLF: The golf course measures 6,038/5,582/4,777 yards and pars at 72/73. It is both scenic and challenging. Keep in mind that you are at about 4,300 feet, and your shots will carry farther than usual.

RATES: (EP) Lodgings - $109/$129/$165. Green fees - $135, including cart. Rates are for May-October.

ARRIVAL: By air - Charlotte or Asheville. By car - Highway 321 to Blowing Rock.

The Grove Park Inn & Resort

290 Macon Avenue, Asheville, NC 28804

(828) 252-2711; (800) 438-5800

ACCOMMODATIONS: 510 guest rooms, including the Club Floor, which features 28 oversized suites, each with a Jacuzzi.

AMENITIES: Two large swimming pools, a sports center, nine tennis courts, two racquetball courts, many retail shops and a children's program. There are four restaurants and two lounges.

GOLF: The Donald Ross-design course rolls out in front of the Inn. The tree-lined, undulating terrain plays 6,500/6,001/4,787 yards with a par of 71. It is a fun layout with a stream that keeps popping up all over. There are also approximately 15 other courses in the immediate area which can be played.

RATES: (EP) Lodgings - $185/$225. Green fees - $65, including cart. Golf package - two nights/three days (includes lodging, green fees, cart, club storage, all taxes), $559/$689 per couple. Rates are for mid-April to mid-November.

ARRIVAL: By air - Asheville.

North Carolina

High Hampton Inn & Country Club

200 Hampton Road, Cashiers, NC 27817

(828) 743-2411; (800) 334-2551

The lobby's huge stone chimney and several fireplaces offer guests a warm and gentle greeting. Should you be in search of nightlife, you may not be overly enthused with High Hampton – nightly entertainment is subdued. It is a quiet, peaceful place.

ACCOMMODATIONS: Rustic with sawmill-finished pine walls and sturdy mountain-crafted furniture. There are also some privately owned two- and three-bedroom homes.

AMENITIES: Eight tennis courts, horseback riding nearby, and a fly-fishing school (tackle is provided for each student). The three lakes on the estate provide 40 acres of water for lake swimming, canoeing, pedal boating and sailing. They also offer well-organized programs for children and teens. The inn serves vegetables from its own garden, as well as homemade pastries and breads. The outstanding meals are served family style. Jackets and ties for men and appropriate attire for ladies are required during the evening hours. The Rocky Mountain Tavern can provide set-ups, but you must bring your own jug. This is a dry area and it's a bit of a drive to a source of supply.

GOLF: The High Hampton Country Club, a George Cobb design, plays 6,012 yards with a par of 71. Do not let the yardage fool you. This layout will give you all you want. The rolling terrain, huge trees (hemlocks, I think), tall pines and water turn this into a shotmaker's affair.

RATES: (FAP) Lodgings - $192/$206 per couple. Green fees - $32, carts $26. Rates quoted are for July-October. A nice plus: the resort has requested that guests do not tip; they also *do not*, as many resorts do, add a gratuity to your bill.

ARRIVAL: By air - Asheville (55 miles). By car - south of US 64 on Highway 107.

Holiday Inn Great Smokies

One Holiday Inn Dr., Asheville, NC 28806

(828) 254-3211; (800) 733-3211

ACCOMMODATIONS: 280 rooms, each offering a balcony view of either the golf course or the mountains.

AMENITIES: Two outdoor pools, a sauna, four indoor and four outdoor lighted tennis courts, and sightseeing in Asheville. For dining try Aunt Minnie's Wisdom Restaurant. The name is rather odd, but the food and service are fine.

GOLF: The course appears to "drop" away from the hotel on all sides, with narrow fairways, huge oak trees, steep inclines and water coming into play on 11 holes. The Bill Lewis design opened in 1976; it plays 5,565/5,100/4,625 yards, with a par of 70/73.

RATES: (EP) Lodgings - $129/$149. Green fees - $30, including carts. Golf package - one night/one day, includes (lodging, breakfast, green fees, cart), $169. Rates are for the April-October period.

ARRIVAL: By air - Asheville airport.

Hound Ears Club

PO Box 188, Blowing Rock, NC 28605

(828) 963-4321

The name of the resort is intriguing, and so is the place. Its name was derived from a unique rock formation resembling huge ears that dominates the high mountain ridge above the club.

ACCOMMODATIONS: Rooms with balconies, which provide spectacular views of the mountains and the golf course. For longer stays, there are Clubhouse suites, privately owned chalets and condominiums.

AMENITIES: All-weather Grass-Tex tennis courts, stable, and bridle trails; a swimming pool adjoins the pavilion. Two dining rooms, upper and lower, offer outstanding food and unequaled service. (Jacket and tie required after 6 PM.) There is a "no tipping" policy; a 15% service charge is automatically added to your bill and covers rooms, meals and beverage service.

North Carolina

This is a dry county; bring your own or go without. If you wish, they will keep your bottle for you at the delightful bar, then mix and serve your drinks on request.

GOLF: The course is one of the prettiest and best maintained we have played. Designed by George Cobb, who performed an ingenious job of fitting it into this lovely valley, it winds past lakes, streams and huge rock outcroppings. From the three tee settings, it plays 6,165/5,639/4,959 yards and pars at 72/73.

RATES: (MAP) Lodgings - $280/$300 per couple. Green fees - $60, carts $36. Rates are for June-October.

ARRIVAL: By air - Charlotte, Greensboro or Asheville, NC. By private aircraft - Elk River Airport, Banner Elk (20 minutes away). By car - off Highway 105 between Boone and Linville in Watauga County.

Hyland Hills Motor Lodge

4110 Highway #1 North, Southern Pines, NC 28387

(910) 692-7615; (800) 841-0638

ACCOMMODATIONS: Regular rooms and some efficiency units. This motel/lodge, overlooking a golf course, is in the heart of the Sandhills of North Carolina.

AMENITIES: Two swimming pools (indoor and outdoor) and tennis courts. The clubhouse serves breakfast and lunch only.

GOLF: Call this golf course easy and it might very well punch your game right in the nose. It boasts the beauty common to this wonderful area, but really looks rather docile. It is, however, anything but. The combination of trees in the wrong places, water where you least expect it and traps where they should not be may expand your vocabulary. Playing 6,422/6,100/4,795 yards, it pars at 72.

RATES: (EP) Lodgings - $49/$55. Golf packages are available. Green fees - $38, carts $36.

ARRIVAL: By air - Fayetteville or Southern Pines. By car -north of Southern Pines on US 1 (two miles).

Maggie Valley Country Club Resort

PO Box 99, Maggie Valley, NC 28751

(828) 926-1616; (800) 438-3861

ACCOMMODATIONS: Motel-type structure. There are also one- or two-bedroom villas featuring living rooms and kitchens.

AMENITIES: Swimming pool and two tennis courts. The main dining room is located in the lodge.

GOLF: The front nine of the course stretches out away from the pro shop and looks very easy. It is not. But when you get to the back nine, not visible from the front side, you will find an entirely different ball game: hills, trees, water, more hills, more trees and yes, more water. While interesting and fun to play, it can eat you alive if you are not careful. By the way, the scenery on the back nine is spectacular. The course measures 6,284/6,004/5,222yards and pars at 71/73.

RATES: (EP) Lodgings - $109/$129/$159. Green fees -$37, carts $30. Golf package - three nights/four days (includes lodging, MAP, green fees), $498/$618 per couple. Rates mid-June to mid-November.

ARRIVAL: By air - Asheville (35 miles). By car - Highway 276 south to Highway 19, then west.

Mid Pines Resort

1010 Midland Road, Southern Pines, NC 28387

(910) 692-2114; (800) 323-2114

ACCOMMODATIONS: A combination of rooms in the stately main hotel, charming cottages, Golfotel, and villas.

AMENITIES: Swimming pool and four lighted tennis courts. The dining facilities are excellent.

GOLF: The course measures 6,515/6,121/5,592 yards, parring at 72/75. Originally built in 1921, the beautiful, fully mature layout has narrow fairways, bunkers and lots of trees. While it is fun to play, watch out for the third hole; it is a zinger. I could explain what the problems are, but it would be more fun for you to find out for yourself.

North Carolina

RATES: (MAP) Lodgings - $240/$270 per couple. Green fees - $85, including cart. Golf package - two nights/three days (includes lodging in hotel, FAP, golf), $1,040 per couple. Same package with lodging in Villa - $1,080 per couple. Rates are for September-November.

ARRIVAL: By air - Fayetteville (30 miles). Raleigh-Durham (55 miles). By car - take North Carolina Route 2, off US 1, then drive a quarter-mile west.

Sand Hills Golf Lodge

PO Box 3246, Pinehurst, NC 28374

(910) 281-3165; (800) 334-4418

ACCOMMODATIONS: A 40-room, two-story structure.

AMENITIES: Swimming pool, two lighted tennis courts, and three stocked lakes for fishing. Champions Dining Room and a lounge are part of the complex.

GOLF: The Pine Bluff Golf Course plays 6,851/6,253/5,680// 5,063 and pars at 72. There are three small lakes that become involved on four holes, and many tall pine trees that seem, at times, to move to the wrong location.

RATES: (BP) Green fees - $45, $34 cart. Golf package - two nights/three days (includes lodging, MAP, green fees and cart), $478 per couple. Rates are for March-May and October-November.

ARRIVAL: By air - Fayetteville (45 miles). Raleigh/Durham (80 miles). By private aircraft - Southern Pines. By car - located on US 1, six miles south of Aberdeen/Southern Pines and one mile south of Pinebluff.

Pinehurst Hotel & Country Club

Box 4000, Pinehurst, NC 28374

(910) 295-6811; (800) 487-4653

Pinehurst Hotel & Country Club has been judged one of our Top 50 resorts.

ACCOMMODATIONS: 310 hotel rooms, 10 four-bedroom villas and over 150 one- to three-bedroom condominiums, which are fully equipped for housekeeping.

AMENITIES: 24 tennis courts (18 clay, six Laykold, four lighted), a riding club offering instructions and carriage rides, trap and skeet shooting, Roman baths, whirlpool and lap pools, five outdoor swimming pools, a health spa, exercise rooms, sauna and steam rooms. From the marina on Lake Pinehurst, you can enjoy windsurfing, sailing, canoeing, swimming, and fishing. The Carolina Dining Room offers outstanding, beautifully presented cuisine. (Jackets required; ties not mandatory, but requested).

GOLF: When you ask for a scorecard, you may well be handed eight of them. There are so many courses they have to number them. *Course 1* has 6,158/5,381 yards and pars at 70/73. *Course 2* stretches out at 7,020/6,401/5,934, with a par of 72/74. *Course 3* measures 6,092/5,261 and has a par of 71/72. *Course 4* reaches out 6,890/6,371/5,726, and *Course 5* measures 6,827/6,355/5,848; both par at 72/73. *Course 6* weighs in at 7,098/6,314/5,400, parring at 72. *Course 7*, a truly championship par-72 layout, stretches out an awesome 7,206/6,783/6,137/5,001 yards. *Course 8*, a Tom Fazio design, opened in the resort's 100th year, so it is named "Centennial." It reaches out 7,066/6,551/6,107/5,400 yards with a par of 72, and offers a little of everything – trees, water in play on five holes, and bunkers.

Yardage and par do not tell the whole story on any of the other courses. Bunkers, trees, water, undulating greens, and elevation changes make all of them fun and interesting. With eight very different courses to explore, you can play almost any type you wish: flat or rolling terrain, lots of water or very little, big greens or small ones, short tees or long. The choice is yours. Courses *1, 2* and *3* were designed by Donald Ross; *Course 4*, originally designed by Ross, was redone in 1973 by Robert Trent Jones and again in 1983 by Rees Jones; *Course 5* is an Ellis Maples layout, redesigned in 1974 by Robert Trent Jones; *Course 6* is a Tom and George Fazio affair; and *Course 7* was designed by Rees Jones. A variety of golf knowledge and a vast amount of expertise is wrapped up in these great layouts. Pinehurst now offers the Golf Advantage School.

RATES: (MAP) Lodgings - $464 per couple. Green fees - $130/ $199, including cart; *Course 2* - $254. Golf package - two nights/

North Carolina

three days (includes lodging, MAP, golf), $1,608 per couple. Rates are for March-June.

ARRIVAL: By air - Raleigh-Durham (55 miles). Fayetteville (30 miles). By private aircraft - Pinehurst-Southern Pines. By car - I-95 or US 1 to Route 211 north.

Pine Needles Resort

PO Box 88, Southern Pines, NC 28387

(910) 692-7111; (800) 659-7677

ACCOMMODATIONS: 75 lodge rooms. A special eight-person arrangement of four bedrooms, five baths and living room is also available.

AMENITIES: Heated swimming pool, two lighted tennis courts, a recreation and game room, and a mini-spa with a steam room. There are two dining rooms: the Split Level for casual dining, and the Crest Dining Room.

GOLF: The very picturesque layout, reaching out 6,603/6,235/4,989 yards, has a par of 71. Traps, water hazards and trees contouring the fairways make this an outstanding golfing experience.

RATES: (FAP) Lodgings - $280/$300 per couple. Green fees - $100, including cart. Golf package - two nights/three days (includes lodging, FAP, green fees, cart, bag storage) $1,000/$1,120 per couple. Rates are for mid-March to mid-June and September-November.

ARRIVAL: By air - Raleigh-Durham (55 miles). Fayetteville (30 miles). By private aircraft - Moore County Airport (three miles). By car - from Raleigh-Durham, North Carolina 70 to US 1, to North Carolina 2 (75 minutes).

Sea Trail Golf Resort

211 Clubhouse Road, Sunset Beach, NC 28468

(910) 287-1100; (800) 624-6601

ACCOMMODATIONS: 75 one-room efficiencies and one-, two-, and three-bedroom villas. Some are located along the fairways; others overlook the Calabash River Creek.

AMENITIES: Swimming pool, sauna, whirlpool spa, two lighted tennis courts, bicycle rentals, a fitness room, along with horseback riding nearby. There are two excellent restaurants, the Jones/Byrd and the Tavern on the Tee.

GOLF: There are three courses – a Dan Maples layout that came into play in 1986, a Rees Jones affair that opened in the spring of 1990, and a Willard Byrd golf course that began play in the fall of 1990.

The Maples design reaches out 6,751/6,332/6,035/5,090 yards. Bringing water into contention on 10 holes, it is extremely well-trapped and lined with trees.

The Jones course, playing to a yardage of 6,761/6,334/5,716/4,912, features large, raised greens with water coming into the act on 11 holes.

The Byrd course measures 6,750/6,263/5,590/4,717 yards. Water is a factor on 10 holes, and it features tree-lined, tight fairways and well-trapped greens. All three courses par at 72.

RATES: (EP) Lodgings - $99/$155/$210. Green fees - $84/$94, including cart. Golf package - one night/one day (includes lodging, one round of golf, breakfast), $206 per couple. Cart $36. Rates quoted are for the spring (March-May) and fall (September-November) periods. Unless you are acclimated to it, this area is too hot and humid during the summer months for golf.

ARRIVAL: By air - Myrtle Beach, SC (35 miles). By car - from Myrtle beach take Highway 17 north to Highway 904. Turn right, drive four miles and turn right onto SR 179. Drive one mile to resort.

Springdale Country Club

Route 2, Box 271, Canton, NC 28716

(828) 235-8451; (800) 553-3027

ACCOMMODATIONS: Range from one-bedroom units to cottages lodging up to 30 people. A nice touch: Upon check-in you are assigned a complimentary golf cart equipped with side curtains and lights, which can be used for transportation around the facility.

AMENITIES: Meals are served family-style in the beautiful dining room.

North Carolina

This resort is in a dry area. You must provide your own or go without. It is quite a drive to a source of supply.

GOLF: The Springdale Country Club Course is a challenging layout, parring at 72/74, and reaching out 6,812/6,437/5,734/5,421 yards. The undulating terrain, large greens, numerous traps, and a wandering stream all combine to make this an interesting and beautiful layout.

RATES: (MAP) Lodgings - $198/$210/$250 per couple. Rates include green fees, carts, breakfast and dinner. Rates are for April to October 31.

ARRIVAL: By air - Asheville. By car - on Highway 276, 11 miles south of Waynesville and six miles south of Route 110 intersection.

Tanglewood Park

PO Box 1040, Clemmons, NC 27012

(336) 778-6370

ACCOMMODATIONS: Motor Lodge, the Manor House, cottages near Lake Mallard, and campground with water and electrical hookups.

AMENITIES: Paddleboats, canoes, trail riding, 10 tennis courts and golf. Tanglewood also has one of the finest dining rooms in the area.

GOLF: The Tanglewood "Championship" layout measures 6,842/6,269/5,566 yards, parring at 70/74, while the East "Reynolds" Course plays 6,649/6,061/5,066 and pars at 72. The combination of narrow fairways, small greens, and enough traps to make you think you are at the beach makes these courses more than just a bit challenging.

RATES: (EP) Lodgings - $45/$105. Cottages - (equipped for housekeeping) $425 per week and up. Green fees - $45, including carts.

ARRIVAL: By air - Winston-Salem, Greensboro. By car - 10 miles west of Winston-Salem on I-40.

The Village at Nags Head

PO Box 1807, Nags Head, NC 27959

(252) 480-2224; (800) 548-9688

The history of the area (which is located a short distance from Kitty Hawk) goes back to the 16th century. Adjacent Roanoke Island was the site of the so-called "Lost Colony." In 1587, 115 English colonists established a settlement there, then vanished without a trace.

ACCOMMODATIONS: The 400-acre resort has private homes ranging from three to eight bedrooms.

AMENITIES: Two lighted tennis courts, Olympic-size pool, and the Ocean Front Beach & Tennis Club. Should you tire of cooking, there is an excellent restaurant at the clubhouse.

GOLF: This is one of the most deceptive golf courses you may ever encounter. Designed by Jerry Turner & Associates, the Nags Head course was created in a true Scottish "links" configuration. The deception is in the yardage. Many a golfer has looked at the scorecard and figured he had an easy conquest at hand. Playing 6,126/5,717/5,354/4,435 yards, it pars at 71.

There are several factors that can turn this apparently easy tour into a raging tiger. First, the wind sometimes seems to come at you from six different directions at once. Next, while the fairways appear to be very open, they are actually very tight. They are shaggy and scrubby, lined with love grass, sea oats, wildflowers and bushes – all of which can destroy a golf shot. Water forms additional challenges on 13 holes.

If you don't think carefully about each shot, you could be seriously embarrassed. Imagine shooting over 100 on a course that plays only 5,717 yards from the men's tees.

RATES: (EP) Lodgings - three- to six-bedroom units. Weekly rentals range from $1,200 to $1,600. Green fees - $89, including cart. Golf packages are available. Fall is the best season for golf here.

ARRIVAL: By air - the nearest major airport is Norfolk (two hours). By private aircraft - Manteo Airport (10 miles). By car - from Norfolk follow 64 E to 168 S (Exit 83B). Continue on 168 S until it turns into 158. Remain on 158. You will cross a long bridge and are now on the Outer Banks. Continue 15 miles after crossing the bridge. Rental check-in is at the Village Realty, which is on the left side of Highway 158.

Washington Duke Inn & Golf Club

3001 Cameron Boulevard, Durham, NC 27706

(919) 490-0999; (800) 443-3853

The last place one expects to find a golf resort is on the grounds of a well-known university, but the five-story inn is, in fact, situated on the campus of Duke University. I'd describe the atmosphere here as "subdued elegance." It is delightful.

ACCOMMODATIONS: 171 rooms and suites.

AMENITIES: Outdoor swimming pool, jogging paths and tennis on nearby courts. The inn's Fairview Restaurant serves a varied selection of specialties and has an excellent wine cellar.

GOLF: The course, a Robert Trent Jones, Sr. design, was later redone by Rees Jones. With a par of 72/74, it reaches out 7,045/6,721/6,207/5,505 yards. While on undulating terrain, the landing areas are fairly open. It is, however, heavily lined with trees. Water also presents a challenge on six holes.

RATES: (EP) Lodgings - $235/$265/$285. Green fees - $63/$78, including cart. Golf packages are available.

ARRIVAL: By air - Raleigh/Durham International Airport (14 miles). By car - take I-40 west toward Durham. Exit onto the Durham Expressway and continue into Durham. Stay on the expressway until it ends, then turn left onto Erwin Road. Stay on Erwin Road until it ends, then turn left onto Cameron Boulevard.

Waynesville Country Club Inn

PO Box 390, Waynesville, NC 28786

(828) 452-2258; (800) 311-8238

ACCOMMODATIONS: Guest rooms or apartments are available in the main lodge or in the Fairway and Brookside buildings. They also offer lodgings in the Senator or Governor Cottages.

AMENITIES: Two tennis courts, a pool, lounge and dining room.

GOLF: The Waynesville Country Club Course was built in the late 1920's. Now a 27-hole course, the Carolina/Blue Ridge combination measures 5,936/5,486/5,013 yards; the Blue Ridge/Dogwood nines reach out 5,791/5,246/4,576 yards; and the final Dogwood/Carolina pairing comes in at 5,793/5,390/4,927 yards. No matter how you mix them, the par remains 70. It is a lovely layout with lush fairways, bent grass greens, water coming into play on 16 holes and a view of the surrounding countryside that is hard to beat.

RATES (MAP) Lodgings - $198/$300 per couple. Villas - (EP) one bedroom, $150. Green fees - $25, carts $30. Golf package - one day/one night, includes lodging, MAP, golf, $202/$232 per couple.

ARRIVAL: By air - Asheville (30 miles). By car - from Atlanta via Sylva, Highway 19-23 to West Waynesville exit.

Wolf Laurel Resort

Route 3, Mars Hill, NC 28754

(828) 689-9212; (800) 221-0409

ACCOMMODATIONS: Log cabins, cottages or A-frame contemporary homes. The homes have from two to five bedrooms and sleep up to 10 or more people.

AMENITIES: Lighted tennis courts, fishing, and hiking. There is an excellent restaurant available.

Another alert: This is a dry county, so bring your own.

GOLF: The Blue Mountain Golf Course measures 6,200/ 5,942/4,627 yards and pars at 72. There are some extremely interesting holes here: a par 3, playing 180 yards, with a drop of 180 feet, or a par-5 double dog-leg, which has a rushing stream protecting your approach to the green.

Keep in mind you are playing at an altitude of almost 5,000 feet. Each tee offers yardage as well as elevation information. Trees and lots of water (at least on the front nine) turn this into a shotmaker's layout.

RATES: (EP) Lodgings - (two-night minimum) $130/$175, weekly $875. Green fees - $55, including cart. Golf packages are available. Rates are for May-October.

ARRIVAL: By air - Asheville. By car - US 23, 27 miles north of Asheville.

North Carolina

Woodlake Country Club

PO Box 648, Vass, NC 28394

(910) 245-4031; (800) 334-1126

ACCOMMODATIONS: One- to three-bedroom villas with living room, kitchen, and dining area; some with washer/dryer.

AMENITIES: Swimming pool, tennis courts and boat docks. There is a restaurant and terrace overlooking the first hole.

GOLF: Woodlake now has 36 holes of golf. The Lakeside/Cypress nines reach out a solid 7,012/6,584/6,144/5,255 yards, the Cypress/Cranes combination is a massive 7,045/6,418/5,895/5,133; the Lakeside/Cranes weighs in at 6,811/6,218/5,695/4,900 yards. No matter how you mix them, the par remains at 72. You will find this layout beautiful as well as challenging, with rolling hills, towering pines and lots of water. Now there is a new 9-hole Palmer/Maples layout as well.

RATES: (EP) Lodgings - $96/$149. Green fees - $46, carts $32. Golf package - two nights/three days (includes lodging, green fees, cart and taxes), $310 per couple.

ARRIVAL: By air - Southern Pines or Fayetteville (28 miles), Raleigh-Durham (60 miles). By car - accessible via US 1, US 74 or I-95; 13 miles north of Southern Pines.

Ohio

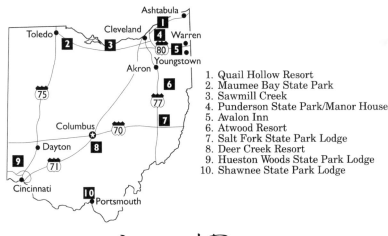

1. Quail Hollow Resort
2. Maumee Bay State Park
3. Sawmill Creek
4. Punderson State Park/Manor House
5. Avalon Inn
6. Atwood Resort
7. Salt Fork State Park Lodge
8. Deer Creek Resort
9. Hueston Woods State Park Lodge
10. Shawnee State Park Lodge

Atwood Resort

2650 Lodge Road, Dellroy, OH 44620

(330) 735-2211; (800) 362-6406

ACCOMMODATIONS: 104 lodge rooms, each with a view of the lake from a balcony or terrace. There are also one- to four-bedroom lakeside cottages.

AMENITIES: Five lighted tennis courts, indoor and outdoor pool, a Nautilus Center, sailing or water-skiing on Lake Atwood, or just some old-fashioned loafing on the sandy beach. Dining is in the Bryce Browning Room.

GOLF: The Atwood Resort's course measures 6,057/5,776/4,188 yards and pars at 70. Rolling terrain, many trees, water coming into play on three holes, and some very interesting dog-legs turn this into a stimulating layout. There is also a lighted, par-3 course.

RATES: (EP) Lodgings - $131/$145. Cottages - weekly, $825. Green fees - $24, carts $39. Golf package - two nights (includes lodging, MAP, green fees, cart), $540 per couple. Rates are for June through September.

ARRIVAL: By air - Akron-Canton. By car - from Canton, south on Route 800 to Route 212, southeast to Route 542, then east.

Avalon Inn

9519 East Market Street, Warren, OH 44484

(330) 856-1900; (800) 221-1549

ACCOMMODATIONS: 144 nicely decorated guest rooms.

AMENITIES: Three indoor/outdoor tennis courts, indoor Olympic-size pool, and saunas. Dining is in the Tall Oaks Restaurant or in the Country Garden.

GOLF: There are two courses. The Avalon South plays 6,106/ 5,295 yards, parring at 71. This layout brings water in on five holes and has some trees where they should not be. The Lakes Course reaches out a more substantial 6,825/6,453/5,393 yards but also pars at 71. This one has water on at least nine holes and sand traps reminiscent of the great Sahara Desert.

RATES: (EP) Lodgings - $73/$100/$135. Green fees - $29/$65, including cart. Golf package - one day/one night (includes lodging, golf, cart, MAP, taxes), $220 per couple per day. Rates are for May-October.

ARRIVAL: By air - Youngstown. By car - five miles east of downtown Warren on East Market Street.

Deer Creek Resort

PO Box 127, Mt. Sterling, OH 43143

(740) 869-2020; (877) 678-3337

ACCOMMODATIONS: 110 guest rooms and 25 cabins, fully equipped for housekeeping.

AMENITIES: Tennis, indoor and outdoor swimming pools, whirlpool, sauna, and a practice putting green. The park is adjacent to 1,277 acres of water and offers swimming, boating, fishing and hunting. There is a dining room, lounge and bar, as well as a coffee shop.

GOLF: The park's 18-hole course reaches out a very impressive 7,134/6,574/5,611 yards, and pars at 72.

RATES: (EP) Lodgings - $105/$199. Cabins - weekly $963. Green fees - $17/$22, carts $24.

ARRIVAL: By air - Columbus. By car - travel south on I-71 to Exit 84. Take State Route 207 to the park (approximately 40 miles total).

Quail Hollow Resort

11080 Concord-Hambden Road, Painesville, OH 44077

(440) 352-6201; (800) 792-0258

ACCOMMODATIONS: 169 comfortably furnished guest rooms.

AMENITIES: Indoor and outdoor swimming pools, men's and women's saunas, lighted tennis courts and, of course, golf. Formal dining is provided in the Quail Wagon (jackets required; ties optional). A more casual atmosphere is found in the Clubhouse Cafe.

GOLF: The Quail Hollow Inn course measures 6,712/6,357/ 5,124/4,389 yards with a par of 72. A Bruce Devlin/Robert Von Hagge layout, it is set on slightly rolling terrain, with trees and water forming a part of the challenge. The newest course is a Weiskopf/Jay Morrish design. Playing to a par of 71, it measures 6,872/6,408/6,019/5,166 yards.

RATES: (EP) Lodgings - $150/$180. Green fees - $65/$75, carts $38. Golf packages are available. Rates are for June-October.

ARRIVAL: By air - Cleveland (30 miles). By car - south of I-90 on Highway 44, east on Concord-Hambden Road.

Sawmill Creek

2401 Cleveland Road West, Huron, OH 44839

(419) 433-3800; (800) 729-6455

ACCOMMODATIONS: 240 guest rooms, including suites.

AMENITIES: Indoor waterfall swimming pool with hydrotherapy pool, adjacent sauna, plus a white sand beach on Lake Erie with sailing, fishing, boating and water-skiing. There are also tennis courts and, of course, golf. For dining there is the Bird Cage restaurant, the Sawmill Steakhouse, and The Smugglers Cove restaurant.

GOLF: The course is a George and Tom Fazio design. Parring at 70/72, it reaches out 6,948/6,351/5,727 yards. While it is flat, the water, bunkers, doglegs and trees (all in the wrong location, or so it seems) will keep your undivided attention.

RATES: (EP) Lodgings - $159/$179 per couple. Green fees - $58/$62, carts $32. Rates are for mid-June through September.

ARRIVAL: Located between Cleveland and Toledo. By car - Ohio Turnpike to Exit 7, then north on 250 to Route 2. Go east on Route 2 to the Rye Beach Road exit.

Ohio State Parks

There are several very fine state parks in Ohio. We are listing only those that offer golf and have lodges or inns. Most of the parks are on lakes and provide an array of water activities. They also happen to be outstanding bargains. For further information, call (800) 282-7275, or write to the Parks Division at 600 W. Spring Street, Columbus, OH 43215. Golf packages are available.

Hueston Woods State Park Lodge

RFD #1, College Corner, OH 45003

(513) 523-6381; (800) 282-7275

ACCOMMODATIONS: 94 rooms in the lodge; 25 deluxe cabins with two bedrooms, bath, kitchen, living room and screened porch; plus 34 standard cabins.

AMENITIES: Game room, indoor and outdoor pools, lighted tennis courts, and boat rentals for fishing. There is also a 1,500-foot swimming beach along with a dining room, lounge and snack bar.

GOLF: The golf course, about eight miles from the park entrance, stretches out a healthy 7,005/6,727/5,176 yards and pars at 72. The yardage alone should tell you this is no pushover.

RATES: (EP) Lodgings - $109/$140. Green fees - $17/$22, carts $24.

ARRIVAL: By air - Cincinnati or Dayton. By car - on Highway 732, eight miles north of Oxford.

Maumee Bay State Park Resort

1750 Park Road #2, Oregon, OH 43618

(419) 836-1466; (800) 282-7275

ACCOMMODATIONS: 120 rooms, and 20 "cottages" that are fully equipped for housekeeping.

AMENITIES: Tennis and racquetball courts, fitness center, whirlpool, sauna, indoor and outdoor swimming pools, boating, fishing and a 1,500-foot beach. The dining room serves breakfast, lunch and dinner.

GOLF: This layout was designed by Arthur Hill. Although the area is relatively flat, the course was built as a links-style affair. With undulating fairways, small multi-level greens, water in play on 13 holes, narrow fairways and tall rough, it will offer you all you can handle – and maybe just a bit more. Parring at 72, it reaches out 6,941/6,557/6,136/5,221 yards. For weekend play, call (419) 836-9009 after 8:00 AM on the Wednesday before.

RATES: (EP) Lodgings - $140/$175/$225. Green fees - $22/$28, carts $24. Weekly rates and golf packages are available.

ARRIVAL: By air - Toledo (10 miles). By car - take State Route 2 east to North Curtice Rd. Turn left – the park entrance is right there.

Punderson State Park Manor House

Route 87, Box 224, Newberry, OH 44065

(216) 564-9144; (800) 282-7275

ACCOMMODATIONS: 35 lodge rooms; there are also 26 cottages, fully equipped for housekeeping.

AMENITIES: Marina, tennis courts, outdoor swimming pool, 18-hole golf course and a dining room.

GOLF: The course measures 6,815/6,600/6,342 yards, with a par of 72.

RATES: (EP) Lodgings - $115/$145. Green fees - $18, carts $24.

ARRIVAL: By air - Cleveland Hopkins Airport (50 minutes). By car - from I-271 take Route 87 east.

Salt Fork State Park Lodge

Box 7, State Route 22, Cambridge, OH 43725

(614) 439-2751; (800) 282-7275

ACCOMMODATIONS: 148 rooms in the lodge, and 54 cottages equipped for housekeeping.

AMENITIES: Saunas, tennis courts, indoor and outdoor pools, horseback riding, swimming beach, the marina and an 18-hole golf course. There is a dining room, lounge and bar.

GOLF: This course plays to a modest yardage of 6,056/5,786/5,446, parring at 71.

RATES: (EP) Lodgings - $118/$160. Green fees - $18, carts $24.

ARRIVAL: By car - eight miles NE of Cambridge off US 32.

Shawnee State Park Lodge

Box 98, Star Route 125, Portsmouth, OH 45662

(614) 858-6621; (800) 282-7275

ACCOMMODATIONS: Shawnee Lodge is a beautiful, modern, three-story inn. There are 50 well-appointed rooms, along with 54 cottages.

AMENITIES: Indoor and outdoor swimming pools, tennis courts, golf course, and swimming beach. The lodge has a dining room and bar.

GOLF: The course plays 6,837/6,407/6,038 yards, with a par of 72/73.

RATES: (EP) Lodgings $95/$125. Green fees - $18, carts $24.

ARRIVAL: By car - on Route 125, northwest of Portsmouth.

Oklahoma

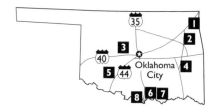

1. Shangri-La Resort
2. Western Hills Guest Ranch
3. Roman Nose State Park
4. Fountainhead Resort
5. Quartz Mountain State Park
6. Lake Murray State Park
7. Lake Texoma State Park
8. Falconhead Resort & CC

Falconhead Resort & Country Club

PO Box 206, Burneyville, OK 73430

(580) 276-9411

ACCOMMODATIONS: Lodgings are available at the Falcon Inn. Falconhead, located in the Red River Valley, is a large residential resort community covering approximately 3,800 acres.

AMENITIES: Four lighted tennis courts, two swimming pools, and golf. Beautiful Lake Falcon adds another dimension to the ranch, providing all types of water sports. The Falcon Inn has a restaurant.

GOLF: The course at Falconhead Country Club pars at 72/71 and measures 6,448/5,992/5,350 yards. While the front nine is flat, the back side brings trees, as well as some rolling terrain, into play. Falcon Lake also gets into the act on four holes.

RATES: (EP) Falcon Inn - $52. Green fees - $20/$24, carts $18. Golf packages are available.

ARRIVAL: By air - Dallas (100 miles). Oklahoma City (125 miles). By car - I-35, 18 miles south of Ardmore exit to Route 32 at Marrietta, then 13 miles west.

Fountainhead Resort

HC 70 Box 1355, Checotah, OK 74426

(918) 689-9173; (800) 345-6343

ACCOMMODATIONS: 202 rooms and suites, plus 22 cottages.

AMENITIES: Boating, fishing, water-skiing, swimming pool, tennis, horseback riding, archery, and golf. The Terrace Room has dining and dancing with entertainment available in the lounge.

GOLF: The Fountainhead State Park course, with a par of 72, reaches out 6,919/6,405/5,885/4,864 yards.

RATES: (EP) Lodgings - $75/$85/$100. Green fees - $14/$17, carts $18.

ARRIVAL: By air - Tulsa (80 miles). By private aircraft - adjacent to the property (a 3,000-foot paved runway). By car - seven miles south of I-40 on Highway 150 and on Lake Eufaula.

Shangri-La Resort

Highway 125 South, Afton, OK 74331

(918) 257-4204; (800) 331-4060

ACCOMMODATIONS: Main Lodge (126 rooms), the Golden Oaks (144 rooms), and the Vista Towers, with 63 two-bedroom suites.

AMENITIES: Indoor and outdoor swimming pools, sand beach, four indoor and outdoor tennis courts, and four bowling lanes. There is a dining room (The Greenery) in the main lodge. There are two other dining spots close by: The Roadhouse, located on Highway 125, (918) 257-8185, and Spats, (918) 257-5903. Both represent a delightful change of pace.

GOLF: The Blue (east course) stretches out 6,972/6,435/5,975 yards and pars at 72/73. This layout has rolling terrain and trees, with well-trapped greens. The Gold (west course) is a bit more modest, playing 5,932/5,431/5,109/4,517 yards and parring at 70/71. While fairly open, with few trees, the well-bunkered course does have its share of water.

RATES: (EP) Lodgings - $134/$174. Green fees - $85/$90, including cart. Golf package - one night/two days (includes lodging, dinner,two rounds of golf, cart, club storage), $349 per couple. Rates quoted are for April-October.

ARRIVAL: By air - Tulsa (65 miles). By car - I-44, take Afton exit to US 59, southeast to Highway 125, then south 11 miles.

Oklahoma's State Parks

500 Will Rogers Building, Oklahoma City, OK 73105

(405) 521-2464; (800) 522-8040

Oklahoma has five resort parks spread throughout the state. They all provide approximately the same amenities: archery, bicycling, boating, golf course, horseback riding, children's playground, swimming pool, tennis, water-skiing (not available at Roman Nose) and private airstrip (not available at Roman Nose or Quartz Mountain). Each resort has a dining room and offers a golf package. These state-operated resorts are not only delightful, but they represent one of the best values for a vacation buck we have seen anywhere in the country.

Lake Murray State Park Resort

The Lodge, Ardmore, OK 73402

(405) 223-6600; (800) 654-8240

ACCOMMODATIONS: 54 rooms in the country-style inn, and 88 cottages. These units have kitchenettes, fireplaces, and color television. There are also 240 RV camping sites and a grocery store. The resort is in a 12,500-acre state park and is located on 5,728-acre Lake Murray.

AMENITIES: Lighted tennis courts and an outdoor swimming pool. The marina offers fishing, paddleboating, sailing, and houseboat rentals. There are also riding stables, with hayrides and trail rides. For dining there is the Quilts restaurant or the Parlor for drinks and lighter fare.

GOLF: The course is now an 18-hole layout.

RATES: (EP) Lodgings - $60/$75/$150. Green fees - $17, carts $20.

ARRIVAL: Two miles east of I-35 and seven miles south of Ardmore on Lake Murray.

Lake Texoma State Park Resort

The Lodge, Durant, OK 74701

(580) 564-2311; (800) 528-0593

ACCOMMODATIONS: 97 rooms, including lodge, poolside, cabana suites, and terrace rooms. There are also 67 one- and two-bedroom cottages.

AMENITIES: Fitness center, lighted tennis courts, a marina offering all types of water sports, as well as horseback riding. For entertainment and dining there is the Waterfront Lounge; food is also served at the Gallery Restaurant and a snack bar at the swimming pool.

GOLF: The course at Texoma State Park is an 18-hole, par 71/74, playing to a yardage of 6,128/5,868/5,145.

RATES: (EP) Lodgings - $60/$95/$99. Green fees - $17, carts $20.

ARRIVAL: On US 70, 13 miles west of Durant, on Lake Texoma.

Quartz Mountain State Park Resort

The Lodge, Lake Altus-Lugert, OK 73522

(580) 563-2238; (800) 654-8240

ACCOMMODATIONS: Overlooking Lake Altus-Lugert, the resort has 45 rooms in the two-story lodge, plus 16 cottages.

AMENITIES: Tennis courts, indoor and outdoor swimming pools, and game room. Watersports include a swimming beach, water-skiing, boating, fishing, paddleboats, canoes, and yak boards. There is a dining room in the lodge.

GOLF: The golf course is now 18 holes, with a par of 69.
RATES: (EP) Lodgings - $69/$125. Green fees $17, carts $20.
ARRIVAL: By car - 141 miles west of Oklahoma City, 20 miles north of Altus on Highway 44 and 44A.

Roman Nose State Park Resort

The Lodge, Watonga, OK 73772

(405) 623-7281; (800) 892-8690

ACCOMMODATIONS: 47 guest rooms in the Lodge, and 10 cottages with kitchenettes. This area, rich in history, was once a campground for the Cheyenne Indian Tribe.
AMENITIES: Tennis, swimming in a natural rock pool, fishing, and boating.
GOLF: The course is a nine-hole layout measuring (when played twice) 5,830/5,202 yards, with a par of 70/72.
RATES: (EP) Lodgings - $60/$150. Green fees - $17, carts $20.
ARRIVAL: By air - Watonga airport. Courtesy transportation to the resort can be arranged. By car - Roman Nose is 81 miles northwest of Oklahoma City, seven miles north of Watonga on Highway 8 and 8A.

Western Hills Guest Ranch Resort

Box 509, Wagoner, OK 74477

(918) 772-2545; (800) 368-1468

ACCOMMODATIONS: 101 rooms, 12 cabanas and 54 cottages. All rooms are air-conditioned and have color TV. There is a trained director for the planned children's programs, which offer various crafts, puppet shows, and water games.
AMENITIES: Two lighted tennis courts, outdoor swimming pool, sailboats, power boats, and paddleboats. There is a western-style dining room, and a grocery store is located on the premises.
GOLF: The 18-hole course measures 5,860/5,555 yards and pars at 70/73.

RATES: (EP) Lodgings - $55/$150. Green fees - $16. Carts: $20.

ARRIVAL: By private aircraft - in the park is a 3,400-foot paved, lighted runway. By car - on Fort Gibson Reservoir, eight miles east of Wagoner on Highway 51.

Oregon

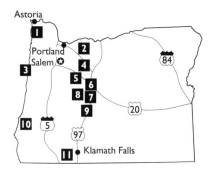

Astoria
Portland
Salem
Klamath Falls

1. Gearheart-by-the-Sea
2. The Resort at the Mountain
3. Westin Salishan Lodge
4. Kah-Nee-Ta
5. Black Butte Resort
6. Eagle Crest Resort
7. The Riverhouse Inn
8. Inn at the Seventh Mountain
9. Sunriver Resort
10. Bandon Dunes Resort
11. The Running Y Resort

Bandon Dunes Resort

Round Lake Drive, Bandon, OR 97411

(541) 347-4380; (888) 345-6008; www.bandondunesgolf.com

Located along the beautiful southern Oregon coast, 26 miles south of Coos Bay, Bandon Dunes Resort enjoys an outstanding setting.

ACCOMMODATIONS: There are 19 single rooms and two four-bedroom suites.

AMENITIES: The clubhouse is the center of activity. This 32,000-square-foot building houses a wonderful restaurant, The Gallery, and The Bunker lounge for cocktailsand snacks. Adjacent to The Gallery is the Tufted Puffin Lounge. There is also a sports pub, a spa facility, a hot tub and an exercise room. Other possible activities include fishing, whale watching, wind surfing and horseback riding.

GOLF: Once you have played this layout, we think you will agree that it is a rare experience. Situated along the Oregon coast, the course overlooks 20 plus miles of sweeping shoreline. On grassy dunes, which roll along the edge of the sea, the entire layout is reminiscent of many of Scotland's golf courses. It has been ranked third in Golf Maganzines's "Top100 You Can Play." An extra: other than the view of the nearby ocean, there is no water coming into play. Reaching out an impressive 7,326/6,844/6,483/6,112/5,691/5178 yards, it pars at 72. With the ocean wind, deep pot bunkers, indigenous vegetation and the distraction of the magnificent ocean views, you will find this layout all you can handle. Another 18-hole course, Pacific Dunes, will be open in 2001.

 Bandon Dunes is a "walking" course. They do, however, have a small number of carts for those who cannot walk. If riding rather than walking is a necessity I suggest you make arrangements when calling for reservations.

RATES: Lodgings - dune view $115; golf/ocean view $165; suites $175/$290. Green fees - $110. Caddy fees - $35, plus gratuities.

ARRIVAL: By air - North Bend Airport (20 miles north car; rentals are available). By car - from Coos Bay, drive south on 101 about 23 miles to the Bandon exit. Guard gate entrance to the resort is two miles before the town of Bandon.

Black Butte Ranch

PO Box 8000, Black Butte Ranch, OR 97759

(541) 595-6211; (800) 452-7455

Black Butte is, in every sense, a "family" resort. From the meadow areas, the view of the many surrounding mountain peaks is spectacular.

ACCOMMODATIONS: Condominiums and many private homes, all equipped for housekeeping. However, should you elect to pass on the housekeeping, you will find the dining room at the lodge an excellent alternative.

AMENITIES: Four swimming pools, 16 miles of bicycle paths, horseback riding (Black Butte is a working ranch), 23 tennis courts, fishing, canoeing, whitewater raft trips, and movies. The fishing, by the way, is barbless fly-fishing, hook and release. The kids love it, and so do the fish.

GOLF: Black Butte has two of the most picturesque golf layouts found anywhere. Big Meadow, stretching out 6,850/6,456/5,678 yards, pars at 72. The newer of the two, Glaze Meadow, measures 6,574/6,273/5,610 yards and also pars at 72. As an added distraction (or attraction), it seems on almost every hole you are looking at one of the many mountain peaks surrounding the ranch. Both courses have been modified: realizing that some of the holes were a bit on the "long" side they have been altered and made more "user friendly."

RATES: (EP) Lodgings - $90/$120/$150/$190. Rates vary for private homes with capacity of six people. Green fees - $60, carts $30.

ARRIVAL: By air - Redmond Airport (30 miles). By car - 135 miles from Portland. Go south on I-5 to Highway 20, then east on Highway 20 (Santiam Pass) for 98 miles.

Eagle Crest Resort

Cline Falls Road, Redmond, OR 97756

(541) 923-2453; (800) 682-4786

ACCOMMODATIONS: 76 rooms in the inn and 75 condominiums.

AMENITIES: Tennis, swimming pool, use of the equestrian center, and miles of hiking and jogging trails. There is an outstanding restaurant in the Canyon Clubhouse.

GOLF: The Eagle Crest Golf Club reaches out a respectable 6,673/6,292/5,395 yards and pars at 72. Your initial impression of this course will be that it is open and should not be too difficult. These two assumptions are incorrect. It is neither. While the first hole will lull you, the second and third will bring you to a fully alert status. The greens throughout the course are multi-level and difficult. All in all it is an entertaining layout, but one that requires your full attention. Water comes into the picture on only four holes.

The newest addition, the Ridge Golf Course, is directly across the road from the resort entrance. It opened in mid-1993 and was designed by John Thronson. Reaching out an awesome 7,011/6,533/5,912/5,087 yards, it pars at 72.

RATES: Lodgings (EP) - $93/$139/$189. Green fees - $32/$49, carts $25.

ARRIVAL: By air - Redmond Airport (six miles). By car - Highway 126 west from Redmond, five miles, then left on Cline Falls Road.

Gearhart by-the-Sea

PO Box 2700, Gearhart, OR 97138

(503) 738-8331; (800) 547-0115

ACCOMMODATIONS: 80 condominium apartments of varying size and floor plan, each with a spacious living room, fireplace, dining area, and fully equipped kitchen.

AMENITIES: Two indoor swimming pools, plus a therapy pool.

GOLF: The Gearhart Golf Links is directly across the road. An 18-hole layout, it plays 6,089/5,882 yards, with a par of 72/74.

RATES: (EP) Lodgings - $126/$148/$194. Green fees - $35/$45, carts $25.

ARRIVAL: By air - Astoria. By car - from Portland, head west on Highway 26 (80 miles) to Highway 101, then north for seven miles to Seaside. Drive three more miles and turn left at Captain Morgans Restaurant. Go west until the road curves south and becomes N. Marion Street. The resort is at N. Marion & 10th.

The Inn of the Seventh Mountain

18575 Century Drive, Bend, OR 97702

(541) 382-8711; (800) 452-6810

ACCOMMODATIONS: Studios and one-, two-, and three-bedroom condominiums. Each has a fireplace and fully equipped kitchen or kitchenette. Washer/dryer units are located in every other condominium building. A convenience grocery store and gas station are located on the property; both operate year-round.

AMENITIES: Seven Plexipave tennis courts, two swimming pools (one with a 65-foot water slide), coed saunas and whirlpools, aerobic and aquatic exercise classes, a roller skating rink, bicycle rentals, horseback riding, hayrides, and whitewater rafting. Children from four to 11 years old can be registered in a professionally supervised day camp. Should you choose not to cook for yourself, there are three alternatives: the Poppy Seed Cafe, El Crab Catcher Restaurant and the clubhouse restaurant and lounge.

During the winter months, skiing is king in this magnificent area. Nearby Mt. Bachelor (14 miles away) has an elevation of 9,065 feet, and features 54 runs, powder snow, three super express quad lifts and the high-speed Summit Chair, along with 60 kilometers of cross-country trails.

GOLF: Designed by Robert Muir Graves, the course plays to a par of 72 and reaches out 6,911/6,483/5,911/5,070 yards. Built on undulating terrain, its multi-level greens and water on 10 holes will challenge you.

RATES: (EP) Lodgings - $69/$125/$189/$299. Green fees - $85, including cart.

ARRIVAL: By air - Redmond Airport (16 miles north of Bend). By car - going south on Highway 97, turn right onto Division Street. Follow signs to Century Drive (Cascade Lake Highway), and continue on Century Drive about five miles to the resort.

Kah-Nee-Ta

PO Box K, Warm Springs, OR 97761

(541) 553-1112; (800) 831-0100

The lodge is owned and operated by the Confederation of Indian Tribes.

ACCOMMODATIONS: 140 rooms and suites, each with private balcony. The village also offers some unique accommodations – tepees! The children will never stop talking about the night they spent in an Indian tepee, and neither will you if you don't bring sleeping bags or cots. The floors are concrete, and there are no beds.

AMENITIES: Horseback riding, two tennis courts, and a huge swimming pool. For dining, the menu offers an unusual and varied selection – everything from lobster tail, rainbow trout, and salmon to game hen, buffalo, or venison.

GOLF: The course plays 6,288/5,418 and pars at 72/73.

RATES: (EP) Lodgings - $130/$145/$210. Green fees - $38, carts $27. Rates are for May-September.

ARRIVAL: By air - Redmond (60 miles); Portland (115 miles). By car - 11 miles north of Warm Springs, with turnoff signs clearly marked.

The Resort at the Mountain

68010 Fairway, Welches, OR 97067

(503) 622-3101; (800) 669-7666

ACCOMMODATIONS: 160 guest rooms and several two- and three-bedroom condominiums.

AMENITIES: Six tennis courts, hiking, swimming, fishing, and whitewater rafting. They also offer a staff-supervised kid haven, which has many electronic games. Dining is available in the Forest Hills Dining Room as well as the lounge.

GOLF: There are 27 holes to play on these gently rolling alpine meadows. The Red/Green combination reaches out 6,394/5,687 yards and pars at 72/74; the Red/Yellow nines play 5,718/5,077 yards with a par of 70/71; and the Green/Yellow plays 6,006/5,246 yards, also parring at 70/71.

RATES: (EP) Lodgings - $99/$179/$249. Green fees - $36, cart $27. Golf packages are available.

ARRIVAL: By air - Portland. By car - head east on I-84 to the Wood Village/Gresham exit. Go three miles to Burnside and turn left. Burnside will become Highway 26. Total travel 25 miles.

The Riverhouse Resort

3075 N. Highway 97, Bend, OR 97701

(541) 389-3111; (800) 547-3928

In the heart of Bend, with the Deschutes River ambling along between the dining areas and the guest rooms, this resort is uniquely situated.

ACCOMMODATIONS: 220 hotel rooms, including luxury suites, some with fireplaces, kitchen units, and spas. The kitchen units have an apartment-size refrigerator, range, and dishwasher, and are fully equipped for housekeeping.

AMENITIES: Indoor and outdoor swimming pools, two outdoor tennis courts, sauna, exercise room, jogging along the river, or trout fishing outside your front door. During the winter months there is downhill and cross-country skiing at Mt. Bachelor (15 miles away). Should you prefer not to cook for yourself, there are three restaurants on the property.

GOLF: Rivers Edge Golf Course (less than a quarter-mile from the resort) was designed by the renowned Robert Muir Graves. Now an 18-hole layout, it plays 6,647/6,428/6,128/5,380 yards and pars at 72/73. Nestled among pine trees, it has rock outcroppings, some substantial elevation changes from tee to green, undulating terrain, and a few extremely difficult greens. The Deschutes River even makes an appearance. Rivers Edge can be a zinger.

RATES: (EP) Lodgings - $89/$215. Green fees - $53, including carts. Golf and skiing packages are available during appropriate times of the year.

ARRIVAL: By air - Redmond Airport (16 miles). By car - the resort is located on the west side of Highway 97 in Bend, Oregon.

The Running Y Ranch Resort

5500 Running Y Road, Running Y, OR 97601

(541) 850-5500; (888) 850-0275

Located a few miles southwest of Klamath Falls in Southern Oregon, the Running Y Ranch Resort enjoys a massive setting on some 3,600 acres. The recorded history of the area dates back to 1825, finally evolving into a ranch/resort in 1997/1998. It still remains a working ranch, however.

ACCOMMODATIONS: The Lodge, built on a ridge overlooking the golf layout, has 83 guest rooms with the suites featuring walk-out balconies, fireplaces and mini-kitchens. Eventually there will be rental of home/condominium suites available.

AMENITIES: The list of activities seems almost endless; there is a 13,000-square-foot sports center, which includes a weight room, aerobics, a spa, a massage therapist, two tennis courts, a swimming pool, as well as a children's wader-pool. There is also horseback riding and bicycle rentals. Canoeing and exploring the shores of Lake Klamath, the largest freshwater lake in the state, is another option. Fishing is an activity you may wish to explore here. The wetlands in the property provide a delightful look at a wide variety of birds and other wildlife. Directly below the hotel is Sugar Pines for lunch, while lunch and dinner are also served at Schatzies on the Green.

GOLF: Designed by Arnold Palmer, and offering five sets of tees, the course plays 7,165/6,679/6,111/5,512/4,886 yards with a par of 72. While water comes into play on only six holes, there are enough bunkers, trees, and rocks to keep your undivided attention. The entire course enjoys a beautiful setting and some unexpected elevation changes. By the way, be advised you are playing at an elevation of approximately 4,200 feet.

RATES: Lodgings - bedroom $115/$229; suites $199/$249. Green fees - $49, carts $26.

 A word of warning: "soft spikes" only are allowed on the course.

There are golf packages available - ask when making reservations.

ARRIVAL: By air - Klamath Falls Airport. By car - from Klamath Falls, take Highway 97 approximately two miles south. Turn off at the Lakeview/Medford exit onto Highway 140. Drive 7.2 miles to entrance (on right side).

Sunriver Resort

PO Box 3609, Sunriver, OR 97707

(541) 593-1221; (800) 547-3922

ACCOMMODATIONS: Bedrooms and suites in the Lodge; private homes; and condominiums.

AMENITIES: 28 tennis courts, 26 miles of paved bike paths, a racquetball club, and riding stables. Canoe trips, fishing, and whitewater rafting on the Deschutes River can also be arranged.

GOLF: There are three 18-hole golf courses. The older South Course measures 6,940/6,502/6,366/5,827 yards and pars at 72. We found it flat, open, and not very interesting. However, the North Course, a Robert Trent Jones design, is an excellent layout. Reaching out 6,823/6,208/5,912/5,446 yards, it also pars at 72.

The newest addition available for play by members and guests of Sunriver is appropriately named the Crosswater Course. The entire layout is either in or alongside wetlands. Ponderosa pine trees and the Deschutes and Little Deschutes rivers spice up the action. Parring at 72, the course reaches out an awesome 7,693/7,305/6,842/6,286/5,389 yards. I doubt that even John Daly would relish the back tees. For advance tee times, call (800) 962-1769.

RATES: (EP) Lodgings - $185/$249. Green fees (including carts) - North Course $70/$80; South Course $75/$85; Crosswater Course $115. Rates are for June-September.

ARRIVAL: By air - Portland (175 miles); Redmond (33 miles). By private aircraft - Sunriver is 4,500 feet, paved and lighted. By car - Highway 97 (15 miles south of Bend).

Westin Salishan Lodge

Highway 101, Gleneden Beach, OR 97388

(514) 764-2371; (800) 452-2300; (800) 937-8461

The Westin Salishan combines the majestic Pacific Ocean and its ever-changing moods on one side with a beautiful golf course on the other.

ACCOMMODATIONS: 205 guest rooms and suites, some with golf course views, others with a view of the bay. Each features a wood-burning fireplace, private balcony, and individual covered parking.

AMENITIES: Three indoor lighted tennis courts, indoor pool, a hydrotherapy pool, and men's and women's exercise rooms. The food is very good at Salishan but, for a change of pace and a delightful experience, try the Bay House. It is a few miles north of Salishan Lodge, located at 5911 SW Highway 101 in Lincoln City; phone (503) 996-3222. Make reservations, as it is popular with the locals.

GOLF: The course plays 6,453/6,203/5,389 yards, with a par of 72. The first nine is tree-lined and tight, while the back side is a links type and more open. It's never easy, and it can be difficult if the wind kicks up. They have added some potential excitement to the back nine with the addition of some pot bunkers and the planting of European grass (similar to pampas grass) near some of the greens. Don't snicker. If you have not had the pleasure of hitting out of this stuff, you have a big surprise coming!

RATES: (EP) Lodgings - $179/$309. Green fees - $55, cart $30. Rates are for June-October.

ARRIVAL: By air - Portland. By private aircraft - Siltzer BayAirport, 3,000-foot paved runway (a half mile away). By car - south on I-5 to the Newberg and Ocean Beach exit, then take Highway 18 to three miles south of the Lincoln City limits.

Oregon

Pennsylvania

1. Cross Creek Resort
2. The Shadow Brook Inn
3. The Holiday Inn
4. Skytop Club
5. Tamiment Resort & CC
6. Pocono Manor Inn & CC
7. Fernwood Resort & CC
8. The Mountain Laurel Resort
9. Mt. Airy & Pocono Garden Lodges
10. Mountain Manor Inn & GC
11. Shawnee Inn & CC
12. The Conley Resort Inn
13. Toftrees Hotel Resort
14. Seven Springs Mountain Resort
15. Hidden Valley Resort
16. Nemacolin Woodlands Resort
17. Hotel Hershey
18. Lancaster Host Resort
19. Carroll Valley Resort Hotel

Carroll Valley Resort Hotel

PO Box 715, Carroll Valley, PA 17320

(717) 642-8211; (800) 548-8504

ACCOMMODATIONS: The motel-like setting has 58 rooms, including 12 "parlor rooms" with Jacuzzi tubs.

AMENITIES: Swimming, spa, tennis, and miniature golf; horseback riding facilities are nearby. Dining is in the Grand Ballroom or the Tiffany Grill.

GOLF: The course, an Edmund Ault design, stretches 6,720/6,425/5,188 yards with a par of 71/72. The well-trapped layout brings water into play on eight of the 18 holes. You can also play The Mountain View Country Club course, which is three miles away. Also an Ed Ault design, it plays 6,305/6,035/5,165 yards, with a par of 71.

RATES: (EP) Lodgings - $89/$119. Green fees - $42/$52, including cart. Golf package - two nights/three days (includes lodging, MAP, three days unlimited golf, cart for three rounds, club storage), $596/$676 per couple. Rates are for mid-April through October.

ARRIVAL: By air - Washington DC (65 miles). By car - from DC, take 270 north to Frederick, MD, then Route 15 north to

Emmitsburg. Make a left at the light onto Route 140 west. Take Route 140 to Route 16; follow Route 16 to Route 116. Turn right on Route 116 and go three miles to Sanders Road. Turn right on Sanders and follow it to the resort.

The Conley Resort Inn

740 Pittsburgh Road, Route 8, Butler, PA 16001

(724) 586-7711; (800) 344-7303

ACCOMMODATIONS: 56 guest rooms, including efficiency apartments.

AMENITIES: 150-foot indoor water slide, whirlpool, sauna, tennis courts and putting green. They have a dining room and lounge, as well as the Irish Pub (the 19th hole).

GOLF: The Conley course plays 6,515/6,200/5,625 yards, with a par of 72.

RATES: (EP) Lodgings - $84/$99. Green fees - $24/$34, carts $26. Golf package - two nights/three days (includes lodging, breakfast, cart, unlimited golf, taxes), $490 per couple. Rates are for May through September.

ARRIVAL: By air - Pittsburgh (32 miles south). By car - the resort is on Route 8, six miles south of Butler and 32 miles north of Pittsburgh.

Cross Creek Resort

PO Box 432, Titusville, PA 16354

(814) 827-9611; (800) 461-3173

ACCOMMODATIONS: 94 motel-type rooms.

AMENITIES: Game room, outdoor heated pool, and tennis courts. There is also a dining room.

GOLF: There are 27 holes to play. Using a crossover system, the Red/White combined nines play 6,480/5,685 yards, with a par of 70/72; the White/Blue layout measures 6,458/5,598 yards, with a par of 71/72; and finally, the Red/Blue nines reach out 6,498/5,833 yards, again with a par of 71/72.

RATES: (EP) Lodgings - $95/$115/$135. Green fees - $52, including cart. Golf packages are available. Rates are for May 16-September 16.

ARRIVAL: By air - Franklin Airport (10 miles). By car - four miles south of Titusville on Route 8.

Fernwood Resort & Country Club

Route 209, Bushkill, PA 18324

(570) 588-9500; (800) 233-8103

ACCOMMODATIONS: Well-furnished rooms, some with sitting room and fireplace. Fernwood is a rambling structure, rather than the typical massive European fortress hotel so common to this area.

AMENITIES: 10 indoor and outdoor tennis courts, three swimming pools, two game rooms, horseback riding, indoor roller skating and two lakes for fishing and boating. Nightly entertainment and dining take place in the Astor Room or the Weathervanes Restaurant and Lounge.

GOLF: The course pars at 72 and plays 6,208/5,822/5,086 yards. Water is very much in play on the back nine. Trees, hilly terrain, and extremely large, well-trapped greens add to the challenge. Fernwood also has a nine-hole, par-28 executive course.

RATES: (MAP) Lodgings - $69/$119/$189 per couple. Green fees - $38/$46, including cart. Golf package - one night/one day (includes lodging, MAP, green fees, cart, nightly entertainment), $200 per couple.

ARRIVAL: By air - Philadelphia. By car - I-84, exit on Route 209, travel south to Bushkill, then on to Fernwood.

Hidden Valley Resort

One Craighead Drive, Somerset, PA 15501

(814) 443-6454; (800) 458-0175

ACCOMMODATIONS: Two- and three-story villas, townhouses and condominiums, some with fully equipped kitchens.

AMENITIES: 12 tennis courts (four lighted), swimming pool, saunas, racquetball courts, exercise facilities, 30 miles of marked biking trails, swimming, fishing and boating. Whitewater raft trips can be arranged on the Youghiogheny River. Should you be able to pronounce its name on the first try you will automatically become the designated driver for the evening. During the winter months the resort turns into a skier's haven. Should you tire of the condo life, there are several fine restaurants: the Hearthside, the Clock Tower, and Mr. Mountain Deli Restaurant.

GOLF: Views from the course, situated on the upper levels of 3,000-foot Hidden Valley Mountain, encompass 20 to 30 miles of the surrounding countryside. This Russell Roberts-designed layout extends 6,640/6,186/5,107 yards and pars at 72/71. There is water on only six holes, but the tree-lined fairways and well-trapped greens will keep your attention.

RATES: (EP) Lodgings - $89/$129/$200. Green fees - $40/$50, including cart. Golf package - one night/one day (includes lodging, green fees, cart), $178 per couple.

ARRIVAL: By air - Latrobe, PA (45 miles). By private aircraft - Somerset, PA (20 miles). By car - from the PA Turnpike, take Exit 9, Donegal. Travel eight miles east to Hidden Valley.

The Holiday Inn

I-80 at Pennsylvania Route 68, Clarion, PA 16214

(814) 226-8850; (800) 465-4329

ACCOMMODATIONS: 122-room motor inn.

AMENITIES: Indoor swimming pool and game parlor. For dining, there is the Fairway Restaurant and the Par IV lounge.

GOLF: The Mayfield Golf Club course, measuring 6,990/6,390/5,780 yards, pars at 72. While the course is fairly flat, the tree-lined fairways and water coming into play produce a challenge. The Mayfield is adjacent to the inn, but there are several other courses in the immediate area: Hi Level in Skippenville; Pine Crest in Brookville; and a nine-hole course in Foxburg. The Foxburg Country Club dates back to 1877 and is now the oldest nine-hole course in existence.

RATES: (EP) Lodgings - $94. Green fees - $45, carts $26. Golf package - two nights/three days (includes lodging, green fees, cart, two days breakfast), $275 per couple.

ARRIVAL: By air - Pittsburgh. By private aircraft - Dubois (35 miles). By car - I-80 to Exit 9, then Highway 322 to Route 68.

Hotel Hershey

PO Box BB, Hershey, PA 17033

(717) 533-2171; (800) 533-3131

ACCOMMODATIONS: 250 rooms and suites in the main hotel, several vacation chalets, and 19 rooms at the Country Club. Located on a hilltop with a view of the surrounding countryside, the hotel is an imposing structure.

AMENITIES: Horseback riding, four tennis courts, saunas, whirlpools, indoor and outdoor swimming pools, exercise equipment, cycling and jogging trails. For dining there is the famous Circular Dining Room, with its 13 original picture windows. Hershey also has an excellent childcare and activity program during the summer months.

GOLF: There are three regulation courses, plus two nine-hole layouts. The East Course extends 7,061/6,363/5,645 yards, parring at 71. While there are only three lakes coming into play, it is heavily trapped (about 100). The West Course plays 6,860/6,480/5,908 yards, parring at 73. From the ladies' tees the par is 77. This is one tough layout – the pars of 73 and 77 give an indication of just how tough. One mile away is the Hershey Parkview Course, which plays a more modest 6,146/5,810/5,230 yards, with a par of 71/72.

RATES: (MAP) Lodgings - $359/$399 per couple. Green fees - $60/$93/$135, including cart. Golf package - two nights/two days (includes lodging in hotel, MAP, green fees), $1,038 per couple. Rates are for April-November.

ARRIVAL: By air - Harrisburg (15 minutes). By car - Hershey can be reached from I-81, I-78, I-83 or the Pennsylvania Turnpike.

Lancaster Host Resort

2300 Lincoln Highway East, Lancaster, PA 17602

(717) 299-5500; (800) 233-0121

ACCOMMODATIONS: 300 rooms.

AMENITIES: Six lighted outdoor and four indoor tennis courts, indoor and outdoor swimming pools, a men's and women's health club, and a game room. The resort has an excellent dining room.

GOLF: The Distlefink course was designed by Geoffrey Cornish in 1965 (don't blame me – I didn't name it). In spite of the name, it is an excellent layout. Playing 7,020/6,345/5,540 yards, it pars at 72. Aside from the yardage, part of the challenge lies in the rolling terrain, traps and water. There is also a nine-hole, par-3 course with a yardage of 2,195.

RATES: (EP) Lodgings - $149/$199. Green fees - $63, including cart. Golf packages are available.

ARRIVAL: By air - Lancaster. By car - from Lancaster, take Highway 30 east to Host Farm.

The Mountain Laurel Resort

PO Box 126, White Haven, PA 18661

(570) 443-8411

ACCOMMODATIONS: 250 very spacious rooms, plus suites.

AMENITIES: Tennis, Olympic-size indoor and outdoor pools, saunas and basketball; horseback riding is available nearby. During summer the resort also has a "Leave the Children to Us" program. The Treetops Dining Room has a spectacular view of the area; there is also the intimate Touch of Vanilla Restaurant. Both are excellent.

GOLF: The Mountain Laurel Resort Course, parring at 72, reaches out 6,798/6,122/5,631 yards. Water comes into play on eight holes, but the real challenge is created by the rolling terrain, trees and difficult greens. A second 18, the Country Club layout, measures 6,910/6,090/5,850; it also pars at 72. The Mountain Laurel operates year-round; it has some of the finest winter action found in the area, including night skiing.

RATES: (MAP) Lodgings - $69/$99 per couple. Green fees - $48, including cart. Rates quoted are for May to mid-November.

ARRIVAL: By air - Wilkes-Barre/Scranton (45 minutes). By car - the resort is at the intersection of I-80 and the northeast extension of the Pennsylvania Turnpike.

Mountain Manor Inn & Golf Club

PO Box 1067, Marshalls Creek, PA 18335

(570) 223-8098; (800) 626-6747

ACCOMMODATIONS: A total of 97 units, including split-level duplexes (living room, fireplace, kitchenette), motel units, club motel units, or main house and clubhouse rooms.

AMENITIES: Indoor and outdoor swimming pools, tennis courts, and bowling; horseback riding is available nearby. Meals are served family-style.

GOLF: There are now four nine-hole courses. Using a cross-over system, the Blue/Yellow layout measures 6,233/5,080 yards, parring at 71; the combination of the Blue/Orange reaches out 6,330/5,207 yards, with a par of 72; and the Orange/Yellow nines play 6,215/5,097 yards, with a par of 71. The newest layout is the Silver nine, playing 3,270/2,534 yards.

RATES: (EP) Lodgings - $139/$159 per couple. Green fees - $30, carts $30. Golf package - four nights/five days (includes lodging, MAP, green fees, cart), $818/$898 per couple. Rates are for June-September.

ARRIVAL: By air - Philadelphia or New York. By car - head west on I-80, take Exit 52 to Marshall's Creek, turn left at the general store, then left again at the firehouse.

Mount Airy & Pocono Garden Lodges

42 Woodland Road, Mount Pocono, PA 18344

(570) 839-8811; (800) 441-4410

ACCOMMODATIONS: Whether you choose to stay at Mount Airy or Pocono Gardens, prepare yourself for some of the most lavish, even exotic, accommodations found anywhere. The lodges offer about 500 rooms and suites. Some of the rather unusual features include heart-shaped sunken tubs and mirrored Roman baths with sunken tubs for two. Some suites have a private indoor/outdoor pool with sauna and fireplace. This is an adults-only resort – children are **not** welcome.

AMENITIES: Should you ever decide to leave your room, you can enjoy tennis on 21 indoor/outdoor courts, water-skiing and trap shooting.

GOLF: The Mount Airy Lodge Course rolls out at 7,123/6,426/5,771 yards, and has a par of 72/73. The combination of rolling terrain, tree-lined fairways, and water coming into play on 11 holes offers plenty of challenge.

RATES: (MAP) Lodgings $154/$290 per couple. Green fees - $45/$55, including carts. Golf package - two nights/two days (includes lodging, MAP, golf, cart, taxes and gratuities), $480/$780 per couple.

ARRIVAL: By air - Scranton or Allentown. By car - north of Stroudsburg on Highway I-80, take Exit 44.

Nemacolin Woodlands Resort & Spa

Rte 40, Box 188, Farmington, PA 15437

(724) 329-8555; (800) 422-2736

ACCOMMODATIONS: 98 rooms and suites in the lodge, plus 66 condominiums. These one- and two-bedroom condos are fully equipped for housekeeping.

AMENITIES: Tennis courts, indoor pool, several outdoor pools, and a state-of-the-art spa offering some 40 different ways to pamper your body. Canoeing, paddleboats and fishing are also offered. The resort has its own equestrian center and has recently completed a polo field. There are five dining locations, including the golf club.

GOLF: Parring at 71, this links-style course extends a respectable 6,814/6,532/6,267/4,835. The front nine has no water hazards and is relatively flat. However, the back side more than makes up for this oversight, as it brings water into play on five holes and has some exceptional elevation changes. A second championship course, designed by Pete Dye, came into play in 1995. Playing 6,832/6,300/5,860/4,800 yards, it pars at 72. With water coming into play on 10 holes, many bunkers, including some pot-bunkers, this layout will give you all you want.

RATES: (EP) Lodgings - $185/$250/$295/$315. Green fees - $79, including cart. Pete Dye course - $125, including cart. Golf package - two nights/two days (includes lodging, breakfast, green fees, cart, bag storage), $740 per couple.

ARRIVAL: By air - Pittsburgh (75 miles). By private aircraft - 4,000-foot paved and lighted landing strip on the property. By car - the resort is in Farmington on Route 40 east.

Pocono Manor Inn & Golf Club

Route 314, Pocono Manor, PA 18349

(717) 839-7111; (800) 233-8150

ACCOMMODATIONS: This is a massive, European-style hotel, with 252 guest rooms.

AMENITIES: 11 tennis courts (two indoor), stable, miles of bridle trails, indoor and outdoor pools, saunas, and racquetball courts. A children's program is provided. There is also an excellent dining room.

GOLF: Two 18-hole courses are available for play. The East plays 6,480/6,310/6,113 yards, with a par of 72/76. The West layout stretches 6,857/6,675/5,706 yards and has a par of 72 from all tee settings. Trees, water, elevation changes, and bunkers (no traps) make these courses interesting and fun.

RATES: (MAP) Lodgings - $248 per couple. Green fees - $28, carts $40. Golf packages are available. Rates are for July-October.

ARRIVAL: By air - Scranton/Wilkes-Barre (45 minutes). By car - take I-80 east to Highway 380 west, turn right and follow signs.

Seven Springs Mountain Resort

RD #1, Champion, PA 15622

(814) 352-7777; (800) 452-2223

ACCOMMODATIONS: 385 guest rooms and suites in the main lodge, plus a 10-story high-rise and 25 Bavarian-style chalets. There are also 80 townhouses within three-quarters of a mile.

AMENITIES: Bowling lanes, 12 tennis courts, handball and racquetball courts, a health spa, roller skating, indoor and outdoor pools, volleyball and horseshoes. They also have four dining rooms, three bars, dancing and entertainment nightly.

GOLF: The Mountain Resort Course, parring at 71/72, reaches out 6,360/6,148/4,934 yards. With rolling hills and heavily wooded terrain, this course will give you all you can handle.

RATES: (EP) Lodgings - $160/$340. Golf packages are available. Green fees - $65, including cart.

ARRIVAL: By air - Pittsburgh (50 miles). By private aircraft - Somerset Airport (approximately 22 miles). By car - from the Pennsylvania Turnpike, take Exit 9 or 10.

The Shadow Brook Inn

Route 6, Tunkhannock, PA 18657

(570) 836-2151; (800) 955-0295

ACCOMMODATIONS: This is a 22-room, motel-type structure in the Endless Mountain region of Pennsylvania.

AMENITIES: Dining room, 12 regulation bowling lanes, swimming pool, and racquetball courts; dancing and live entertainment are offered on the weekends.

GOLF: The Shadow Brook Course, a very short layout, plays 5,888/5,583/4,700 yards, with a par of 71.

RATES: (EP) Lodgings - $67/$127. Green fees - $20, carts $20. Golf packages are available.

ARRIVAL: By air - Scranton/Wilkes-Barre. By car - 1½ miles east of Tunkhannock on US 6.

Shawnee Inn & Country Club

River Road, Shawnee-On-Delaware, PA 18356

(570) 424-4000

ACCOMMODATIONS: Inn and townhouses.

AMENITIES: Indoor and outdoor tennis courts, indoor and outdoor pools, horseback riding, racquetball and canoeing. The dining room, which offers evening dining, also serves indoor and outdoor buffets and brunches.

GOLF: There are 27 holes to play. The Red/White nines measure 6,589/6,086/5,424 yards; the combination of the Red/Blue plays 6,800/6,390/5,650 yards; and the White/Blue mix comes in at 6,665/6,350/5,398 yards. All three layouts par at 72 for the men and 74 for the ladies.

RATES: (MAP) Lodgings - $188/$218/$356 per couple. Green fees - $43/$53, including cart. Golf packages are available. Rates are for May-October.

ARRIVAL: By air - Scranton (1¼ hours) By car - from I-80, take Exit 52 at Marshalls Creek and follow the signs.

Skytop Club

Route 390, Skytop, PA 18357

(570) 595-7401; (800) 345-7759

ACCOMMODATIONS: 196 guest rooms in the multi-story resort, some adjacent to the golf course.

AMENITIES: Seven tennis courts, swimming, sunbathing, and facilities for rowing, canoeing and fishing. Dining is offered in the Pine Room. There is also a children's program.

GOLF: The course measures 6,256/5,683 yards and pars at 71/75. Skytop Lake and Lower Lake come into play and the greens are extremely large.

RATES (FAP) Lodgings - $375/$450 per couple. Green fees - $40, including cart. Golf packages are available. Rates are for peak season May-October.

ARRIVAL: By air - Wilkes-Barre/Scranton (45 minutes). By car - on Route 390, 20 miles north of Stroudsburg.

Tamiment Resort & Country Club

Tamiment, PA 18371

(570) 588-6652; (800) 233-8105

ACCOMMODATIONS: Lodging is available in Tamiment House, which is a modern hotel, as well as in cottages located throughout the complex.

AMENITIES: 10 tennis courts, indoor and outdoor swimming pools, a 90-acre stocked private lake (sailing and canoeing), sports complex, men's and women's health clubs. There are five dining rooms.

GOLF: The Robert Trent Jones layout plays 6,858/6,599/5,598 yards, and has a par of 72. The course is relatively flat, but has tree-lined fairways, water in play on four holes and plenty of traps.

RATES: (MAP) Lodgings - $182/$230 per couple. Green fees - $45, including cart. Golf packages are available. Rates are for May-October.

ARRIVAL: By air - Allentown. By car - take I-80 to Exit 52, then head north on 209 to Bushkill. Turn left at the blinker light in Bushkill and proceed to Tamiment.

Toftrees Hotel Resort

One Country Club Lane, State College, PA 16803

(814) 234-8000; (800) 252-3551

ACCOMMODATIONS: Three-story, three-wing lodge, as well as some fully equipped condominiums. Toftrees is bordered by state gamelands on one side and Pennsylvania State University on the other. Should you want reservations during the college football season, I suggest you request them at least two years in advance.

AMENITIES: Heated swimming pool, and tennis on four courts (two lighted). Country French dining and nightly entertainment are offered in Le Papillon restaurant.

GOLF: The lush, well-maintained Toftrees Course plays a hefty 7,018/6,427/5,593/5,555 yards, and pars at 72. With trees, a couple of ponds and rolling terrain, it is not an easy layout.

RATES: (EP) Lodgings - $109/$135. Green fees - $55/$75, including cart. Golf package - two nights/three days (includes lodging, green fees, cart, bag storage), $536/$676 per couple. Rates are for mid-March to October.

ARRIVAL: By air - University Park Airport. By car - take I-80 to Exit 24; go to Route 26, then follow the signs to Pennsylvania State University. Turn onto Route 322 W, then travel approximately three miles.

South Carolina

1. Myrtle Beach
Anderson Inn/Beach Colony Resort/Atlantic Paradise Inn/Beach Cove Resort/
The Beach Dunes/Bel-Aire Motel/Bluewater Resort/Breakers North Towers/
Breakers Resort Hotel/Captains Quarters/Caravell Resort Hotel/CaribbeanMotel/
Carolina Beach Resort/Cherry Grove Manor/Condos Unltd./Compass Cove Resort/
Condotels/Coral Beach Resort/Crown Reef Resort/Days Inn North/Days Inn
Oceanfront/Dayton House/Driftwood Resort/Dunes Village/Hartford Motor Inn/
The Helms/Holiday Inn North/Holiday Inn Downtown/Indigo Inn/The Inn/Landmark
Resort/Marion Earl Resort/Montego Inn/Myrtle Beach Hilton/Myrtle Beach
Martinique/Mystic Sea Hotel/Ocean Creek Resort/Ocean Dunes-Sand Dunes Resort
Ocean Forest Villa Resort/The Palace/Palms Condos/Pan American/Patricia Grand/
The Poindexter/Polynesian Beach Resort/Radisson Resort Hotel/Ramada Ocean Forest
Resort/Sands Beach Club/Sands Ocean Club/Sea Crest/Sea Island Inn/Sea Mist
Resort/Seaside Inn/ Sheraton Myrtle Beach/Ship Ahoy Resort Motel/ South WindVillas/
Tea & Sea Golf Plantation

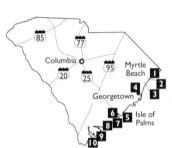

2. Surfside Beach
   Plantation Resort
3. Pawleys Island
   Litchfield Beach & Golf Club/Pawleys
   Plantation/Ramada Pawleys
   Island/Waccamaw House & Inn/
   Litchfield Inn
4. Georgetown
   Wedgefield Plantation
5. Wild Dunes Resort
6. Kiawah Island Golf & Tennis Resort
7. Seabrook Island Resort
8. Fairfield Ocean Ridge
9. Fripp Island Resort
10. Hilton Head Island
    Crown Plaza Resort/Daufuskie
    Island Resort/Hyatt Regency
    Hilton Head/Hilton Resort/Palmetto
    Dunes Resort/Sea Pines Plantation/
    Shipyard Plantation/The Westin
    Resort, Hilton Head

There are a great many golf resorts scattered throughout the state of South Carolina. But there is a concentration of them in two areas – Hilton Head Island and Myrtle Beach. We have listed the various resorts throughout the state in alphabetical order, followed by Hilton Head Island's eight properties, then by the Myrtle Beach area, with its large number of resorts and hotels.

Fairfield Ocean Ridge

#1 King Cotton Road, Edisto Island, SC 29438

(843) 869-2561; (800) 845-8500

ACCOMMODATIONS: Efficiencies, one-bedroom condominiums, and cottages.

AMENITIES: Five tennis courts, a pool, oceanfront beach cabana and a fully equipped playground. For dining there is the Planter's Oak Restaurant.

GOLF: The course plays 6,312/6,016/5,412 yards, parring at 71/72. With water coming into play throughout the entire layout, there is a real need for careful placement here, rather than power.

RATES: (EP) Lodgings - $255/$275/$465 (three-night minimum). Golf packages are offered. Green fees - $50, including cart.

ARRIVAL: By air - Charleston. By car - 45 miles south of Charleston, 95 miles north of Savannah. Highway 17 to 174, then east.

Fripp Island Resort

1 Tarpon Blvd., Fripp Island, SC 29920

(843) 838-3535; (800) 845-4100

ACCOMMODATIONS: There is a wide choice of well-equipped accommodations, ranging from villas overlooking the Atlantic and the tidal marshes to homes adjoining the golf course.

AMENITIES: Swimming pools, bicycling on paved trails, fishing, and 10 tennis courts (two lighted). In addition to the Loggerhead Restaurant, there are dining facilities at the Marina and at the Golf Club.

GOLF: The Ocean Point Links, a George Cobb design, reaches out a rather respectable 6,590/6,060/4,951 yards and pars at 72. With trees, traps and water coming into play on 16 holes, if you do not stay alert you will most certainly perish.

RATES: (EP) Lodgings - $195/$340. Green fees - $58, including carts. Rates are for March through August.

ARRIVAL: By air - Savannah, Georgia. By car - from Beaufort, take Highway 21 to Fripp Island.

Kiawah Island Golf & Tennis Resort

12 Kiawah Beach Drive, Kiawah Island, SC 29455

(843) 768-2121; (800) 845-2471

Kiawah Island has been judged one of our Top 50 resorts.

ACCOMMODATIONS: 150 rooms at the inn, along with 500 villas and several private homes. Those who enjoy preparing their own meals will appreciate the full-service grocery store located only five miles from the resort. Just prior to publication we found that a complete and comprehensive reconstruction is planned for

Kiawah. The hotel is to be demolished as well as the present dining areas – to be replaced by new and much larger facilities. In the meantime, the condominiums will suffice as quarters and the existing dining rooms are more than adequate. All is scheduled to be complete in mid-2001.

AMENITIES: Swimming pools, 23 composition tennis courts, five all-weather tennis courts, and a comprehensive tennis school under the direction of Roy Barth. There are also bicycle rentals and ocean beaches. The restaurants are numerous (now eight) and include the Jasmine Porch, Sundancer's, and the Sweetgrass Café. For those who are interested in wildlife, there are egrets by the thousands, loggerhead turtles and enough alligators to keep everyone alert.

GOLF: You have a choice of touring courses designed by Pete Dye, Tom Fazio, Jack Nicklaus or Gary Player. Marsh Point (Player-designed) measures 6,472/6,203/4,944 yards and pars at 71. Introducing water on 13 holes, it also seems to have trees where they should not be. The newer, Jack Nicklaus-designed Turtle Point course plays 6,919/6,489/6,025/5,285, with a par of 72. It is a links affair featuring several oceanfront holes. A third layout, Osprey Point (a Tom Fazio design), plays 6,678/6,015/5,122 yards and also pars at 72. It introduces golfers to water on 15 holes, along with trees and marsh areas. The Nicklaus/Flick golf school is also here.

The fourth course, called the Ocean Course, was designed by Pete Dye. A railroad tie layout, it stretches along three miles of oceanfront. Each hole offers a view of the ocean, and there are 10 holes running right along the beach. This layout was selected for the 1991 Ryder Cup Matches. It was drawing recognition even prior to play. It really must be seen to be fully appreciated. Parring at 72, it stretches out an awesome 7,371/6,824/6,244/5,327 yards.

There is a new course, the Oak Point, designed by Clyde Johnston. Reaching out 6,759/6,468/5,952/4,956 yards, it has a par of 72. With the water and the wetlands, the correct way to play this layout is to "navigate" with care.

Bring insect repellent, as they do not pre-feed their mosquitoes, but depend on visitors to fill this void. On the serious side: Don't fool with the alligators. They will not bother you if you keep your distance, but they are not as slow as they might appear and can move at an incredible speed for short distances. They are very dangerous.

RATES: (EP) Lodgings - $125/$275/$315. Green fees - $110/$260, including cart. Rates are for September-November.

ARRIVAL: By air - Charleston (21 miles). By private aircraft - Johns Island, with two 5,000-foot runways (10 miles). By car - take I-5 to I-26, then head east for 35 miles to the Cosgrove Avenue Exit. Take South Carolina 7 for five miles, then US 17 south for five miles; turn left on Main Road and follow the signs (17 miles).

Seabrook Island Resort

1002 Landfall Way, Johns Island, SC 29455

(843) 768-1000; (800) 845-2475

This resort stretches out along the beautiful Carolina coast with 3½ miles of white beach. There is a guard gate to pass through that provides complete security; most unusual is the fact that the guards are friendly and helpful.

ACCOMMODATIONS: Well-furnished one-, two- and three-bedroom villas, cottages, and beach houses, all fully equipped for housekeeping.

AMENITIES: 13 Har-Tru courts, equestrian program, bicycling, sport fishing, and walking along the beautiful beaches. The resort offers a children's program designed to keep the kids amused and you smiling. Should you choose not to "condo it," restaurants include Cap'n Sams and the more formal Island House Restaurant.

GOLF: The Crooked Oaks Course reaches out 6,832/6,387/6,037/5,250 yards from its four tee settings. The Ocean Winds Course measures 6,805/6,395/6,027/5,524 yards. Each pars at 72. While both are very good, I preferred the Ocean Winds. The small greens are guarded by traps and trees; water comes into play on 10 holes. A few of the greens offer a spectacular view of the ocean.

RATES: (EP) Villas, one bedroom - $175/$250. Weekly rates are available. Green fees - $120, including cart. Golf package - two nights/two days (includes lodging, green fees and cart for two rounds, bag storage), $560/$700 per couple. Rates are mid-March to June.

ARRIVAL: By air - Charleston. By car - I-95 exit to I-26, then exit at Cosgrove Avenue south. Follow SC Route 7 for five miles to US 17 south. Go five more miles, then turn left at the traffic light. You are now on the main road. Follow signs for 17 miles.

Wild Dunes Resort

PO Box 503, Isle of Palms, SC 29451

(843) 886-6000; (800) 845-8880

ACCOMMODATIONS: Cottages or villas, each fully equipped for housekeeping. Private homes are also available. There is also a 93-room hotel called the Boardwalk Inn.

AMENITIES: 19 Har-Tru tennis courts (four lighted), two Olympic-size pools, jogging paths, a 200-slip yacht harbor and sand beaches. Dining is available in the Links Restaurant. A possible dining alternative is the One-Eyed Parrot, less than two miles away at 1300 Ocean Boulevard; telephone (803) 886-4360. It presents one of the finest seafood selections we have seen.

GOLF: Rather than "cutting" the course out of the naturally undulating terrain, Fazio used what nature had so beautifully provided and has the fairways following the natural contour of the sand dunes. Some of the tees atop these dunes provide a spectacular ocean view. The course plays 6,722/6,131/5,280 with a par of 72. From the ladies' tees the yardage is 4,849. Do not allow the yardage from the white tees to fool you; it will offer all you can handle. The second Tom Fazio-designed course, the Harbor Course, is quite different from the links layout. It has large well-trapped greens, and features nine holes along the Intracoastal Waterway. Parring at 70, it shows a more modest yardage of 6,446/5,900/4,774.

RATES: (EP) Lodgings - $195/$259. Green fees - $89, including cart. Rates are for mid-June through mid-August.

ARRIVAL: By air - Charleston. By car - from Charleston over the Cooper River Bridge, turn on Highway 17, which will become Highway 703 (Sullivan's Highway). Continue to Sullivan's Island. Turn left on Jasper Blvd. Then go straight ahead to Isle of Palms and Wild Dunes.

Hilton Head Island

An island of some 45 square miles, Hilton Head has a great many attractions: over 12 miles of excellent beaches, a better-than-average year-round climate, seven "major" resorts and a great many motels, as well as enough restaurants, shops, and businesses to keep a large city satisfied. Hilton Head Island is the second largest island on the eastern seaboard, surpassed in size only by Long Island.

Crowne Plaza Resort

130 Shipyard Drive, Hilton Head Island, SC 29928

(843) 842-2400; (800) 334-1881

ACCOMMODATIONS: 338 rooms, including 25 suites. The Crowne Plaza is within Shipyard Plantation's 800 acres, and adjacent to 12 miles of beach.

AMENITIES: 24 tennis courts, health spa with saunas, hydrotherapy pool, indoor and outdoor swimming pools, bicycle rentals with miles of riding paths, sailing, excellent fishing and, of course, golf. For dining there is Portz, Brella's Café and Signals. Stellini's, only a short distance away at 8 Pope Avenue, is an excellent dining alternative and offers Italian cuisine; telephone (803) 785-7006.

GOLF: For details on these courses, refer to Shipyard Plantation.

RATES: (EP) Lodgings - $249/$279. Green fees - $95, including cart. Golf packages are available. Rates are for March-November.

ARRIVAL: By air - Savannah (35 miles). By car - Highway 278 to Hilton Head Island; continue on 278 to the Shipyard Plantation entrance.

Daufuskie Island Club Resort

PO Box 23285

Hilton Head Island, SC 29925

(843) 842-2000; (800) 648-6778

This resort is not actually located on Hilton Head Island. It is, however, only one mile away and is accessible via the resort's water taxi and ferry service.

The facility came into being as a resort in 1997.

ACCOMMODATIONS: The Inn has 50 rooms featuring dressing room and sitting area, many offering ocean views. There are also cottages ranging from two to four bedrooms, equipped with full-service kitchens, living rooms, washer/dryers, fireplaces and porches.

AMENITIES: Two tennis centers, three outdoor pools, a fitness center, para-sailing, water skiing, sailing and, of course, fishing. There is an equestrian center as well as bicycle tours available. There are also several children's programs. The list of dining facilities is impressive: The Stoddard Room located at the Inn (breakfast and dinner), Jack's Place at the golf course (lunch and dinner), and the Beach Club for casual dining. There are also many wonderful restaurants on Hilton Head Island to explore.

GOLF: There are two championship golf courses available to guests of the resort. The Melrose layout plays 7,081/6,688/6,245/5,575 yards, with a par of 72. Designed by Jack Nicklaus, it is a semi-links-style affair with small greens, some very long par 4s and par 5s, and with the 17th and 18th holes running directly along the Atlantic Ocean. The second course is called the Bloody Point. Reaching out an impressive 6,900/6,470/5,940/5,220 yards, it also has a par of 72. This is a Weiskopf/Morrish design and a more conventional layout with trees, water and marshes coming into play.

RATES: Lodging - The Inn, $195 per couple; cottages, $410. Green fees - $85, including cart. Golf packages are available. Rates are for high season, mid-March through October.

ARRIVAL: By air - Savannah (31 miles). By private aircraft - Hilton Head Island Airport. By car - take Highway 278 to Hilton Head Island. Drive eight miles after crossing the James Byrnes Bridge. From Hilton Head Island Airport, turn left onto Beach City Rd. Follow it to the end, taking a right on Highway 278.

South Carolina

Drive to Gumtree and follow to its end. Take right on Squire Pope Rd. Embarkation center is a quarter-mile on left side.

Hilton Resort

23 Ocean Lane, Hilton Head Island, SC 29938

(843) 842-8000; (800) 845-8001

ACCOMMODATIONS: 324 oceanview rooms and suites, located on the Palmetto Dunes Resort complex.

AMENITIES: 25 tennis courts (23 clay, two hard), canoeing and paddleboating through miles of lagoons, bicycling over moss-draped lanes, fishing, sailing, excursion boat tours, use of the health club and saunas. Dining at this resort can include seafood prepared over mesquite charcoal or a more formal candlelit dinner.

GOLF: There are three courses, each designed by a different architect, and each with its own distinctive character. For yardage and more detail, refer to Palmetto Dunes Resort.

RATES: (EP) Lodgings - $149/$184. Green fees - $95, including cart. Golf packages are available. Rates are March through May.

ARRIVAL: By air - Savannah (31 miles). By private aircraft - Hilton Head Island Airport. By car - Highway 278 to Hilton Head Island. Drive eight miles after crossing the James Byrnes Bridge.

Hyatt Regency Hilton Head

PO Box 6167, Hilton Head Island, SC 29938

(843) 785-1234; (800) 233-1234

ACCOMMODATIONS: 505 rooms within the Palmetto Dunes Resort complex.

AMENITIES: The hotel is surrounded by golf, swimming, tennis, and several miles of beach.

GOLF: For details on these courses, refer to Palmetto Dunes Resort.

RATES: (EP) Lodgings - $220/$265/$280. Green fees - $86/$95, including cart. Golf packages are available.

ARRIVAL: By air - Savannah (31 miles). By private aircraft - Hilton Head Island. By car - Highway 278 to Hilton Head Island. Drive eight miles after crossing the James Byrnes Bridge.

Palmetto Dunes Resort

PO Box 5616, Hilton Head Island, SC 29938

(843) 785-7300; (800) 845-6130

ACCOMMODATIONS: One- to four-bedroom villas, well-equipped for housekeeping. Each villa cluster has its own swimming pool.

AMENITIES: Canoeing and fishing in the man-made lagoon systems, and 25 tennis courts (six lighted). Palmetto offers the superb Hugo's Rotisserie and the Golf Grill.

GOLF: Three 18-hole courses are available. The George Fazio course, with its four tee settings, plays 6,873/6,534/6,239/5,273 yards, parring at 70. The challenge on this layout is presented by extremely small greens, narrow and undulating fairways, lots of water and 71 traps. The Robert Trent Jones course stretches out 6,710/6,148/5,425 yards, with a par of 72. Again, water is a factor, as are the dogleg holes, trees and traps. The third course is an Arthur Hill design. Also parring at 72, this one measures 6,651/6,122/4,999 yards. Water comes into the action on only nine holes. The pro shop has its own toll-free number: (800) 827-3006.

RATES: (EP) Lodgings - $195/$255 (two-night minimum). Green fees (including cart) - $67/$95; for the Arthur Hill course, $100. Golf packages are available. Rates are for May-September.

ARRIVAL: By air - Savannah. By private aircraft - Hilton Head. By car - take Highway 278 to Hilton Head Island. Drive eight miles after crossing the James Byrnes Bridge.

Sea Pines Plantation

PO Box 7000, Hilton Head Island, SC 29938

(843) 785-3333; (800) 845-6131

ACCOMMODATIONS: Approximately 500 one- to four-bedroom villas, as well as homes ranging from two to six bedrooms. Sea Pines Plantation occupies nearly 5,000 acres on the southernmost tip of the island.

AMENITIES: Nearly five miles of ocean beaches, 40 tennis courts, three golf courses, 25 swimming pools, two marinas with over 150 boat slips, equestrian center, miles of bicycle and jogging paths, fishing, boating and ocean swimming. There are a variety of restaurants on the Plantation property.

GOLF: The three courses include the Ocean Course, playing 6,614/6,213/5,284 yards, parring at 72; the Sea Marsh, measuring 6,372/6,086/5,527 yards, also with a par of 72; and the Harbour Town Golf Links, home of the MCI Heritage Classic. Harbour Town, a par 71, stretches out an awesome 6,912/6,119/5,019 yards. Do not allow the regular tee yardage to lull you. The trees, sea breezes, water on 16 holes and Dye's small, firm greens can be catastrophic to your game. I enjoyed playing all three courses, but found Harbour Town the most interesting.

RATES: (EP) Lodgings - $100/$225. Green fees - $85/$125, including cart. Harbour Town Green fees $165, including. Golf packages are available. Rates are for April-August.

ARRIVAL: By air - Savannah (43 miles). Charleston (95 miles). By car - southbound on I-95, exit to Highway 462; follow signs along Highway 170 and 278 to the island. Sea Pines is at the southernmost tip of the island.

Shipyard Plantation

PO Box 7000, Hilton Head Island, SC 29938

(843) 785-3333; (800) 845-6131

ACCOMMODATIONS: One- to three-bedroom villas, each with kitchen, living room and washer/dryer.

AMENITIES: Swimming pools, fishing, boating, horseback riding and four tennis courts.

GOLF: Within the resort, courses include the Brigantine, the Galleon and the Clipper nines. The Brigantine/Galleon combination plays 6,716/5,994/5,115 yards; the Galleon/Clipper duo stretches out a healthy 6,830/6,167/5,391 yards; and the Brigantine/Clipper combo weighs in with a substantial 6,818/6,091/5,190 yards. No matter how you join them you end up with a par of 72. Each combination presents an interesting challenge, with huge oaks, a great deal of water, and oceanside play.

RATES: (EP) Lodgings - $160. Green fees - $80/$135, including cart. Golf packages are available. Rates are for March-August.

ARRIVAL: By air - Savannah (35 miles). By car - from I-95, exit on Highway 462 and follow the signs along Highways 170 and 278 to the island.

Westin Resort Hilton Head

2 Grasslawn Avenue, Hilton Head Island, SC 29928

(843) 681-4000; (800) 228-3000

ACCOMMODATIONS: 410 rooms in a five-story structure overlooking the Atlantic Ocean. There are also two- and three-bedroom villas available. For villa information, call (800) 933-3102.

AMENITIES: 16 tennis courts, three swimming pools (one is indoor), fishing, boating, full use of the health club and exercise equipment, sauna, steam rooms, massage therapists, charter fishing, aqua-cycles, floats, 16-foot Prindles, Sunfish, and Aqua Cats. For dining, you may select the Baroney Grille or the Carolina Cafe.

GOLF: Three championship courses are offered: the Robber's Row, a par-72 layout measuring 6,711/6,188/5,299 yards; the Baroney, also a par-72 course, stretching out 6,530/6,038/5,253 yards; and the Planters Row, weighing in at 6,520/6,009/5,126 yards. While the courses are pretty flat, each offers a mixture of water, huge oak trees and oceanside fairways to keep your attention.

RATES: (EP) Lodgings - $205/$265/$315. Green fees - $85/$95, including cart. Golf packages are available. Rates are for mid-March to mid-November.

ARRIVAL: By air - Savannah (35 miles). By car - from I-95, exit on Highway 462. Follow signs along Highway 170 and 278 to the island. The entrance to Port Royal Plantation will be on your left.

South Carolina

Myrtle Beach, Pawleys Island, Georgetown

Within this section on Myrtle Beach, we cover about 90 golf courses and a great many motels/hotels. The number of golf courses is anticipated to increase to 100 within a short time. While Myrtle Beach has often been described as a "golfer's super-market," it also could be called a "golfer's smorgasbord."

In addition to golf facilities, there are some 50,000 motel/hotel rooms in the immediate vicinity. A number have access to start-ing times at the various golf courses. Many also offer golf pack-ages. Check prior to making reservations as to which courses you can play and if prices include golf fees, cart fees, etc. These golf layouts are not run-of-the-mill affairs; many rank among the best in the country.

There is also a great deal to do in Myrtle Beach other than play-ing golf: 50-plus miles of beautiful beaches, several hundred res-taurants (someone said 750 – but we didn't count), amusement parks, over 2,000 outlet shops and much more.

RATES: It is not practical to list rates for this number of resorts. There are many golf packages available. Peak golf season is September-October and March through May.

ARRIVAL: Myrtle Beach is located on US 17 (business route) with easy access to I-95.

Anderson Inn

2600 North Ocean Beach Blvd., Myrtle Beach, SC 29577

(843) 448-1535; (800) 437-7376

Beachfront, multi-story, restaurant, swimming pool, exercise room.

Atlantic Paradise Inn

1401 So. Ocean Blvd., Myrtle Beach, SC 29577

(843) 444-0346; (800) 992-0269

Oceanfront, indoor pool, whirlpool. One- and two-bedroom units.

Beach Colony Resort

5308 North Ocean Blvd., Myrtle Beach, SC 29577

(843) 449-4010; (800) 222-2141

Beachfront, multi-story, restaurant and lounge, room service, suites and apartments, outdoor and indoor swimming pools, saunas, whirlpools.

The Beach Cove Resort

Oceanfront at 48th Ave. So., North Myrtle Beach, SC 29582

(843) 272-4044; (800) 331-6533

Multi-story beachfront hotel. Two-room condo/suites. Indoor and outdoor swimming pools, dining rooms, lounge, room service, racquetball, whirlpools and saunas. Tennis nearby.

The Beach Dunes

1807 S Ocean Blvd., Myrtle Beach, SC 29577

(843) 626-3653; (800) 334-3055

Beachfront, some units with kitchens, indoor pool, guest laundry.

South Carolina

Bel-Aire Motel

102 North Ocean Blvd., North Myrtle Beach, SC 29582

(843) 249-1434; (800) 342-0078

Three-story, beachfront, two swimming pools, fully equipped kitchens, coin-operated laundry.

Bluewater Resort

2001 South Ocean Blvd., Myrtle Beach, SC 29578

(843) 626-8345; (800) 845-6994

High-rise, beachfront, rooms and villas, indoor and outdoor swimming pools, racquetball, saunas, whirlpools, rooftop lounge, restaurant.

The Breakers North Towers

27th Avenue North & Ocean Blvd., Myrtle Beach, SC 29578

(843) 626-5000; (800) 845-0688

Multi-story, beachfront, restaurant, poolside bar, heated swimming pool.

The Breakers Resort Hotel

21st Avenue & Ocean Blvd., Myrtle Beach, SC 29578

(843) 626-5000; (800) 845-0688

Multi-story, beachfront, restaurant, whirlpool, sauna, exercise rooms, heated pool.

The Captain's Quarters

901 South Ocean Blvd., Myrtle Beach, SC 29578

(843) 448-1404; (800) 843-3561

Oceanfront, high-rise, restaurant, indoor and outdoor swimming pools, bowling lanes on premises.

The Caravelle Resort

70th Avenue North, Myrtle Beach, SC 29577

(843) 449-3331; (800) 845-0893

Beachfront, multi-story, 320 rooms and suites, indoor and outdoor swimming pools, restaurant and lounge.

Caribbean Motel

Ocean Front at 30th Ave. N., Myrtle Beach, SC 29577

(843) 448-7181; (800) 845-0883

High-rise, beachfront, villas, restaurant, swimming pool.

Carolina Beach Resort

16 Causeway Drive, Ocean Isle Beach, NC 28459

(843) 579-7181; (800) 222-1524

95 units, one- and two-bedroom fully equipped condominiums, tennis, swimming pool, Jacuzzi.

South Carolina

Cherry Grove Manor

2104 N. Ocean Blvd., North Myrtle Beach, SC 29582

(843) 249-2731; (800) 727-2322

46 one- , two- , and three-bedroom units; oceanfront; heated swimming pool; outdoor grill and picnic area. There are also some beach cottages and bungalows.

Compass Cove Resort

2311 South Ocean Blvd., Myrtle Beach, SC 29577

(843) 448-8373; (800) 222-9894

Oceanfront. Multi-story hotel, with four outdoor and two indoor swimming pools, Jacuzzi, exercise room and restaurant. Formerly called the Swamp Fox Resort.

Condos Unlimited

6th & 7th Ocean Blvd., North Myrtle Beach, SC 29597

(843) 272-7176; (800) 845-2398

One- to three-bedroom oceanfront condominium units.

Condotels

PO Box 3196, Myrtle Beach, SC 29582

(843) 272-8400; (800) 852-6636

Condominium hotel, beachfront, high-rise, dining room.

Coral Beach Resort

1105 South Ocean Blvd., Myrtle Beach, SC 29578

(843) 448-8421; (800) 843-2684

Multi-story, beachfront, indoor swimming pool, steam room, sauna, exercise room, eight bowling lanes, restaurant.

Crown Reef Resort

2913 S Ocean Blvd., Myrtle Beach, SC 29577

(843) 626-8077; (888) 500-6600

Rooms, suites, efficiencies, indoor pool, two restaurants, lounge, fitness center, some fully equipped kitchen units.

Days Inn North

1321 South Ocean Blvd., North Myrtle Beach, SC 29597

(843) 272-5131; (800) 845-0605

Beachfront, 75 units (some efficiencies), multi-story, swimming pool.

Days Inn Ocean Front

77th Avenue North, Myrtle Beach, SC 29577

(843) 449-7431; (800) 845-0656

Oceanfront, high-rise, 99 units, restaurant, lounge, swimming pool.

South Carolina

Dayton House

2400 North Ocean Blvd., Myrtle Beach, SC 29578

(843) 448-2441; (800) 258-7963

High-rise hotel (some efficiencies), tennis, swimming pool, Jacuzzi, children's pool.

Driftwood Resort

1600 North Ocean Blvd., Myrtle Beach, SC 29578

(843) 448-1544; (800) 942-3456

Beachfront high-rise. Resort can arrange play on the famous Dunes Course.

Dunes Village

5200 North Ocean Blvd., Myrtle Beach, SC 29577

(843) 449-5275; (800) 648-3539

High-rise oceanfront, indoor and outdoor swimming pools, whirlpool and tennis courts.

Hartford Motor Inn

5310 North Ocean Blvd., N. Myrtle Beach, SC 29582

(843) 249-3408; (800) 422-2710

Three-story, oceanfront, swimming pool. All rooms are efficiency units.

The Helms

304 North Ocean Blvd., North Myrtle Beach, SC 29582

(843) 249-2521; (800) 968-8986

Oceanfront, 75 units, two swimming pools.

Holiday Inn Downtown

6th Ave. S. & South Ocean Blvd., Myrtle Beach, SC 29577

(843) 448-4481; (800) 845-0313

Oceanfront, multi-story, swimming pool, sauna, whirlpool, exercise room, snack bar, restaurant.

Holiday Inn North

2713 South Ocean Blvd., North Myrtle Beach, SC 29582

(843) 272-6153; (800) 845-9700

Oceanfront, multi-story, dock, fishing charters, restaurant, swimming pool.

Indigo Inn

2209 South Ocean Blvd., Myrtle Beach, SC 29577

(843) 448-5101; (800) 448-1631

High-rise, beachfront, efficiency rooms and apartments, swimming pool. Restaurant next door.

The Inn

7300 North Ocean Blvd., Myrtle Beach, SC 29577

(843) 449-3361; (800) 845-0664

Multi-story, beachfront, 123 guest rooms (some efficiencies), swimming pool, dining room.

Landmark Resort

Ocean Beach & 15th S., Myrtle Beach, SC 29577

(843) 448-9441; (800) 845-0658

High-rise, beachfront, 376 rooms, restaurant, lounge, sauna.

South Carolina

Litchfield Beach & Golf Club

PO Drawer 320, Pawleys Island, SC 29585

(843) 237-3000; (800) 854-1897

Lodgings consist of 10 fully equipped cottages. Condo rentals are handled by Waccamaw House, (803) 237-8402 or (800) 845-1897. There are two courses on the premises, as well as four or five more in the immediate area. This location is about 20 miles from Myrtle Beach. There are also several tennis courts nearby.

Litchfield Inn

1 Norris Drive, Litchfield Beach, SC 29585

(843) 237-4311; (800) 637-4211

Oceanfront, 140 rooms, including suites, dining room, swimming pool and children's pool. Access to all of the Litchfield Beach & Golf Resort amenities.

The Marion Earl Resort Motel

1401 South Ocean Blvd., Myrtle Beach, SC 29582

(843) 272-5181; (800) 843-0096

Beachfront three-story motel with 51 rooms, many with kitchen. Swimming pool. About a mile to closest restaurant.

Montego Inn

1305 S. Ocean Blvd., Myrtle Beach, SC 29578

(843) 448-8551; (800) 472-0081

Multi-story beachfront, efficiency units, restaurant, indoor and outdoor swimming pools, children's pool, whirlpool.

Myrtle Beach Martinique

7100 North Ocean Blvd., Myrtle Beach, SC 29578

(843) 449-4441; (800) 542-0048

16-story oceanfront, 197 rooms, workout room, restaurant, outdoor and indoor swimming pools, tennis nearby.

Mystic Sea Motel

2105 South Ocean Blvd., Myrtle Beach, SC 29578

(843) 448-8446; (800) 822-7050

Oceanfront motel, swimming pool, refrigerators in rooms.

Ocean Creek Resort

10600 N. Kings Hwy, North Myrtle Beach, SC 29572

(843) 272-7724; (800) 845-0353

Three-story, 800 condos, dining room, swimming pool, on-premises putting green.

Ocean Dunes-Sand Dunes Resort

74th Avenue & Ocean Blvd., Myrtle Beach, SC 29577

(843) 449-7441; (800) 845-6701

Multi-story buildings; most are beachfront. Over 300 rooms, plus 310 efficiency units and 45 apartments. Indoor and outdoor swimming pools, two restaurants, racquetball, saunas, whirlpools, steam rooms.

Ocean Forest Villa Resort

5601 North Ocean Blvd., Myrtle Beach, SC 29577

(843) 449-9661; (800) 845-6701

Oceanfront villas, two swimming pools, whirlpools. They also offer a supervised children's program.

The Palace

1605 South Ocean Blvd., Myrtle Beach, SC 29577

(843) 448-4300; (800) 334-1397

High-rise, on the beach, 298 studios and one- and two-bedroom suites. Two swimming pools, five whirlpools, sauna, steam room, restaurant.

Palms Condos

2500 North Ocean Blvd., Myrtle Beach, SC 29578

(843) 626-8334; (800) 528-0451

High-rise, oceanfront, suites and villas, indoor and outdoor swimming pools, exercise room, and sauna. Restaurants are nearby.

Pan American

5300 N. Ocean Blvd., Myrtle Beach, SC 29578

(843) 449-7411; (800) 845-4501

Oceanfront, high-rise, 84 rooms. Swimming pool and six tennis courts on premises.

Patricia Grand

27101 North Ocean Blvd., Myrtle Beach, SC 29578

(843) 448-8453; (800) 255-4763

Oceanfront, high-rise. Rooms, efficiency apartments, suites, dining room, lounge, indoor and outdoor swimming pools, whirlpool, exercise room, sauna.

Pawleys Plantation

PO Box 2070, Highway 17, Pawleys Island, SC 29585

(843) 237-8497; (800) 367-9959

ACCOMMODATIONS: Two- and three-bedroom villas, dining room, swimming pool, tennis courts and biking trails.

GOLF: The course is a Nicklaus design, measuring a substantial 7,026/6,522/6,127/5,560 yards and parring at 72. The terrain in this area is generally flat. In a successful attempt to introduce challenges, they have used many sand traps, the natural growth of oak and pine trees, and water on 11 holes. On at least one hole you may find your ball nestled on beautiful white sand, hiding behind a tree.

RATES: (EP) Lodgings - $150/$190. Green fees - $65, carts $32.

ARRIVAL: By air - Myrtle Beach. By private aircraft - Georgetown (nine miles). By car - from Georgetown on Highway 17, south nine miles.

Plantation Resort

1250 US Highway 17 North, Surfside Beach, SC 29575

(843) 238-3556; (800) 845-5039

Golf course condominiums, 16,000-square-foot swimming pool, saunas, steam rooms. Restaurants nearby.

South Carolina

The Poindexter

1702 North Ocean Blvd., Myrtle Beach, SC 29577

(843) 448-8327; (800) 248-0003

Beachfront, high-rise, 227 rooms, three outdoor and one indoor swimming pools, restaurant, game room and an exercise room.

Polynesian Beach Resort

10th Avenue South & Ocean Blvd., Myrtle Beach, NC 29577

(843) 448-1781; (800) 845-6971

Beachfront, high-rise hotel, with fully equipped efficiencies, two swimming pools, and Jacuzzi. Restaurant nearby.

Radisson Resort Hotel

9800 Lake Drive, Myrtle Beach, SC 29577

(843) 449-0006; (800) 289-4300

Beachfront, high-rise, 255 one-bedroom suites, restaurant, nightly entertainment, lounge, health club.

Ramada Ocean Forest Resort

5523 North Ocean Blvd., Myrtle Beach, SC 29578

(843) 497-0044; (800) 522-0818

High-rise, with 195 two-bedroom suites, health club, exercise rooms, indoor and outdoor swimming pools, Jacuzzi, restaurant and lounge.

Ramada Pawleys Island

PO Box 2217, Pawleys Island, SC 29585

(843) 237-4261; (800) 553-7008

ACCOMMODATIONS: 100-room motel-style resort.
AMENITIES: Tennis, fishing facilities, pool, and a restaurant.
GOLF: The Seagull Golf Club, a par-72 layout, plays 6,910/
6,295/5,375 yards. It is an interesting course, and rambles
throughout this old Southern plantation. Water either crosses or
laterally comes into play on 12 holes.
RATES: (EP) Lodgings - $69/$79. Rates are for March-April.
ARRIVAL: By air - Myrtle Beach (12 miles). By car - Highway
17 Bypass, south of Myrtle Beach.

Sands Beach Club

1000 Shore Drive, Myrtle Beach, SC 29572

(843) 449-1531; (800) 845-6701

Fronts on beach. 225 suites, washers/dryers, restaurant, outdoor and indoor/outdoor swimming pools. Whirlpool, racquetball and two tennis courts.

Sands Ocean Club

500 Shore Drive, Myrtle Beach, SC 29572

(843) 449-6461; (800) 845-6701

Beachfront, 355 rooms, restaurant and cafe, indoor/outdoor
swimming pool, children's pool, Jacuzzi, fitness center, two tennis courts.

South Carolina

Sea Crest Resort

803 South Ocean Blvd., Myrtle Beach, SC 29577

(843) 626-3515; (800) 845-1112

Oceanfront high-rise, 90 units, restaurant, and swimming pool; mini-mart on premises.

Sea Island Inn

6000 North Ocean Blvd., Myrtle Beach, SC 29577

(843) 449-6406; (800) 548-0767

Multi-story, oceanfront, rooms and efficiencies, swimming pool, dining room.

Sea Mist Resort

1200 South Ocean Blvd., Myrtle Beach, SC 29578

(843) 448-1551; (800) 732-6478

Very large complex, with 12 high-rise buildings, indoor pool, six outdoor pools, tennis court, Jacuzzi, and restaurant.

Seaside Inn

2301 South Ocean Blvd., North Myrtle Beach, SC 29582

(843) 272-5166; (800) 433-5710

Three-story oceanfront motel, with swimming pool and hot tub.

Sheraton Myrtle Beach

2701 South Ocean Blvd., Myrtle Beach, SC 29577

(843) 448-2518; (800) 992-1055

Oceanfront 14-story hotel with 232 guest rooms, restaurant, lounge, outdoor and indoor swimming pools.

Ship Ahoy Resort Motel

3400 North Ocean Blvd., Myrtle Beach, SC 29582

(843) 249-3551; (800) 255-5490

Three-story oceanfront motel (some units with fully equipped kitchens), with a swimming pool.

South Wind Villas

5310 North Ocean Beach Blvd., Myrtle Beach, SC 29577

(843) 449-5211; (800) 842-1871

56 units, some oceanfront. Villas have fully equipped kitchens. There is a coin laundry, sauna and putting green.

Tea & Sea Golf Plantation

Box 4338, One Plantation Dr., North Myrtle Beach, SC 29597

(843) 249-8572; (800) 845-6191

One- , two- , and three-bedroom condominiums, with two swimming pools, two tennis courts, snack bar at the pro shop, and 54 holes of golf on the premises. Five-minute drive to the beach.

South Carolina

Waccamaw House & Inn

Highway 17 & S. Litchfield Beach, Pawleys Island, SC 29585

(843) 237-8402; (800) 845-1897

ACCOMMODATIONS: Located 20 miles from Myrtle Beach, Waccamaw House & Inn offers 96 suites. There are also condominiums at Litchfield Country Club, less than a mile away.

AMENITIES: Restaurant, indoor and outdoor swimming pools, fitness center, steam room, and sauna.

GOLF: At least five championship golf courses are available for play.

Wedgefield Plantation

100 Manor Drive, Georgetown, SC 29440

(843) 922-8085; (800) 849-3343

ACCOMMODATIONS: Villas range from two-bedroom units with one bath to three-bedroom units with 2½ baths.

AMENITIES: All-weather tennis courts, swimming pool, biking and jogging trails. Dining is provided in Wedgefield's Manor House.

GOLF: The Wedgefield Plantation course plays 7,077/6,689/6,199/5,111 yards and pars at 72. It is a delightful but testing layout, with moss-draped oaks lining the fairway and many traps. After you have played it, you will understand why it has been host to the South Carolina Open and amateur championships.

ARRIVAL: By air - Charleston (65 miles south) or Myrtle Beach (30 miles north). By private aircraft - Georgetown (paved runway). By car - Highway 701, just north of Georgetown.

Wyndham Myrtle Beach Resort

10000 Beach Club Drive, Myrtle Beach, SC 29572

(843) 449-5000; (800) 996-3426

ACCOMMODATIONS: 393 rooms.

AMENITIES: Tennis, swimming (both pool and ocean), charter fishing and sailing. For dining there is Alfredo's and the coffee shop.

GOLF: The Wyndham owns Arcadian Shores Golf Club, which stretches out 6,960 to 5,721 yards, with a par of 72. This is an interesting course, well-trapped, with water and trees very much in play.

RATES: (EP) Lodgings - $159/$189/$209. Rates April-September.

ARRIVAL: By air - Myrtle Beach. By car - located on Highway 17 (business route) at Arcadian Shores.

Tennessee

1. Paris Landing State Resort Park
2. Montgomery Bell State Resort Park
3. Opryland Hotel
4. Fairfield Glade
5. Bent Creek Golf Resort
6. Baneberry Resort
7. Buffalo Mountain Resort
8. Henry Horton State Resort Park
9. Fall Creek Falls State Resort Park
10. Pickwick Landing State Resort Park

Baneberry Resort

Route 2, Harrison Ferry Road, White Pine, TN 37890

(865) 674-2500

ACCOMMODATIONS: Villas bordering the golf course. Each two-bedroom/two-bath unit is fully equipped for housekeeping.

AMENITIES: Restaurant and lounge, along with tennis courts and a swimming pool.

GOLF: The Baneberry Resort Course reaches out 6,707/6,678/6,060/4,928 yards and pars at 71. While the front nine is pretty flat and open, the back side has rolling terrain and is lined with trees.

RATES: (EP) Lodgings - $90/$102 per night; weekly, seventh night free. Green fees are included in the lodging rates. Carts $26.

ARRIVAL: By air - Knoxville. By car - 40 miles east of Knoxville on Highway 81.

Bent Creek Golf Resort

3919 E. Parkway D, Gatlinburg, TN 37738

(865) 436-2875; (800) 251-9336

ACCOMMODATIONS: Large rooms with sitting areas and queen-size beds; some with fireplaces.

AMENITIES: Four lighted tennis courts and a large swimming pool; horseback riding nearby. Bent Creek offers an excellent dining room. By the way, this is a dry county, so bring your own.

GOLF: The Davis, Kirby & Gary Player-designed layout reaches out a modest 6,182/5,802/5,111 yards and pars at 72/73. The testy part of this course is due partly to traps and trees. The primary challenge, however, comes in the form of water. A pesky little creek comes into play on 14 holes, occasionally crossing the same fairway more than once. This is an interesting course with a beautiful setting.

RATES: (EP) Lodgings - $95/$120/$165. Green fees - $50, including cart. Golf package - one night/one day (including lodging, MAP, unlimited green fees), $175 per couple. Rates are for June-October.

ARRIVAL: By air - Knoxville. By private aircraft - Sevier-Gatlinburg, a 3,500-foot paved runway. By car - from Gatlinburg, Route 321 N for 11 miles.

Buffalo Mountain Resort

Route 2, 100 Country Club Drive, Unicoi, TN 37692

(865) 928-6531; (800) 545-3311

ACCOMMODATIONS: This 69-room motel is in the Appalachian Mountains of Eastern Tennessee.

AMENITIES: Olympic-size swimming pool, indoor and outdoor tennis courts, a large restaurant and lounge.

GOLF: The Buffalo Valley Course plays 6,599/6,193/5,389 yards, parring at 71/75. It is a well-trapped layout, bringing water into play on six holes.

RATES: (EP) Lodgings - $50/$69. Golf packages are available.

ARRIVAL: By air - Asheville, North Carolina (80 miles). By car - 5½ miles south of Johnson City on Highway 23 South.

Tennessee

Fairfield Glade

PO Box 1500, Fairfield Glade, TN 38557

(931) 484-3723; (800) 624-8755

ACCOMMODATIONS: The Glade Lodge (motel-type rooms) and the Country Club Villas (two- and three-bedroom units).

AMENITIES: Indoor and outdoor swimming pools, a health club, whirlpools, basketball, volleyball, badminton, arts and craft workshops, tennis (two indoor and six outdoor courts), fishing, and boating (at their own marina). For dining, choose from the Druid Hills Country Club, Stonehenge Restaurant or the Sassafras Restaurant.

GOLF: While the Dorchester course is restricted to member play, three other excellent golf courses are now open for guest play. The Druid Hills layout weighs in at a gentle 6,329/5,946/4,948 yards, with a par of 72. The Stonehenge Golf Club, coming into play in late 1984, measures 6,549/6,202/4,900 yards with a par of 72. The newest is the Heatherhurst course, a Gary Baird design. Reaching out 6,500/6,250/5,650 yards, it also pars at 72. For tee times, call (800) 624-8755.

RATES: (EP) Lodgings - $120/$175. Green fees - $55/$69, including cart. Rates are for mid-April to October. Golf packages are available.

ARRIVAL: By air - Knoxville (88 miles). By private aircraft - Crossville Airport has a 6,000-foot paved runway (13 miles). By car - take Exit 332 off I-40 at Peavine Road near Crossville, then follow the signs six miles north.

Opryland Hotel

2800 Opryland Drive, Nashville, TN 37214

(615) 889-1000

ACCOMMODATIONS: Approximately 2,300 rooms, many offering a view of the garden or overlooking the conservatory, a two-acre Victorian garden under glass with fountains, waterfalls, and bridges.

AMENITIES: Three swimming pools. There is also the Opryland showpark with its various presentations, as well as theme park activities for the younger set. Dining possibilities are numerous: The Old Hickory Room, the Cascades Restaurant, Rhett's, Rachel's, and the Veranda for poolside meals. The new Springhouse Golf Club is open for lunch.

GOLF: The Springhouse Golf Course, designed by US Open champion Larry Nelson, plays a very hefty 7,007/6,588/6,185/5,788 /5,126 yards and pars at 72. While definitely a links-style layout, very open with few trees, it presents more than its share of problems – mounds, moguls, sand traps, grass bunkers and, of course, water. Although water comes into action on only six holes on the front side, the back nine makes up for it with the wet stuff coming into play on eight fairways. Golf operations are supported by a 43,000-square-foot clubhouse complete with locker rooms, a beautiful restaurant, lounge and golf shop. For tee times, call (615) 871-7759.

RATES: (EP) Lodgings - $195/$245/$279/$550 and up. Golf packages are available. Rates are for June through October.

ARRIVAL: By air - Nashville International Airport. By car - the resort is nine miles northeast of downtown Nashville. From Briley Parkway, take Exit 12B for the hotel. The golf course exit is 12A.

Tennessee State Parks

Although Tennessee has 54 state parks, we are listing only those with resort inns and golf courses. Rates quoted are for peak season (April-October). All rates shown are EP; MAP plans are available. Golf fees are the same at each park; green fees are $35, including carts. For additional information, call (888) 867-2757 or (615) 532-0001.

Fall Creek Falls State Resort Park

State Highway 30, Route 3, Pikeville, TN 37367

(423) 881-5241; (800) 250-8610

ACCOMMODATIONS: There are 72 rooms, as well as suites with kitchenettes. Cabins are available for up to eight people. At 16,000 acres, this is the second largest park in the system and offers some spectacular scenery.

AMENITIES: Olympic-size pool, tennis courts, marina and restaurant.

GOLF: This is one zinger of a golf course. Playing 6,706/6,378/6,060 yards, it pars at 72. *Golf Digest* has placed it among the top 50 public courses in the nation. For tee times, call (423) 881-5706.

RATES: (EP) Lodgings - $75/$140.

ARRIVAL: 11 miles east of Spencer and 18 miles west of Pikeville. Enter from Highway 111 or 30.

Henry Horton State Resort Park

PO Box 128, Chapel Hill, TN 37034

(931) 364-2222; (800) 250-8612

ACCOMMODATIONS: The inn has 72 rooms, including four with kitchenettes. There are also five cabins, fully equipped for housekeeping.

AMENITIES: Trap and skeet shooting, swimming, lighted tennis courts and marina.

GOLF: The Buford Ellington Golf Course was the site of the NJCAA tournaments in 1978 and 1981. It plays 7,151/6,580/5,905 yards with a par of 72/73. For tee times, call 931-364-2319.

RATES: (EP) Lodgings - $60/$85.

ARRIVAL: 40 miles south of Nashville on Highway 31A, between Chapel Hill and Lewisburg.

Montgomery Bell State Resort Park

Route 1, Burns, TN 37029

(615) 797-3101; (800) 250-8613

ACCOMMODATIONS: The lodge is a large stone structure with 40 guest rooms.

AMENITIES: Marina (boating and fishing), tennis courts and a dining room.

GOLF: The Frank G. Clement-designed course has a par of 72 and plays 6,377/6,056/5,586/4,994 yards. For tee times, call (615) 797-2578.

RATES: (EP) Lodgings - $70/$75/$80. Golf packages are available.

ARRIVAL: By car - Seven miles east of Dickson on Highway 70. From I-40, take Montgomery Bell Park exit and follow signs.

Paris Landing State Resort Park

Route 1, Buchanan, TN 38222

(901) 642-4311; (800) 250-8614

ACCOMMODATIONS: 100 rooms in the inn.

AMENITIES: Two swimming pools, lighted tennis courts and a modern full-service marina. There is also an excellent dining room.

GOLF: The course, parring at 72/76, measures 6,762/6,479/5,723 yards. For tee times, call (901) 644-1332.

RATES: (EP) Lodgings - $65/$75/$125.

ARRIVAL: By car - 16 miles northeast of the town of Paris, on US 79.

Tennessee

Pickwick Landing State Resort Park

State Highway 57, PO Box 10, Pickwick Dam, TN 38365

(901) 689-3135; (800) 250-8615

ACCOMMODATIONS: The inn offers rooms, and there are also cabins equipped for housekeeping.

AMENITIES: Full-service marina, a swimming pool, a popular beach area, tennis courts, and a restaurant.

GOLF: The course weighs in at a hefty 6,616/6,401/5,793 yards, with a par of 72/74. For tee times, call (901) 689-3149.

RATES: (EP) Inn - $62/$68/$160; suites $150. Cabins - $100/$125.

ARRIVAL: By car - In western Tennessee on State Highway 57, south of I-40.

Texas

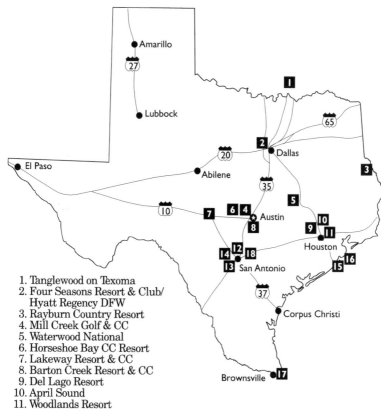

1. Tanglewood on Texoma
2. Four Seasons Resort & Club/
   Hyatt Regency DFW
3. Rayburn Country Resort
4. Mill Creek Golf & CC
5. Waterwood National
6. Horseshoe Bay CC Resort
7. Lakeway Resort & CC
8. Barton Creek Resort & CC
9. Del Lago Resort
10. April Sound
11. Woodlands Resort
12. Woodcreek Resort
13. Flying L Guest Ranch
14. Tapatio Springs Resort & CC
15. South Shore Harbour
16. Columbia Lakes
17. Rancho Viejo Resort
18. Hyatt Regency Hill Country
    Resort/Westin La Cantera Resort

April Sound

Box 253 Highway 105 West, Conroe, TX 77301

(409) 588-1101

ACCOMMODATIONS: Villas (hotel-type) with verandas or balconies, and one- to three- bedroom townhouses, complete -

with living rooms and kitchens. On the shores of 21,000-acre Lake Conroe, 50 miles northwest of Houston, April Sound offers an almost endless variety of water activities.

AMENITIES: 17 tennis courts (four covered and nine lighted). The main dining room, the Fernery, overlooks the cove and part of the golf course.

GOLF: The Lakeview Course, parring at 71 and reaching out 6,189/5,807/5,323 yards, borders on April Sound. Water only becomes a factor on seven holes. There is also a nine-hole, par-3 executive layout.

RATES: (EP) Lodgings - $79/$249. Rates given are for February 15 through November 15. Green fees - $60, carts $24.

ARRIVAL: By air - Houston. By car - from Houston (50 miles), take I-45 north, then head west on Highway 105 (eight miles).

Barton Creek Resort & Country Club

8212 Barton Club Drive, Austin, TX 78735

(512) 329-4000; (800) 336-6158

ACCOMMODATIONS: 147 guest rooms, each with sitting area, and three suites. Five of the rooms have fireplaces. The resort is 15 minutes from downtown Austin.

AMENITIES: Fitness center with spa, steam rooms, sauna, whirlpools, loofah scrubs, herbal wraps, massage, indoor running track, Lifecyles and Stairmasters. There are 10 lighted tennis courts, one indoor pool and two outdoor swimming pools. The dining rooms include the Terrace Room, the Tejas Room (in the clubhouse), the Palm Court, and The Gourmet (open for dinner only).

GOLF: The course was designed by Ben Crenshaw and Bill Coore. It reaches out a respectable 6,678/6,066/4,483 yards, with a par of 71. Water is a factor on only three holes. However, on the second course, a Fazio design, water comes into action on at least nine holes. The par-72 course measures 6,956/6,513/6,231/5,875/5,905 yards. Now a third Fazio-designed course has been added. Called Canyon, it reaches out a substantial 7,161/6,872/6,504/6,100/5,149 yards, with a par of 72.

RATES: (EP) Lodgings - $230/$345. Green fees - Crenshaw Course, $65; Fazio Course, $135/$175, including carts. Golf packages are available.

ARRIVAL: By air - Austin International Airport (15 miles). By car - take Bee Caves Road (RM 2244), 11 miles west of Austin.

Columbia Lakes

188 Freeman Boulevard, West Columbia, TX 77486

(979) 345-5151; (800) 231-1030

ACCOMMODATIONS: Cottages, many along the golf course, provide anything from a single bedroom to an eight-plex with living room.

AMENITIES: Four lighted tennis courts, swimming pool, bicycle and boat rentals, a marina, and some excellent fishing. The restaurant and lounge are in the clubhouse.

GOLF: The Columbia Lakes Country Club course measures 6,967/6,300/5,280 yards and pars at 72. This well-trapped layout can test you with its many trees and generous amount of water.

RATES: (EP) Lodgings - $99/$150. Green fees - $50/$65, including cart. Golf package - two nights/three days (includes lodging, green fees and cart), $538 per couple. Rates are for September-November and March-May.

ARRIVAL: By air - Houston (60 minutes). By car - Highway 288 south to Highway 35, then west to Country Road 25. North to Columbia Lakes.

Del Lago Resort

600 Del Lago Blvd., Montgomery, TX 77356

(936) 582-6100; (800) 833-3078

ACCOMMODATIONS: 310 one-bedroom Tower Suites. The units in these 22-story towers have kitchenettes. There are also 48 two-bedroom golf course cottages, each with a woodburning fireplace, fully equipped kitchen, washer/dryer, and dining/living area. The lakeside villas include the same amenities as the cottages, but have private boat slips.

AMENITIES: 13 tennis courts, two racquetball courts, an exercise room complete with Nautilus and Universal equipment, and a massage therapist. Also available: a health spa, swimming pool, bicycling, horseshoes, and all manner of fishing and boating. Dining is provided in the Lago Vista or the less formal Café Verde.

GOLF: Designed by Dave Marr and Jay Riviere, the course plays 6,907/6,467/5,829 yards and pars at 71. You might encounter water on 11 holes.

RATES: (EP) Lodgings - $99/$159/$170/$190. Lakeside villas - $600/$750. Green fees - $50/$65, including cart. Golf packages are available. Rates shown are April through mid-October.

ARRIVAL: By air - Houston (40 miles). By car - from Houston, take I-45 north. Exit to Highway 105. Turn left (west) and go 13 miles. Turn right onto Walden Road for two miles. Look for signs to resort.

Flying L Guest Ranch

Highway 173, Bandera, TX 78003

(830) 460-3001; (800) 292-5134

ACCOMMODATIONS: One- to three-bedroom villas, some with two double beds, others with king-size beds. Some feature fireplaces.

AMENITIES: Two lighted tennis courts, swimming, horseback riding, hayrides, and fishing. They can also provide a few hours of entertainment for children while you try a round of golf. The resort has a dining room and lounge. Should you go hungry here it's your own fault. The food is great, both in quantity and quality.

GOLF: The Flying L Country Club course, parring at 72, plays a hefty 6,635/6,273/5,442 yards.

RATES: (MAP) Rooms - $216 per couple, includes discounted green fees. Green fees - $22/$31, including cart. Golf packages are available.

ARRIVAL: By air - San Antonio. By car - from San Antonio, 40 miles west on Highway 410 to Highway 16 (Bandera Rd.). North on 16 into Bandera. Turn left onto Highway 173 for one mile.

Four Seasons Resort & Club

4150 North MacArthur Blvd., Irving, TX 75038

(972) 717-0700; (800) 332-3442

The Four Seasons Resort & Club has been judged one of our Top 50 resorts.

ACCOMMODATIONS: 357 guest rooms, including 13 suites. There are also 50 Golf Villas overlooking the 18th green of the TPC course. These represent the ultimate in luxurious accommodations.

AMENITIES: Four indoor and eight outdoor tennis courts, one indoor and three outdoor swimming pools, children's pool, two squash courts, and four racquetball courts. There is a wonderful health spa with dry and wet saunas, whirlpools, herbal wraps, massages, weight room and exercise room. They also have a children's care center. Four restaurants are available for dining.

GOLF: The TPC Player's Course, home of the Byron Nelson Golf Classic, was designed by Jay Morrish with consultation from Byron Nelson and Ben Crenshaw. Stretching out 6,899/6,500/6,004/5,340 yards, it pars at 70. The 74 sand bunkers and water located throughout the course make it an interesting layout.

A second 18, the Cottonwood Valley Course, was designed by Robert Trent Jones. This course is also available for guest play. Parring at 71/72, it reaches out 6,862/6,367/5,961/5,320 yards. The first green is in the shape of the state of Texas, while the bunker immediately behind forms the state of Oklahoma. The resort features the Byron Nelson Golf School, which has an outstanding program. The Director of Golf is Mike Abbott.

RATES: (EP) Lodgings - $305/$395 and up. Green fees - $125, carts $36. Golf package - one day/one night (includes lodging, green fees for one round per person with cart, bag storage), $370/$450 per couple. Unusual is the fact that the rate is lower on weekends.

ARRIVAL: By air - Dallas/Ft. Worth. By car - from the north exit of the airport take 114 E. Exit at MacArthur Blvd. South and drive approximately two miles south. The resort will be on your left.

Texas

Horseshoe Bay Country Club Resort

Box 7766, Horseshoe Bay, TX 78657

(830) 598-2511; (800) 531-5105

ACCOMMODATIONS: Guest rooms at the inn, and some 200 one- to three-bedroom condominiums with fully equipped kitchens.

AMENITIES: They have one of the most unusual pools we have seen – an enormous black marble basin. At first glance it looks as if it had been constructed by the Romans. Horseback riding and 14 lighted tennis courts are also available. There is a full-service marina and, with more than 22 miles of lake, you can sail, water-ski, or fish. The Yacht Club Restaurant offers good food and a spectacular view of the bay.

GOLF: All three courses were designed by Robert Trent Jones. The Slick Rock course, parring at 72, reaches out 6,839/6,358/5,858 yards. The front nine is heavily wooded, while the back side is a little more open. You can rest assured that the 72 traps, along with water coming into contention on 10 holes, will keep you occupied.

The Ram Rock course is one of the tougher layouts in Texas. Parring at 71, it plays 6,946/6,408/5,954/5,305 yards. With its 68 traps, heavily wooded fairways, and water hazards on eight holes, this gem is a stemwinder. The Apple Rock course, the newest addition, weighs in at 6,999/6,536/6,038/5,480 yards, also with a par of 72.

RATES: (EP) Lodgings - $165/$577. Green fees - $95/$105, cart $21. Golf package - two nights/three days, available weekdays only (includes lodging, three rounds of golf with cart, two dinners, all taxes and gratuities), $960 per couple. Rates are for mid-March to November.

ARRIVAL: By air - Austin. By private aircraft - Horseshoe Bay Airport. By car - from Austin, take Route 71 northwest 55 miles.

Hyatt Regency DFW

International Parkway, DFW Airport, TX 75261

(972) 453-1234; (800) 233-1234

ACCOMMODATIONS: 1,370 guest rooms.

AMENITIES: Health spa, swimming pool, three lighted indoor and four outdoor tennis courts, 10 racquetball courts, and golf. Four restaurants offer a wide variety of cuisine; there are also three bars.

GOLF: Two golf courses are located five minutes from the hotel. The Bear Creek Club West reaches out 6,677/6,261/5,597 yards; the East Course measures 6,670/6,282/5,620 yards. Each pars at 72. Undulating terrain, many traps, and water combine to produce two fine layouts.

RATES: (EP) Lodgings - $214/$375 and up. Green fees - $78/$88, carts $24. Golf packages are available.

ARRIVAL: Dallas/Ft. Worth Airport.

Hyatt Regency Hill Country Resort

9800 Hyatt Resort Drive, San Antonio, TX 78251

(210) 647-1234; (800) 233-1234

ACCOMMODATIONS: 500 rooms, including 56 suites. They also have a concierge level providing VIP service.

AMENITIES: Two swimming pools, three tennis courts, walking and biking paths, and a health club providing state-of-the-art workout equipment plus Swedish and sports massage. The resort offers dining in the Springhouse Café in the hotel and the Antlers Lodge at the clubhouse.

GOLF: Unlike the stereotypical perception of Texas geography, this area has craggy, rolling hills, stone cliffs, live oak, cedar, Spanish oak trees, and an abundance of water in the form of lakes and rivers.

The golf course, designed by Arthur Hills, plays to a substantial 6,913/6,481/5,747/4,781 yards and pars at 72. Mr. Hills took full advantage of the terrain and the diabolically placed lakes and ponds. He also sprinkled in a great number of bunkers to keep everyone honest.

RATES: (EP) Lodgings - $190/$285/$310/$1,250. Green fees - $120, including cart. Golf packages are available.

ARRIVAL: By air - San Antonio International Airport (20 minutes). By car - take Loop 410 to State Highway 151; get off at Sea World exit. Travel north to resort.

Lakeway Resorts & Conference Center

101 Lakeway Drive, Austin, TX 78734

(512) 261-6600; (800) 525-3929

ACCOMMODATIONS: Motel-type rooms and hotel suites at the inn. There are also the "Hillcourt Villas" condominiums at the World of Tennis, as well as other homes and condominiums. A word of caution: If you are driving, do not plan to arrive at night. This is a large complex and it is extremely difficult to find your way around.

AMENITIES: 32 lighted tennis courts (two indoor), steam and whirlpool baths, and an equestrian center providing instruction and trail rides. Dining is a relaxing affair in the Inn's Travis Room; seldom have we had better service. The Trophy Room at the Yacht Club is also available.

GOLF: The Live Oaks has a yardage of 6,643/6,228/5,472 and pars at 72/73; the Yaupon 18 plays 6,595/5,988/5,032 yards, parring at 72. Both are available for guest play.

RATES: (EP) Lodgings - $160/$179/$240. Green fees - $64/$74, including carts. Golf package - one night/one day (includes lodgings, green fees and cart), $380 per couple. Rates are for peak golf season, April to October.

ARRIVAL: By air - Austin. By private aircraft - Lakeway's own airport. By car - (20 miles northwest of Austin) I-35, exit on Highway 620, continue five miles after you cross the Mansfield Dam.

Mill Creek Golf & Country Club

PO Box 67, Salado, TX 76571

(254) 947-5141; (800) 736-3441

ACCOMMODATIONS: Mill Creek Guest Homes, Mill Creek Inn, as well as a number of one- , two- , and three-bedroom private homes. Mill Creek Golf & Country Club, while private, allows guests use of all facilities.

AMENITIES: Swimming, tennis, golf, and attendant social activities. The Mill Creek Restaurant offers a relaxed and casual atmosphere.

GOLF: The beautifully maintained course, designed by Robert Trent Jones, Jr., measures 6,486/6,052/5,250 yards and pars at 71/73. Salado Creek wanders throughout the entire layout and adds both beauty and challenge to the course.

RATES: (EP) Lodgings - $83/$93. Green fees - $55/$65, including cart. Golf package - one night/one day (includes lodging, green fees, and cart), weekdays $141; weekends $182 per couple.

ARRIVAL: By air - Austin. By car - I-35 to exit on 285, then travel half a mile.

Rancho Viejo Resort

One Rancho Viejo Drive, Rancho Viejo, TX 78575

(956) 350-4000; (800) 531-7400

ACCOMMODATIONS: Luxurious poolside suites, and one- , two- , or three-bedroom fully equipped fairway villas. Flowering hibiscus, oleanders, and bougainvillea welcome you.

AMENITIES: Huge swimming pool with swim-up bar and two lighted tennis courts. Dining takes place in the Casa Grande Supper Club. For less formal dining, there is the Ranchero Room at the main clubhouse. You can also have fun aboard the *Delta Dawn* riverboat.

GOLF: Golf is played on two championship courses – the El Diablo, 6,899/6,213/5,575 yards, parring at 70/72, and the El Angel. The latter is, regardless of its name, no angel, measuring 6,647/6,003/5,387 yards, again with a par of 70/72. Each of them will challenge you in its own way, with fairways that wind through citrus orchards and pines.

Texas

RATES: (EP) Lodgings - $125/$175. Green fees - $40, carts $24. Golf package - one night/one day (includes lodging, breakfast, green fees, cart, club storage and taxes), $224/$292 per couple. Rates are for January-March.

ARRIVAL: By air - Brownsville (15 minutes). By car - three miles off Highway 100 and less than one mile off Highway 511.

Rayburn Country Resort

1000 Wingate, Sam Rayburn, TX 75951

(409) 698-2444; (800) 882-1442

ACCOMMODATIONS: 50 hotel rooms and 54 villa rooms, some located near the Country Club, with others along the lush golf course.

AMENITIES: Four lighted tennis courts, a 25-meter pool, and fishing and sailing on Lake Sam Rayburn. Dining is in the Rayburn Country Club.

GOLF: The 27-hole crossover system offers a variety of play. The Green/Blue combination of nines measures 6,754/6,266/5,524 yards; the Green/Gold plays 6,741/6,236/5,301 yards; and the Blue/Gold Course weighs in at 6,754/6,266/5,524 yards. All three par at 72. There are more than enough water hazards, traps, dogleg holes, and trees to hold your undivided attention. These are not easy courses.

RATES: (EP) Hotel: $75/$225. Villas (one bedroom), $100. Green fees - $25/$35, carts $22. Golf package - two nights/three days (includes lodging, green fees, and cart), $528/$624 weekdays, $599/$678 weekends, per couple.

ARRIVAL: By air - Beaumont (88 miles). By private aircraft - Pineland/Jasper Airport. By car - from Beaumont, north on US 96, left on Highway 255.

South Shore Harbour Resort

2500 South Shore Boulevard, League City, TX 77573

(281) 334-1000; (800) 442-5005

ACCOMMODATIONS: 250 guest rooms and suites. These units are equipped with two phones and in-room movies; many have excellent views of the yacht basin fronting the hotel. The resort is an impressive 11-story structure with a stone circular drive entrance.

AMENITIES: There is a large tropical pool on the property. The adjacent marina has 750 boat slips and offers charter fishing trips. A 70,000-square-foot fitness center, located a short distance away, features a multitude of ways to destroy yourself. Included is a 25-meter lap pool, a coed whirlpool, eight lighted tennis courts (two indoor), along with racquetball courts. The Paradise Reef Restaurant has a varied menu ranging from seafood to beef. The Harbour Club has a more formal setting. There is also the poolside "Hooker's Nook" for lighter fare. The name refers to a "fishing" hook (at least that's what they told me).

GOLF: The course rolls out from the clubhouse for 6,663/6,040/5,374 yards and plays to a par of 71. It brings water into play on 15 holes. Play can also be arranged on several other golf courses in the area.

RATES: (EP) Lodgings $135/$145/$155. Green fees - $65/$70, including cart. Golf packages are available.

ARRIVAL: By air - Houston International. By car - take Bay Area Blvd. to El Camino Egret Bay Blvd. Turn left onto Marina Bay Drive. Drive to the resort entrance.

Tanglewood on Texoma

PO Box 265, Pottsboro, TX 75076

(903) 786-2968; (800) 833-6569

ACCOMMODATIONS: 65 rooms, including five master suites in the unique nine-story "Lighthouse," as well as 120 fully equipped condominiums. Tanglewood is a resort community nestled among wooded hills on the shore of Lake Texoma.

AMENITIES: Three-tiered swimming pool, two lighted tennis courts, an equestrian center and a 21-foot ski boat. Guests can dine in the elegant Captain's Table Restaurant or The Seachest Room.

GOLF: The Ralph Plummer-designed course has three tee settings, and covers 6,997/6,354/5,572 yards, with a par of 72/73. In addition to the yardage, additional challenges are provided by some tree-lined fairways and water hazards on six holes.

RATES: (EP) Lodgings - $85/$370. Green fees - $50/$60, including carts. Golf packages are available. Rates are for April-October.

ARRIVAL: By air - Dallas/Ft. Worth. By private aircraft - Grayson County Airport. By car - 80 miles north of Dallas on Highway 75.

Tapatio Springs Resort & Country Club

PO Box 550, Boerne, TX 78006

(830) 537-4611; (800) 999-3299

ACCOMMODATIONS: 96 rooms in the hotel.

AMENITIES: Swimming, tennis, sauna, Jacuzzi, and exercise rooms. Dining is in the Clubhouse Restaurant.

GOLF: The 18-hole championship course is both fun and beautiful. With a par of 72, it plays 6,543/6,233/5,849/5,277 yards.

RATES: (EP) Lodgings - $135/$175/$250. Green fees - $75, carts $26. Golf package - two nights/two days (includes lodging, green fees, cart, club storage), $258/$400 per couple.

ARRIVAL: By air - San Antonio (25 minutes). By car - I-10 north to Boerne, turn left (west) on John's Road to Tapatio Springs.

Waterwood National Resort

Waterwood Box One, Huntsville, TX 77340

(936) 891-5211; (877) 441-5211

ACCOMMODATIONS: Rooms are available in the lodge area, as well as in lodge cabanas that are equipped with refrigerator and wet bar. Waterwood, with miles of shoreline, is located in one of the most picturesque areas of Lake Livingston.

AMENITIES: Four lighted tennis courts, Olympic-sized pool, marina, boat rentals, paddleboats, canoes, water-skiing, and fishing. There is also a dining room.

GOLF: Carved from the east Texas pine woods, the rolling tree-lined fairways and typical Pete Dye greens layout will challenge you. Stretching across half of Texas, it plays 6,872/6,258/5,480/5,029 yards and pars at 71/73.

RATES: (EP) Lodgings - $70/$110. Green fees - $40/$60, carts $20. Golf package - two nights/three days in the lodge (includes lodging, green fees, dinner each evening, cart, club storage), $506/$590 per couple. Rates are for March-October.

ARRIVAL: By air - Houston (98 miles). By car - I-45 from Houston north to exit 190. East at Huntsville. Continue east until you see signs.

Westin La Cantera Resort

16641 La Cantera Parkway, San Antonio, TX 78256

(210) 558-6500; (800) 937-8461

La Cantera, which opened in 1999, has a great deal to offer its guests.

ACCOMMODATIONS: 508 rooms, including 25 suites plus 38 rooms in a Casita Village.

AMENITIES: Two tennis courts, four swimming pools including a 14-foot waterfall, two outdoor hot tubs, an exercise and fitness center and a children's program. Restaurants include the main dining room, a specialty restaurant, a poolside snack bar and La Cantera Grille at the clubhouse. Be sure to set aside time to visit the wonderful "River Walk" area, as well as the Alamo.

GOLF: Designed by Jay Morrish/Tom Weiskopf, La Cantera plays to a substantial 7,001/6,406/6,026/5,581/4,940 yards, with a par of 72. As this layout is located at the southern end of the "Hill Country," it offers several elevation changes. Opened in 1995, it is fully mature and happens to be the home of the Western Texas Open, a PGA Tournament event. Now under construction and set to be open by the time you read this is a second golf layout. A championship 18-hole affair, designed by Arnold Palmer, it will stretch over 250 acres and will be supported by a separate clubhouse and driving range.

RATES: (EP) Rooms - $334/$380. Green fees - $115, including cart. Golf package - (includes one night/one day, room, breakfast, golf cart, green fees, golf clinic), $419 per couple.

ARRIVAL: By air - San Antonio Airport. By car - from the airport take Highway 420 west; continue on to I-10 until you exit onto La Cantera Parkway (approximately 15 miles); turn left. En-

Texas

trance to resort is approximately three-quarters of a mile farther on the right side.

Woodcreek Resort

One Woodcreek Drive, Wimberley, TX 78676

(512) 847-7176; (800) 870-5678

ACCOMMODATIONS: Lodge rooms, cabins or townhouses. The townhouses each have a living room and fully equipped kitchen.

AMENITIES: Canoeing, paddleboating, fishing, 10 tennis courts, handball, hot tubs, and swimming pool. Although there is more than one place to eat, the Sam Houston Dining Room serves as good a meal as you will find.

GOLF: The Woodcreek Resort course, measuring a modest 6,470/5,973/5,287 yards, pars at 72. The pesky little Cypress Creek runs throughout the entire 18, creating some rather interesting golf shots.

RATES: (EP) Lodgings - $60/$86/$207. Green fees - $34/$44, including cart.

ARRIVAL: By air - Austin (43 miles) or San Antonio (63 miles). By car - from either I-10 or I-35, turn northwest at San Marcus to Wimberley.

The Woodlands Resort

2301 N. Millbend Drive, The Woodlands, TX 77380

(281) 367-1100; (800) 433-2624

ACCOMMODATIONS: 364 rooms and suites, many with kitchenettes. They have recently added an additional 95 rooms.

AMENITIES: Health club, saunas, steam room, herbal baths, whirlpools and Swedish massage. Tennis is served up on 17 outdoor and seven indoor courts, supported by a well-stocked tennis shop. Swimming and basketball are also offered. While there are several restaurants on the premises, the standout is the Glass Menagerie, with a view of the lake. There is also a dining room at the Country Club.

GOLF: Woodlands now offers play on 54 holes. The North Course reaches out 6,881/6,339/5,765 yards with a par of 72; the West 18, parring at 72/73, plays 7,010/6,591/6,196/5,351 yards. The TPC layout (formerly the East Course) covers 7,045/6,367/5,302 yards, with the par set at 72. The introduction of water, bunkers, and tree-lined fairways makes these courses intriguing.

RATES: (EP) Lodgings - $199/$219/$239/$350. Green fees - $85, including cart; TPC course - $145, including cart. Golf package - two nights/three days (includes lodging, green fees, cart, golf clinic, bag storage, unlimited golf on the north course and one round on the TPC course), $636 per couple. Rates are for mid-March through May and September through mid-November.

ARRIVAL: By air - Houston (25 miles). By car - I-45 north to Woodlands/Robinson Road exit. Turn west back over I-45 to Grogan's Mill Road. Take a left, go to the second stoplight, and turn right on N. Millbend Road.

Utah

Homestead Resort & Golf Club

700 North Homestead Drive, Midway, UT 84049

(801) 654-1102; (800) 327-7220

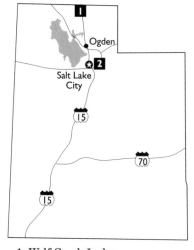

1. Wolf Creek Lodge
2. Homestead Resort & Golf Club

ACCOMMODATIONS: 130 rooms located in cottages, executive cottages, cottage suites and condominiums; the latter are fully equipped for housekeeping. There are also some two- and three-bedroom condominium units. The Homestead enjoys a lovely setting among a profusion of trees. Pines, oaks, dogwoods, aspens, spruce, maples and walnuts surround the entire area.

AMENITIES: Two lighted tennis courts, indoor and outdoor swimming pools, mineral baths, whirlpools, a hot tub, saunas, horseback riding, hay, buggy and barnyard rides (for the small fry). Nearby Deer Creek reservoir is used for boating, fishing, and water-skiing. The resort also has a children's program. Simon's, a beautiful dining room, is available for candlelight dining; for lighter fare you might consider The Grill Room at the golf club. In the winter, there is snowmobiling, a sleigh ride/dinner package, and cross-country skiing. The snowmobile and ski programs include rental equipment, instruction and supervision.

GOLF: The course plays 6,967/6,159/5,131 yards with a par of 72. The front nine is definitely a mountain layout, with elevations ranging from 5,000 to 6,000 feet. While the greens are of average size they are also multi-level affairs. The good news is that water comes into play on only three holes. The bad news – they make up for it on the back nine. While the back side is relatively flat, Snake Creek wanders all over the place and makes a nuisance of itself on all nine holes. For tee times, call (435) 654-5588. The John Jacobs' Practical Golf School is available. A second golf facility is located less than a mile away – the outstanding 27-hole Wasatch Mountain State Park Course.

RATES: (EP) Lodgings $139/$219. Green fees - $25/$35, including carts. Various package plans and seasonal memberships are available.

ARRIVAL: By air - Salt Lake City (55 minutes). By private aircraft - Heber City Airport (paved runway five miles from the resort). By car - take I-80 east from Salt Lake City. Continue past the Park City exit. Exit right onto US 40, and drive about 18 miles to the Homestead/Midway exit. Turn right on River Road and follow signs to the resort (five miles).

Wolf Lodge

3615 North Wolf Creek Drive, Eden, UT 84310

(435) 745-2621; (800) 345-8824

ACCOMMODATIONS: Condominiums, all with fully equipped kitchens and woodburning fireplaces. Most border on the golf course.

AMENITIES: During the winter, this area offers some of the finest skiing in the country. In summer, guests can enjoy swimming (two pools), sailing and boating on Pine View Lake, tennis, racquetball, and horseback riding. There are also weight rooms and a sauna.

GOLF: The Wolf Creek Country Club Resort course reaches out a healthy 6,825/6,459/5,816 yards and pars at 72/74. Whoever designed this layout obviously liked water, as it comes into play on 13 holes.

RATES: (EP) Lodgings - $100/$110. Green fees - $30/$35, carts $24.

ARRIVAL: By air - Salt Lake City. By car - from Ogden, take Highway 39 east to 166, north to Highway 162. Follow 162 to the resort.

Utah

Vermont

1. The Green Mountain Resort/Mt. Mansfield Resort/Mt. Snow Resort/ Stowehof Inn
2. Basin Harbor Inn
3. Sugarbush Inn
4. Lake Morey Inn & CC
5. Quechee Inn at Marshland Farm
6. The Woodstock Inn & Resort
7. The Equinox Resort & Spa
8. Stratton Mountain Resorts

Basin Harbor Club

Lake Champlain, Vergennes, VT 05491

(802) 475-2311; (800) 622-4000

ACCOMMODATIONS: The Main Lodge, the Champlain House, the Homestead and approximately 77 lakeview cottages. The resort is located on the eastern shore of beautiful Lake Champlain.

AMENITIES: Sailing, swimming, fishing, water-skiing, and five tennis courts. Jackets and ties are required in the main dining room.

GOLF: The Basin Harbor course, which starts right at your door, has a modest yardage of 6,513/6,232/5,745, with a par of 72. With trees lining five fairways, as well as an abundance of traps, it is an entertaining but challenging layout. Two water hazards, some devious bunkers and fiendish tree placements are there to spice up the action.

RATES: (FAP) Lodgings - $219/$240/$255/$265/$285 per couple. Green fees - $37, carts $25. Golf package - three nights/three days (includes lodging, FAP, green fees and cart for one round per night of stay, club storage), $1,005/$1,540 per couple. Rates are for July to mid-October.

ARRIVAL: By air - Burlington. By private aircraft - Basin Harbor (3,200-foot runway, grass/not lighted). By car - from Vergennes, follow the signs to 22A through town and over the bridge; turn right at the caution light and drive six miles to Basin Harbor.

The Equinox Resort & Spa

Route 7A, Manchester Village, VT 05254

(802) 362-4700; (800) 362-4747

To appreciate the flavor of the Equinox, a little historical background is in order. I am not sure how long this place has been in operation, but Mrs. Lincoln, wife of our 16th President, spent some time here during the summer of 1863 with her children. With painstaking attention to detail, the resort was restored and reopened in 1985. Every post and bit of wallpaper was brought back to its original state.

ACCOMMODATIONS: 154 rooms and suites, as well as 10 three-bedroom condominiums just west of the hotel.

AMENITIES: Heated swimming pool, a steam room, saunas, whirlpool, aerobics, weight rooms, massage, facial and herbal wraps, and three tennis courts, as well as fly-fishing and shooting schools. They also folded some of yesteryear into the mix in the form of nostalgic carriage rides, bicycle touring and canoeing. Horseback riding is available nearby. The dining facilities are excellent.

During the winter, The Equinox offers the perfect setting for cross-country as well as alpine skiing on nearby Stratton or Bromley Mountains.

GOLF: The course, parring at 71, measures 6,423/6,069/5,082 yards. Originally designed by Walter Travis, it has been around since 1927. Completely redone by Rees Jones, it was renamed Gleneagles Country Club. Built on rolling terrain, one of its major challenges is the scenery. The beautiful surrounding mountains can become a definite distraction.

Vermont

RATES: (EP) Lodgings - $189/$259/$339. Green fees - $70/
$75, carts $40. Golf package - two nights/three days (includes
lodging, green fees, club storage), $836/$980 per couple.

ARRIVAL: By air - Rutland or Burlington. By car - from Manchester Village, take Route 7A south to the resort.

The Green Mountain Resort

Main Street, Box 60, Stowe, VT 05672

(802) 253-7301; (800) 445-6629

ACCOMMODATIONS: 72 guest rooms, each reflecting the
warmth of the past.

AMENITIES: Use of the inn's full-service health club, swimming in the outdoor heated pool, or visiting the many antique
shops and boutiques that abound in this area. The resort boasts
two excellent restaurants.

GOLF: Golf is available at the Stowe Country Club. For details
on this layout, refer to the Stowehof Inn.

RATES: (EP) Lodgings - $110/$275/$300. Various package
plans are available.

ARRIVAL: By air - Burlington (45 minutes away). By car - the
resort is at the intersection of Mountain Road (Route 108) and
Route 100.

Lake Morey Inn & Country Club

PO Box 48, Fairlee, VT 05045

(802) 333-4311; (800) 423-1211

This country club resort has a beautiful setting, with 600-acre
Lake Morey at the back door and a championship golf layout at
the front.

ACCOMMODATIONS: Lodging is available in the main
building, the Morey Wings, the Edgewater, or the lakeside cottages; the latter are equipped with fireplaces.

AMENITIES: Lake swimming, canoeing, fishing, water-
skiing, four all-weather tennis courts, racquetball facilities, a

health club and an indoor pool. Dining facilities include the Steamboat and the Lakeview rooms.

GOLF: The course has been the site of the Vermont Open for over 40 years. Both the 13th and 15th tees are cut back into the woods. The course plays 6,024/5,807/5,007 yards and pars at 70.

RATES: (MAP) Lodgings - $188/$282 per day, per couple. There are several package plans available. Green fees are included with lodging rates; carts $30. Rates are for late June through late October.

ARRIVAL: By air - Lebanon, New Hampshire. By car - Route I-91, Exit 15, 20 miles north of White River junction.

Mount Mansfield Resort

5781 Mountain Road, Stowe, VT 05672

(802) 253-3000; (800) 253-4754

ACCOMMODATIONS: 38 rooms at the inn, plus 40 town-houses and lodge condominium units.

AMENITIES: Six clay tennis courts, three heated swimming pools, saunas, a whirlpool, an Alpine slide, a game room and a health spa. Dining is provided in the Toll House and the Cliff House dining rooms.

GOLF: The Stowe Country Club Course is owned and operated by the Inn. It plays 6,213/5,851/5,365 yards and pars at 72/74.

RATES: (EP) Lodgings - $131/$161/$250. Green fees - $65, including cart. Golf packages are available. Rates are for June-September.

ARRIVAL: By air - Burlington International Airport (45 minutes). Amtrak - Waterbury. By car - the Inn is on Route 108, five miles west of Stowe Village.

Mount Snow Resort

500 Mountain Road, Mount Snow, VT 05356

(802) 464-7788; (800) 451-4211

ACCOMMODATIONS: Snow Lake Lodge (105 rooms) or the Snowtree condominiums and townhouses, with units ranging from studios for two to full townhouses for 10.

AMENITIES: Indoor and outdoor swimming pools, 10 lighted tennis courts. Boating and lake swimming are also available. The Lakeside Dining Room serves a combination of American and continental cuisine.

GOLF: Parring at 72/74, the golf course reaches out 6,894/6,443/5,829 yards. It is more than just an interesting layout. It is well trapped, with tree-lined fairways. That, combined with water coming into play on 11 holes, will test you.

RATES: (EP) Lodgings - $88/$156/$166. Golf vacation packages and golf school packages are available. Green fees - $50, carts $32. Rates are for June-October.

ARRIVAL: By air - Albany, New York (68 miles). By car - take Route 9 to Wilmington, then head north on Route 100 for approximately nine miles.

Quechee Inn at Marshland Farm

Clubhouse Road, Quechee, VT 05059

(802) 295-3133; (800) 235-3133

ACCOMMODATIONS: Although small (24 guest rooms), this resort can only be described as intimate and charming.

AMENITIES: All guests have privileges at the Quechee Club, including the use of indoor and outdoor swimming pools, tennis, an exercise room, squash courts and boating. Their restaurants are known throughout the area.

GOLF: The Highland and Lakeland golf courses are available for play. For complete details, refer to Quechee Lakes Resort.

RATES: (BP) Lodgings - $130/$160/$190 per couple. Green fees - $100, including cart. Rates are for May-October.

ARRIVAL: By air - Lebanon Regional Airport. By car - I-89 north. Take Route 4 to Woodstock, and turn left (west) on Route 4 for 1.3 miles.

Quechee Lakes Resort

PO Box 432, Quechee, VT 05059

(802) 295-9356; (800) 262-3186

ACCOMMODATIONS: 1,100 well-equipped two- and three-bedroom homes and condominiums, many with washer/dryer.

AMENITIES: 10 tennis courts, squash and racquetball, sailing, fishing, horseback riding and golf. Summer theater, a New England tradition, is held in nearby White River, Woodstock, and Hanover and in Lake Sunapee, New Hampshire. The dining facilities are located in the clubhouse.

During the winter months, when golf and sailing are no longer possible, consider skating parties at the lighted ice rink, torchlight skiing or curling up by a crackling fire.

GOLF: The Highland and the Lakeland courses were designed by Geoffrey Cornish. Highland plays 6,765/6,342/5,439 yards, parring at 72. The Lakeland course, also with a par of 72, is a bit more modest at 6,569/6,016/5,399 yards. Lakeland tries to live up to its name with water on 13 holes.

The Highland course has been rated one of the top courses in the country. Quechee Lakes has been host to the New England PGA Tournament for the past several years.

RATES: (EP) Lodgings - $500 for two nights. Green fees - $100, including cart.

ARRIVAL: The resort is four miles west from I-89 on Route 4, midway between Woodstock (six miles west) and Dartmouth College at Hanover, New Hampshire (10 miles east).

Stowehof Inn

Box 1108, Edson Hill Road, Stowe, VT 05672

(802) 253-9722; (800) 932-7136

ACCOMMODATIONS: 50 rooms and suites, each with balcony or patio; some have a fireplace and kitchenette.

AMENITIES: Heated swimming pool and tennis on four courts. Once you have dined here, you will know why they continue to earn the AAA Four Diamond award.

Vermont

GOLF: Guests may use the Stowe Country Club course, which measures 6,252/5,844/5,364 and has a par of 72/74. There is a clubhouse with dining room, bar and locker rooms.

RATES: (MAP) Lodgings - $188/$300 per couple. Green fees - $57/$67, carts $32.

ARRIVAL: By air - Burlington (45 minutes away). By car - Route 108, just 3½ miles from Stowe Village. Turn right onto Edson Hill Road.

Stratton Mountain Resorts

Stratton Mountain, VT 05155

(802) 297-2200; (800) 843-6867

ACCOMMODATIONS: The 100-room Stratton Mountain Inn; the Liftline Lodge (95 rooms); the Long Trail Condo (65 rooms); or the new Village Lodge, a condo/hotel with 91 units. There are also some fully equipped condominiums and three- and four-bedroom homes.

AMENITIES: Health spa with hot tubs and Nautilus gym, a fly-fishing school for novices and experts (videotape analysis is available), 15 outdoor and four indoor tennis courts, horseback riding, swimming, sailing and golf. The new Stratton Sports Center added more indoor tennis and racquetball courts. There are a number of good restaurants and night spots.

GOLF: The Country Club course is now a 27-hole layout. The Lake/Mountain nines reach out a respectable 6,602/6,107/5,410 yards. The combined Mountain/Forest courses play 6,478/6,019/5,163 yards, while the final matchup of the Lake/Forest layouts measures 6,526/6,044/5,153 yards. Any way you want to mix them, the par comes out to 72/74. This layout can test you, with a brook that seems to traverse the courses at will, as well as trees, traps and a few double dogleg holes.

RATES: (EP) Lodgings - $69/$109/$129. Green fees - $82/$99, including cart. Golf packages are available. Rates are for the summer.

ARRIVAL: By air - Keene, New Hampshire, Rutland or Springfield, Vermont (15 miles). By car - head north on I-91 and take Exit 2 at Brattleboro, then follow the signs to Route 30 north to Bondville. Turn onto Stratton Mountain Road, then drive four miles to the resort.

Sugarbush Inn

RR 1, Box 350, Warren, VT 05674

(802) 583-2301; (800) 451-4320

ACCOMMODATIONS: 50 rooms and suites at the inn. There are also many one- to three-bedroom condominiums featuring fully equipped kitchens, fireplaces, and other amenities.

AMENITIES: 14 tennis courts, indoor or outdoor pools, Jacuzzis and saunas; horseback riding is available nearby. The fishing is reputed to be excellent. Northland Trout Tours can be arranged, and fly-fishing schools are open from May through September. Skiing becomes king during the winter months.

Excellent dining is available in the Colonial Room, which features continental cuisine, or the Onion Patch.

GOLF: The Sugarbush course, a Robert Trent Jones design, plays 6,524/5,886/5,187 yards, parring at 72. The mix of dogleg holes, water, trees and rolling hills, plus the fabulous view, make this one of the better layouts around.

RATES: (EP) Lodgings - $86/$100/$240. Green fees - $49/$52, cart $34. Golf packages are available. Rates are for late June to mid-September.

ARRIVAL: By air - Burlington (43 miles) or Montpelier (27 miles). By car - the inn is two miles west of Vermont Route 100 on Sugarbush Valley Access Road.

The Woodstock Inn & Resort

14 The Green, Woodstock, VT 05091

(802) 457-1100; (800) 448-7900

The village has long been acclaimed one of the most beautiful in America. When you first arrive you may well feel that you have stepped back to an earlier time in our history.

ACCOMMODATIONS: 146 guest rooms, including suites.

AMENITIES: Horseback riding, swimming, and 10 tennis courts. The new 40,000-square-foot Sports Center is adjacent to the golf course and provides many facilities, including squash, tennis and racquetball courts, a 30-by-60-foot swimming pool, saunas, steam rooms, a Nautilus exercise room, a 900-square-

Vermont

foot aerobics room, massage room, and men's and ladies' locker rooms. There is also a small restaurant and bar.

Fine dining is a tradition here, with Continental and New England dishes offered in the dining room (jackets and ties required in the evening). The coffee shop is available for less formal dining.

GOLF: The course dates back to the late 1800s, but was redesigned in 1969 by Robert Trent Jones, Sr. Parring at 69/71, it plays a relatively short 6,001/5,555/4,956 yards. With a creek wandering throughout (water on 12 holes), plus trees and a narrow valley setting, it is not short on challenge.

RATES: (EP) Lodgings - $169/$212/$249/$299. Green fees - $46/$58, carts $36. Golf package weekdays only - two nights/three days (includes lodging, three days of golf, and club storage; does not include cart), $518 per couple. Golf package rates are for June-September.

ARRIVAL: By air - Lebanon, New Hampshire (15 miles). By car - on Route 4, 15 miles west of the junction of I-89 and I-91.

Virginia

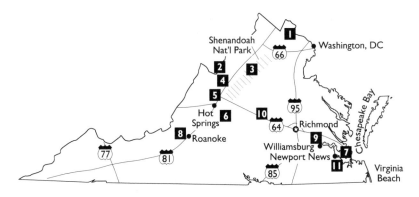

1. Lansdowne Resort
2. Bryce Mountain Resort
3. Cavern CC/Luray Caverns Resort
4. Massanutten Resort
5. The Homestead
6. Wintergreen
7. Tides Inn/The Tides Lodge Resort & CC
8. Olde Mill Golf Club
9. Colonial Williamsburg Inn/Ford's Colony at Williamsburg/Kingsmill Resort
10. The Boar's Head Inn
11. Lake Wright Quality Inn Resort

The Boar's Head Inn

Route 250 West, Charlottesville, VA 22903

(804) 296-2181; (800) 476-1988

ACCOMMODATIONS: 175 rooms.

AMENITIES: Indoor and outdoor tennis courts, squash, swimming pools, saunas, a fitness room and aerobics classes. There are two dining rooms.

GOLF: The course, designed by Lindsay Irvin in 1981, plays 6,820/6,259/5,739/5,041 yards with a par of 72. The front nine might best be described as undulating and open, while the back side is hilly and tree-lined. Water comes into the picture on three holes of the front nine and four holes on the second nine.

RATES: (EP) Lodgings - $179/$360. Green fees - $40/$50, carts $30. Golf packages are available.

ARRIVAL: By air - Charlottesville Airport. By car - take I-64 west to Exit 118B. Drive to US 250. Go west 1½ miles and turn left to the Inn.

Bryce Mountain Resort

PO Box 3, Basye, VA 22810

(540) 856-2143; (800) 307-3938

ACCOMMODATIONS: One-bedroom studio condominiums with kitchenettes, two- and three-bedroom units with full kitchens, and chalets facing the golf course.The resort now has 30 townhouses, 76 Aspen East condominiums, 104 Bryce Hill condos and 607 chalets.

AMENITIES: Swimming in Lake Laura or the two pools, canoeing, grass skiing, fishing, horseback riding, tennis and golf. Should you elect not to cook for yourself, the 200-seat restaurant offers Old Virginia-style cooking and special buffets.

GOLF: Renowned golf architect Edmund Ault designed this golf course in 1970. It is still considered one of the best in the state of Virginia. While the terrain around the resort is rugged, providing excellent skiing, the golf course is on the floor of the valley. It plays 6,175/5,950/5,295 yards, with a par of 71. It is well-trapped and has enough water to more than keep your attention – Stoney Creek seems to run all over the place. The pro shop telephone number is (540) 856-2124.

RATES: (EP) Lodgings - $70/$75 (two nights minimum. Green fees - $45, including cart. Golf packages are available. Rates are for April-November.

ARRIVAL: By air - Washington DC (110 air miles to the resort). By private aircraft - Sky Bryce Airport (2,500-foot runway), within walking distance of the pro shop. By car - from Washington DC, take I-66, then go south on I-81 to Exit 69. Follow Route 263 (11 miles) to Basye and Bryce Resort.

Caverns Country Club/ Luray Caverns Resort

PO Box 748, Luray, VA 22835

(540) 743-6551

ACCOMMODATIONS: The Luray Caverns Resort is a mile from the golf course. Virginia's Blue Ridge Mountains and the Shenandoah Valley create a beautiful setting for this resort.

AMENITIES: Swimming pools and tennis courts, with horseback riding available nearby. A number of fine restaurants are within five minutes of the resort.

GOLF: The course stretches out 6,743/6,409/6,299/5,725 yards, parring at 72/73. The backdrop of the Shenandoah River and the Blue Ridge Mountains, along with water, trees and large greens, makes this a beautiful course.

RATES: (EP) Lodgings - $59/$69. Green fees - $22/$33, carts $24. Golf packages are available. Rates are for mid-March through November.

ARRIVAL: By air - Dulles Airport (two hours). By private aircraft - Luray Caverns. By car - US 211, 15 minutes from I-81 at New Market, Virginia.

The Homestead

PO Box 2000, Hot Springs, VA 24445

(540) 839-1766; (800) 838-1766

The Homestead has been judged one of our Top 50 resorts. Steeped in history, it stretches back to the mid-1700s and the Revolutionary War period. It reached world class status in the early 1900s, and has grown and matured since that time.

ACCOMMODATIONS: Rooms and suites in the Main Section, the East Wing, the West Wing, the Tower, and the newest addition, the South Wing, for a total of 521 rooms.

AMENITIES: Twelve tennis courts, horseback or carriage riding throughout the delightful countryside, skeet and trap shooting, fishing, swimming (two outdoor and one huge indoor pool), bowling (eight 10-pin lanes) and, of course, the original reason for the Homestead's existence, the historic Warm Springs pools. The

Spa offers steam rooms, saunas, whirlpools, hot packs, tub bath, and massage. The variety and presentation in the dining rooms is superb. Jackets and ties are required in the evening. While the dining room is excellent, you might consider the more intimate Homestead Grille for a change of pace. The Casino serves one of the better patio luncheons.

On the lower level of the hotel and reaching out to the wings are some of the most elegant shops we have seen. Additional boutiques are located on the back side of Homestead within the "Village," also the location of Sam Snead's Tavern. A visit here is an absolute must. There is a year-round children's program, enabling those with younger ones to enjoy at least a few of the amenities.

GOLF: There are three 18-hole courses. The Cascade stretches out 6,566/6,282/5,448 yards with a par of 70/71. Designed by William Flynn, it came into play in 1924. The Lower Cascade Course, parring at 72/70, weighs in at 6,619/6,240/4,726 yards. This layout was put together by Robert Trent Jones, Sr. and came into play in 1963. The Homestead, with a par of 71/72, plays a short 6,211/5,796/4,852 yards.

The Homestead course is a modest affair, but the Cascade is something else. It could be called many things, but never modest. The general terrain is such that you can rarely see one fairway from another, so you feel you "own" the course. You will use every shot and shot combination you have heard of, and probably some you've never even thought of using. It is not only one of the most beautiful but also one of the finest golf courses I have played.

The Lower Cascade Course, while not as difficult as the upper layout, offers its own challenges. Should there be some question as to the relative difficulty of each, please note the course ratings measured from the men's middle tees: Homestead, 108; Lower Cascade, 124; Upper Cascade, 134. Each course has its own pro shop, clubhouse, restaurant and locker rooms.

RATES (MAP) Lodgings - $368/$410/$468 per couple. Green fees - $100/$160, including cart. All lodging rates include bag storage charges. Golf package - two nights/two days (includes MAP, unlimited golf with cart, club storage), $572/$796 per couple. Rates are for April-November.

ARRIVAL: By air - Washington DC, then Trans World Express to Ingalls Field (18 miles) or Roanoke (80 miles). By car - US 220 from north or south.

Lake Wright Quality Inn Resort

6280 Northampton Boulevard, Norfolk, VA 23502

(757) 461-6251; (800) 228-5157

ACCOMMODATIONS: 304 rooms, including suites.

AMENITIES: Swimming pool, two tennis courts, a jogging track, and a men's and women's styling salon. There is a full-service restaurant and lounge. The Lake Wright Inn is a short drive from Virginia Beach and the incomparable Colonial Williamsburg area.

GOLF: The Lake Wright Course plays to a par of 70 and reaches out a modest 6,174/5,874/5,297 yards. While flat, the front nine is open with water coming into play on six holes. The back side introduces water on two holes, but makes up for that careless oversight by bringing trees into contention. Within a short distance are four other golf courses which may be played: Ocean View, a par 70; Red Wing, a par 72 layout; Stumpey Lake, also a par 72 course; and Bow Creek, playing to a par of 71.

RATES: (EP) Lodgings - $79/$99/$145. Green fees - $25/$30, including cart.

ARRIVAL: By air - Norfolk International Airport. By car - the resort is on Northampton Blvd., at the intersection of I-64 and State Route 13.

Lansdowne Resort

44050 Woodridge Parkway, Leesburg, VA 22075

(703) 729-8400; (800) 541-4801

ACCOMMODATIONS: 305 rooms, including suites. The hotel has two five-story wings with a nine-story tower section. This particularly beautiful part of Virginia is rich in history.

AMENITIES: Outdoor and indoor swimming pools, five lighted tennis courts, squash and racquetball courts, a men's and women's health facility featuring a spa, steam room and sauna, and enough exercise equipment to completely destroy yourself. There are two dining rooms: The Riverside Hearth and the more formal Potomac Grille. Lansdowne also provides a children's program called the "Resort Rascals."

GOLF: The course is a Robert Trent Jones, Jr. design. Showing a substantial yardage of 7,057/6,552/5,954/5,213, it pars at 72. The terrain is undulating with the back side bringing trees into play. While the greens are considered average in size, some of them are elevated. Water, in the form of a rock-lined creek, comes into the picture on eight holes. It is a beautiful golf layout, one that will test you from the first tee to the 18th green. The course is supported by a well-equipped pro shop.

RATES: (EP) Lodgings - $199/$289 and up. Green fees - $85, including cart. Golf package - one night/one day (includes MAP, lodging, one round of golf with cart, golf clinic), $439 per couple.

ARRIVAL: By air - Dulles International Airport (15 miles). By car - from Dulles take I-28 north to Route 7. Turn left onto 7. Travel approximately 3½ miles, then turn right onto Lansdowne Boulevard.

Massanutten Resort

PO Box 1227, Harrisonburg, VA 22801

(540) 289-9441

ACCOMMODATIONS: 60 well-appointed hotel rooms. There are also a number of Shenandoah and Mountainside Villas, along with condominiums and cottages.

AMENITIES: Indoor swimming pool, outdoor hot tubs, racquetball courts, basketball, volleyball, saunas, tennis courts, tanning room, weight room and restaurant.

GOLF: Massanutten's Mountain Green Course is an 18-hole layout, with tree-lined fairways (white oak and hardwood), large greens protected by bunkers and an occasional stream to keep your attention. Parring at 72/73, it plays 6,408/5,956/5,157 yards.

RATES: (EP) Lodgings - $90/$225. Green fees - $50, including cart. Golf packages are available.

ARRIVAL: By air - Washington DC, or the Shenandoah Valley airport just 18 miles away. By car - from Washington DC, take Beltway 495 to Route 66 west, then Route 29 south, to Route 33 west. Entrance is six miles past Elkton, VA.

Olde Mill Golf Club

Route 1, Box 84, Laurel Fork, VA 24352

(540) 398-2638; (800) 753-5005

This is a quiet resort in the Blue Ridge Mountains, set among pine forests and running streams.

ACCOMMODATIONS: Two-bedroom/two-bath cottages with living room, dining room, kitchen and daily maid service.

AMENITIES: Tennis courts and a swimming pool. The lodge has a dining room.

GOLF: The Ellis Maples-designed course is beautiful, with pine trees, rock outcroppings and rhododendrons in abundance. It is extremely well bunkered. Wandering through tree-lined fairways at Groundhog Mountain, it has spectacular elevation changes along with some 64 acres of water to spice up the action. Reaching out a substantial 7,002/6,266/5,426 yards, the par is 72.

RATES: (EP) Lodgings $100/$150. Green fees - $42/$55, including cart. Golf package - two nights/two days (includes lodging, green fees, cart, club storage), $280/$432 per couple. Rates are for April-September.

ARRIVAL: By air - Roanoke (65 miles). By car - head north on The Parkway, take the second left turn, just beyond milepost #187 on State Road 631. Turn left on 638, then take another left at Kimble's on 645. The resort is on Highway 58.

The Tides Inn

Route 3, Irvington, VA 22480

(804) 438-5000; (800) 843-3746

ACCOMMODATIONS: 110 guest rooms and suites. The Tides Lodge and The Tides Inn have joined together. They operate a boat between the two locations, allowing guests to use the combined facilities. It's a delightful move.

AMENITIES: Saltwater swimming, canoeing, sailboating, a children's playground, golf and tennis. Dining is a superb experience, with fine linen, china, and crystal, and service that is rarely equaled. Jackets and ties are required in the evening.

GOLF: The newer Golden Eagle Course, parring at 72, reaches out 6,943/6,523/6,035/5,383 yards. A George Cobb design, it introduces the challenge (fun) of a 50-acre lake, with several sharp dogleg holes and exceptionally well-trapped greens. There is also a nine-hole, par-3 course available at the inn.

RATES: (MAP) Lodgings - $355/$384 per couple, including gratuities. Green fees - $55, cart $32. Rates include tennis, canoes, bicycles and par-3 golf. Golf package - two nights/three days (includes lodging, MAP, green fees, cart), $800/$880 per couple. Rates are for mid-April through mid-October.

ARRIVAL: By air - Norfolk or Richmond. By car - from the north, US 301 to Virginia Route 3, 12 miles south of the Potomac. From the Richmond area, take I-64 and Highway 33 to West Point and Saluda, turn right on Saluda to the Rappahannock River Bridge.

The Tides Lodge Resort
& Country Club

Top 50

Irvington, VA 22480

(804) 438-6000; (800) 248-4337

The Tides Lodge is one of our Top 50. It is on Carter's Creek just off the Rappahannock Rive, nine miles from Chesapeake Bay. Many years ago, the Coast Guard stopped the use of boats between The Tides Lodge and The Tides Inn. It has since been resumed and the two resorts have been joined. Guests can eat at one resort, sign the check and return to the other. The water taxi operates from 8 am until 10 pm.

ACCOMMODATIONS: 60 rooms, most with a view of the inlet or the river.

AMENITIES: Bicycling, lighted tennis courts, swimming in a heated freshwater or saltwater pool, canoeing or sailing (the resort has a full-service 45-slip marina), all of which are complimentary. All manner of bay or river fishing charters can be arranged, and there are daytime or evening(regularly scheduled) cruises aboard either of two yachts (the 60-foot *High Tide II* or the 46-foot *Highland Fling*). The food, which is provided in either the Royal Stewart Dining Room (jackets are required for dinner on weekends,but not during the week) or the less formal Binnacle Restaurant, is superb, and the service is even better.

GOLF: The Tides Tartan course was originally designed by Sir Guy Campbell, the famous resident architect of the Royal and Ancient in St. Andrews, Scotland. Unfortunately, while work was in progress, he passed away. Due to the fact that Sir Guy was held in such high esteem, the golf course and, in fact, the entire lodge, reflects a Scottish motif. The well-known George Cobb completed the course, which is quite unusual in its layout. With water coming into play on 10 holes, rolling terrain, tree-lined fairways, and several dogleg holes, it will definitely not put you to sleep. This layout will require your full attention. Weighing in at 6,586/6,308/5,608/5,121 yards, it pars at 72. The Golden Eagle course, three miles from The Tides Inn, is also at your disposal. For details refer to The Tides Inn.

RATES: (MAP) Lodgings - $299 per couple, including gratuities. Green fees -$40/$50, carts $32. Golf package - two nights/two days (includes lodging, MAP, golf, cart, tennis), $864 per couple. Rates are for spring and fall.

ARRIVAL: By air - Norfolk or Richmond. By car - from the north, US 301 to Virginia Route 3, 12 miles south of the Potomac. From Richmond area, I-64 and Highway 33 to West Point and Saluda, right on Saluda to the Rappahannock River Bridge.

Wintergreen Resort

PO Box 706, Wintergreen, VA 22958

(804) 325-2200; (800) 325-2200

Wintergreen has been judged one of our Top 50 resorts. In recent years, it has received many well-deserved accolades. *Golf Digest* ranked it as one of the outstanding golf courses, and it has won awards from *Tennis* and *Ski* magazines – the list is a long one. With its 3,800-foot elevation, this 11,000-acre resort enjoys unobstructed and stunning views in all directions, encompassing Virginia's Blue Ridge Mountains as well as the Shenandoah and Rockfish Valleys.

ACCOMMODATIONS: 350 privately owned condominiums and homes (ranging from studios to six-bedroom units). All units are well-equipped for housekeeping, and most feature full-size woodburning fireplaces. A convenient extra is the Black Rock Market, which is located on the premises and provides a wide selection of food items.

AMENITIES: 28 tennis courts (23 fast-dry clay, five Laykold), one indoor and five outdoor swimming pools, 20-acre Lake Monocan for fishing, swimming and canoeing, an equestrian center, and 20 miles of hiking trails (there is a seven-mile stretch of the Appalachian Trail which winds through the grounds). At the Wintergarden Complex there is a complete indoor sports center, featuring a 30-by-50-foot indoor swimming pool, three six-foot hot tubs, a 180-square-foot whirlpool and an exercise room. Bicycle rentals are also available. You may select from five dining locations: The Copper Mine (continental cuisine), The Cooper's Vantage (casual dining), The Verandah, The Garden Terrace, or The Rodes Farm Inn restaurant, in a restored 19th-century farmhouse in the valley. The winter facilities are excellent. With 17 ski slopes, trails equipped for night skiing, and a vertical drop of 1,000 feet, their ski area is one of the best.

GOLF: The Devil's Knob golf course, at 3,800 feet, offers a spectacular view in all directions. Set high on the mountain, this is one of the most beautiful golf layouts I have played. There is very little rough, with lush, manicured fairways giving way to stands of timber (maple and oak) lining each fairway. These same trees form a backdrop for almost every green. The course architect was Ellis Maples, a former professional on the PGA tour and architect of some 50 or more courses. Playing 6,576/6,003/5,101 yards, it pars at 70. If you are a hooker, you are going to have problems on the front nine. On the back nine, the course chastises a slicer. A new 10,000-square-foot club house is in place, with a fine dining restaurant, modern pro shop and locker facilities.

A second course is available, the par-72 Stoney Creek Golf Club. Designed by Rees Jones, it reaches out an impressive 7,005/6,740/6,312/5,500 yards. The name Stoney Creek may give you a clue about a few of the problems on this layout. Lake Monocan, aided and abetted by Allen and Stoney Creeks, brings water into play on at least 11 holes. The entire complex, which includes a large clubhouse, driving range, golf shop, restaurant and lounge, is on the floor of the valley directly below Wintergreen. Set amid rolling hills and verdant fields, with deer and other wildlife in attendance and the mountains forming a spectacular backdrop, it is most impressive. Stoney Creek offers a perfect balance to the Devils Knob layout. A new nine was put into play several years ago at the Stoney Creek location, turning this into a 27-hole facility.

The resort offers the Wintergreen Golf Academy. It covers all facets of the game with two-night/three-day or four-night/five-day programs, and is gaining widespread recognition.

RATES: (EP) Lodgings - $170/$200. Green fees - $74/$89, carts included. Golf package - two nights/two days (includes lodging, one round of golf per person with cart), $476/$608 per couple (more on weekends). Rates quoted are for April-November.

ARRIVAL: By air - Washington DC (168 miles), or Charlottesville (43 miles). By car - from the south, Route 29 to Route 151; travel north 21 miles to Route 664; go left on 664 for 4½ miles.

The Williamsburg Area

We have visited several restored historical towns, but none equals Williamsburg. The restoration of this 18th-century village by the Rockefeller family preserved the heritage of a significant and creative period in our nation's history. In addition to the many buildings and over 100 beautiful gardens, the magnificent Governor's Palace and the Capitol were carefully brought back to original condition.

Within the immediate area are three outstanding resorts: Colonial Williamsburg Inn, Kingsmill Resort and Ford's Colony Country Club. All three are described in detail on the following pages.

Colonial Williamsburg Inn

PO Drawer B, Williamsburg, VA 23187

(757) 229-1000; (800) 447-8679

Top 50

The Williamsburg Inn has been judged one of our Top 50 resorts. One of the biggest problems with this magnificent place is that there are so many things to do and see that golf almost takes a back seat.

ACCOMMODATIONS: In addition to the lodgings in the Williamsburg Inn (Main Building, 102 rooms; Colonial House, 47 rooms; Colonial Taverns, 38 rooms; and the Providence Hall Wings, 48 rooms), there are accommodations in the Lodge with its many wings (311 rooms), The Woodlands (219 rooms), the Cascades (96 rooms), and the Governor's Inn (72 rooms). The grand total is 933 guest rooms and suites.

AMENITIES: The surrounding grounds are a manicured wonderland. Facilities include eight tennis courts, two outdoor pools plus an indoor pool at the fitness center, badminton, lawn bowling, saunas, steam, whirlpools and training room. Dining is superb, and choices include the elegant Inn Regency Dining Room, the Cascades Restaurant, Williamsburg Lodge Dining Room and the Golden Horseshoe Clubhouse Grill.

GOLF: The Golden Horseshoe Gold Course is a Robert Trent Jones, Sr. design. Measuring 6,700/6,443/6,179/5,159 yards, it pars at 71. This little beauty spreads over 125 acres of rolling terrain, traversing ravines and dense woodland valleys, bringing water into play on seven holes. The foregoing challenges, along with very large greens, turn this into a testing experience. There is also an "Executive" par-31, nine-hole affair, the Spotswood. Another course, designed by Rees Jones, is called the "Green" Course. It is a traditional layout, tree-lined, well-trapped and with extremely large greens. It plays to an awesome 7,120/6,722/6,244/5,348 yards, with a par of 72. An unexpected plus is the fact that water becomes a factor on only four holes.

RATES (EP) Main Building: $399/$425. Providence Hall Wing - $340. Colonial Houses - $185/$325. Lodge - $175/$225. Woodlands: $112/$125. Suites are available. Green fees - $80/$115, including cart. Rates vary by location but are the same year-round. There are many different package plans available.

ARRIVAL: By air - Newport News, Richmond, Norfolk. By car - on I-64, midway between Richmond and Norfolk.

Ford's Colony at Williamsburg

101 St. Andrew Drive, Williamsburg, VA 23188

(757) 258-1120; (800) 228-9290

ACCOMMODATIONS: Rooms and villas in Marriott's Manor Club. Ford's Colony is a 2,200-acre premier recreation/resort community.

AMENITIES: Swimming pool and four tennis courts.

GOLF: There are now 36 holes of golf to play. The White/Red course measures 6,755/6,237/5,579 and pars at 72. The Blue/

Gold layout plays out at 6,769/6,182/5,398, with a par of 71. For tee times, call (757) 258-4130.

RATES: (EP) Lodgings - $169/$269. Green fees - $95/$125, including cart. Golf packages are available.

ARRIVAL: By air - Richmond or Norfolk. By car - off I-64 northwest of Williamsburg. Richmond and Norfolk are 50 miles away.

Kingsmill Resort

1010 Kingsmill Road, Williamsburg, VA 23185

(757) 253-1703; (800) 832-5665

Kingsmill has been judged one of our Top 50 resorts.

ACCOMMODATIONS: Condominium/villas. Some overlook the fairways, others the tennis complex or the James River. A nice plus: the grounds are protected by 24-hour guard gates.

AMENITIES: Indoor and outdoor swimming pools, two racquetball courts, 13 tennis courts, game room (withbilliards, darts and shuffleboard), and fully equipped health club. The marina has all of the amenities expected, including pump-out service, electrical hookups, showers, restrooms, etc. Fishing charters can also be arranged. The "Kingsmill Kamper" program entertains the younger set. For your dining pleasure, try the Kingsmill Cafe, The Bray Dining Room, Moody's Tavern, and The Peyton Grille.

GOLF: The River Course, a Pete Dye design, is the home of the Michelob Championship each July. Reaching out 6,797/6,022/4,968/4,606 yards, it pars at 71. This layout has several unique features: a tee box on a wooden platform, a trap 300-plus yards long, trees and narrow fairways, plus some multi-level greens. I also found water hazards in some very unexpected places. A second 18, designed by Arnold Palmer and Ed Seay, came into play several years ago.

The Plantation Course weighs in with a yardage of 6,605/6,092/5,503/4,880, and pars at 72. It is a beautiful layout with tree-lined, undulating fairways and more than its share of sand and water. A third course has now joined the group. Designed by Tom Clark and Curtis Strange, "The Woods" plays 6,784/6,393/6,030/5,140 yards with a par of 72. Play is complimentary on the nine-hole, par 3, Bray Links course. Designed in a true links style, it runs right along the edge of the James River.

RATES: (EP) Lodgings - $199/$279/$458. Green fees - $90/$125, including cart. Golf package - two nights/two days (includes lodging, golf, cart, bag storage, golf clinic Tuesday afternoon), $652/$784 per couple. Rates are for April-November.

ARRIVAL: By air - Richmond, Norfolk, Newport News. By car - 2½ miles east of Williamsburg on Route 60. Follow signs to Busch Gardens and turn right just before its entrance.

Washington

1. The Resort Semiahmoo
2. The Resort at Port Ludlow
3. Alderbrook Inn Resort
4. Skamania Lodge
5. Homestead Farm Golf & CC
6. Heron Beach Inn

Alderbrook Inn Resort

E 7101, Highway 106, Union, WA 98592

(360) 898-2200; (800) 622-9370

ACCOMMODATIONS: 103 guest accommodations, 21 of which are cottages, each with two bedrooms, living room, fully equipped kitchen and fireplace. Alderbrook is on the shores of Hood Canal, a fjord-like inlet of Puget Sound.

AMENITIES: Four tennis courts, sauna, and therapy pool. There is also a swimming pool enclosed in a year-round greenhouse. The dining room offers the standard fare, but does a special job with seafood.

GOLF: This course is an experience you will long remember. Parring at 72/73, this little gem covers a modest yardage of 6,312/6,133/5,506. But don't allow the yardage to mislead you. The professional smiles quietly (or maybe it's a snicker) when he hears someone threaten to "tear up" this course. While the second nine is easy, the front nine is another kettle of fish. The tight fairways, towering trees, and sharp doglegs will test your nerves. I have seen a few golfers pray for a triple bogey on certain holes of the first nine.

RATES: (EP) Lodgings - $99/$109/$139/$209. Green fees - $25/$30, carts $24.

ARRIVAL: By car - from Seattle take the Bremerton Ferry, then Highway 101 to Highway 106. Turn right on 106 and drive 15 miles.

Homestead Farm Golf & Country Club

115 E. Homestead Boulevard

Lynden, WA 98264

(360) 354-1196; (800) 354-1196

ACCOMMODATIONS: One- and two-bedroom condominiums, each with fireplace and fully equipped for housekeeping.

AMENITIES: A fitness center, an indoor/outdoor swimming pool, a children's wading pool, a hot tub and a new clubhouse and restaurant.

GOLF: Parring at 72, this layout reaches out 6,927/6,504/6,033/5,570 yards. While flat with no trees, it brings enough water and traps into play to keep you alert. The wind, which becomes a factor on most days, will also test you. The course boasts about its par 5 hole that winds up on an island green.

RATES: Range from $99/$119/$149. Green fees - $50, cart $20. **ARRIVAL:** Take the Lynden exit from I-5 (Exit 256). You are now on Meridian. Turn right and head north approximately 12 miles to Hwy 546. Turn right and go 1½ miles to Depot Road. Clubhouse is on left about a quarter of a mile.

The Resorts at Port Ludlow

There are now two resorts from which to choose: The Resort at Port Ludlow, with its 180 condominium rooms, and the newer Heron Beach Inn. These two separate properties are virtually one on top of the other. Both front along the marina and guests may use the dining facilities of each.

The Ludlow course was designed by one of the best golf architects on the scene: Robert Muir Graves. With a total of 27 holes, it plays as follows: the Tide/Timber combination measures 6,787/6,262/5,598 yards; the Timber/Trail nines play 6,848/6,333/

5,326 yards and the Tide/Trail duo weighs in at 6,775/6,263/ 5,408 yards. It is, without a doubt, one of the most beautiful golf layouts we have played. Watching deer feed on the edge of the fairway and, in some cases, crossing in front of you can be a delightful distraction. I would suggest you use a cart, as it is extremely hilly.

Heron Beach Jnn

One Heron Road, Port Ludlow, WA 98365

(360) 437-0411

ACCOMMODATIONS: 37 guest rooms, including suites. Each room is equipped with a gas-burning fireplace and a sitting area, oversized whirlpooth bath jetted tub, and refrigerator, as well as water and mountain views.

AMENITIES: Two tennis courts located at the Port Ludlow Golf Course, kayaks in Port Ludlow Bay, bicycle rentals are available, charter boats (sail and power can be rented). Or curl up with a good book or a friend in front of your in-room fireplace. The dinning facilities as well as the service are outstanding.

GOLF: For details on the golf facilities refer to the above section: Port Ludlow Resorts.

RATES: Rooms - $165/$225. Suites - $300/$450. Green fees - $55, carts $30.

ARRIVAL: From Seattle - take the ferry to Bainbridge Island. Then Highway 305 to Paulsbo (15.4 miles). Turn right (north) onto Highway 3 to Hoods Canal Bridge. After crossing the bridge, take the first right turn onto Paradise Bay Road. Drive six miles to Oak Bay Road. Turn right and follow signs.

The Resort at Port Ludlow

9483 Oak Bay Road, Port Ludlow, WA 98365

(360) 437-2222; (800) 732-1239

ACCOMMODATIONS: 180 guest rooms, ranging from one room to suites with living room, fully equipped kitchen, fireplace, and private decks on up to four bedrooms. Set on a hillside dense with towering trees, the resort overlooks Ludlow Bay and a 300-slip marina.

AMENITIES: Two tennis courts, large heated pool, clam digging, fishing, boating, hiking, beachcombing, or maybe just relaxing on the beach. The Harbormaster restaurant and lounge offers entertainment from Tuesday through Saturday during the summer.

GOLF: For details on the golf facilities, see The Resorts at Port Ludlow, above.

RATES: (EP) Lodgings - $105/$475. Green fees - $55, carts $30. Golf package - one night/one day (includes lodging, green fees), weekdays $190/$230 per couple. Rates are for May-October.

ARRIVAL: By car - from Seattle, take the Seattle-Winslow or Edmonds-Kingston ferry and cross the Hood Canal bridge; 300 yards past the bridge, turn right and follow the signs for about eight miles.

The Resort Semiahmoo

9665 Semiahmoo Parkway, Blaine, WA 98230

(360) 371-2000; (800) 770-7992

ACCOMMODATIONS: 200-room resort hotel, as well as a number of townhouse condominiums.

AMENITIES: Two tennis courts, two indoor racquetball courts, squash courts, an exercise room, and the most unusual indoor-outdoor swimming pool we have seen. There are three restaurants: Stars, Packers, and the Oyster Bar & Lounge, serving local seafood.

GOLF: Designed by Arnold Palmer/Ed Seay and built on fully wooded and rolling terrain, the course reaches out a healthy 7,005/6,435/6,003/5,288 yards, with a par of 72. As if the contoured hillsides and densely wooded areas were not enough, four lakes come into play on six different holes. Even though my game was a bit shaky, I found it to be one of the better and more relaxing rounds I have played in some time. For tee times, call (306) 371-7005.

RATES: (EP) Lodgings - $159/$189/$229 and up. Green fees - $80, including cart. Golf package - one day/one night (includes lodging, one round of golf, breakfast), $209/$379 per couple. Rates indicated are for the peak golf season, mid-June through September.

ARRIVAL: By car - from Seattle, north on I-5, then take Exit 270. Continue left to Birch Bay/Linder, then on to Harbor View Road. Turn right at the waterslide. Follow signs.

Skamania Lodge

1131 Skamania Way, Stevenson, WA 98648

(509) 427-7700; (800) 221-7117

Skamania Lodge opened in 1993. Built of heavy timber and natural stone, the four-story lodge blends well within its setting.

ACCOMMODATIONS: 195 guest rooms, including 34 fireplace units, four parlor suites, six family rooms, and a grand suite.

AMENITIES: Two tennis courts, full-service spa with indoor pool, exercise rooms, a sauna, private whirlpool, massage rooms and an outside whirlpool with a natural rock setting. The 200-seat dining room and lounge provides a spectacular view of the Columbia River. Room service is also available. An additional attraction: you can catch a ride on the sternwheeler *Columbia Gorge* from the town of Stevenson.

GOLF: The course is a creation of Gene C. (Bunny) Mason, designer of the spectacular Glaze Meadows course, one of two at Black Butte Ranch in central Oregon. Starting at the pro shop near the main lodge, it meanders through the Gorge, providing views of the river and mountains, rolling out past water hazards and two small lakes. Built on undulating terrain, it plays to a modest 6,243/5,865/5,470/4,876 yards, parring at 70.

RATES: (EP) Lodgings - $159/$189/$229. Green fees - $45, carts $26. Golf packages are available.

ARRIVAL: By air - Portland International Airport (45 minutes). By car - from Portland, take I-84 to the Bridge of the Gods (just west of the Cascade Locks). Cross over the bridge to the Washington side. Turn right (east) on Highway 14 for 1¼ miles. Turn left on Rock Creek Drive.

West Virginia

1. Wilson Lodge
2. The Lakeview Resort
3. Cacapon State Park
4. Canaan Valley Resort Park
5. Glade Springs
6. The Greenbrier
7. Twin Falls State Park
8. Pipestream Resort State Park

Glade Springs

PO Box D, Daniels, WV 25832

(304) 763-2000; (800) 634-5233

ACCOMMODATIONS: Well-appointed, individually designed executive suites or one- to three-bedroom villas. This 4,000-acre property is nestled on a plateau atop the Appalachian Mountains.

AMENITIES: Eight tennis courts (three indoor), squash and racquetball courts, Olympic-size pool, saunas, steam baths, whirlpools, horseback riding and three delightful restaurants.

GOLF: The course is well-trapped, with water and variable tee placements that can test your mettle and, at times, your vocabulary. It plays 6,841/6,176/5,466/4,884 yards, parring at 72.

RATES: (EP) Lodgings - $119/$179/$400. Green fees - $60/$70, including carts. Golf package - two nights/two days (includes lodging in an executive suite, two days golf, cart), $416 per couple. Rates are for April-October.

ARRIVAL: By air - Raleigh County Airport (seven miles). Served by Aeromech Airlines. By car - I-77, exit at Flat Top, travel north to Glade Springs.

The Greenbrier

West Main Street,

White Sulphur Springs, WV 24986

(304) 536-1110; (800) 624-6070

The Greenbrier has been judged one of our Top 50 resorts. The vast grounds and formal gardens can only be described as breathtaking.

ACCOMMODATIONS: 650 guest rooms, including 40 suites at the hotel as well as approximately 69 spacious cottages. The cottages are not equipped for housekeeping. A nice extra: children sharing a room with their parents receive complimentary breakfast, dinner and accommodations.

AMENITIES: Eight bowling lanes, three golf courses, a fitness center, horseback riding, carriage rides, fishing, swimming in indoor or outdoor pools, trap and skeet shooting, mountain biking, whitewater rafting, a hunting preserve and 20 tennis courts. Then there is the basis of Greenbrier's very existence – the soothing mineral baths and massage. Or perhaps a slow relaxing stroll through the glorious formal gardens would be more to your liking. The resort also has a well-organized children's program. Once you have visited and dined here, you will fully understand why they continue year after year to earn Mobil Five Star and AAA Five Diamond awards.

GOLF: While each of the courses is a pleasure to navigate, none could be called easy. The Greenbrier reaches out 6,681/6,311/5,280 yards and pars at 72. Well-trapped, with tree-lined fairways, it brings water either in play or threatening on 14 holes. The Lakeside, playing 6,336/6,608/5,175 yards and parring at 70, lives up to its name (water on 15 holes); and the Old White, rolling out 6,640/6,353/5,658 yards and also parring at 70, sports its share of water on eight holes. All begin and end at the magnificent clubhouse – one of the finest we have seen, with a restaurant and lounge, men's and ladies locker rooms and an excellent golf shop.

The resort has a rather unusual program known as the Greenbrier Clinic. In operation since 1948, with a staff of over 50 people, it is headed up by dedicated physicians specializing in diagnostic internal medicine and diagnostic radiology. They can offer a complete health examination and evaluation for both men and women while you are under the restful influence of the Greenbrier.

West Virginia

RATES: (MAP) Lodgings - $486/$546/$596 per couple. Green fees - $145, including cart. Golf package - two nights/three days (includes lodging, MAP, three days unlimited green fees, club storage, carts not included), $1,290/$1,576 per couple. Rates are for April-October.

ARRIVAL: By air - Greenbrier Valley Airport (12 minutes). By car - just off I-64. Another alternative is provided by Amtrak. Running between Washington and Chicago, The Cardinal stops at the recently refurbished 1925 train station directly across from the main entrance to Greenbrier.

The Lakeview Resort

Route 6, Box 88A, Morgantown, WV 26505

(304) 594-1111; (800) 624-8300

ACCOMMODATIONS: The three-story structure has 187 guest rooms and suites.

AMENITIES: Tennis, indoor and outdoor swimming pools, men's and women's exercise rooms, whirlpools, saunas and a steam room. If you care to step outside, you can add fishing, boating, and water-skiing. The Reflections-On-The-Lake restaurant sets a mood of contemporary elegance.

GOLF: The championship Lakeview course, parring at 72, measures 6,760/6,357/5,432 yards. This tree-lined, typically beautiful West Virginia countryside layout is well worth playing. The Mountain Course, the newer of the two, also pars at 72 and weighs in at a more modest 6,447/6,152/5,242 yards.

RATES: (EP) Lodgings - $149/$175/$395. Green fees - $40/$52, carts $30. Golf package - two nights/three days (includes lodgings, MAP, golf, cart), $608/$664 per couple.

ARRIVAL: By air - Pittsburgh (75 miles); Morgantown (eight miles). By car - the resort is southeast of I-79 at Exit 10 of US Highway 48.

Wilson Lodge

Wheeling City Park, Wheeling, WV 26003

(304) 242-3000; (800) 624-6988

ACCOMMODATIONS: 210 guest rooms and suites. There are also 32 four-bedroom deluxe cabins, fully equipped for housekeeping. Wilson Lodge is located in the heart of the beautiful Oglebay area.

AMENITIES: 10 lighted tennis courts, fishing, riding, swimming, boating and golf. The Ihlenfeld Restaurant seats 200.

GOLF: The Crispin Course, parring at 71, measures a modest 5,670/5,100 yards. The second course, The Speidel, is a Robert Trent Jones championship design. From its multiple tee settings, it weighs in at a healthy 7,010/6,555/6,085/5,515 yards, parring at 72. There is also a par-3 affair, lighted for night play. Now a new tester has been added. Designed by the Arnold Palmer group, parring at 71/72 and featuring five tee settings, this layout plays 6,725/6,498/6,165/5,125/4,569 yards.

RATES: (EP) Lodgings - $115/$150. Golf package - two nights/two days (mid-week only; includes lodging, breakfast, unlimited golf on all courses, cart), $552 per couple. Green fees - $30/$65, including carts. Rates are for June 17-October 15.

ARRIVAL: By air - Pittsburgh (55 minutes) or Wheeling-Ohio County Airport. By car - State Route 88, two miles north of the Oglebay exit, off I-70.

State Parks of West Virginia

West Virginia offers one of the finest state park systems in the US. Each resort operates its individual program, but they all use a national, toll-free central reservations number: (800) 225-5982. Our list does not include all the parks – only those with appropriate lodging facilities and a golf course. Rates quoted are for the summer period.

West Virginia

Cacapon State Park

Berkeley Springs, WV 25411

(304) 258-1022

ACCOMMODATIONS: 50 rooms plus cabins.

AMENITIES: Tennis courts, and swimming, boating and fishingon the lake. They have a fine restaurant and a lounge.

GOLF: The rolling terrain at the foot of Cacapon Mountain is an ideal location for their new Robert Trent Jones-designed golf course. It plays at 6,940/6,410/5,410 yards and pars at 72.

RATES: (EP) Lodgings - $62/$75. Cabins - $340 weekly. Green fees - $26, carts $22.

ARRIVAL: By car - west of Hagerstown, Maryland on I-70, then south on State 522.

Canaan Valley Resort Park

Route 1, Box 39, Davis, WV 26260

(304) 866-4121

ACCOMMODATIONS: 250 guest rooms plus 15 deluxe cabins equipped for housekeeping.

AMENITIES: Tennis, bicycling, fishing, hayrides, swimming and roller skating on a lighted outdoor rink. The main lodge has a dining room and coffee shop.

GOLF: There is a beautiful 18-hole championship golf course. While water comes into play on seven holes, the greatest challenge is to keep your mind on the game. With the Allegheny Mountains forming the backdrop and white-tailed deer and Canadian geese in almost constant view, it is not easy to pay attention. The course weighs in at 6,982/6,436/5,820 yards, with a par of 72.

RATES: (EP) Lodgings - $81/$137. Green fees - $26, carts $22.

ARRIVAL: By air - Elkins (25 minutes). By car - from Elkins, take Route 33 north to intersect Route 32. Follow Route 32 (15 minutes) south to Davis.

Pipestem Resort State Park

Pipestem, WV 25979

(304) 466-1800

ACCOMMODATIONS: The Pipestem Lodge or the Mountain Creek Lodge. The Mountain Creek Lodge, while beautiful, presents a slight problem in that it is at the bottom of a 1,000-foot-deep canyon and accessible only via a scenic aerial tram.

AMENITIES: Horseback riding, hiking, tennis, archery, bicycling, swimming in either indoor or outdoor pools and golf.

GOLF: The park's own course pars at 72 and stretches out a respectable 6,884/6,131/5,623 yards. There is also a nine-hole, par-3, 1,716-yard affair near the pool and recreation center.

RATES: (EP) Lodgings - $78/$109. Green fees - $26, carts $24.

ARRIVAL: By car - the resort is located in the southeastern corner of the state, 20 miles north of Princeton on Route 20.

Twin Falls State Park

PO Box 1023, Mullens, WV 25881

(304) 294-4000

ACCOMMODATIONS: Rooms in the lodge, as well as 13 deluxe cabins. Twin Falls Lodge is on one of the highest points in the park.

AMENITIES: Tennis, swimming and an archery range. The lodge has a dining room along with a gift shop and lounge.

GOLF: The golf course is now an 18-hole layout. Parring at 71, it reaches out a modest 6,382/5,987/5,202 yards.

RATES: (EP) Lodgings - Golf package, two nights/three days (includes lodgings, green fees) $202 per couple. Carts - $24.

ARRIVAL: By car - located southwest of Beckley. From the West Virginia Turnpike, take Route 16 from Beckley to Route 54. At Maben take Route 97 to the park.

Wisconsin

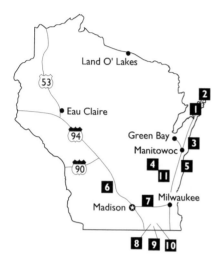

1. The Alpine Resort
2. Maxwelton Braes Resort & CC
3. Fox Hills Resort
4. The Heidel House
5. American Club
6. Devil's Head Lodge
7. Olympia Resort & Spa
8. Lake Lawn Lodge
9. The Abby on Lake Geneva/
   Grand Geneva Resort & Spa
10. Nippersink Manor Resort
11. The Osthoff Resort

The Abbey on Lake Geneva

Fontana, WI 53125

(262) 275-6811; (800) 558-2405

ACCOMMODATIONS: 340 guest rooms and approximately 32 condominiums; the condos have fully equipped kitchens and fireplaces.

AMENITIES: Six lighted tennis courts, one indoor and four outdoor swimming pools, along with an indoor recreation and amusement arcade. The Fontana Spa offers loofah scrubs, Swiss showers, Scotch hose, massage, and on and on (I was afraid to ask what a Scotch hose was). The 400-slip marina provides boats for fishing, water-skiing, or just cruising the beautiful lake. For dining there is La Tour DeBois, the Monaco and the Waterfront Café.

GOLF: Abbey, while having no golf course of its own, can arrange play for guests at the Lake Lawn Lodge course a few miles away. For details on this course refer to Lake Lawn Lodge. In fact, there are four additional courses, including the Abbey Springs Country Club less than two miles away.

RATES: (EP) Rooms - $175/$195 per couple. Suites - $350/$475. Green fees - Abbey Springs $80, including cart. Rates are for June-September.

ARRIVAL: By air - Chicago (90 minutes). Airport limousine service is available. By private aircraft - paved runway that can accommodating Lear jets, adjacent to the Lake Lawn Lodge (seven miles). By car - from Milwaukee, take Highway 15 west to 67; go south on 67 to Fontana.

The Alpine Resort

PO Box 200, Egg Harbor, WI 45209

(920) 868-3000

ACCOMMODATIONS: 60 rooms in the lodge, and 40 cottages scattered throughout the grounds.

AMENITIES: Tennis, riding, boating, just plain loafing, or swimming. The gently sloping beach is safe for children, and the resort recently added an outdoor heated pool. The Alpine dining room prepares home-cooked meals and fresh pastries.

GOLF: The challenge on this 27-hole golf course is found primarily in the rolling fairways and many trees. Using a crossover system, you can play the Red/White combination, measuring 6,047/5,879 yards and parring at 70/73; the Red/Blue 18, playing 5,858/5,440 yards, with a par of 71/70; and the Blue/White nines, parring at 71/73, with a yardage of 6,207/5,837.

RATES: (EP) Lodgings - $77/$101. Cottages - $698 per couple per week. Green fees - $24/$27, carts $22. Rates are for June 22-September 3.

ARRIVAL: By air - Milwaukee. By car - from Milwaukee on I-43 to Manitowoc, then Highway 42 through Sturgeon Bay to Egg Harbor.

The American Club

Highland Drive, Kohler, WI 53044

(920) 457-8000; (800) 344-2838

The American Club has been judged as one of our Top 50 resorts. The hotel has an interesting history. Originally housing immigrant workers of the Kohler Company, it was converted into a luxury hotel. The interior decor is highlighted by stained glass, crystal chandeliers, and oak paneling, which may well be one of the reasons AAA has given this hotel a Five Diamond rating.

ACCOMMODATIONS: 236 rooms, each with private whirlpool bath. The "special" suites include fireplace and elaborate baths (Kohler whirlpool baths for two). It had better be a "Kohler" or it won't be tolerated for long in this place. A 60-room hotel, the Inn on Woodlake is located within Kohler Village. It offers its guests all of the amenities mentioned below.

AMENITIES: Six blocks away is a complete health spa and fitness facility. With 85,000 square feet, it is reputed to be one of the most complete spas, sports and fitness centers in the country. There are six outdoor and six indoor tennis courts, swimming, whirlpools, racquetball courts, an outdoor two-mile jogging path, an indoor track, and a complete Nautilus training circuit. Spa offerings include Swedish massage, herbal wraps, manicures, pedicures and facials, along with European tanning systems, steam rooms and more. You may also enjoy horseback riding, trap shooting and canoeing.

During winter there are 30 miles of cross-country ski trails. Also ice skating (bring your own skates). The dining facilities at this resort are among the very best we have encountered. There four restaurants on the premises and another five in the village nearby. Also available is the Blackwolf Run clubhouse with its country-style restaurant (a fun place to dine).

GOLF: Both courses are Pete Dye designs. You know you are going to be challenged (maybe punished is more accurate) by small, fast and hard greens, railroad ties all over the place, undulating terrain, and a surplus of water. The River Course, parring at 72, plays to a substantial yardage of 6,991/6,607/6,101/5,090. Its name should give you a clue – the Sheboygan River gets into the act on 14 holes. Mr. Dye did a masterful job of laying the course out along the river. There are trees on one side, the river on the other, rolling terrain, traps where they should not be (usually where your ball just stopped), and small greens. The Meadow Valleys course, while longer, is more open and brings water into play on only five holes. Reaching out a hefty 7,142/6,735/6,169/5,065 yards, it also pars at 72. A new course should be in play by the time you read this – Whistling Straights. A links type layout, it is approximately five miles away on the shores of the Michigan.

As to the Meadow Valleys course, I get a bit jumpy when I find the opening hole called "Fishing Hole" and the 18th referred to as the "Salmon Trap." The River Course is not a great deal more reassuring, as the first hole is named the "Snake" and number 17 the "Snapping Turtle."

RATES: (EP) Lodgings - $230/$310/$355/$385/$465. Green fees - $140 (River Course) and $106 (Meadow Course), including cart. Golf package - two nights/two days (includes lodging, two rounds of golf, cart, bag storage), $1,219/$1,375/$1,445 per couple. Rates shown are for late May through September.

ARRIVAL: By air - Milwaukee International Airport (60 miles). By private aircraft - Sheboygan Memorial Airport (10 miles). By car - take I-43 north to Exit #126. Go west on Highway 23 to Exit Y. Take Y south to Kohler.

Devil's Head Lodge

S 6330 Bluff Road, Merrimac, WI 53561

(608) 493-2251; (800) 472-6670

ACCOMMODATIONS: 238-room motel.

AMENITIES: Tennis, swimming (indoor and outdoor pools), a fitness room, sauna, whirlpool, biking, sailing, and golf. Dining is available at the unique In-The-Round Chalet.

GOLF: The Devil's Head course measures 6,725/6,336/5,141 yards, with a par of 73. Not too much water, but dogleg holes and trees add to the tension (or fun).

RATES: (EP) Lodgings - $122/$270. Green fees - $54/$64, including carts. Golf packages are available. Rates are for June-September.

ARRIVAL: By air - Madison (40 miles). By car - from I-90/94, head southwest on 78.

Fox Hills Resort

PO Box 129, Mishicot, WI 54228

(920) 755-2376; (800) 950-7615

ACCOMMODATIONS: 160 rooms, including executive suites. All have Jacuzzis and woodburning fireplaces.

AMENITIES: Tennis, game room, charter fishing on Lake Michigan, an indoor and an outdoor swimming pool, a health club, golf and, in the winter, cross-country skiing. They have an excellent dining room and lounge.

GOLF: Parring at 72, the Fox Hills National Course plays an ample 7,017/6,574/6,267/5,366 yards. It is definitely a Scottish links course. With undulating mounded terrain and water on 10 holes, the exceptionally well-trapped course has long been recognized as one of the best layouts in the area.

The Fox Hills Resort course (27 holes) plays the front/back nine at 6,374/6,107/5,688 yards with a par of 72/73. The combination of the Back/Blue nines measures 6,410/6,081/5,721 yards, parring at 71/73. The Front/Blue courses reach out a more modest 6,224/5,597/5,597 yards, with a par of 71/72.

RATES: (EP) Lodgings - $119/$299. Green fees - $18/$20, carts $20. There are several different golf packages available. Rates are for May 15-September 15.

ARRIVAL: By air - Milwaukee or Green Bay. By car - from Milwaukee, take I-43, exit onto Highway 82 and travel east.

Grand Geneva Resort & Spa

Highway 50 and 12, Lake Geneva, WI 53147

(262) 248-8811; (800) 558-3417

ACCOMMODATIONS: 355 well-appointed rooms, featuring balconies or patios, each with a view of the lush Wisconsin countryside.

AMENITIES: Indoor and outdoor swimming pools plus a lap pool, indoor and outdoor tennis courts, horseback riding and hayrides, a health and fitness center, an outstanding spa program, saunas, and an electronic game room. Dining is in The Newport Grill and the Ristorante Brissago. During the winter months downhill and cross-country skiing take over.There is also a "Grand Adventure Club" to entertain the younger set.

GOLF: Two championship 18-hole courses are available. The Brute, a par 72/74 playing 6,997/6,554/5,408 yards, was designed by Robert Bruce Harris. This aptly named course will confront you with some 70 bunkers, many water hazards, rolling terrain, and an abundance of trees. The greens are reputed to be among the largest in the world, at an average of 10,000 square feet. The Highlands, a Dye/Nicklaus design parring at 71, plays a more modest 6,665/6,167/5,701/5,161 yards. Unlike the Brute, it has little water, few trees, and small greens.

RATES: (EP) Lodgings - $199/$229/$289. Suites- $389. Green fees - $110/$125, including cart. Golf package - two nights/two days (includes lodging, two rounds of golf, cart, club storage), $879 per couple. Rates are for June-September.

ARRIVAL: By air - Milwaukee. By private aircraft - Lake Geneva, a 4,100-foot runway. By car - from Milwaukee take I-94 south. Exit onto Highway 50 west. Drive approximately 40 miles and the resort will be on your right side.

The Heidel House

643 Illinois Avenue, Green Lake, WI 54941

(920) 294-3344; (800) 444-2812

ACCOMMODATIONS: Varied, ranging from rooms, to semi-suites, to suites.

AMENITIES: From spring through fall, they offer excursions and charter parties on the Heidel House yacht. There is also an indoor pool, saunas, and a tennis program. You have a choice of three dining areas: the Grey Rock Mansion Restaurant, the Boat Lounge, and the Sun Room.

GOLF: The Tuscumbia Golf & Country Club's course, in operation since 1896, weighs in at 6,301/5,833 yards, and pars at 71/72. There are two other courses where play can be arranged, the Mascoutin Golf Club and the 27-hole layout at Lawsonia.

RATES: (EP) Lodgings - $229/$279/$379. Green fees - $42/$56, including cart. Golf package - two nights/two days (includes lodging, breakfast, two days green fees covering choice of 63 holes of golf, and cart), $699/$739 per couple. Rates are for June 16-September 5.

ARRIVAL: By air - Milwaukee or Madison. By car - from Milwaukee, take 41, left on 23 to Green Lake.

Wisconsin

Lake Lawn Lodge

2400 E Geneva St. (HWY 50 E), Delavan, WI 53115

(262) 728-5511; (800) 338-5253

ACCOMMODATIONS: 284 guest rooms, including suites and loft rooms. Each unit has wood paneling, vaulted ceilings, and natural stone. The lodge is nestled on 275 prime wooded acres fronting on Lake Delavan.

AMENITIES: Boating, water-skiing, fishing, two indoor swimming pools, seven indoor tennis courts, horseback riding, and a health spa with steam room, sauna, and hydrotherapy pools. Dining is available in the Frontier Room and the coffee shop.

GOLF: An attractive layout, the Lake Lawn Golf Course plays 6,418/6,173/5,215 yards and pars at 70. You will, however, find it a challenge, with traps and trees in abundance.

RATES: (EP) Lodging: $169/$209/$229/$319. Green fees - $57/ $67, including cart. Golf package - two nights/three days (includes lodging, breakfast, green fees, club storage, and gratuities on food), $468/$588 per couple. Rates are for June-September.

ARRIVAL: By air - Chicago (75 miles). Milwaukee (50 miles). By private aircraft - the Lodge has a 4,400-foot, lighted runway. By car - from Chicago, take I-94 north to Highway 50, then head west to Delavan.

Maxwelton Braes Resort & Golf Club

Bonnie Brae Road, Baileys Harbor, WI 54202

(920) 839-2321

The name Maxwelton Braes comes from the song *Annie Laurie*, whose home near St. Andrew's Golf Course was called Maxwelton House.

ACCOMMODATIONS: Lodge rooms or cottages, with living room, two bedrooms, and either one or two baths.

AMENITIES: Two lighted tennis courts, a large swimming pool, boating, horseback riding, bicycling and excellent fishing. Dining is provided in the new Scottish Grill & Lounge.

GOLF: The Maxwelton Braes Country Club course is a links layout, with rolling fairways and unusually large bent grass greens. It is dotted with bunkers, and plays a modest 6,019/5,867 yards, with a par of 70/74.

RATES: (EP) Lodgings - $99/$119. Green fees - $28, carts $22. Golf packages are available. Rates are for June-September.

ARRIVAL: By air - Green Bay. By car - from Green Bay, north on Highway 57.

Nippersink Country Club & Lodge

PO Box 130, Genoa City, WI 53128

(262) 279-5281

ACCOMMODATIONS: Hotel rooms, new suites, and recently renovated cottages.

AMENITIES: Outdoor pool, boating and water-skiing on adjacent Lake Tombeau, six tennis courts, and horseback riding nearby. The resort's dining room provides an excellent and diversified menu.

GOLF: The course, parring at 71/76, weighs in at 6,289/5,905 yards. Although there is little water on this layout, it features small greens, many traps, and rolling terrain.

RATES (EP) Lodgings - $72/$87/$155. Green fees - $20/$30, carts $26. Rates are for the July-August period.

ARRIVAL: By air - Chicago (60 miles). By car - go north on US 41 or I-94 to Illinois 173, then west to US 12, right for a quarter-mile, and turn right on Burlington Road (Highway "P"). Follow signs for three miles.

Olympia Resort & Spa

1350 Royale Mile Road, Oconomowoc, WI 53066

(262) 567-0311; (800) 558-9573

ACCOMMODATIONS: 400 rooms and suites.

AMENITIES: Four indoor and seven outdoor lighted tennis courts, four racquetball courts, indoor and outdoor swimming pools, and spa. For dining, there are four restaurants to choose from.

GOLF: If you are having "control" problems with your golf game, you might consider taking up sailing. There is enough water to accommodate you right on the course. Playing at 6,368/6,177/5,899 yards, it pars at 71/74. With water a factor on 10 holes, lots of trees and traps, you will find this a most stimulating layout.

RATES: (EP) Lodgings - $99/$159/$209. Green fees - $26/$30, carts $25. Golf package - two nights/two days (includes lodging, breakfast, two rounds of golf with cart, gratuities and taxes), $355 per couple. Rates are for late June to mid-September.

ARRIVAL: By air - Milwaukee (30 minutes). Chicago (two hours). By car - from Milwaukee, take I- 94 to Exit 282, then continue on Route 67 for 1½ miles.

The Osthoff

101 Osthoff Avenue, Elkhart Lake, WI 53020

(920) 876-3366; (800) 876-3399

ACCOMMODATIONS: This is a condominium resort with lodging ranging from one- to three-bedroom units – each fully equipped for housekeeping. There are gas fireplaces. Some two- and three-bedroom units also have a washer/dryer.

AMENITIES: Indoor and outdoor swimming pools, a fitness center, tennis courts, canoes, paddleboats, sailboats and bicycle rentals. Horseback riding is nearby. During the winter, activities include: cross-country skiing, snowmobiling, sleigh and hayrides and ice skating. Just Otto's Restaurant is available for your dining pleasure, serving three meals daily.

GOLF: The Quit Qui Oc golf course (I know the name is odd but I didn't name it) is an 18-hole layout. Reaching out 6,178/5,969/5,134 yards and parring at 70/71, it is a traditional course – tree-lined with some water in play and very well bunkered.

RATES: (EP) One bedroom unit - $169/$399. Green fees - $22/$28; carts $26. Two-night minimum stay during July-August. Golf packages are available.

ARRIVAL: By air - Milwaukee (65 miles). By car - from Milwaukee, take Highway 43 north to 23 west. Turn onto Highway 67 and drive six miles to resort.

Wyoming

Grand Teton/ Jackson Hole Area

The sheer, stark, beauty of this area is difficult to describe. It is truly "High Country." The highest point in Wyoming is 13,804 feet (Gannett Peak), but what is not generally realized is that the lowest point is still 3,100 feet above sea level (Belle Fourche River).

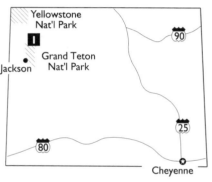

1. Grand Teton - Jackson Hole Area
   Jackson Hole Racquet Club
   Teton Pines Resort

Located on the floor of the valley, surrounded by mountains on all sides, the Arnold Palmer-designed Teton Pines Golf Course will give you all you can handle. With its undulating fairways, the course plays 7,401/6,888/6,333/5,486 yards, parring at 72, and is without a doubt one of the most beautiful layouts we have seen. A few of its more challenging features include the distraction of the magnificent Teton Mountain views, 40 acres of water either threatening or coming into play on 11 holes, and three acres of sand spread over 50 bunkers. There is more than enough water to make you think you are in Florida.

The tennis pavilion offers use of the private athletic club, including saunas, whirlpools, steam rooms, a Nautilus-equipped workout room and outdoor heated swimming pool. Racquetball and tennis are also available; court fees are charged. A separate structure houses the seven-court complex (three indoor courts with a center stadium court). There is another unusual attraction – a fly-fishing school. Headed up by nationally recognized fly-fishing expert Jack Dennis, instruction covers how to tie a fly, read a stream, cast for trout, and all the other fine points. There is also access to river rafting, horse-back riding, and polo.

As for winter sports, the property has a 10-kilometer cross-country ski course; Teton Village, which has downhill skiing, is only four miles away. This is one of the largest ski areas in the United States, and has a vertical drop of 4,139 feet. Both resorts provide shuttle service during the winter.

In addition to the Country Club restaurants, there are two eating experiences awaiting you. The Blue Lion in Jackson is open for lunch as well as dinner. One of their specialties is Jalapeño Garlic Shrimp – it is as good as it sounds. Another good restaurant is Stieglers at the Racquet Club Resort, which serves Austrian/Continental cuisine. Listed below are two possible places to stay. Both are on the golf course, but their accommodations are quite different.

Jackson Hole Racquet Club Resort

Star Route Box 3647, Jackson, WY 83001

(307) 733-3990; (800) 443-8616

ACCOMMODATIONS: 120 well-appointed condominiums, ranging in size from studio and one-bedroom units to luxurious three-bedroom/loft townhouses. Each condo (including studios) features a fully equipped kitchen, cable TV, washer/dryer, and woodburning fireplace.

AMENITIES: All the activities (including golf), referred to in Grand Teton-Jackson Hole Area.

RATES: (EP) Lodgings - $160/$190/$200/$350. Rates are for July and August. Green fees - $110, including cart.

ARRIVAL: By air - Jackson Hole Airport (eight miles). By car - seven miles from Jackson on Highway 390 (also known as the Teton Village Highway), 13 miles to Grand Teton National Park, and 63 miles to the south entrance of Yellowstone National Park.

Teton Pines Resort

Star Route Box 3669, Jackson, WY 83001

(307) 733-1005; (800) 238-2223

ACCOMMODATIONS: Country Club Suites with bedrooms, or full suites. The units are not equipped for housekeeping.

AMENITIES: Heated swimming pool and all of the activities, including golf, listed in the Grand Teton-Jackson Hole Area.

RATES: (EP) Lodgings - $350/$695. Green fees - $110, including cart.Weekly rates are available.

ARRIVAL: By air - Jackson Hole Airport (eight miles). By car - seven miles west of Jackson (on Highway 390, also referred to as the Teton Village Highway).

Wyoming

Canada

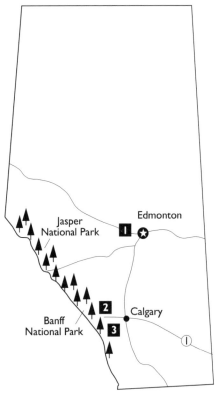

1. Jasper Park Lodge
2. Banff Springs Hotel
3. Delta Lodge at Kananaskis
   Kananaskis Inn

Alberta

Banff Springs Hotel

PO Box 960, Banff, Alberta, Canada T0L 0C0

(403) 762-2211; (800) 866-5577

    The Banff Springs Hotel has been judged one of our Top 50 resorts. The architect of Banff Springs confronted the same breathtaking scenery as did the architect of Jasper Lodge. But, rather than attempting to blend the buildings in with the surroundings, he took these massive mountains head on. The result was a magnificent fortress-like structure.

ACCOMMODATIONS: 846 hotel rooms and suites.

AMENITIES: Indoor Olympic-size swimming pool, a smaller outdoor pool, Jacuzzis, sauna, exercise area, five tennis courts, horseback riding (including overnight pack trips and a morning breakfast ride), bicycling, and, of course, hiking and mountain climbing. Among the dining options are the Alberta Dining Room, the Alhambra Room, the Rob Roy Room for intimate dining, and the Samurai Japanese Restaurant for a taste of the Orient. The Pavilion Restaurant is at the Manor Wing. If you are still hungry, there is the Expresso Café and, weather permitting, the Red Terrace for outdoor barbecues and cocktails. The Waldhaus Restaurant (formerly the Golf Clubhouse) was added in 1991 and serves German specialties. Room service is available 17 hours a day. Bars include the Rundle Lounge, the Grapes Wine Bar, and King Henry's.

There must be 40 different shops or services available between the lobby, the arcade, and the lower arcade. Services include a tanning salon, masseuse, post office, a money exchange bank, and a beauty and barber shop. This is one busy place. I recommend that you spend the time to really explore its many delightful shops, alcoves, and levels.

GOLF: The entire area is surrounded by mile upon rolling mile of beautiful dense forests. Beautiful, that is, until a few trees get in front of you on the golf course. At that point they lose some of their appeal. It is not at all uncommon to see elk on this course, particularly in the morning. Nor is it unusual to find huge bear paw prints in some of the sand traps early in the morning. It keeps you alert.

The Banff Golf Course now consists of three nines. Using a crossover pattern, you can play the Rundle/Sulphur combination, stretching 6,626/6,391/6,282/5,964 yards, with a par of 71. The Sulphur/Tunnel nines weigh in at 6,721/6,420/6,014 yards, also parring at 71. The final combination is the Rundle/Tunnel course, which reaches out 6,443/6,117/5,652 yards and pars at 72. The Rundle and the Tunnel nines each bring water into play on only three holes. However, on the Sulphur layout the Bow and the Spray Rivers present an interesting challenge on at least six holes. The architects, Cornish/Robinson, went to great lengths to blend the new creation with the original Stanley Thompson de-

Canada

sign; the new nine has views even more spectacular than those on the original layout.

RATES: (FAP) Banff is now an "all inclusive" resort with rates covering all meals and activities; two days/two nights – $959/ $1,264. Rates are for peak season June-October.

ARRIVAL: By air - Calgary (about 85 miles). By car - from the south take Highway 2 to Calgary. From Calgary go west on the four-lane Trans-Canada Highway 1.

Jasper Park Lodge

PO Box 40, Jasper, Alberta T0E 1E0 Canada

(780) 852-3301; (800) 866-5577

We were pleasantly surprised by our first view of the Jasper Park Lodge. After visiting Banff Springs, I think we expected something more massive and stately.

ACCOMMODATIONS: 437 guest rooms, including the deluxe Beauvert Suites. Suites include sitting rooms, living and dining rooms, patios, and woodburning fireplaces. The lodge, including nearby chalets, can accommodate up to 950 guests.

AMENITIES: Four hard-surfaced tennis courts, heated outdoor swimming pool, exercise rooms, whirlpool, saunas, steam rooms, table tennis, shuffleboard and various video games. Additional activities include croquet, a fully equipped equestrian center offering trail and overnight rides, bicycling, jogging and hiking on the 3.8-kilometer trail surrounding Lac Beauvert. They also offer fishing, rowboats,canoes, sailboats, windsurfing, and pedal boats. If you really want to get serious, whitewater paddle rafting can be arranged on the mighty Athabasca River. During the winter months you can add skating parties on Lac Beauvert, sleigh rides, snowmobiling, cross- country skiing, and downhill skiing at Marmot Basin. There are four dining rooms to choose from – The Beauvert, Moose's Nook, The Edith Cavell Room, The Meadows and a new coffee shop on the promenade level.

GOLF: The Jasper Golf Course, designed by renowned golf architect Stanley Thompson, originally came into being in 1925. It was virtually plowed under at the end of World War II, then completely rebuilt; the present clubhouse opened in May of 1968. Parring at 71/75, it measures 6,598/6,323/6,037 yards. With gently rolling terrain, each fairway lined by trees, more than a fair number of sand bunkers, and water becoming a nuisance on four holes, this layout will keep your attention.

It is not unusual to see elk, deer, or a flock of geese in the early morning, or to find a bear print in the sand traps. These prints are big. As a matter of fact, they are huge. Someone suggested the professional staff attempt to teach the grizzlies a little golf etiquette and show them how to rake traps. So far there have been no volunteers.

RATES: (EP) Lodgings - $459/$689 per couple. Green fees - $117, including cart. Golf packages are available.

ARRIVAL: By air - Jasper Hinton Airport (30 minutes). By car - from Calgary take Highway 1 west to the junction of Highway 93. Take Highway 93 (Banff/Jasper Road) north to Jasper. It's a total of 260 miles.

Kananaskis Village

Approximately 55 miles west of Calgary, Kananaskis Village was created for the prime purpose of supporting the 1988 Winter Olympics. Each of the facilities operates year-round. Adjacent to Nakiska at Mount Allan (location of the 1988 Winter Olympics), the area includes a ski run with a vertical drop of 2,493 feet, one fixed-grip double chair, one fixed-grip triple chair, two detachable quad chairs, and one free-handle tow.

It is aptly named a village, as it offers lodgings in the Delta Lodge at Kananaskis and the Kananaskis Inn. There is also a Village Center Building that provides visitors and overnight hotel guests with some of the essential services.

It's difficult to describe the surrounding area, as it is not easy to do justice to this scenery. I have seen the rugged mountains in Alaska, China, and Japan, and the magnificent mountains of western Colorado. While all of them are breathtakingly beautiful, none comes close to these mountains.

Within five minutes of the village, in the midst of this magnificent area, are two of the most interesting golf courses you will find anywhere. The Kananaskis Country Club has two superb 18-hole layouts. The Mt. Lorette course plays to a mighty 7,102/6,643/6,155/5,429 yards and pars at 72. Designed by Robert Trent Jones, Sr., it must have been conceived during a period in which he discovered that water can be a definite irritant to golfers. On

Canada

the front nine, eight holes bring water into play. On the back side, the Kananaskis River gets involved on five holes. Then, to add to the excitement that nature provided in the form of trees, Mr. Jones scattered sand bunkers around both courses like snowflakes. There are some 136 in total.

The Mt. Kidd layout operates out of the same clubhouse. It measures a masochistic 7,049/6,604/6,068/5,539 yards. Like the Mt. Lorette course, it pars at 72. Water is in play on eight holes of the front nine, and on two of the back nine. Mt. Kidd's greens are somewhat smaller than Mt. Lorette's. Keep in mind that your drives are carrying so far because of the elevation, which is a bit over 4,800 feet. For tee times, call (403) 591-7070. The courses are public and are open to guests of all of the hotels. Green fees - $65, carts $30.

ARRIVAL: By air - Calgary (one hour, 55 miles). By car - from Calgary travel Highway 1 west to Highway 40. Turn south to Kananaskis. The resort complex is 49 miles from Banff via Highway 1 and 40.

Delta Lodge at Kananaskis

Kananaskis Village Resort

PO Box 249, Alberta, Canada T0L 0C0

(403) 591-7711; (800) 268-1133

ACCOMMODATIONS: 321 rooms, including 64 suites with fireplaces.

AMENITIES: Fully equipped health club, steam rooms, a tanning salon, an exercise room, an indoor swimming pool, whirlpools, and a sauna. The main guest dining room can handle 300 people. There is also a Japanese restaurant and bar, the Sushi & Shabu Shabu.

GOLF: For details on the golf courses and green fees, refer to Kananaskis Village.

RATES: (EP) Lodgings - $240/$280. Green fees - $65, cart $30. Golf package - two nights/two days (includes lodging, two rounds of golf with cart, club storage), $430/$644 per couple. Rates quoted are for the peak golf season, late June through early October.

Kananaskis Inn

Kananaskis Village, Alberta, Canada T0L 2H0

(403) 591-7500; (888) 591-7501

ACCOMMODATIONS: 96 rooms and suites. Many of the suites have fireplaces, private whirlpool baths, and balconies. Thirty-two of the suites are equipped with kitchenettes.

AMENITIES: Indoor swimming pool, hot tubs, steam room, Jacuzzi, a patio deck for sunning, a gift shop and access to the shopping plaza of the village. There is also an underground parking garage. The glass-enclosed dining room affords a stunning view of the surrounding area.

GOLF: For details on the golf courses and green fees refer to Kananaskis Village.

RATES: (EP) Standard - $160/$295. Rates are for the period of June through September. Green fees -$65, cart $30.

British Columbia

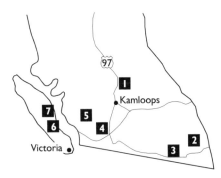

1. Mile 108 Golf & Country Inn
2. Fairmont Hot Springs Resort
3. Kohanee Springs Golf Resort
4. Harrison Hot Springs Hotel
5. Whistler Resorts
   (40 hotels, B&Bs and condos)
6. Schooner Cover Resort Hotel
7. The Qualicum College Inn

Best Western 108 Resort

RR 1, 100 Mile House, Caribou, BC, Canada V0K 2E0

(250) 791-5211; (800) 667-5233

ACCOMMODATIONS: 63 rooms and one suite. This resort surprised us a bit; it had more to offer than we had expected.

AMENITIES: Saunas, whirlpools, outdoor heated pool, barbecue pits, volleyball, horseshoes, a large children's playground, and much more. There are also five Plexipave tennis courts, bicycle rentals, horseback riding (they have a large stable of horses with one to match every level of expertise – or lack thereof), open country riding, barbecues, and bonfire sing-a-long rides. The beach is on a 360-acre lake just 500 yards from the resort, and boat rentals are available. The 108 Restaurant has a beautiful view and diverse menu, as well as cocktail service.

GOLF: The Ranch Course virtually surrounds the resort and plays 6,669/6,401/6,246 yards, with a par of 72/75. At first glance it looks easy, but that is misleading. Winding its way over slightly undulating terrain and bordered by pine and maple trees, it is no pushover. The rough is deep and you can be punished even more by straying into marsh-like areas next to some of the fairways. There is not much water on the front side (just two holes as I recall), but the back side has a lateral ditch and a stream providing a challenge on six holes.

RATES: (EP) Lodgings - $125/$250. Green fees - $35, carts $24. Golf packages are available. Rates are for June-September.

ARRIVAL: By air - Vancouver or Williams Lake. By private aircraft - a one-mile-long paved runway at the resort. By car - take Highway 97 north to Mile 108 BC.

Fairmont Hot Springs Resort

PO Box 10, Fairmont Hot Springs, BC, Canada VOB 1L0

(250) 345-6311; (800) 663-4979

ACCOMMODATIONS: 140-room lodge, 265-unit trailer park (135 units with full service), and about 116 time-share one- and two-bedroom villas, the latter fully equipped for housekeeping. Sixty condos have now been added next to the Riverside course. For information on villas, call (604) 345-6341. We were pleasantly surprised by the excellent condition of the Canadian roads in this area.

AMENITIES: Swimming in four natural hot mineral outdoor pools, two tennis courts, horseback riding, and hiking. The resort recently added a new Sportsplex that offers squash, racquetball, weight rooms, an indoor swimming pool, three Jacuzzi pools, and a sauna. Nearby Windermere and Columbia Lakes offer swimming, windsurfing, sailing, and water-skiing.

GOLF: The resort has two championship layouts. The Fairmont Mountain Course's two tee settings measure 6,510/5,938 yards and par at 72. The view from the fairways is magnificent and can be a distraction to your game. The Riverside Course came into play in early 1989 and is a par-3 course. The Columbia River comes into play on at least 14 holes, and you have to cross the river no less than four times. The Riverside layout plays 6,507/6,102/5,349 yards and has a par of 71.

RATES: (EP) Lodgings - $159/$169/$199. Green fees - $50, carts $30. Golf packages available. Rates shown are for late March-September.

ARRIVAL: By air - Calgary (190 miles). By private aircraft - a 6,000-foot paved runway within a half-mile of the resort. By car - from Calgary, go west on Canada 1 to Highway 93. Turn south and continue to Radium Junction. Intersect Highway 95 south to Fairmont Hot Springs (190 miles). From Spokane, go east on I-90 to Coeur d'Alene, then north on Highway 95 to the resort (260 miles).

Harrison Hot Springs Hotel

Harrison Hot Springs, BC, Canada V0M 1K0

(604) 796-2244; (800) 663-2266

ACCOMMODATIONS: 81 rooms in the main hotel, 80 in the Tower, 40 in the West Wing, and 14 in the Lodge, plus 15 suites and Executive Bungalows.

AMENITIES: Horseback riding, tennis, sauna, whirlpools, massage, croquet, bicycling, shuffleboard, ping-pong, swimming in the outdoor heated pool, and their famous natural hot springs. At the lake there is power boating, sailing, water-skiing, fishing, and two miles of sand beaches for sunbathing and swimming. The Lakeside Terrace Dining Room serves breakfast, lunch, and dinner, while the Terrace Lounge is available for cocktails and live entertainment.

GOLF: The nine-hole golf course is an interesting layout. With more than an ample number of trees, underbrush, OB stakes, and lateral water hazards, this par-36 layout will keep you busy. It plays 3,420/3,241/2,930 yards.

RATES: (EP) Lodgings - $149/$169/$219. Bungalows - $150. Green fees - (18 holes) $35, carts $28. Golf packages are available. Rates are for May-September.

ARRIVAL: By air - Vancouver (80 miles). By private aircraft - seaplane landing facilities in front of the hotel. By car - take Highway 1 (Trans-Canada) east. Watch for Agassiz-Harrison turnoff signs beyond Chilliwack. From Vancouver, 129 kilometers (80 miles).

Kokanee Springs Golf Resort

PO Box 96, Crawford Bay, BC, Canada V0B 1E0

(250) 227-9226; (800) 979-7999

Spread along the shores of Kootenay Lake, the resort provides a magnificent vista of the Kokanee Glacier as well as the lake.

ACCOMMODATIONS: Chalet rooms and suites, each fully equipped for housekeeping. The tent and trailer park has water, electricity, fire pits, a children's playground, washrooms with showers, a coin-operated laundry, and a sani-sump. There is also a 26-room hotel on the golf course.

AMENITIES: Sandy beach, fishing and a public boat launch ramp at nearby Fishhawk Bay Marina.

GOLF: The course was designed by Norman R. Woods in 1967. It plays 6,537/6,193/5,747 yards; the men's par is 71, ladies' is 76. The yardage is only a sample of the challenge awaiting you. The immense rolling greens (some of the largest in Canada) have 66 sand traps and 12 water hazards, with ash, chestnut, oak, and beech trees sprinkled throughout the course. These factors combine to make any golfer more cautious and alert than normal.

RATES: (EP) Lodgings - $125/$150. Green fees - $49/52, carts $25. There are a variety of golf packages available. Rates quoted are for late May to early September. This resort is open from mid-April to mid-October.

ARRIVAL: By air - a 2,700-foot grass airstrip, maintained in the spring, summer, and fall. By car - 45 miles north of Creston, BC on Highway 3A. Located about 177 miles from Spokane, WA.

Schooner Cove Resort Hotel & Marina

3521 Dolphin Drive (Box 12), Nanoose Bay, BC, Canada V0R 2R0

(250) 468-7691; (800) 663-7060

ACCOMMODATIONS: Oversized guest rooms, many overlooking the marina. This resort consists of Fairwinds (a 1,300-acre residential resort community), a marina and golf course.

AMENITIES: Heated outdoor swimming pool, hot tub, sauna, tennis courts and a universal gym. Bicycle rentals are also provided. The 400-berth marina adds another dimension. The marina can accommodate boats of up to 120 feet in length and has 30- and 50-amp power available. Dining is offered in the Schooner Cove Room with a view of the ocean and the marina; there is also the Pirates Pub, where golf tales flow almost as freely as the drinks. The golf clubhouse has a full-service dining room and lounge.

GOLF: The Fairwinds Golf & Country Club is one of the finest courses on Vancouver Island. Playing 6,141/5,683/5,173 yards, it pars at 71. The course was built on slightly undulating terrain, and with its tree-lined fairways, liberal sprinkling of sand traps and water in play on all but one hole, you won't get bored. The greens are quite large and many of them are contoured.

RATES: ((EP) Lodgings - $129/$149. Green fees - $46/$49, carts $26. Golf package - two nights/two days (includes lodging, two rounds of golf per guest, two dinners, two breakfasts, room tax; does not include cart), $558 per couple.

ARRIVAL: By air - Vancouver International Airport which is not on Vancouver Island but on the mainland. By car - from the ferry terminal at Nanaimo drive north on the Island Highway. When you come to the Petro-Canada service station at the Nanoose Junction, turn right and follow signs to resort, approximately 11 kilometers.

The Qualicum College Inn

427 College Road, Qualicum Beach, BC, Canada VOR 2T0

(250) 752-9262; (800) 663-7306

ACCOMMODATIONS: 70 guest rooms. The Inn, a classic structure, was at one time a boarding school for boys.

AMENITIES: Indoor swimming pool, whirlpool, table tennis and badminton. Within 10 minutes there are tennis courts, beaches, fishing charters, horseback riding, live theater, three golf courses and a great deal more. Dining facilities include Oliver's and Chippendale's Pub. Each of the golf courses also has dining facilities.

GOLF: Eaglecrest, playing to a par of 71, reaches out 6,313/6,048/5,431 yards. Although relatively flat, the course is tree-lined and well trapped, and brings some water into action. The Morningstar course weighs in with a healthy yardage of 7,018/6,385/5,882/5,313, parring at 72. It ranges from open links to rolling mounds, and has tree-lined fairways, lakes and a generous sprinkling of traps. Morningstar was selected for the Canadian Professional Tour Qualifying School from 1992 through 1997.

RATES: (EP) Lodgings - $99/$119. Golf package - two nights/three days (includes lodging, two rounds of golf at your choice of course, two breakfasts, one dinner; does not include cart), $480 per couple. Rates are for June through September.

ARRIVAL: By air - Nanaimo Airport. By car - from Nanaimo take the Islands Highway 45 minutes north (50 kilometers). Resort will be on your right.

Whistler Mountain

Whistler Village is generally considered one of the finest ski areas in Canada or, for that matter, in North America. The alpine-style village offers many different types of accommodations, from hotels to condominiums to chalets. In fact, within the village itself there are 18 different types of lodgings, while outside the village proper (the so-called Valley Accommodations), there are another 16 hotels of various kinds. In total, there are approximately 5,600 rooms.

Some of the hotels provide amenities such as swimming pools, saunas, Jacuzzis, fireplaces, fully equipped kitchens, on-premises restaurants, lounges, and tennis courts. When making reservations make your requirements clear. While a few of the inns within the village have their own restaurants, they are all grouped near a number of places to eat. The food selection is almost limitless, extending from the most sophisticated European cuisine to fast food.

Activities are almost as varied as the accommodations. Whistler's five lakes and nearby rivers offer whitewater canoeing, kayaking, river rafting, sailing, windsurfing, swimming, and fishing. Should you tire of water action, you can try tennis, horseback riding, hiking, walking trails, guided mountain tours, chairlift rides, helicopter glacier skiing (that's right – glacier skiing in the summer), jogging, and cycling paths. In addition, arrangements can be made to pan for gold, tour a mine, climb a giant monolith, watch logging championships, visit hot springs, take a train to the desert-like Southern Caribou, or explore the interior of British Columbia by car. During the winter months Whistler Mountain really comes into its own. The resort area offers some of the finest skiing in North America.

Finally, to the main focus of interest (as far as we are concerned): golf. The Whistler Golf Course officially opened in 1983 with a demonstration round by Arnold Palmer. Designed by Palmer & Associates, it measures 6,502/6,074/5,381 yards and pars at 72. This layout is fun, but the second nine can give you problems. At one time this was a swamp area and a great deal of water was redirected to form hazards. One creek really becomes a nuisance, paralleling and then crossing one fairway no less than three times. As I recall, it was the par-5 11th hole. For tee times call (604) 932-4544.

 A word of warning: be sure to take a supply of mosquito repellent with you.

A Robert Trent Jones, Jr. golf course came into play in early 1993. Measuring 6,635/6,243/5,692/5,157 yards, it pars at 72. Literally carved out of a rugged forest setting, it uses abrupt elevation changes (up to 300 feet); water is a factor on 12 holes. Along with ancient Douglas firs and massive granite outcroppings, this course may eventually be judged one of the finest golf courses in the country. Another championship layout came into operation in 1996. Designed by Jack Nicklaus and named the Nicklaus North Course, the par-71 course reaches out a substantial 6,925/ 6,438/6,046/5,503/4,693 yards.

ARRIVAL: By air - Vancouver, BC (75 miles from town, 95 miles from airport). By car - from Vancouver, take Highway 99 northbound along Howe Sound (allow about two hours). Avis has a car rental office at Whistler. Taxi service operates year-round from Whistler Village to Vancouver International Airport; call (604) 932-5455.

Chateau Whistler Resort

4599 Chateau Blvd., Whistler, BC, Canada V0N 1B0

(604) 938-8000; (800) 866-5577

ACCOMMODATIONS: 343 guest rooms, including 36 suites.

AMENITIES: Health club, indoor-outdoor swimming pool, whirlpools, exercise room, massage, saunas, steam rooms, tennis, hiking, fishing, biking, canoeing, rafting, horseback riding, and mountain biking. Restaurants include The Wildflower and La Fiesta. We also suggest a super place called Trattoria Di Umberto in the village. It serves some of the finest Italian food we have tasted and is modestly priced. For breakfast, try The Glacier Lodge Cafe & Deli, directly across from the hotel.

GOLF: For details on the golf courses, refer to Whistler Mountain on the foregoing pages.

RATES: (EP) Lodgings - $249/$349. Green fees - $160, including cart. Golf packages are available. Rates quoted are for June-September.

ARRIVAL: By air - Vancouver (airport is 90 miles away).

Whistler Area Lodging

Reservations can be made at the following hotels using the Whistler Resort Association telephone numbers (604) 932-4222 or, within the US & Canada, (800) 944-7853.

Blackcomb Lodge - 72 rooms, indoor swimming pool, common-use sauna and Jacuzzi. Fireplaces in some units, kitchens in most.

Carleton Lodge - 16 rooms, most with Jacuzzi, fireplace, and kitchen. Satellite TV, restaurant, and lounge.

Clocktower Hotel - 15 rooms, common-use sauna, kitchen in most units, restaurant and lounge.

Delta Mountain Inn - 290 rooms, outdoor pool, sauna, Jacuzzi, fireplace, and kitchen in some units. Satellite TV, restaurant, lounge.

Fairways Hotel - 194 rooms, outdoor pool, sauna, Jacuzzi, restaurant and lounge. Cable TV.

Fireplace Inn - 37 rooms, most with Jacuzzi, fireplace, and kitchen. Restaurant, lounge, cable TV.

Fitzsimmons Condos - 10 units, with sauna, Jacuzzi, fireplace,and kitchen in most units. Cable TV. Restaurant and lounge.

Hearthstone Lodge - 10 units, with sauna, fireplace, and kitchen in most units. Satellite TV.

Listel Whistler Hotel - 97 rooms, sauna and Jacuzzi. Restaurant, lounge, and satellite TV.

Mountainside Lodge - 90 units, outdoor swimming pool. Sauna, Jacuzzi, fireplace, and kitchen in most units. Restaurant, lounge, and satellite TV.

Nancy Greene Lodge - 137 units, outdoor swimming pool, sauna, and Jacuzzi. Fireplace and kitchen available in some units. Restaurant, lounge, and satellite TV.

Tantalus Lodge - 76 units, outdoor swimming pool, sauna and Jacuzzi. Fireplace and kitchen in most units. Cable TV.

Timberline Lodge - 42 units, outdoor swimming pool, sauna and Jacuzzi. Fireplace in some units. Restaurant, lounge, and cable TV.

Village Gate House - 20 units, somewith Jacuzzi. Fireplace, kitchen in most units. Cable TV.

Westbrook Whistler - 49 units, some with Jacuzzi. Fireplace and kitchen in most units. Cable TV.

Whistlerview - Nine units, with sauna, fireplace, and kitchen in most. Jacuzzi in some units. Restaurant, lounge, cable TV.

Whistler Village Inn - 88 units, outdoor swimming pool, sauna and Jacuzzi. Fireplace and kitchen in most units. Restaurant, lounge, and cable TV.

Windwhistle Condos - Four units, with Jacuzzi, fireplace, kitchen and satellite TV. Restaurant and lounge.

Resorts on Blackcomb Mountain

Foxglove - 36 units, with fireplace, kitchen, and cable TV.

Gables - Nine units; Jacuzzi, fireplace, and kitchen in most. No TV.

Glacier Lodge - 112 units, ranging from lodge rooms to two-bedroom suites (some with fireplace and fully equipped kitchen), outdoor swimming, laundry facilities.

Le Chamois - 50 studios and suites, with kitchenettes, microwaves, small refrigerators. Bell service and room service are available. There is a heated outdoor pool, underground parking, laundry, two restaurants, and ski facilities.

The Marquise - 90 units with one or two bedrooms, fully equipped kitchen, gas fireplace, and cable TV. Outdoor heated pool, indoor hot tub and sauna, underground parking.

Stoneridge - Nine units, with fireplace and kitchen in all units. No TV.

Wildwood Lodge - 33 units, outdoor swimming pool. Fireplace and kitchen in all units. Cable TV.

Lodgings Outside the Village

Fitzsimmons Creek Lodge - 45 units, some with kitchen. Restaurant, lounge, and cable TV.

Gondola Village - 45 units, most with fireplace and kitchen. Cable TV.

Highland Vale - 55 units, a sauna and Jacuzzi. Fireplace and kitchen in some units. Restaurant, lounge, and satellite TV.

Lake Placid Lodge - 104 units, outdoor swimming pool, Jacuzzi. Kitchen in most units. Cable TV.

The Seasons - 13 units, most with fireplace and kitchen. Cable TV.

Whistler Creek Lodge - 43 units, outdoor swimming pool, a sauna, Jacuzzi, tennis courts. Fireplace and kitchen in most units. Restaurant, lounge, cable TV.

Whistler On The Lake - 24 units, most with fireplace and kitchen. Cable TV.

Whistler Resort & Club - 42 units, outdoor swimming pool, a sauna, Jacuzzi and tennis courts. Fireplace and kitchen in most units. Restaurant, lounge and cable TV.

Whiski Jack Resorts - 15 units, most with fireplace and kitchen, some with Jacuzzi. Sauna, cable TV.

Bed & Breakfast Jnns

Alta Vista Chalet - Six units, sauna, Jacuzzi and fireplaces. Cable TV.

Chalet Luise - Six units, sauna, Jacuzzi. Fireplace in most units. No TV.

Durlacher Hof - Seven units, sauna. Fireplace in most units. No TV.

Edelweiss - Six units, sauna, fireplaces. No TV.

Haus Heidi - Six units, sauna, Jacuzzi. Fireplace in most units. No TV.

In addition to the above, homes are available to rent. For information, call Whistler Chalets at (604) 683-7799 (from Vancouver) or toll-free at (800) 663-7711.

Manitoba

Falcon Lake Resort & Club

Falcon Boulevard, Falcon Lake, Manitoba, Canada R0E 0N0

(204) 349-8400; (888) 552-2299

1. Gull Harbour Resort
2. Falcon Lake Resort & Club

ACCOMMODATIONS: Motel rooms, or executive apartments with kitchenette, patio, and air-conditioning. Falcon Lake Resort is located at the southern end of Whiteshell Provincial Park.

AMENITIES: Indoor heated swimming pool, a spa and sauna, boating, lake swimming, and fishing. During the winter months there is downhill and cross-country skiing, snowmobiling, ice fishing, and indoor curling. A professionally maintained sports complex is a short walk away, offering tennis, horseback riding, lawn bowling, and miniature golf. There is a dining room and lounge available, as well as a game room and a children's arcade.

GOLF: The Falcon Beach Course is operated by the Provincial Parks Department. The well-trapped, par-72 layout reaches out a substantial 6,964/6,540/5,917 yards. Falcon Creek becomes a nuisance on about seven holes.

RATES: (EP) Lodgings - $73/$83/$103. Green fees - $25, carts $24. Rates quoted are for the peak summer season of late June through early September.

ARRIVAL: By air - Winnipeg (90 miles). By car - take Trans-Canada Highway 1 due east to Falcon Lake.

Gull Harbour Resort

General Delivery, Riverton, Manitoba, Canada R0C 2R0

(204) 279-2041; (800) 267-6700

ACCOMMODATIONS: There are 91 guest rooms plus two suites. Most ground floor rooms provide a patio area, while the suites have spacious living areas and fireplaces. The resort is 110 miles north of Winnipeg on the northeastern tip of Hecla Island.

AMENITIES: Swimming pool, sauna, whirlpool, tennis, baseball, shuffleboard, windsurfing, and even horseshoes. In the gym, there is basketball, volleyball, or badminton. For the children they provide a wading pool, arts and crafts program, and scavenger hunts. The resort is open year-round.

Winter activities include cross-country skiing, ice fishing, tobogganing, ice skating and snowshoeing. The dining room has a wide choice of cuisine, ranging from country fare and seafood to Icelandic baked goods. There is also a lounge and a coffee shop. During the summer months, the resort operates an outside bar and grill for quick lunches and occasional evening barbecues.

GOLF: The Hecla golf course is adjacent to the parking lot of the lodge and runs along the lake itself. Parring at 72, it measures 6,022/5,735/5,060 yards. There is a fair amount of water on this layout with ponds in play on holes 15, 16,and 17. An inlet from Lake Winnipeg becomes a nuisance on numbers 10, 11, and 12.

RATES: (EP) Lodgings - $95/$105. The resort also offers golf packages. Green fees - $30, carts $27.

ARRIVAL: By air - Winnipeg (110 miles). By private aircraft - Riverton (limited airstrip). By car - from Winnipeg, take Highway 8 north.

Canada

New Brunswick

The Algonquin

St. Andrews-by-the-Sea

New Brunswick, Canada EOG 2X0

(506) 529-8823; (800) 441-1414; sales@alg.cphotels.ca

Fredericton

Fundy Nat'l Park

St. George

1. The Algonquin

ACCOMMODATIONS:
258 rooms, including suites, with private baths and showers. The town of St. Andrews-by-the-Sea is over 200 years old. Situated along the Bay of Fundy, it was founded by the Loyalists at the time of the American Revolution. You can take a trip back in time by visiting the cottage craft shops, St. Andrews Block House, Greenock Church, or the wharf at the biological station.

AMENITIES: Fishing, boating, tennis, swimming pool, health spa, whirlpool, saunas, aerobics classes, cycling, and golf. Tours are available by bus, rental car or boat. The Algonquin has children's programs from July-August. For dining there is the Passamaquoddy Veranda, the Coffee House and the Van Horne Veranda (ties optional; jackets required).

GOLF: The Algonquin Golf Course weighs in at 6,546/6,226/6,021 yards, with a par of 72/74. Many think, due to its name and location, that it might be typical of the famed St. Andrews "Old Course" in Scotland. That is not the case, as this course has more hazards and more undulating terrain. The course offers a wonderful view of the harbor and Passamaquoddy Bay, but water comes into play on only six holes. Be advised that, although the greens are in excellent shape, several of them entice golf balls to defy gravity. The combination of trees, bunkers and distracting views make this an entertaining layout. The Woodland nine-hole course is also available.

RATES: (EP) Lodgings - $259/$299. Green fees - $100, including carts. Golf packages are available. The resort is open from May through October.

ARRIVAL: By air - St. John (70 miles). By private aircraft - St. Stephen Airport, a 3,000-foot surfaced runway (20 miles). By car - from St. John, take Provincial Highway 1 west to Highway 127. Head south on 127 (five miles) to St. Andrews-by-the-Sea.

Nova Scotia

Dundee Resort

RR #2 West Bay, Cape Breton, Nova Scotia, Canada B0E 3K0

(902) 345-2697; (800) 565-1774

This resort on the shores of Bras d'Or Lakes has evolved considerably since it started in 1977 with a few cottages and a nine-hole golf course.

ACCOMMODATIONS: 40 cottage units, ranging from one to two bedrooms, with baths and fully equipped kitchens and a 60-unit hotel.

AMENITIES: Heated pool, tennis courts, a 32-boat floating dock and marina, surfboards, canoes, and an intro-

1. Dundee Resort
2. Keltic Lodge
3. The Pines Resort Hotel

ductory sailing program. There is also a children's playground. The fully licensed dining room is open for lunch and dinner each day.

GOLF: The course, parring at 72, plays 6,475/5,940/5,236 yards. Although it is already a beautiful layout lined with magnificent pine, maple and spruce trees, plans are underway to improve the sand traps and to lengthen the course with new tee construction. The resort opens in May and closes in October.

Canada

Due to the growing popularity of Dundee, I suggest you arrange reservations as far in advance as possible.

RATES: (EP) Lodgings - $110/$120/$200. Green fees - $45/$50, carts $32. There are several different golf packages, with weekly rates on green fees and carts, senior rates, and a monthly golf pass.

ARRIVAL: By air - Sydney Airport (75 miles) or Halifax Airport (180 miles). By private aircraft - Port Hawkesbury (20 miles).

Keltic Lodge

PO Box 70, Ingonish Beach, Nova Scotia, Canada B0C 1L0

(902) 285-2880; (800) 565-0000

ACCOMMODATIONS: 32 rooms in the Main Lodge, 40 air-conditioned rooms with private baths in the White Birch Inn, or deluxe two- to four-bedroom cottages. Keltic Lodge is on the northern tip of Cape Breton and is operated by the Nova Scotia Department of Tourism.

AMENITIES: Tennis, shuffleboard and lawn croquet, and swimming at the lake, the ocean beach, or in the heated saltwater pool. The Keltic Lodge's fully licensed dining room is well known for the quality and diversity of its food. The resort is closed from November through May each year.

GOLF: The Cape Breton Highlands Golf Links is one of the finest layouts in Canada, and has been judged among the 10 best in the world. It was designed by Stanley Thompson, who is the architect of over 200 wonderful golf courses, including Banff Springs, Jasper Park and the lovely Capilano in West Vancouver. In the Scottish tradition, each of the fairways has been named. The seventh hole is "Killiecrankie" (a long and narrow pass), the 16th, a par five, is "Sair Fecht" (hard work), while number 18 is named "Hame Noo" (what else?). The links plays, from its one tee setting, 6,193 yards with a par of 71. For the ladies, the yardage remains the same but the par is 76, and includes something not normally seen – two par-6 holes. By the way, one of those par-6 gems is called "Tattie Bogle" (potato pits). That is a nice way to put it, though I have heard certain golf holes described in much more strident terms.

RATES: (MAP) Lodgings - $283/$299 per couple. Green fees - $35/$40. Golf packages are available.

ARRIVAL: By air - Sydney (two hours drive). By private aircraft - Margaree Airport, a 2,500-foot paved runway (one hour). By car - from Sidney take Highway 125 north. Join Highway 105 and continue westerly. At South Gut, St. Ann's, turn onto Cabot Trail Highway north, and continue to the lodge.

The Pines Resort Hotel

PO Box 70, Digby, Nova Scotia, Canada B0V 1A0

(902) 245-2511; (800) 565-0000

Overlooking the beautiful Annapolis Basin, the multi-storied main lodge was done in an impressive French Norman architectural style.

ACCOMMODATIONS: 90 rooms in the hotel, each with private bath, plus 30 cottages.

AMENITIES: Two lighted tennis courts, heated outdoor pool, lawn croquet, shuffleboard, putting green, hiking trails and a children's play area. The resort presents a diverse menu in the Annapolis Dining Room, butits specialty is seafood.

GOLF: The course, weighing in at a modest 6,204/5,940 yards, pars at 71/76. Sited on slightly rolling terrain, it is well trapped with water coming into play on four holes.

RATES: (EP) Lodgings - $125/$250. MAP meal plan is also available. Green fees - $35/$45, carts $26. Golf packages are available. The resort is open June through mid-October.

ARRIVAL: By air - Halifax and Yarmouth, Nova Scotia. By private aircraft - Digby Municipal Airport. By car - There is frequent daily car-ferry service between Digby and Saint John, New Brunswick, as well as between Yarmouth and Bar Harbor and Portland, Maine.

Canada

Ontario

1. Deerhurst Inn & CC/
   Best Western Hidden Valley Resort
2. The Baldwins/Windemere House
3. Shamrock Lodge
4. Pinestone Inn & CC
5. Brooklea Motor Hotel & Inn/
   Wig-A-Mog Inn
6. Horseshoe Valley Resort
7. The Briars Inn & CC
8. Nottawasaga Inn
9. Oakwood Inn & Golf Club
10. Forest Golf & Country Hotel

The Baldwins

Box 61, Windermere, Ontario Canada P0B 1P0

(705) 769-3371; (800) 461-1728

ACCOMMODATIONS: One- and two-bedroom units in the lodge, as well as cottages.

AMENITIES: Indoor pool, whirlpool/sauna, lighted outdoor shuffleboard, badminton, ping-pong, horseshoes, two tennis courts, a sandy beach, canoes and pedal boats. Motorboats can be rented for fishing. The resort also provides a supervised children's program. The food here is superb. Nice added touches are the outdoor barbecues, hot and cold buffets, or evening wiener roasts by the lake.

GOLF: It is a two-minute walk from the resort to the first tee of the Windermere Golf & Country Club. For details on this golf course, refer to Windermere House, page 471.

RATES: (MAP) Lodgings - $1,284 weekly per couple. Green fees - $55, carts $30.

ARRIVAL: By air - Toronto (135 miles). By car - take Highway 401 to 400 and drive north to Highway 11 north. West on 141 to 24, then 4 to The Baldwins.

Best Western Hidden Valley Resort

RR 4, Huntsville, Ontario, Canada P0A 1K0

(705) 789-2301; Toronto (416) 364-2011

ACCOMMODATIONS: There are 100 well-appointed rooms, plus eight deluxe suites featuring fireplaces and whirlpools. The resort is 2½ hours from Toronto.

AMENITIES: Originally planned as a winter sports complex, Hidden Valley Resort now welcomes summer golfers, tennis nuts and those occasionally referred to as the waterlogged set. Located along Peninsula Lake, it offers a great variety of water-oriented sports: sailing, canoeing, windsurfing, rowing, fishing, lake swimming, paddleboats, motor boat rentals, and water-skiing. There are also indoor and outdoor heated pools, a mixed sauna, a giant whirlpool, four tennis courts (two lighted), squash and racquetball courts, jogging trails, an exercise room and a games room. The dining room overlooks the lake and the outdoor swimming pool, and has a delightful menu.

GOLF: The two Deerhurst Country Club courses are less than a half-mile away. For details, refer to Deerhurst Inn & Country Club.

RATES: (EP) Lodgings - $118/$135. Green fees - $108/$125, including cart. Rates shown are for June-September.

ARRIVAL: By air - Toronto (160 miles). By private aircraft - Huntsville. By car - from Toronto take Highway 400/11 north. Turn east on Highway 60 for five miles, then follow signs.

Canada

The Briars Inn & Country Club

55 Hedge Road RR 1, Jackson Point, Ontario, Canada L0E 1L0

(905) 722-3271; (800) 465-2376

Its beautiful grounds reflect the attention lavished on this resort. One of the reasons this resort is so popular is the warmth and gracious attitude of the entire staff. I suggest you take the time to walk through the "old manor house" section to see their collection of antiques. These are some of the finest to be found anywhere.

ACCOMMODATIONS: Varied, both in type and location. They range from rooms and suites at the Inn, the Bourchier Wing, or the Leacock Wing, and cottages at the Country Club. The names selected for these cottages – Birdie, Eagle, Shelter, Divot and Chip Shot – show how golf-oriented they really are.

AMENITIES: The proximity of Lake Simcoe, with its 144 miles of shoreline, makes possible every kind of water activity. You can choose from swimming, sailing, windsurfing, boating, water-skiing and fishing. Other facilities or activities include billiards, shuffleboard, heated indoor pool, two heated outdoor pools, five all-weather tennis courts (some lighted), bicycle rentals, a sauna, and whirlpool, From July-August there are live, professional summer theater productions. The Briars also offers a children's program. The dining facilities are outstanding. During the summer months you can also dine at the Country Club. Winter activities include cross-country skiing, skating, tobogganing, and snowshoeing (the greatest way in the world to disable yourself).

GOLF: The resort offers a championship layout that plays 6,229/6,017/5,450 yards, with a par of 71/72. It has been the host course for Peter Gzowski's Invitational Tournaments since 1986. The original nine was put in place in 1922 by the well-known golf architect, Stanley Thompson. The full 18 was completed in 1973 by C. E. Robinson.

RATES: (FAP) Lodgings - $378/$418 per couple. Weekend (two-day minimum) - $716/$791 per couple. Green fees - $50/$60, carts $30. Golf packages are available. Rates shown are for July through September 5th.

ARRIVAL: By air - Toronto (45 miles). By car - from the south travel north on Markham Road (Highway 48) to Sutton. Go through the village to the traffic lights at Dalton Road. Turn right on Dalton Road to Jackson Point. At the second stoplight (Lakeshore Road) turn right. Drive one km to the Briars gates (Hedge Road).

Brooklea Motor Hotel & Country Club

751 Yonge Street West, Midland, Ontario, Canada L4R 4L1

(705) 526-3075; Clubhouse (705) 526-9872

ACCOMMODATIONS: Seven suites adjacent to the clubhouse, and 52 additional rooms in the Park Villa Motel in Midland. Brooklea is about 90 miles north of Toronto and a bit more than a mile south of Midland.

AMENITIES: Putting green, driving range, and swimming pool. The large clubhouse has a dining room, fully licensed lounge and snack bar.

GOLF: The well-groomed 18-hole Brooklea Golf & Country Club course is one of the better layouts in this part of Canada. The exceptional condition of the course is due, in no small part, to its fully automatic irrigation system. The course plays 6,501/ 6,199/5,857/5,464 yards and pars at 72. It is well-trapped, with water coming into play on six holes. Also available is an executive nine-hole with a par of 32.

RATES: (EP) Golf package - one night/one day (includes lodging at Park Villa Motel or Brooklea, green fees), $75/$90. Green fees without golf package - $45/$48, carts $32. Rates quoted are for the peak summer season.

ARRIVAL: By air - Toronto (90 miles). By car - from Toronto take Highway 400 north to Highway 93. Brooklea is on Highway 93, 1½ miles south of Midland.

Deerhurst Resort

RR #4, Huntsville, Ontario, Canada P0A 1K0

(705) 789-6411; (800) 461-4393

ACCOMMODATIONS: 108 hotel units, as well as luxurious condominiums and villas, giving the resort a total capacity of 465 bedrooms.

AMENITIES: Eight tennis courts (four indoor), three international squash courts, racquetball court, fitness center, health spa, beauty salon, two indoor and three outdoor swimming pools. The resort is located on Peninsula Lake, and offers canoeing, water-skiing and kayaking. There are about 50 boats available. The riding stables, while on resort property, are located across the bay. Both English and Western saddle riding lessons can be arranged. They also offer trail, wagon and hayrides. Several dining options are available, and the menus are quite varied; there is the Dining Room at The Lodge, Steamers for more casual dining and The Pub for lighter snacks. The inn offers a children's program during the summer and Christmas break.

GOLF: The Deerhurst Lakeside Golf Course, a fun executive layout, plays 4,667/4,142/3,737 yards with a par of 65. Although short on yardage, it offers some unexpected challenges with multi-level, undulating greens and some deep bunkers. The Deerhurst Highlands course is also available. Designed by Robert Cupp and Thomas McBroom, it is truly of championship caliber. Parring at 72/74, it reaches out an impressive 7,011/6,506/6,012/5,393 yards. Carved out of rugged terrain and located on the northern portion of the resort property, it winds through dense woods, meandering creeks and outcroppings of huge granite bedrock. While water comes into action on only two holes on the front nine, the back side has plenty. One example of its many challenges is the fifth hole – a 601-yard par 5.

RATES: (EP) Lodgings - $149/$209/$249/$289/$517. MAP plan is also available. Green fees - $108/$125, including cart. Golf packages are available. Rates are for June to mid-October.

ARRIVAL: By air - Toronto (approximately 160 miles). By private aircraft - Huntsville. By car - from Toronto take Highway 11 north. Turn east on Highway 60, five miles to Canal Road. Turn right and travel one mile, then angle left onto Deerhurst Road.

Forest Golf & Country Hotel

102 Main Street South, Forest, Ontario, Canada N0N 1J0

(519) 786-2397; (800) 265-0214

ACCOMMODATIONS: Each of the extra-large rooms features individually controlled air-conditioning and full bath facilities. Forest, Ontario is 30 minutes east of Blue Water Bridge, between Port Huron, Sarnia and Grand Bend.

AMENITIES: Sauna, whirlpool, indoor pool, and coed weight room; tennis courts are adjacent to the hotel. Dining is in the King & I room.

GOLF: The Forest Country Club course, contiguous to the hotel, is an 18-hole layout on slightly rolling terrain. It plays 4,470 yards with a par of 66. A new nine-hole executive layout has just been completed.

RATES: (EP) Lodgings - $77/$87 per couple per night. Green fees - $18/$20, carts $25. Golf packages are available.

ARRIVAL: By air - London. By car - take Highway 401 to Highway 21. Travel on 21 north to Forest and follow signs to the resort.

Horseshoe Valley Resort

Box 10, Horseshoe Valley RR #1, Barrie, Ontario, Canada L4M 4Y8

(705) 835-2790; (800) 461-5627

ACCOMMODATIONS: 142 well-appointed, two-bedroom condominiums. There are also "lodge condominiums" available. Each two-bedroom, two-bath unit accommodates up to six people and features a log-burning fireplace, living room and fully equipped kitchen.

AMENITIES: Two lighted Plexipave tennis courts, indoor and outdoor swimming pools, squash courts, a whirlpool, exercise and fitness room, and hiking trails; horseback riding is nearby. The resort, developed originally as a winter destination, remains one of the premier ski areas in the province. There is a main dining room as well as The Terrace (weather permitting).

GOLF: The course was carved out of rolling woodlands. Weighing in at 6,130/5,800/5,282 yards, it pars at 72. While there is water coming into contention on only two holes, the challenge arises from tight fairways, sloping greens and sand traps placed where they should not be. The beauty and lush quality of this layout is enhanced by its irrigation system. The new Highlands Course came into play in mid-1992.

RATES: (EP) Lodgings - $129/$169/$250. Green fees - $46/$62, carts $32. Golf package - two nights/two days (includes lodging, breakfast, two rounds of golf, carts, taxes and gratuities), $666/$746 per couple.

ARRIVAL: By air - Toronto (60 miles). By car - north on Highway 400. Take exit 117 onto Horseshoe Road. Cross Highway 93 and continue on to the resort.

Canada

Nottawasaga Inn

Box 1110 Highway 89, Alliston, Ontario, Canada L0M 1A0

(705) 435-5501

ACCOMMODATIONS: 162 rooms.

AMENITIES: Indoor and outdoor pools, sauna, whirlpool, exercise room, fitness center, racquetball courts, volleyball, hiking, and an 18-hole miniature golf course. Dining is offered in The Amber Glow Dining Room and the Coffee Shop.

GOLF: The Nottawasaga Inn course came into play during the summer of 1986; it weighs in at 6,319/5,856/5,321 yards, with a par of 70/71.

RATES: (EP) Lodgings - $129/$265. Green fees - $33/$58, including carts. Golf package - two nights/three days (includes lodging, three days unlimited golf), $416 per couple.

ARRIVAL: By air - Toronto (one hour). By car - go north on Highway 400 to Highway 89. Take a left onto 89, then travel seven miles to the resort.

Oakwood Inn & Golf Club

Highway 21 N, Box 400, Grand Bend, Ontario, Canada N0M 1T0

(519) 238-2324; (800) 387-2324

ACCOMMODATIONS: The motel offers a choice of single, double, or two double beds. There are also duplex cabins. Surrounded by beaches and forests, Grand Bend has become one of the most popular vacation areas on Lake Huron.

AMENITIES: Swimming and fishing at Oakwood Beach. Four tennis courts are available at the adjacent Lakeside Tennis Club. A spacious log building houses the main dining room, the Falcon Room.

GOLF: The Oakwood course plays 5,356/4,897 yards and pars at 70. It is a well-kept layout, with water, in the form of a creek, coming into play on 10 holes.

RATES (EP) Lodgings - $117/$159. Green fees - $25, carts $25. Golf packages are available.

ARRIVAL: By air - London (about one hour) By car - from London take Highway 4 north to Highway 7. Turn west on 7 to Highway 81, then head north on 81 to the Inn.

Pinestone Inn & Country Club

Highway 121, Haliburton, Ontario, Canada K0M 1S0

(705) 457-1800; (800) 461-0357

The Pinestone Inn, about 2½ hours northeast of Toronto and about four miles from Haliburton Village, is between Pinestone Lake and Lake Kashagawigamog. The Royal Canadian Mounted Police use the lake's name as a test. If you can pronounce it on the first try you are sober enough to drive.

ACCOMMODATIONS: The oversize rooms in the two-story Inn have two double beds. There are also golf course villas and one-and two-bedroom chalets featuring Jacuzzi bath, living room and fireplace.

AMENITIES: All-weather tennis courts, indoor/outdoor pool, horseshoes, shuffleboard, nature trails, and a 1¼-mile jogging trail around Little Pinestone Lake. There are docking facilities and a sandy beach. The dining room and Golden Slipper lounge are highlighted by a double fireplace and offer nightly entertainment in a warm and friendly atmosphere.

GOLF: The course, less than 75 paces from the hotel lobby, is a full 18-hole, par-71/73 layout measuring 6,023/5,533. Do not allow the yardage to lull you, as this course is not a pushover. The course winds its way among the tree-lined fairways and brings a great quantity of water into play, particularly on the back side. Not only is it fun to play, but it is one of the better courses in Ontario.

RATES: (EP) Lodgings - $119/$139/$239. Green fees -$52, carts $30. Golf package - three nights/three days (includes MAP, lodging, green fees and cart) $810/$900 per couple. Rates quoted are for June-October.

ARRIVAL: By air - Toronto (2½ hours). By car - from Toronto, east on Highway 401 to exit 436 (Newcastle). North on Highway 35/115 to Minden. Just past Minden turn right (east) on Highway 121 for 11 miles to Haliburton Village. Turn right at resort sign.

Canada

Shamrock Lodge

Box 218, Port Carling, Ontario, Canada P0B 1J0

(705) 765-3177

ACCOMMODATIONS: Rooms in the main lodge, the Elmwood, the Kelly House, the Tam O'Shanter, the Driftwood, the Pinewood and Pinewood #4. Muskoka Lakes is considered by many to be one of the best vacation areas in Ontario.

AMENITIES: Canoes, paddleboats, sailboats, a sandy beach, indoor heated pool and whirlpool, a sauna complex, lighted tennis courts, volleyball, shuffleboard, horseshoes and table tennis. There is also a supervised children's program. You will have to work at going hungry here; they usually offer a wide selection of entrées, accompanied by a choice of salad and vegetable dishes.

GOLF: There are a total of five golf courses within a short distance of the resort, including one within walking distance. The Muskoka Lakes Golf & Country Club, one of the closest courses, has a par of 70/72 and weighs in at 5,905/5,761/5,025 yards. The course is laid out well, and brings lateral water into play on six holes. There are also several ponds and the lake itself to keep your attention.

RATES: (FAP) Lodgings (three-night minimum) - $190/$290 per couple, per night. Weekly rates are also available. Green fees - $95, including carts.

ARRIVAL: By air - Toronto (2½ hours). By car - from Toronto take Highway 400 north to Highway 11 to Bracebridge. Go through Bracebridge and turn left onto Highway 118 west. Continue over the locks at Port Carling and through the business district. At the foot of the hill turn right onto Muskoka Road #27, then drive 2½ miles to the lodge.

Wig-A-Mog Inn

North Lake Kashagawigamog Rd.

Haliburton, Ontario, Canada K0M 1S0

(705) 457-2000; (800) 661-2010

ACCOMMODATIONS: Rooms in the main inn, or Georgian Suites.

AMENITIES: Three tennis courts, outdoor heated swimming pool (with patio, deck chairs, and umbrella tables), indoor pool, saunas, whirlpool and a billiard room. The lake provides numerous water activities. The Georgian Dining Room offers a beautiful view of the lake.

GOLF: The Pinestone Inn & Country Club course is just a short walk through the woods. For detail on the course, refer to Pinestone Inn & Country Club.

RATES: (MAP) Lodgings (five-day minimum) - $900/$1,420 per couple for the five days. Green fees - $52, carts $30. Rates are for late June through August.

ARRIVAL: By air - Toronto (135 miles). By private aircraft - Haliburton Air Service (float planes only). By car - from Toronto travel east on Highway 401. Take Exit #436. Travel north to Highway 121 (Minden), turn right (east), then drive 11 miles. Turn right onto Kashagawigamog Road North, and go one mile to resort.

Windermere House

Box 68, Windermere, Ontario, Canada P0B 1P0

(705) 769-3611; (888) 946-3376

ACCOMMODATIONS: Rooms or Executive Suites in the main lodge; Garden Suites; Lake View Veranda Suites; The Terrace (fireplace, private decks); or the one-bedroom Settler's Bay units. On the shores of Lake Rosseau, surrounded by wooded terrain, this "Grand Dowager" has much to offer its guests.

AMENITIES: Windsurfing, sailing, water-skiing, fishing, heated outdoor pool or sunbathing at the sandy beach. There are also two tennis courts. Dining is in the Main Room; for lunch or snacks, choose from the Cottage Lounge under the trees on the patio, or the pool deck.

GOLF: The adjoining Windermere Golf & Country Club's championship course has been judged one of the better golf layouts in this part of Canada. It plays 6,402/6,189/5,689 yards, parring at 72/73.

RATES: (MAP) Lodgings - $240/$280/$320/$350 per couple. Weekdays slightly less. Green fees - $55, carts $35. Golf packages are not available during the peak golf season. Rates quoted are for the July-August peak season.

Canada

ARRIVAL: By air - Toronto (140 miles). By private aircraft - Muskoka Airport (Bracebridge). Pontoon aircraft can dock at Windermere. By car - from Toronto, travel north on Highway 400/11 past Bracebridge and turn off to Highway 141. Head west on 141 to Highway 4 and follow signs to the resort.

Prince Edward Island

Rodd's Brudenell River Resort

PO Box 67, Cardigan, Prince Edward Island, Canada C0A 1G0

(902) 652-2332; (800) 565-7633

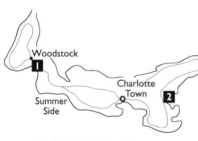

1. Rodd's Mill River Resort
2. Rodd's Brudenell River Resort

ACCOMMODATIONS: 50 riverside chalets (14 equipped for housekeeping).

AMENITIES: Tennis, outdoor heated adult pool, trail riding, bicycle rentals, lawn bowling, canoeing and windsurfing. If you prefer not to cook, the Gordon Dining Room and the Par 5 Lounge are excellent alternatives.

GOLF: The Brudenell River Provincial Course, on the premises, skirts the shores of the beautiful Brudenell River. Water is either in play or a threat on eight or nine holes; that plus the trees makes this an intriguing course. Watch out for the huge white birch that sits smack dab in the middle of the 11th fairway; it has been known to eat golf balls. Parring at 72/69, the course measures 6,517/6,037/5,662/5,082 yards.

RATES: (EP) Lodgings - $118/$399. Green fees - $52, carts $29. Golf packages are available. Rates are for July-August.

ARRIVAL: By air - Charlottetown. By car - take Canada 1 to Canada 3, to Cardigan.

Rodd's Mill River Resort

Route 2, Woodstock, Prince Edward Island, Canada C0B 1V0

(902) 859-3555; (800) 565-7633

ACCOMMODATIONS: The Mill River Resort has 80 twin rooms, plus suites.

AMENITIES: Six lighted tennis courts, indoor pool, sauna and whirlpool, canoeing, windsurfing, and bicycle rentals. For dining, the resort offers the Hernewood Dining Room and the Club On The Green Lounge. Drinks are served in the Lobby or the Down Under bars. The Mill River Inn, with nine separate breakout rooms, can accommodate groups up to 200 for meetings.

GOLF: The on-premises Mill River Provincial Golf Course is considered by many to be one of the better layouts in Canada. Measuring 6,588/6,022/5,896/5,354 yards, it pars at 72. While water is a factor on only seven holes, there is enough of it on the eighth hole to float the QE II. The well-trapped course has fairways lined by fir, pine and maple trees; it will give you plenty to think about.

RATES: (EP) Lodgings - $115/$143/$228. Green fees - $52, carts $29. Golf packages are available. Rates quoted are for the peak golf season, July-August.

ARRIVAL: By air - Charlottetown. By car - on Route 2, in West Country, about 57 kilometers west of Summerside.

Quebec

Auberge Gray Rocks

PO Box 1000, St. Jovite, Quebec, Canada J0T 2H0

(819) 425-2771; (800) 567-6767

ACCOMMODATIONS: Varied; choose from rooms in the main lodge, the deluxe Chalet Suisse, a log cabin with rustic interior and fireplace, or Le Chateau. The Gray Rocks Inn is a delightful French-Canadian resort on the shores of beautiful Lac Ouimet.

Canada

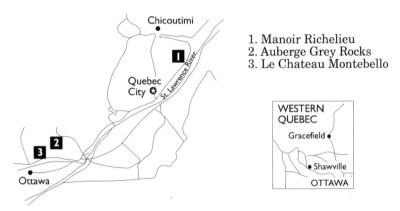

1. Manoir Richelieu
2. Auberge Grey Rocks
3. Le Chateau Montebello

AMENITIES: Sunfish boats, canoeing, windsurfing, water-skiing and, of course, swimming. In addition to the water sports, there are 20 tennis courts, volleyball, croquet, shuffleboard, lawn bowling, horseback riding, indoor fitness center with indoor heated swimming pool, hot tub, sauna, and two exercise rooms. There are free supervised children's programs. The resort is basically informal, but jackets are required in the dining rooms during the evening hours.

GOLF: The interesting Gray Rock Golf Club course, now an 18-hole championship affair, plays 6,320/6,152/5,785, with a par of 72/73 (a pretty fair reach for the ladies). The original nine was designed and laid out by Robert Williams in 1922. There was no heavy equipment available at that time to clear the land, and all rocks and boulders had to be moved by hand or horse. In the beginning, a flock of sheep kept the grass cut, as well as fertilized. Since the putting greens and fairways were the same length, putting was quite an art. Today, most of the greens are quite small and very well trapped. A few of the other delightful diversions include: an occasional tree in the middle of the fairway, a variety of side hill lies, rolling terrain, and magnificent scenery that makes it extremely difficult to keep your mind on the game.

RATES: (FAP) Lodgings - $302/$406 per couple. Green fees $74, carts $32. There are several golf and tennis package plans available. Rates quoted are for late June through August.

ARRIVAL: By air - Montreal (120 kms). By private aircraft - a 3,200-foot licensed strip (within half a mile) and a seaplane base at the resort. By car - from Montreal, take Highway 15 northwest to St. Jovite.

Le Chateau Montebello

392 Rue Notre-Dame,

Montebello, Quebec, Canada J0V 1L0

(819) 423-6341; (800) 866-5577

This is one of our Top 50 resorts. Located on the northern shore of the Ottawa River between Montreal and Ottawa, it is one of the most luxurious resorts in Canada. While the chronicle of this area stretches far back into French Canadian history, the resort itself came into being in 1930. It now offers all of the modern amenities one would expect. The lobby area is quite unusual, with a towering six-sided fireplace as the centerpiece of the huge open atrium area. The charming countryside cultivates a rustic, restful setting.

ACCOMMODATIONS: 210 newly renovated rooms, ranging from twins to doubles to suites. Six very deluxe suites have been added. Rooms have individual heating and air-conditioning.

AMENITIES: Indoor and outdoor swimming pools, six tennis courts, whirlpools, outdoor track, badminton, croquet, volleyball, a miniature golf layout, putting green, children's playground, bicycling, horseback riding, hunting and fishing. The Sports Complex offers squash courts and an equipped exercise studio. It is adjacent to the indoor pool. For meals, Aux Chantignoles is a gourmet's delight, and the Café Habitant serves lunch and light snacks.

GOLF: Le Chateau Montebello Club de Golf plays 6,046/5,614/5,539 yards and pars at 70/72. Designed by Stanley Thompson, it offers 18 holes of rolling wooded hills and valleys, bringing water into play on eight. It is a fun layout, but can be quite treacherous if you don't concentrate. A great deal of money and effort was expended and many changes completed in 1992, turning this into one of the premier layouts in Canada.

RATES: (EP) Lodgings - $185/$205/$235 per couple. Green fees - $69, including cart. Golf packages are available. Rates are for peak summer season.

ARRIVAL: By air - Montreal (64 miles) or Ottawa (approximately 50 miles). By car - from Ottawa, take Provincial Highway 148 east. From Montreal take Highway 148 west.

Manoir Richelieu

181 Richelieu Street, Pointe-au-Pic, Quebec, Canada G0T 1M0

(418) 665-3703; (800) 463-2613

ACCOMMODATIONS: 325 guest rooms, plus 12 suites, span three wings and rise five stories. There are also four six-bedroom cottages and several apartments.

Manoir Richelieu, built in the manner of a European castle, is on a knoll some 700 feet directly above the St. Lawrence River.

 This is a French-speaking area and very few of the hotel employees either can or will speak English. It can become difficult, particularly when you know they are able to speak English but refuse to do so.

AMENITIES: Outdoor heated saltwater pool, indoor freshwater pool, horseback riding and tennis. For dining there is Le St. Laurent or the main dining room, and Le Doyen (The Parasol) for snacks or a light meal.

GOLF: The Manoir Richelieu Course, a Herbert Strong design, opened for play in 1928. The first group to tour this layout was led by President William Howard Taft. Playing 6,110/5,780/5,680 yards, it is a manicured par-70/73 affair. It is not only beautiful, but its dogleg holes and fairways lined with cypress, pine and spruce will test you. There is not a great deal of water coming into play, but a creek wanders along the side of several fairways. The clubhouse, an unusual structure, is itself a miniature chateau.

RATES: (EP) Lodgings - $174/$465 and up. MAP is also available. Green fees - $80, including cart. Rates quoted are for late June to mid-October.

ARRIVAL: By air - Quebec. By private aircraft - St. Irenee (10 miles). By car - take Route 138 to Baie St. Paul, then Route 362, a newly paved and scenic highway, along the coast to Pointe-au-Pic.

The Caribbean

The Bahamas

Grand Bahama Island

The Bahamas were originally discovered by Columbus and later colonized by the British. They were subsequently retaken by the Spain and, during one short period, by the United States. The Bahamas became a Crown Colony until independence was attained in 1973.

There are some 700 islands in the Bahamas, but only 22 have any appreciable population. The islands begin 50 miles off the coast of Florida and reach out in a 750-mile arc; the southeast extension ends approximately 50 miles from Haiti. Grand Bahama Island, with its popular resort town of Freeport, is the closest island to Florida; it has an excellent selection of resorts and golf courses.

US citizens visiting the Bahamas do not need to have a passport, but proof of citizenship (birth certificate or voter registration card, accompanied by a social security card and a driver's license) is required. If you do have a passport, bring it; it will simplify things.

If you are not already aware, the Bahamas are a British colony, so cars drive on the left side of the road. It can be a bit confusing. Sometimes a taxi becomes the most attractive method of transportation.

Lucayan Beach & Golf Resort

Lucaya, Grand Bahama

(242) 373-1333 US; (800) 622-6770 Canada; (800) 848-3315

ACCOMMODATIONS: 175 guest rooms, including 52 suites.

1. Bermuda
   Fairmont Southampton Princess
2. Grand Bahama
   Lucayan Beach & Golf Resort/The Resort at Bahamia
3. Abaco
   Treasure Cay Beach Hotel
4. Eleuthera
   Cotton Bay Club
5. New Providence Island, Nassau/Atlantis Resort & Casino/
   Nassau Beach Hotel/Clarion Resort South Ocean Beach/Nassau Marriott
   Resort & Casino
6. Turks & Caicos
   Grace Bay Club
7. Grand Cayman
   Holiday Inn Grand Cayman/Hyatt Regency Grand Cayman/Westin
   Casuarina Resort
8. Jamaica
   Franklin D. Resort/Half Moon Club/Breezes Runaway Bay Resort/
   Tryall Beach Club/Wyndham Rose Hotel
9. Dominican Republic
   Casa De Campo Resort/Jack Tar Village
10. Puerto Rico
    Wyndham El Conquistador Resort/Hyatt Dorado Beach/Hyatt Regency
    Cerromar Beach/Palmas Del Mar Resort/Westin Rio Mar Beach Resort
11. St. Thomas
    Marriott Frenchman's Reef/Renaissance Grand Beach Resort
12. St. Martin/St. Maarten
    Mullet Bay Resort & Casino
13. St. Croix
    The Buccaneer Hotel/Sunterra Carambola Beach Resort
14. St. Kitts/Nevis
    Jack Tar Resort/Sun 'n Sand Village/Timothy Beach Resort/Four Seasons
    Resort
15. Barbados
    Coral Reef Club/Glitter Bay Hotel/Almond Beach Club/Sandy Lane Hotel/
    Royal Pavilion

AMENITIES: Pool and swimming beach, four tennis courts, scuba diving snorkeling, parasailing, water-skiing, paddleboats and Hobie Cat rentals. There are two dining facilities – Arawak Dining Room (reservations and jackets required) and Butterfly Brasserie, serving on the terrace.

GOLF: The Lucaya Country Club layout adjacent to the hotel was built in 1962 by Dick Wilson. The terrain is generally flat but well bunkered, with elevated greens and fairways lined by dense tropical underbrush and pine trees. Water comes into the picture only on the 17th hole. Parring at 72/75, the course measures 6,824/6,488/5,978 yards.

RATES: (BP) Lodgings - $155/$185/$235. Golf package (two nights/two days, includes lodging, one round of golf daily with cart, breakfast, taxes, gratuities), $698/$778 per couple.

ARRIVAL: By air - Freeport International Airport.

The Resort at Bahamia

Princess Country Club, PO Box F-207, Freeport, Grand Bahama

(242) 352-6721; (800) 545-1300

The Resort at Bahamia is actually two resorts. The one listed above is the Country Club. Directly across the street is the Princess Tower.

ACCOMMODATIONS: 10-story tower with 400 rooms, including 20 suites; the country club location consists of two- and three-story low-rise structures with over 560 rooms and suites.

AMENITIES: 12 tennis courts and two swimming pools. Transportation is provided to the beach area, which offers a multitude of water sports. For casual dining there is Guanahani's, the Rib Room, and a variety of restaurants in the Tower.

GOLF: 36 holes of tropical golf will keep you busy. The Emerald Course, adjacent to the Country Club, plays 6,679/6,402/5,722 yards and pars at 72/75. Designed in 1965 by Dick Wilson, the Emerald has been the site of the PGA Bahamas National Open. The pros play from the back tees, but this layout is a lot more fun from the white tees. Stretching out from the Tower is the Princess Ruby Course, with yardage of 6,750/6,385/5,622 and par of 72/74. The Ruby was designed by Joe Lee and came into play in 1966. It has also been the location of several prestigious tournaments, including PGA's Hennessy Cup, the Daiwa

Canadian PGA Championship and the Hoerman Cup (the Caribbean Championship matches). Although water comes into contention on only five holes, the fairways are lined by extremely tall Arawak pines and lush tropical growth (a favorite hiding place for golf balls).

RATES: (EP) Lodgings - $125/$155/$300. Green fees - $85, including cart. Golf packages are available. Rates quoted are for January 1st through April 14th.

ARRIVAL: By air - Freeport International Airport.

Treasure Cay Beach Hotel

Treasure Cay, Abaco, Bahamas

(242) 365-8535; (800) 327-1584

ACCOMMODATIONS: Suites, rooms, and beachside TreasureHouses.

AMENITIES: Six tennis courts, bicycle rentals, freshwater pools, 150-slip marina (accommodating boats up to 100 feet), and golf. Should you choose not to cook for yourself, there are several restaurants: The Spinnaker, Typsy Seagull (poolside), or the Beach Sandbar.

GOLF: The Treasure Cay Golf & Country Club, a Dick Wilson design, reaches out 6,985/6,650/5,690 yards with a par of 72/73. The course is long, but water comes into contention on only four holes.

RATES: (EP) Lodgings - $155/$225/$315. Green fees - $65, carts $35.

ARRIVAL: By air - Treasure Cay International Airport. A number of commercial flights and charter trips can also be arranged. By car - taxi to the hotel is about 45 minutes.

Nassau

Very few people refer to this island as New Providence. Most call it Nassau. But Nassau is, in fact, the capital city – not only of New Providence, but of the entire Bahamas.

Atlantis Resort & Casino

PO Box N-4777, Paradise Island, Bahamas

(242) 363-3000; (800) 285-2684

AMENITIES: The complex extends over three miles of white sand beach and is divided into three locations: the Resort & Casino, the Ocean Golf & Tennis Resort and the Atlantis Beach Resort. Room rates include sailing, snorkeling, windsurfing, water-skiing, day and night tennis (12 courts) and bicycling. Several restaurants offer a variety of cuisines, including American, French, Italian, Chinese/Polynesian and Bahamian. There is also a 30,000-square-foot casino, with roulette, 24-hour blackjack, slot machines and Baccarat.

GOLF: The Paradise Island Golf Club layout was designed by Dick Wilson, who took full advantage of the island's natural beauty. Lush tropical foliage surrounds each green. The course is bordered on three sides by the mother of all water hazards, the Atlantic Ocean, and water (in the form of ponds) becomes a challenge on 13 holes. There are over 80 sand traps, along with beach areas to keep you alert. The prevailing tradewinds seem to change each time you play. The course measures 6,976/6,562/5,880 yards and pars at 72.

RATES: (EP) Lodgings - $285/$360/$410. Green fees - $120, including cart. There are so many different package plans it is not practical to list them all. Rates shown are for the peak winter season of late December through April.

ARRIVAL: By air - Nassau International Airport.

Clarion Resort South Ocean Beach

PO Box N-8191, Adelaide Road, Nassau, New Providence, Bahamas

(242) 362-4391; (800) 424-6423

ACCOMMODATIONS: 120 rooms, plus 130 oceanfront luxury rooms.

AMENITIES: The resort has over 1,500 feet of white sand beach fronting the property. There are four tennis courts (two lighted), two swimming pools, scuba diving (ranging from

Caribbean

structured reef diving to mile-deep dropoffs), windsurfing, boating, fishing and, of course, golf. Dining takes place at the hotel's Casuarina and Papagayo Restaurants.

GOLF: The Joe Lee-designed course plays 6,707/6,292/5,908 yards, with a par of 72/74. Most of the fairways on this relatively flat layout are bordered by trees. It is well-bunkered and brings water into play on five holes. As on most of the islands, wind can become a definite factor.

RATES: (EP) Lodgings - $195/$295. Green fees - $95, including cart. Rates are for January through April.

ARRIVAL: By air - Nassau International Airport (10 minutes).

Nassau Beach Hotel

PO Box N-7756, Nassau, New Providence, Bahamas

(242) 327-7711; (888) 627-7282

ACCOMMODATIONS: 410 rooms, including suites and penthouse suites.

AMENITIES: Windsurfing, paddleboating, Hobie Cat and Sunfish rentals, aquabikes, water- skiing, parasailing, snorkeling and scuba diving. Daily programs are offered, including water sports clinics. There are also six lighted tennis courts. Dining facilities at this hotel and within the immediate area include Frilsham House (jackets required), the Lobster Pot, The Beef Cellar, the Beachcomber Grill & Pizzeria, Hibiscus and Pineapple Place.

GOLF: Nassau Beach Hotel is directly across the street from the Cable Beach Golf Course. Parring at 72, it plays 6,534 yards. Watch these greens – they are extremely fast.

RATES: (EP) Lodgings - $145/$170. Green fees - $85, carts $30. Golf packages are available. Rates are for January through April.

ARRIVAL: By air - Nassau International Airport.

Nassau Marriott Resort & Casino

West Bay Street (Box N-8306), Nassau, New Providence, Bahamas

(242) 327-6200; (800) 453-5301

ACCOMMODATIONS: Several multi-storied beachside hotels with 1,550 rooms and suites.

AMENITIES: Two swimming pools, parasailing, water-skiing, Hobie Cat and Sunfish rentals, windsurfing, snorkel trips and deep-sea fishing. There are also saunas, steam rooms, a Jacuzzi, weight lifting or massage therapy. A variety of dining locations are available, along with a huge casino and discotheque.

GOLF: Atlantis Paradise Island (18 holes, par 72, seven miles away); Cable Beach Golf Course (18 holes, par 72, one mile away); South Ocean Beach Golf Course (18 holes, par 72, seven miles away).

RATES: (EP) Lodgings - $259/$299 and up. Green fees - $110, including cart. Golf packages are available.

ARRIVAL: By air - Nassau International Airport.

Barbados

Barbados, which is about 21 miles long and 14 miles wide, is one of the few islands our good friend Columbus actually missed.

Almond Beach Club

Vaux Hall, St. James, Barbados, West Indies

(246) 432-7840; (800) 223-9815

ACCOMMODATIONS: One- and two-bedroom suites.

 This is an adult facility; children under the age of six are not permitted.

AMENITIES: Two lighted tennis courts, three freshwater pools, and numerous types of water activities; all are complimentary. There is also a Nautilus fitness center, squash courts, saunas and a masseuse. Dining and evening entertainment are offered in the Sand Dollar Restaurant.

GOLF: The Sandy Lane Golf Club is located across the street. For details on the course, refer to Sandy Lane Hotel & Golf Club.

RATES: (FAP) Lodgings - $660/$710/$790. Green fees - $82, carts $50. Rates quoted are for mid-December through March 30th.

ARRIVAL: By air - Grantley Adams Airport. Taxi service is available (distance is 18 miles).

Coral Reef Club

St. James, Barbados, West Indies

(246) 422-2372; (800) 223-1108

Although small (12 acres), this family-owned and operated hotel has many amenities.

 Children under 12 cannot be accommodated from mid-January through mid-March.

ACCOMMODATIONS: Villa-style buildings (71 units) with cottages, rooms and two-to four- bedroom apartments. Some units have a dining room and fully equipped kitchen.

AMENITIES: Water-skiing, scuba school, snorkeling, Hobie Cat and Sunfish rentals, pool and ocean swimming, and two lighted tennis courts. Nice extras: a boutique, hairdressing salon and a beauty/body clinic on the premises. The food here is unusually good.

GOLF: Guests may use the Sandy Lane Golf Course, approximately one mile away. For complete details on this interesting course, refer to Sandy Lane Hotel & Golf Club on the following pages.

RATES: (MAP) Lodgings - $385/$815. Green fees - $85, carts $50, caddies $20. Rates quoted are for the peak season, mid-December through mid-April.

ARRIVAL: By air - Grantley Adams Airport (18 miles). Taxi service is available.

Glitter Bay Hotel

St. James, Barbados, West Indies

(246) 422-4111; (800) 866-5577

ACCOMMODATIONS: 83 units, ranging from hotel rooms to three-bedroom suites.

AMENITIES: Lighted tennis courts, fitness center, two swimming pools, catamaran sailing, water-skiing, snorkeling, and windsurfing. Scuba diving and deep-sea fishing can also be arranged. Or you can just sunbathe on the beach. Dining is available in the Piperade Restaurant. Guests also have signing privileges at the at the Royal Pavilion restaurants.

GOLF: The Royal Westmoreland course, designed by Robert Trent Jones II, measures a healthy 6,870/6,497/5,968/5,333 yards and pars at 72. Guests may also use the Sandy Lane Golf Club, described below.

RATES: (EP) Lodgings - $385/$410 per couple. Green fees - $195, including cart. Rates shown are for the peak season, mid-December through April.

ARRIVAL: By air - Grantley Adams Airport.

Royal Pavilion

Porters, St. James, Barbados, West Indies

(246) 422-4444; (800) 866-5577

ACCOMMODATIONS: 72 oceanfront junior suites.

AMENITIES: Two tennis courts, outdoor swimming pool, fitness center featuring LifeCycle and LifeStep equipment, and a half-mile of sand beach. Dining facilities area available at the resort as well as at the directly adjacent Glitter Bay Hotel.

GOLF: Guests may use the Royal Westmoreland Course at the Glitter Bay Hotel (see preceding entry).

RATES: (EP) Lodgings - $280/$470. Green fees - $195, including cart.

ARRIVAL: By air - Grantley Adams Airport.

Caribbean

Sandy Lane Hotel

St. James, Barbados, West Indies

(246) 432-1311; (800) 223-6800

ACCOMMODATIONS: 112 rooms, including 27 suites and three penthouse suites. Sandy Lane is on the sheltered west coast of Barbados, about 15 minutes from Bridgetown, the capital city.

 The hotel is built on several levels connected by stairs, so it might pose problems for guests with disabilities.

AMENITIES: Five tennis courts (two lighted), swimming pool, water-skiing, scuba diving, snorkeling, windsurfing, sailing, and deep-sea fishing. There are two restaurants, the Sandy Bay and the Seashell, as well as a poolside snackbar. Children six or under may dine in the Seashell Restaurant between the hours of 7 and 7:30 and are not allowed in the Sandy Bay Restaurant. What a wonderful and thoughtful arrangement!

GOLF: Parring at 72, the Sandy Lane Course plays 6,576/6,206/5,536 yards. It is stunningly beautiful; the profusion of tropical trees and plants includes mahogany, breadfruit, avocado, Barbados ebony, towering royal palms, wild orchid and hibiscus. The signature hole is number seven; the par 3 of some 130 yards (blue tees) features a substantial drop from tee to green.

RATES: (EP) Lodgings - At press time the resort was undergoing renovations and no rates had been set. Call for details.

ARRIVAL: By air - Grantley Adams Airport.

Bermuda

Bermuda, an archipelago approximately 22 miles in length and a bit over a mile wide, consists of seven major and many lesser islands. The capital city is Hamilton. While it is close to the US in geographical terms, culturally it is more British than England.

Although Bermuda is a British colony, it has a great degree of autonomy. Visiting US citizens must present proof of citizenship, preferably a passport; visa or vaccination records are not required. No rental cars are available on Bermuda. Transportation is provided by taxi, boat taxi (which runs in and out of Hamilton and serves the entire area), or by bus (which is excellent). Visitors may also rent mopeds and pray, as the roads are extremely narrow and the traffic pattern is on the left side.

In addition to the resorts listed, there are many housekeeping cottages, apartments, and guest houses available for rent. For a list of these lodgings, write to the Bermuda Department of Tourism, Globe House, 43 Church Street, Hamilton HM 12, Bermuda, or call (800) 233-6106.

Fairmont Southampton Princess

PO Box HM 1379, Hamilton 5, Bermuda HM FX

(441) 238-8000; (800) 866-5577

Located on the highest point in Bermuda, the Southampton Princess commands a breathtaking view of the Great Sound and the Atlantic Ocean.

ACCOMMODATIONS: The nine-story hotel has 563 guest rooms and 37 suites. Recently added is the Newport Club, a concierge level arrangement.

AMENITIES: 11 tennis courts (three lighted), health club with sauna, two heated freshwater pools (one indoor, one outdoor) and use of their private beach club with its locker rooms, chaise longues, etc. Scuba diving, snorkeling, sailing and sport fishing can be arranged. They have a children's program, as well as a plan wherein children stay and eat for free. There are many delightful places to dine or to be entertained: The Windows on the Sound, the Newport Room (considered by many to be the finest on the island; jacket and tie required) and the lovely Waterlot Inn dining room.

GOLF: The Southampton Princess has an 18-hole, par-3 course, measuring 2,684 yards and parring at 54. This layout has one of the most scenic settings on the island, but the wind and 60-plus traps can make it a most difficult golf course to navigate.

A word of caution: Should you approach this course expecting an easy conquest, you are in for a rude awakening.

Two other golf facilities are also available: the Port Royal Golf Club and the Riddell's Bay Club.

RATES: (EP) Lodgings - $479/$529/$759 per couple. Green fees - $59, carts $35. Golf packages are available. Rates shown are for the peak season, April-November.

ARRIVAL: By air - Bermuda Airport (on Saint Davids Island), approximately 40 minutes. By car - taxi service is available to the hotel.

Cayman Islands

The Caymans are 500 miles south of Miami and 150 miles northeast of Jamaica. A British Crown Colony, the group consists of Grand Cayman and, about 80 miles east, Little Cayman and Cayman Brac islands. The cost of living is high because most food and basic necessities must be imported.

A passport is required. Visitors must also have either a return or continuing ticket in their possession. Both Canadian and American dollars are considered legal tender and are readily accepted.

The language spoken on the Caymans is English. At least I think it is. The English pronunciation is interlaced with flavors of Cornish, Welsh, Irish and Scottish. You may also encounter regional British variations along with some American Southern intonations.

Golf is played on the Britannia Golf Course, which is the only course on Grand Cayman. Nicklaus created a beautiful layout with a Scottish flair, using grassy mounds, rolling dunes, lakes, lateral water and large bunkers. It is a single course, but is played in three different configurations. The Championship Course (nine holes) reaches out 6,206/5,398 yards with a par of 70. By playing the very forward tees and shorter greens, it becomes an 18-hole executive affair with a yardage of 2,911/2,466 and a par of 58. Finally, it can be played as the Cayman 18-hole Course. This play requires the revolutionary Cayman Ball, developed by Jack Nicklaus (the ball travels half the distance of a regulation golf ball). With this configuration, the course plays 3,092/2,662 yards and pars at 71. The way my game comes and goes, I think someone slipped a Cayman Ball into my bag.

The course plays as a Championship affair on Tuesdays, Thursdays and Saturdays; an Executive layout on Mondays and Fridays after 1 PM, and all day on Wednesdays and Sundays; it plays as a Cayman Course on Mondays and Fridays before 11 AM.

The Holiday Inn Grand Cayman

PO Box 904, Grand Cayman Island, British West Indies

(859) 578-1114; (800) 465-4329

The Holiday Inn fronts directly on the ocean and has over 1,000 feet of white sand beach; its location is one of the best on the island.

ACCOMMODATIONS: 215 well-appointed rooms.

AMENITIES: Freeform freshwater pool, jet skiing, sailing, glass-bottom boat rides and dinner and cocktail cruises. Dining takes place in the Veranda Dining Room. Lighter fare is available in the oceanside Cabana.

GOLF: For details on the Britannia Course, refer to the introductory section on the Cayman Islands.

RATES: (EP) Lodgings - $150/$360. Green fees - $110, including cart. Rates are January to mid-April.

ARRIVAL: By air - Owen Roberts International Airport. Taxi service runs approximately $15 (for one to four people).

Hyatt Regency Grand Cayman

PO Box 1698, Grand Cayman Island, British West Indies

(345) 949-1234; (800) 233-1234

The Hyatt Regency is located on an 88-acre tract adjacent to the Britannia Golf Course.

ACCOMMODATIONS: 236 luxury hotel rooms, including 43 Regency Club rooms and a few studio suites. There are also a number of two- and three-bedroom fully equipped villas.

AMENITIES: Paddleboats, aqua trikes, windsurfing, Sunfish and Hobie Cats, day sailers, catamarans, freshwater swimming pool, two Plexipave, hard-surface, lighted tennis courts. The Hyatt has its own 176-slip private marina. For dining, select from The Garden Loggia Cafe or Hemingway's Restaurant.

GOLF: Details on the Britannia Golf Course are above in the introductory section on the Cayman Islands.

RATES: (EP) Lodgings - $375/$425/$460. Green fees - $110, including cart. Executive and Cayman play: $55, carts $36.

ARRIVAL: By air - Owen Roberts International Airport (10 minutes). By car - taxi service is available from the airport. Moorage can also be arranged at the Hyatt's Marina.

The Westin Casuarina Resort

West Bay Road, Grand Cayman Island, B.W.I.

(345) 945-3800; (800) 228-3000

ACCOMMODATIONS: 340 guest rooms, including suites. Most open onto balconies.

AMENITIES: Lighted tennis courts, two freshwater pools, a swim-up bar, a fitness center, several dining rooms, and 24-hour room service.

GOLF: Details on the Britannia Golf Course are above in the introductory section on the Cayman Islands.

RATES: $429/$600. Green fees - $110, including cart. Rates are for peak season.

Dominican Republic

The Dominican Republic continues to reflect an old-world charm. Siesta is still observed and all businesses close between the hours of 1 and 3 PM. You will find the capital, Santo Domingo, a treasure trove of ancient cathedrals, palaces, forts, museums, and restored mansions.

It has a population of over 6,000,000 people and a land area of 19,100 square miles. The language is Spanish, the time zone is Atlantic and the currency is the peso. A US driver's license is valid; driving is on the right. Upon entry, visitors must show a passport.

The Dominican Republic charges entrance and departure taxes of $10 per person. They will accept nothing but US funds for these fees, so be sure to save enough to pay the exit fee. Also, when you attempt to change your pesos back into dollars, you will find they refund only up to 30% of the total you changed from US dollars.

Casa de Campo Resort

PO Box 140, La Romana, Dominican Republic

(809) 523-3333; (800) 877-3643

Casa de Campo has been judged one of our Top 50 resorts. The large complex has 7,000 acres, and is adjacent to the small sea town of La Romana. Since the resort is spread over such a large area, guests will need either a rental car or golf cart, which can be arranged.

ACCOMMODATIONS: 900 units, divided among many one- and two-story red-roofed casitas. You can also choose from many two- to four-bedroom villas.

AMENITIES: Swimming at their hidden beach, several swimming pools, deep-sea fishing, scuba diving, sailing, Hobie Cats, windsurfing, paddleboats, snorkeling, skeet and trap shooting, and a tennis complex featuring 11 composition/clay and four Laykold courts. The resort also has a stable of quarter horses, with riding facilities for beginners as well as for polo matches and rodeos. Dining facilities are numerous: El Tropicana, the tropical café El Patio, the Lago Grill, El Pescador and, of course, the 19th Hole.

GOLF: There are two championship golf courses, both put together by Pete Dye. They are beautiful, and not as punishing as the average Dye layout. "The Teeth of the Dog" is a fun course, measuring more than a respectable 6,888/6,057/5,571 yards with a par of 72. Seven holes either cross a portion of or run alongside the Caribbean. Three play downwind, while four play against the prevailing wind. The greens are small, extremely fast and multi-leveled. You may even find a sand dune, rather than a sand trap, running the entire length of the fairway. Use extreme caution on holes five and 16. These are two testers you will not soon forget. You will love the 18th hole. From the regular tees you drive across the La Romana airport runway. There are, however, guards to keep you from bashing into aircraft. The "Links Course" is a refreshing change of pace. Parring at 71, it reaches out a relatively modest 6,461/5,597/4,521 yards.

RATES: (EP) Lodgings - $225/$295. Green fees - Teeth of the Dog Course, $132; Links Course, $100; both include cart. Various package plans are available. Rates shown are for January through April 7th.

ARRIVAL: By air - Santa Domingo International Airport (two hours). Arrange for van pickup when making reservations; the cost is $34 round trip. A taxi will cost about $80. There are also flights from San Juan directly to Casa de Campo at La Romana Airport (5,348-foot paved runway). This is a best bet; flying in and out of La Romana will avoid the two-hour trip from Santa Domingo.

Jack Tar Village

PO Box 368, Puerto Plata, Dominican Republic

(809) 586-3557; (800) 999-9182

ACCOMMODATIONS: 280 rooms, including a few suites. The Jack Tar Puerto Plata is on the north shore of the Dominican Republic.

AMENITIES: Freshwater pool and poolside bar, a newly added adults-only swimming pool complete with swim-up bar, tennis courts, beach, snorkeling, sailing, windsurfing, horseback riding, and organized tours of the island. There is a gourmet restaurant located in the casino.

GOLF: Four holes of El Campo de Golf de Playa Dorada surround the Jack Tar Resort. A Robert Trent Jones design, it plays to a yardage of 6,992/6,302/5,361 and pars at 72. Built on relatively flat terrain and well bunkered, it wends its way throughout the resort grounds, along the beach and inland through a tropical growth area.

RATES: (FAP) Lodgings - $232/$366. These rates are for January 4th through April 7th.

 Rates indicated cover all meals, cocktails or soft drinks, transportation to and from the airport, nightly entertainment, bicycle rentals, green fees, gratuities, and taxes. Golf carts are $40.

ARRIVAL: By air - Puerto Plata International Airport. Do not fly into Santa Domingo, as it is much too far from the resort (four hours by car).

Jamaica

Jamaica's topography ranges from beautiful white sand beaches to the rugged ridges of the Blue Mountains. The island population is about 2.3 million. The rainy months are May and October, with temperatures of 70-88° at sea level and approximately 5° cooler in the mountainous area. The peak season is from mid-December through April.

Three 18-hole championship layouts are located in the Montego Bay area: the Ironshore, the Wyndham Rose and the Half Moon Golf Club. Two additional 18-hole courses can be found in the Ocho Rios region. The Kingston area has two more – The Caymanas and the Constant Springs Clubs. There is also a nine-hole affair located in Mandeville, the Manchester Club.

Spectator activities include cricket, horse racing, soccer and boxing. Of course, you can always just relax and do nothing more strenuous than lift a cool one.

While the language is English, it is strongly laced with Jamaican patois. The traffic pattern is also English. Be careful when driving, but also be sure to look in the correct direction prior to stepping off a curb. Not realizing that traffic is coming from the other direction can be extremely hazardous to your health.

Jamaica is only 90 minutes by air from the Florida coast and has international airports in Montego Bay and Kingston. Visitors must have a current passport.

Rental cars are available, as well as many different tours, including half-day and full-day trips. Medical facilities are excellent and available in each major area.

 Many of the hotels do not accept children under 16 years of age.

In addition to the major resort properties, there are many individually owned villas available for rent. Most come complete with a staff, including a maid, cook and gardener. For details call the Jamaica Tour Office at (800) 526-2422.

Caribbean

Breezes Runaway Bay Resort

PO Box 58, Runaway Bay, Jamaica, West Indies

(876) 973-2436; US (800) 858-8009; Canada (800) 553-4320

Breezes Resort, set on 214 acres, has over 2,000 feet of beach-front.

ACCOMMODATIONS: 238 rooms including suites; all are air-conditioned and have a private terrace.

 The resort does not accept guests under 16 years of age.

AMENITIES: Sunbathing, ocean swimming, water-skiing, scuba diving, snorkeling, windsurfing, Sunfish, catamaran cruises and kayaking. There are also three swimming pools, Jacuzzis, four lighted tennis courts, horseback as well as donkey riding and bicycling. Dining facilities are provided by the informal beach terrace and the resort's more formal dining room.

GOLF: The Runaway Bay course, designed by British Naval Commander James Harris, is referred to as a placement affair. Extremely well-trapped and parring at 72, the yardage is 6,884/6,602/6,093. The resort offers an outstanding golf school.

RATES: Lodging - $1,530/$2,670 per couple, for three nights, all-inclusive. There are no green fees; carts are $60.

ARRIVAL: By air - Sir Donald Sangster Airport (Montego Bay). Complimentary hotel bus transportation to and from the airport (one hour).

Franklin D. Resort

PO St. Ann, Runaway Bay, Jamaica, West Indies

(876) 973-3067; (800) 654-1337

ACCOMMODATIONS: One- , two- and three-bedroom suites, fully equipped for housekeeping. Rates include lodging, three meals per day, wine, beer and cocktails and the use of all sporting facilities

AMENITIES: Tennis, pool, windsurfing, sailing, snorkeling, scuba diving, bicycles, unlimited green fees, transfer from the airport to the resort, tours of the area and much more. For children, there is a playground, arts and crafts center and beach program. Dinner is served in the oceanside restaurant. There is a nightly show at the Reef Garden Night Club, featuring singers, acrobats, limbo dancing, etc.

GOLF: The Runaway Bay Golf Course is less than a mile from the resort. For details, see Breezes Runaway Bay Resort.

RATES (FAP) Lodgings - $350/$400 per adult per night. Children under 16, free. Green fees - $60, carts $60. Rates are for mid-December through April.

ARRIVAL: By air - Sir Donald Sangster Airport (Montego Bay). Complimentary transportation is available from the airport; when making reservations, advise the hotel of your flight number and arrival time.

The Half Moon Club

PO Box 80, Montego Bay, Jamaica, West Indies

(876) 953-2211; (800) 626-0592

Situated on 400 acres of tropical gardens and manicured lawns, Half Moon Bay Club has over a mile of white sand private beach property.

ACCOMMODATIONS: 90 guest rooms, 79 suites and 36 one- to three-bedroom golf villas. Some of the cottages and villas come equipped with kitchen and maid/cook service.

AMENITIES: 13 tennis courts (four lighted), four squash courts, fishing, snorkeling, sailing, scuba diving, windsurfing, saunas and horseback riding. Elegant dining is available at the Club House Grill, overlooking the 18th green.

GOLF: The Robert Trent Jones-designed layout reaches out 7,115/6,582/5,992 yards and pars at 72. Although it has wide rolling fairways, the wind can turn it into a tiger.

RATES: (EP) Lodgings - $390/$490/$590. Green fees - $100, carts $35. Caddy (mandatory), $15. Golf packages are available. Rates shown are for December 15 through April 15.

ARRIVAL: By air - Sir Donald Sangster International Airport (Montego Bay), about 10 minutes away.

Caribbean

Tryall Beach Club

Sandy Bay Post Office, Hanover Parish, Jamaica, West Indies

(876) 956-5660; (800) 238-5290

ACCOMMODATIONS: 44 rooms in the Great House, and over 40 two- , three- , and four-bedroom villas. Villas are staffed with cook, chambermaid, laundress, and gardener. About 12 miles west of Montego Bay, the Tryall Club is spread over 2,200 rolling acres of Jamaica's north coast.

AMENITIES: Six tennis courts (two lighted), pool or beach swimming, snorkeling, sailing, water-skiing, windsurfing, scuba diving and deep-sea fishing. Breakfast and dinner are served in the formal dining room of the Great House.

GOLF: The Tryall Club has long been recognized as one of the finest courses in the Caribbean. Parring at 71/73, it reaches out 6,407/6,104/5,764 yards. The well-trapped layout has fairways lined with palm trees and introduces water on eight holes.

RATES: (EP) Lodgings - $500/$625. Green fees - $80, carts $30.

ARRIVAL: By air - Sir Donald Sangster International Airport (Montego Bay 14 miles). By car - taxi service is available to the hotel.

Wyndham Rose Hotel

PO Box 999, Montego Bay, Jamaica, West Indies

(876) 953-2650; US (800) 822-4200; CANADA (800) 631-4200

ACCOMMODATIONS: 480 hotel guest rooms, including suites. The hotel fronts on 30 acres of private beach, but its backdrop is formed by heavily timbered slopes.

AMENITIES: Tennis, complete health club, snorkeling, water-skiing, large freshwater swimming pool, beach swimming, scuba diving, deep-sea fishing and sailing. Dining ranges from very casual (the swim-up bar and snack bar at the pool) to the more formal Country Club and Great House Veranda.

GOLF: The course has been described as a remarkable combination of highland (mountainside) and links (seaside) layouts. Parring at 72, it reaches out 6,598/6,162/5,309 yards. This layout will offer you some unusual and challenging golf shots. Several greens are beside waterfalls, one is surrounded by the turquoise waters of the Caribbean, and some fairways are bordered by jagged mountains.

RATES: (EP) Lodgings - $215/$775. Green fees - $75, carts $40, caddy $20.

ARRIVAL: By air - Sir Donald Sangster International Airport (Montego Bay 16 miles).

Puerto Rico

Puerto Rico is the most easterly of the major islands of the Greater Antilles. Approximately 1,000 miles southeast of Miami, it measures about 100 miles long and 35 miles wide. It is located in the Atlantic Standard time zone. The year-round temperature is 80°. In summer months the humidity can become oppressive, but in prime season (late December through April) it is usually very pleasant. Certainly a vast improvement over slipping and sliding behind that snowplow on your local ice-covered freeway.

There are many resorts along with some excellent golf courses described in the following pages.

Hyatt Dorado Beach

Dorado Beach, Puerto Rico 00646

(787) 796-1234; (800) 233-1234

ACCOMMODATIONS: 298 rooms, including beachfront units, 17 casitas and a two-bedroom suite casita. The Hyatt Dorado is 22 miles west of San Juan and three miles from the town of Dorado.

AMENITIES: Two swimming pools, snorkeling, scuba diving, pelican boats, 21 tennis courts (four lighted), bicycling, jogging, aerobics and a health club. For dining, choose from The Ocean Front Cafe, The Surf Room, Su Casa, or the à la carte menu at the golf course.

GOLF: The two layouts were designed by Robert Trent Jones. The East course reaches out a monstrous 7,005/6,430/5,805

Caribbean

yards and pars at 72/74, with water coming into play on 10 holes. The West course appears a little more modest but is really not. Also parring at 72/74, it reaches out 6,913/6,431/5,883 yards. Should you be one of those poor devils who has a tendency to hook, I suggest you acquire some floating golf balls and keep the betting very low.

RATES: (MAP) Lodgings - $535/$635 per couple. Green fees - $130, including cart. Golf packages are available. Rates are for late December through late April.

ARRIVAL: By air - San Juan International Airport. Dorado Transport Company charges $13 per person each way to the hotel. By private aircraft - a 3,600-foot paved, lighted runway on property.

Hyatt Regency Cerromar Beach

Golf & Tennis Resort, Dorado, Puerto Rico 00646

(787) 796-1234; (800) 233-1234

ACCOMMODATIONS: 506 rooms, including 19 suites.

AMENITIES: 21 tennis courts (four lighted), snorkeling, scuba diving, freeform water playground with swim-up bar, Olympic-size swimming pool and The Spa Caribe Health Club. For dining there is the Swan Café, Medici's for a bit more formal dining and the Casita de Oro.

GOLF: Both courses were designed by Robert Trent Jones. The North Course, with water in play on seven holes, reaches out 6,841/6,249/5,547 yards and pars at 72. The South layout plays 7,047/6,298/5,486 yards, also with a par 72. Both courses are flat and, while not easy, they are not very interesting. Last year Raymond Floyd redesigned both the North and the South courses. A much-needed update, as these layouts were set up originally in 1956.

RATES: (EP) Lodgings - $375/$485. Green fees - $130, including cart.

ARRIVAL: By air - San Juan International Airport. By private aircraft - a 3,600-foot paved and lighted runway on property. The Dorado Transportation Company provides transport to the hotel.

ARRIVAL: By air - San Juan International Airport. By private aircraft - a 3,600-foot paved and lighted runway on the property. The Dorado Transportation Company provides transport to the hotel.

Palmas Del Mar Resort

PO Box 2020, Humacao, Puerto Rico 00792

(787) 852-6000; (800) 468-3331

Set on 2,700 acres on the Caribbean side of Puerto Rico, Palmas Del Mar is about 45 miles from San Juan.

ACCOMMODATIONS: 102 rooms in the Candelero Hotel, 23 suites in the Palmas Inn, and 195 one- to three-bedroom villas.

AMENITIES: Large tennis complex (20 courts, six lighted), seven swimming pools, an equestrian center, 3½ miles of beach, rental bikes, deep-sea fishing, sailing, water-skiing and scuba diving. There are several restaurants at Palmas Del Mar: The Palm Terrace; the Blue Hawaii; Chez Daniel Restaurant; Beach Bohio; the Tennis Bar and the Club Deli.

GOLF: A Gary Player design, the Palmas Del Mar Course plays 6,830/6,247/5,432 yards with a par of 72. Although it does not have a great many bunkers, it does bring water into contention on 12 of the 18 holes. The undulating terrain, relatively fast greens and wind all combine to create a great deal of challenge. The views along the shores of the Caribbean Sea can also be distracting.

RATES: (EP) $225/$370. Green fees - $145 including cart. Package plans are available. Rates quoted are for the winter season of January 2nd-April 30th.

ARRIVAL: By air - San Juan International Airport. When making reservations, request ground transportation from the airport.

Westin Rio Mar Beach Resort

6000 Rio Mar Blvd., Rio Grande, PR 00745

(787) 888-6000; (800) 228-3000

The Westin Rio Mar Beach has been judged as one of our Top 50 resorts.

ACCOMMODATIONS: 600 rooms, including 72 suites, all with mountain, ocean or golf course views. This 481-acre facility runs directly along Luquillo Beach.

AMENITIES: Beachfront swimming pools, extensive water sports and beach activities, including scuba lessons, Hobie Cats, water skiing, 13 tennis courts, complete spa program, fitness center and a full service casino. There is also a youth activity program. Dining rooms include the superb Marbella, The Grille Room at the clubhouse, the Club Coqui for poolside dining and, for lighter fare, La Estancia, atop the tennis complex.

GOLF: The Rio Mar Beach Resort Course was designed by George and Tom Fazio. Rolling out 6,782/6,435/6,083/5,450 yards, it pars at 72. It's very well bunkered, and water becomes a challenge on 14 holes. The newest layout is called the River Course. Designed by Greg Norman, it plays 6,945/6,343/5,826/5,119 yards and also pars at 72.

RATES: (EP) Rooms - $245/$465. Beach Club - $625/$645. Green fees - $175. River Course - $135. Golf, spa and tennis packages are available.

ARRIVAL: By air - San Juan International Airport. Transportation to the resort can be arranged prior to your arrival.

Wyndham El Conquistador Resort

Las Croabas, Fajardo, Puerto Rico 00738

(787) 863-1000; (800) 468-8365

El Conquistador Resort is situated on a promontory with the Atlantic Ocean on one side and the Caribbean on the other. The views from this 300-foot vantage point are quite dramatic. The registration procedure is also unique. El Conquistador has a welcome center at the San Juan International Airport. The resort's buses transport guests to the hotel, and hotel staff pre-registers them en route; upon arrival, visitors can proceed directly to their lodgings.

ACCOMMODATIONS: 74 cliffside units, 144 rooms in La Manna Village, and the hotel. There are a total of 926 rooms, including over 70 suites.

AMENITIES: Six pools, seven-court tennis center, luxury spa, jogging track, solarium, fitness and aerobics center, white sand beaches, and private 55-slip marina with boat charters and deep-sea fishing available. There is also a marvelous casino, evening entertainment, and, of course, golf. For dining, guests can choose from 16 different restaurants and lounges.

GOLF: The course was rebuilt by Arthur Hill, who requires that the resort maintain the course properly. In other words, impeccably manicured. Mr. Hill has created a most exciting golf layout using the natural undulating terrain, many trees, and vertical elevation changes of over 200 feet. Parring at 72, it measures 6,600/6,300/5,800 yards.

RATES: (EP) Lodgings - $395/$475/$555. Green fees - $175, including cart.

ARRIVAL: By air - San Juan International Airport. By private aircraft - Fajardo Airport (10 miles). When making reservations, advise the resort of your flight number and arrival time to arrange for airport pickup.

St. Kitts - Nevis

The island of St. Kitts is approximately 20 miles long, encompasses 65 square miles, and has a population of about 37,000. The entire island, which is quite mountainous, is dominated by 3,790-foot Mount Liamuiga.

Nevis, with an area of 36 square miles, is less than two miles from St. Kitts. Of volcanic origin and surrounded by coral reefs, it remains virtually untouched by tourism. A small island, it offers a quiet, peaceful setting with forested slopes rising from the beach area.

Caribbean

The two islands became independent in 1983 and have the distinction of being one of the world's smallest nations. Visitors must have passports, but visas are not usually required of US citizens.

Jack Tar Resort

PO Box 406, Frigate Bay, St. Kitts, West Indies

(869) 465-8651; (800) 999-9182

The resort is on the northeastern portion of the island overlooking Lake Zuliani and has beaches fronting on the Atlantic and the Caribbean.

ACCOMMODATIONS: 242 air-conditioned rooms, including a few suites.

AMENITIES: Four tennis courts (two lighted), two swimming pools, bicycling and complimentary scuba lessons, catamaran cruises, tours of the island, sunset cruises and deep-sea fishing. Horseback riding is available for a fee. Dinner is served in the Village Dining Room and the Garden Restaurant, which also serves breakfast and lunch. The resort's Village Casino features blackjack, roulette, slots and crap tables.

GOLF: The Royal St. Kitts-Frigate Bay Golf Course borders the resort. Its front nine is along the Atlantic Ocean, while the back side borders the Caribbean Sea. Reaching out 6,918/6,476/6,033/5,349 yards, it pars at 72. Water becomes a factor on 12 holes. It looks generally open but is well-trapped, with a profusion of palm trees. The course is a great deal of fun to play and, although at first glance it appears to be quite easy, it is not.

RATES: (FAP) Lodgings - $306/$334. Golf carts - $40. Rates are for the period of December 23rd through April 6th.

 Rates indicated also cover all meals, cocktails, transportation to and from the airport, nightly entertainment, bicycle rentals, green fees, gratuities, and all taxes

ARRIVAL: By air - Golden Rock Airport (four miles). When making reservations arrange for transfer to resort.

Sun 'N Sand Village

PO Box 341, Basseterre, St. Kitts, West Indies

(869) 465-8037; (800) 621-1270

ACCOMMODATIONS: Two-bedroom cottages or studio apartments.

AMENITIES: Beach activities, two tennis courts, and swimming pool. The Royal St. Kitts Casino offers an evening diversion.

GOLF: For details on the golf facilities, refer to the Jack Tar Resort & Casino.

RATES: (EP) $130/$280. Green fees - $50, carts $40.

ARRIVAL: By air - Golden Rock Airport (four miles). Taxi service is available to the resort.

Timothy Beach Resort

PO Box 81, Basseterre, St. Kitts, West Indies

(869) 465-8597; (800) 621-1270

ACCOMMODATIONS: Rooms and two-bedroom/three-bath townhouses. This beachfront resort also overlooks a portion of the golf course.

AMENITIES: Tennis court, swimming pool, and restaurant and bar on premises.

GOLF: For details on the golf course, refer to the Jack Tar Resort & Casino, page 502.

RATES: (EP) Lodgings - $100/$125/$150/$175. Green fees - $80, including cart.

ARRIVAL: By air - Golden Rock Airport (four miles). Taxi service is available from the airport to the resort.

The Four Seasons Resort

PO Box 565, Nevis, West Indies

(869) 469-1111; US (800) 332-3442; Canada (800) 268-6282

The Four Seasons Resort has been judged one of our Top 50 resorts. To get here, fly to St. Kitts, then board a new 52-foot private catamaran for a 40-minute cruise to the resort's dock. If you want to bypass this delightful scenario, access is available from Puerto Rico, Antigua, St. Maarten and several other islands using inter-island airlines directly to Nevis Airport.

ACCOMMODATIONS: 12 clusters of guest cottages, providing a total of 196 rooms and suites. Ten provide ocean views, while the remaining two overlook the third fairway. A washer/dryer is located in each cluster. There are also some villas and private homes (with two, three and four bedrooms).

AMENITIES: Freeform swimming pools, lap pool, 10 lighted tennis courts (with a variety of surfaces, including clay and cushioned rubber), fitness center, exercise rooms, saunas, whirlpool, massage rooms, and a beauty salon in the Great House. The resort has one of the most beautiful beaches in the world, and the waters around Nevis offer some of the finest snorkeling and scuba diving you will find anywhere. Many other activities can be arranged: deep-sea fishing charters, sailing, windsurfing, water-skiing, horseback riding, and bicycling. A complete children's activity program is provided seven days a week. For dining, there are two excellent restaurants: The Dining Room and the Grille. Lighter fare is offered in the sports pavilion and the poolside/beachside cabana.

GOLF: The course was designed by Robert Trent Jones II. It contours around the resort, and offers spectacular ocean and mountain views. Reaching out 6,766/6,199/5,623/5,153 yards, it pars at 71. From the very first tee this layout starts an almost imperceptible climb, reaching a pinnacle at the 15th tee where you can see the contour and outline of the world (at least it appears that way). The view is breathtaking. On the green, when putting toward the mountain you must be very firm, as it will be slow. When putting away from the mountain, it will be extremely fast. While the course itself is difficult enough, there is the added distraction of spectacular views from almost every vantage point, along with wild monkeys (very much in evidence early in the morning), donkeys and wild goats on the course. I have seen almost everything that slithers, runs, flys or jumps on a golf course, but this is the only place we have encountered donkeys, monkeys and goats.

RATES: (EP) Lodgings - $675/$750/$1,275. Green fees - $130, including cart. The resort also offers MAP and FAP plans. Golf package - seven nights/seven days (includes lodging, MAP, boat transfer from St. Kitts to Nevis, unlimited golf with cart, daily golf clinic), $6,575/$7,100 per couple. Rates are for January 3 through April 15.

ARRIVAL: By air - from the US, you can fly via San Juan to St. Kitts, then take the resort's catamaran to their dock, or take a connecting flight to the Nevis airport.

US Virgin Islands

This group of islands consists basically of St. Thomas, St. John and St. Croix. It is 1,000 miles from Miami, a bit over 1,500 miles from New York, and 18 degrees north of the equator. *Be aware:* driving is on the left side and the roads are mountainous and extremely narrow.

The history of the area follows a familiar pattern. Discovered by Christopher Columbus, then becoming a virtual shopping mall for privateers and pirates, and later coming under the influence of Denmark, the islands were finally purchased by the United States in 1917.

St. Thomas and St. Croix have golf courses; St. John does not. The Mahogany Run Golf course is probably as well known as any in the world. George and Tom Fazio used one of the most beautiful locations in the Caribbean for this course. The valleys, hills and rugged coastline of St. Thomas turn this into one of the most spectacular golf layouts you may ever find. Playing to a modest yardage of 6,022/5,609/4,873, it pars at 70. The yardage is the only "modest" part of this course. Cut from solid forest, running in some cases beside steep drop-offs to the sea, it is as tight, tree-lined and as difficult as you could conjure up in your wildest dreams. There is *no* room for error. Your shot is either straight or you're dead. The course is extremely well-trapped, and the sand bunkers can, on occasion, save you from sheer disaster. As a resting place for your ball, they are infinitely preferred over the water hazards that influence play on 10 holes. The shifting, buffeting and almost constant wind is also very much a factor.

The course offers any golfer a "Devil's Triangle Award" – provided they complete play on holes 13 through 15 without incurring a penalty stroke. I do not think that is achievable by a mortal, much less the average hacker. There is a regularly scheduled beverage cart on the course. After you have played the "triangle" it is often referred to as the "survival wagon."

Marriott's Frenchman's Reef and the Renaissance Grand Beach Resort are recommended places to stay on St. Thomas. Both are excellent destination-resorts and have a reciprocal arrangement with the course.

St. Thomas

Marriott's Frenchman's Reef

PO Box 7100, St. Thomas, US Virgin Islands 00801

(340) 776-8500; (800) 524-2000

On the eastern point of St. Thomas Harbor, Frenchman's Reef commands a view of the passing parade of stately cruise ships entering and exiting the port of Charlotte Amalie.

ACCOMMODATIONS: 425 rooms, including 18 suites, most offering an ocean or harbor view. There are also 96 luxury units in the Morning Star Beach Resort.

AMENITIES: Four lighted tennis courts, various tours (including helicopter trips), two pools, ocean swimming, snorkeling, scuba diving, sailing, deep-sea fishing, sunset cruises and catamaran sailing. There is also a 46-foot submarine, allowing navigation of the reef at Buck Island in a safe and comfortable cabin. The resort provides a complimentary program for children under 12 years of age. There are many excellent restaurants to choose from.

GOLF: For details on the golf facilities, refer to The US Virgin Islands on the foregoing pages.

RATES: (EP) Lodgings - $299/$329/$399. Green fees - $110, including cart.

ARRIVAL: By air - Cyril E. King Airport (five miles). Taxi service is available to the resort.

Renaissance Grand Beach Resort

Smith Bay Road, PO Box 8267, St. Thomas, USVI

(340) 775-1510; (800) 468-3571

The Grand is on a hillside reaching out along Pineapple Beach and overlooking the sea, about 20 minutes outside Charlotte Amalie.

ACCOMMODATIONS: 86 units in seven two-story structures at poolside; and 211 in the hibiscus area, terraced into the hillside.

AMENITIES: Six lighted tennis courts, two freshwater swimming pools, a 100-foot private dock, scuba diving, snorkeling, sailing, powerboats and world-class fishing. A Kids Club operates seven days a week. There are two restaurants: the Smuggler's Bar & Grill for casual poolside dining, or the Baywinds Restaurant.

GOLF: For details on the fabled and spectacular Mahogany Run Golf Course, refer to the US Virgin Islands.

RATES: (EP) Lodgings - $251/$279/$289/$400. Green fees - $110, including cart. Golf packages are available. Rates quoted are for the peak season and are lower at other times of the year.

ARRIVAL: By air - Cyril E. King Airport (nine miles). Taxi service is available.

St. Croix

The largest of the three US Virgin Islands, St. Croix offers a variety of spectacular scenery. Once again, remember to drive on the left side of the road.

The Buccaneer Hotel

PO Box 25200, Gallows Bay, St. Croix, USVI 00824

(340) 773-2100; (800) 223-1108

Most of the resorts experienced severe damage to their grounds and buildings from Hurricane Hugo's visit a few years back. However, when the damage was repaired, some welcome changes and additions were also made.

ACCOMMODATIONS: 150 rooms, including 14 suites. Each room has ceiling fan, air-conditioning, and cable TV.

AMENITIES: Three wonderful beaches, eight tennis courts (two lighted), two outdoor swimming pools, scuba diving, snorkeling, windsurfing, and health club with sauna and massage facilities. Dining takes place in the Terrace Restaurant (dress is casual), or the more intimate Brass Parrot (slacks and closed shoes required).

 Children are welcome at this resort, provided they know how to behave in public areas.

GOLF: The Buccaneer Golf Course is a Bob Joyce design; parring at 71, it plays 6,117/5,504/4,490 yards.

 Prior to teeing off, be sure to ask for the "How To Enjoy This Course" flyer from the pro shop. This useful guide covers each hole, describing suggested approaches and the various problem areas to avoid. It also mentions wind conditions, which are a definite factor in this area.

RATES: (EP) Lodgings - $250/$330/$450/$600, including breakfast. Green fees - $65, carts $30. Golf packages are available. Rates shown are for the peak season.

ARRIVAL: By air - Alexander Hamilton Airport (40 minutes). Taxis meet all incoming flights. If you book a golf package, make transportation arrangements when making your reservations.

Sunterra Carambola Beach Resort

PO Box 3031, Kingshill, St. Croix, USVI 00851

(340) 778-3800; (888) 503-8760; (800) 424-1943

Carambola, like most properties, suffered under the lashing of Hurricane Hugo a few years back. However, this 1,000-acre resort has come back better than ever. The resort's setting is reminiscent of a fishing village, with a mixture of Dutch, French and Spanish accents.

ACCOMMODATIONS: Six-unit clusters, each unit with its own sitting area and screened-in porch. There are also a number of two- and three-bedroom villas, with full-sized kitchen, living area, washer/dryer, etc. For information on villa rentals, call (809) 778-0797 or (800) 323-7241.

AMENITIES: Beach activities include scuba diving, snorkeling and swimming in Davis Bay. There are also four lighted tennis courts and a freshwater pool. Carambola's dining facilities are the Saman and the Mahogany Dining Room.

GOLF: The course is known as one of the finest in the Caribbean. A Robert Trent Jones Sr. design, it reaches out a very substantial 6,843/6,228/5,687/5,424 yards and pars at 72/73. Water becomes a factor on only eight holes, but Jones more than compensated for this oversight by installing many traps and extending the length of certain holes. Number 15 plays 593 yards from the blue tees and 554 from the white tees, with a par of 5.

RATES: (EP) Lodgings - $160/$190/$220. Green fees - $60, carts $28. Golf package (two nights/three days; includes lodging, green fees, cart) - $400 per couple. Rates quoted are for January through April.

ARRIVAL: By air - St. Croix International Airport.

The Turks & Caicos Islands

This group of islands has experienced a mixed history. At one time considered part of the Bahamas, they were first under French, then Spanish, influence. In 1874, they came under the rule of Jamaica, and in 1962 became a British Crown Colony.

Consisting of some 35 islands (eight are inhabited), they support a population of nearly 14,000 and are 575 miles from Miami, 286 miles due north of the Dominican Republic and 465 miles west-northwest of San Juan, Puerto Rico. The temperature ranges from 77°-83°. American Airlines flies from Miami to the

Providenciales Airport. There are also several feeder flights from San Juan and the Dominican Republic.

Grace Bay Club

PO Box 128, Providenciales, Turks and Caicos Islands, BWI

(649) 946-5757; (800) 946-5757

ACCOMMODATIONS: 21 suites, ranging from junior to two-bedroom luxury units, each with private terrace.

AMENITIES: Two lighted tennis courts, two freshwater pools, snorkeling, scuba diving, sailing, parasailing, massage and body treatment, and miles of beach area. Dining is provided in Anacoana, an open air restaurant, and the clubhouse.

GOLF: Designed by Karl Litten in 1991, the Provo Club Course measures 6,529/6,217/5,753/4,979 yards, with a par of 72. Water comes into play on at least 12 holes. The numerous freshwater ponds provide a habitat for many species of migrant birds. Knowing that, you shouldn't be so upset when you fish your ball out.

RATES: (EP) Lodgings - $635/$1,395. MAP plan is also available. Green fees - $120, including cart. There are no golf packages during peak season.

ARRIVAL: By air - Providenciales Airport (10 miles).

Mexico

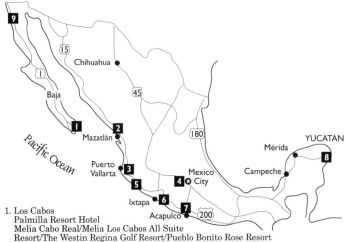

1. Los Cabos
   Palmilla Resort Hotel
   Melia Cabo Real/Melia Los Cabos All Suite
   Resort/The Westin Regina Golf Resort/Pueblo Bonito Rose Resort
2. Mazatlan
   Camino Real Mazatlan/El Cid Resort
3. Puerto Vallarta
   Marriott CasaMagna/The Westin Regina Resort/Four Seasons Resort
   Punta Mita
4. Valle De Bravo
   Avandaro Golf & Spa Resort
5. Manzanillo
   Las Hadas
6. Ixtapa-Zihuatanejo
   Westin Brisas Ixtapa
7. Acapulco
   Fairmont Acapulco Princess Resort/Las Brisas Resort/Fairmont Pierre
   Marques Resort
8. Cancún
   Camino Real/Casa Maya Cancún/Hyatt Cancún Caribe/Hilton Cancún Resort/
   Krystal Cancún/Marriott Casa Magna Resort/Presidente Inter-Continental Cancún
9. Bajamar Ocean Front Golf Resort

Mexico is a country of some 760,000 square miles, bordered on the north by the United States, on the south by Guatemala and Belize, on the east by the Gulf of Mexico and Caribbean Sea, and on the west by the majestic Pacific Ocean. It is a land of rich and ancient history, now reaching for a more modern society.

The flatlands of Mexico are situated between the two Sierra Madre mountain ranges. At an elevation of 2,500 to 10,000 feet, this area enjoys a moderate climate. Most of the larger cities and the bulk of Mexico's almost 70 million people can be found in this area.

Most of the major resorts are situated in the coastal lowland areas, where the climate is definitely tropical. While extremely warm and humid during the summer months, the temperature is pleasant during the winter.

Don't be reluctant to shop – Mexico is a bargainer's paradise. Take the tours, as they will offer you a good selection of sights at a relatively low cost. And when the sun goes down, Mexico comes alive. Take part, as there is much to see and do.

The best part of Mexico is the people. They are warm and friendly, and graciously tolerant when we mutilate their beautiful language.

Things You Need To Know

- For international flights, arrive at the airport at least an hour and half prior to departure. For flights within Mexico, one hour is fine. Baggage is limited to two checked pieces and one carry-on.
- To avoid hassles, be sure to bring your passport. You must have a "tourist card" to enter Mexico. Once you have filled it out, do not misplace it. You must present it upon departure.
- The electricity is 120 volts/60 cycle (same as US), so there is no need to bring converters.
- The climate is mild, even warm, but the nights can get cool. It is wise to have a jacket or sweater for the evening hours.
- There are certain remote areas where travel by private vehicle is not recommended and can even be dangerous. Check with your resort management.

Acapulco – Guerrero Area

Acapulco, 150 miles south of Zihuatanejo/Ixtapa, has been referred to as one of the world's greatest playgrounds. With its magnificent bay, miles of beaches, shops galore, and many beautiful resorts, that is an appropriate description.

Fairmont Acapulco Princess Resort

PO Box 1351, Acapulco, Guerrero, Mexico 39868

011-52-748-4-31-00; (800) 866-5577

ACCOMMODATIONS: The main building is in the shape of an Aztec Pyramid with an atrium soaring 16 stories. Within this structure are 423 rooms, junior suites and six penthouses. Additional rooms and suites are available a short distance away in the 10-story Princess Tower; it is connected to the main building by a covered walkway. In total there are 1,020 rooms. Set on 480 acres along Revolcadero Beach, the Princess is one of the largest resorts in Mexico.

AMENITIES: Nine outdoor and two indoor tennis courts, four freshwater swimming pools, a saltwater lagoon, and a children's wading pool. Other activities that can be arranged are scuba diving, deep-sea fishing, parasailing, water-skiing, sailing, catamaran cruises, a yacht cruise, and even nightclub tours. Eight restaurants offer a wide variety of cuisine.

GOLF: There are two golf layouts: the Acapulco Princess course and the testier Pierre Marques. The two, side by side, are directly across the street from their respective hotels. The Acapulco, playing 6,355/6,085/5,400, pars at 72. A Ted Robinson design, it presents its own challenge in the form of water on 10 holes and many trees. For detailed coverage of the more difficult Pierre Marques course, refer to the Pierre Marques Resort below.

RATES: (MAP) Lodgings - $259/$490 per couple. Green fees - $85, including cart. Golf packages are available.

ARRIVAL: By air - Acapulco International Airport. Government-run taxi service is available from the airport to the hotel.

Las Brisas Resort

PO Box 281, Acapulco, Guerrero, Mexico 39868

011-52-748-4-15-80; (800) 223-6800

Las Brisas has been judged one of the top 50 resorts. I think our love affair with Las Brisas began upon arrival. By the time we had flown from Mexico City and then driven to the hotel, our tongues were literally hanging out. Before I could even get my room confirmation forms out, some delightful person placed a tall, cool, tropical drink in my hand. What a great way to start a relationship.

ACCOMMODATIONS: 300 casitas on top of Las Brisas hill. These views, outstanding during the daylight hours, are beyond description at night. There are 250 pools on the property; only 96 casitas share a pool, while all others have their own. A few of the thoughtful amenities include: fresh flowers flown in from Mexico City each day are placed on your pillows and sprinkled in your swimming pool; continental breakfast left in a little slide-through door of your room each morning; a complimentary bowl of fresh fruit replenished daily; and a fully stocked bar. In each casita is a louvered wall that glides back to reveal a delightful pool (either private or shared).

AMENITIES: Five lighted tennis courts; a jeep caravan excursion to the bullfights (available only during the winter season); a jeep safari to nearby fishing villages, plantations, or tropical lagoons; or you can arrange for your own jeep to explore the area. Descend to the beach area and another world opens up. At the foot of the bluff is the Concha Beach Club. Available only to members and guests of the resort, there is windsurfing, parasailing, water-skiing, snorkeling, sailing, and even a private scuba diving club. La Concha Restaurant is something to remember. The main dining room, Bella Vista, is a terrace patio open on three sides. There is also El Mexicano.

GOLF: Guests of Las Brisas can arrange play at either the Acapulco Princess or the Pierre Marques golf courses. For details on either of these layouts, refer to the sections on these resorts.

Las Brisas Resort now has its own championship 18-hole course located much closer to the resort. Designed by the Robert von Hagge group and called Tres Vidas, it plays to 7,040/6,597/5,960/5,056 yards and with a par of 72.

RATES: (EP) Lodgings $315/$515 and up. All rates include continental breakfast. A fee (about $20) is charged for each day of your stay to cover all tipping, including check-in and departure.

ARRIVAL: By air - Acapulco International Airport (20 minutes). Government-operated taxi service is available from the airport to the resort.

Fairmont Pierre Marques Resort

PO Box 474, Acapulco, Guerrero, Mexico 39868

011-52-748-4-20-00; (800) 866-5577

ACCOMMODATIONS: 344 rooms, plus suites.

AMENITIES: Five lighted tennis courts, three freshwater pools, children's wading pool, aerobic classes, Spanish orientation classes, scuba diving, deep-sea fishing, water-skiing, parasailing, catamaran or yacht cruises, and night club tours. There are several dining options: La Terraza, the Tabachin Room and the Amigo Restaurant.

GOLF: Originally designed by well-known golf architect Percy Clifford, the course was redone by Robert Trent Jones, Jr. in time for the 1982 World Cup Tournament. While fun to navigate (water in play on 13 holes), it places a premium on accuracy off the tee and delivers immediate chastisement for erratic shots. The yardage alone should give you some indication of its difficulty; measuring 6,855/6,557/6,112/5,197 yards, it pars at 72/73.

RATES: (MAP) Lodgings - $265/$599 per couple. Golf packages are available.

ARRIVAL: By air - Acapulco International Airport. Government-operated taxi service is available from the airport to the hotel.

Los Cabos, Baja California Sur

Los Cabos is at the southern tip of the Baja California peninsula. It is a fast-growing community of just over 25,000 people. The area has long been recognized as one of the world's premier sport-fishing areas. There are about 850 different species in the area; prize catches include marlin, sailfish, tuna, dorado, wahoo, and roosterfish. The best time for sport fishing is summer; whale watching is popular in the winter. Golf season runs from mid-

October through mid-May. Development of several spectacular destination resorts is underway, which will also bring new golf courses to the area.

Melia Cabo Real

Carretera Cabo San Lucas, San Jose del Cabo

Baja California Sur, 23410

011-52-114-400-00; (800) 336-3542

ACCOMMODATIONS: 302 guest rooms, including eight junior suites and seven master suites. The hotel is situated on the beach between San Jose del Cabo and Cabo San Lucas.

AMENITIES: Tennis, a very large swimming pool, horseback riding, cycling, windsurfing, scuba diving, water-skiing and, of course, deep-sea fishing. There is also a health center, featuring massages. Dining facilities include a seafood grill as well as a dining room and coffee shop.

GOLF: The Cabo Real Golf Club was designed by Robert Trent Jones II. Parring at 72, the course reaches out a very respectable 6,921/6,439/5,956/5,050 yards. While water becomes a factor on only two holes, there are enough traps to keep your full attention. A second 18 – a Jack Nicklaus design – known as the El Dorado Golf Course, reaches out 7,050/6,593/6,240/5,771/4,855 yards, parring at 72.

RATES: Lodgings - $270/$305; Jr. Suites - $580. Green fees - $190, including cart. The resort offers a variety of package programs and rates – ask when making reservations.

ARRIVAL: By air - San Jose del Cabo International Airport (15 miles).

Melia Los Cabos All Suite Beach & Golf Resort

Carretera Transpeninsular CSL-SJC Km 18.5

Los Cabos, Baja California Sur 23400, Mexico

(11) 52 114-40202; (800) 336-3542

Melia Los Cabos, an all suite hotel is located along the corridor between San Jose del Cabo and Cabo San Lucas, facing on one of the most beautiful beaches in Cabo.

ACCOMMODATIONS:136 suites, including 90 studios, 30 executive, 13 luxury and three corner suites. All ocean-view with private terrace, kitchenette, safe deposit box, and 24-hour room service.

AMENITIES: A Gym & Spa featuring massage, facials, etc., two tennis courts, swimming pools, beach-front swimming and, for dining, Los Terrazos, featuring international cuisine. There are also two bars – El Mirado and El Chapuzon, located at the main pool.

GOLF: There are several courses available to you. Please refer to the Melia Cabo Real Resort for details.

RATES: Lodgings - Studio $224/$260; Executive Suites $290/$375; Corner Suites $395. Green fees - $190, including carts.

ARRIVAL: By air - San Jose del Cabo International Airport.

Palmilla Resort Hotel

San Jose del Cabo, Baja California Sur, Mexico 23400

011-52-684-205-82; (800) 637-2226

The Palmilla Resort has been judged one of the top 50 resorts. We grossly underestimated this resort – it is in every measure, a world-class destination. Completely remodeled in 1996, it comes very close to being "the jewel of Baja." The lush tropical setting is complemented by the hacienda-style white stuccoed wall and red-tiled roofs. It is a magnificent setting. I believe one of the things that makes this resort so special is the quiet, soft warmth of the entire resort and its people.

ACCOMMODATIONS: 115 luxuriously appointed guest accommodations in the hotel, plus eight two-bedroom suites and two five-bedroom villas. All units are air-conditioned and have patios or balconies; some include sitting rooms. About five kilometers from San Jose del Cabo, this 900-acre golf community development, has over two miles of coastline fronting on the Sea of Cortez.

AMENITIES: Two tennis courts, croquet, volleyball, swimming pool with a swim-up bar, scuba diving, snorkeling, and some of the most fabulous sportfishing in the world. A two-mile stretch of beach is only a short walk from the hotel. The dining rooms offer an extensive menu, ranging from continental to Mexican specialties and include La Paloma and El Jardin Restaurants. The musical entertainment during the evening is outstanding, as is the food selection and presentation.

GOLF: Palmilla now has 27 holes of championship golf designed by Jack Nicklaus. A variety of distractions and challenges await you, such as spectacular views of the ocean, mountains, and lakes, deep arroyos, a variety of cacti and more than a quorum of sand bunkers. The three nine-hole combinations are the Arroyo, playing 3,337/3,134/2,918/2,703/2,334 yards. The Mountain nine reaches out a very robust 3,602/3,348/3,212/2,970/2,254 and the Ocean Course measures 3,548/3,373/3,227/2987/2,645. Each layout pars at 36; thus, no matter how you mix them, they par at 72. Be prepared for some spectacular elevation changes as this is primarily a mountainous affair. There are several other courses nearby.

RATES: (EP) Lodgings - $395/$595. Jr. suites - $690. Suites - $950/$1,250. Casa Christina - $2,750. Green fees - $175, including cart.

ARRIVAL: By air - San Jose International Airport (25 minutes). Ask for pickup service when you make reservations.

Pueblo Bonito Rose Resort

Playa El Medano, Cabo San Lucas, BCS Mexico, 23410

011-52-114 35500; (800) 990-8250

Located at the southern tip of Baja, California, the Rose Resort enjoys a magnificent setting overlooking the Sea of Cortez. In the form of an open "U," with a huge freeform swimming pool occupying the center. It is a most impressive structure.

ACCOMMODATIONS: This is an all-suite hotel. There are 260 suites – each equipped for housekeeping, with full kitchens and private balconies or patios. Each room also has a safe-deposit box.

AMENITIES: There is a Spa & Fitness program with massages, facials and body treatments. Along with the aforementioned huge swimming pool, there is a wonderful beach, tennis courts (lighted), room service, as well as several restaurants: Mare Nostrum and L'Orangerie, featuring French cuisine and poolside dining. Watersports, such as fishing, scuba diving, Jet skiing and parasailing, can be arranged. Horseback riding is also available. For those who bring little ones along, there is babysitting service available.

The best news: The Pueblo Bonito Rose has its own purified water system.

GOLF: The Cabo San Lucas Country Club course was designed by the Pete Dye group. Playing to a par of 72, it stretches out 7,220/6,862/6,603/6,135/5,302 yards. This is the closest golf course to the resort (10 minutes), but several more are available nearby: Cabo del Sol (15 minutes), Palmilla, (25 minutes), El Dorado (20 minutes), Cabo Real (20 minutes).

RATES: Lodgings - Junior Suites $300/$350; Luxury Suites $350 and up. Green fees - $155, including cart.

ARRIVAL: By air - San Jose Del Cabo Airport. Arrange pickup with the hotel when making reservations, or take a local taxi.

The Westin Regina Golf & Beach Resort

Carretera Trans Peninsula KM 22.5, Box 145

San Jose del Cabo B.C.S, 23400, Mexico

011 (52) 114-29000; (800) 937-8461

The hotel property consists of 15 acres graced by the most unusual structure. Even though it is a huge hotel, it blends so well into the surroundings that from a distance it is difficult to see.

ACCOMMODATIONS: The hotel has 295 rooms, including suites and villas. Each unit has a view of the sea. All have private balconies, in-room safes, handcrafted furniture and original art works. Junior suites have Jacuzzis.

AMENITIES: A full-service fitness center and a spa with sauna, steam rooms, and professional massage services. In addition to the ocean, there are seven outdoor swimming pools. There are also two tennis courts, and the hotel staff can arrange for all manner of water activities (scuba, deep-sea fishing, sailing, water and Jet Skiing). If you are not out of gas, there is also horseback riding, hiking and hunting. The excellent dining facilities, in addition to 24-hour room service, include La Cascada, for Mexican as well as international fare, Arrecifes, La Playa and El Set poolside dining.

GOLF: There are a total of five championship courses at your disposal: A Dye 18, two courses designed by Jack Nicklaus and one by Robert Trent Jones, Jr. The El Dorado, designed by Jack Nicklaus, reaches out a very substantial 7,050/6,593/6,240/5,771/4,855 yards, parring at 72. With seven holes fronting the Sea of Cortez, five holes with water in play, a liberal sprinkling of traps, plus elevation changes that may require your ball to obtain clearance from NASA, this layout will test your nerves.

RATES: Lodgings - Rooms $332/$350; Royal Beach Club $415/$475; Suites $670/$1,445. Green fees - $214, including cart. Golf packages are available. Check when making reservations.

ARRIVAL: By air - San Jose del Cabo International Airport (10 minutes). Ask for pickup at the airport when making reservations.

Bajamar Ocean Front Golf Resort

Hacienda Las Glorias, Km 77 Carretera Cuota

Tijuana-Ensenada, B.C.S, Mexico

011-52-615 501-52; (800) 225-2418

The resort is located 77 km south of the US-Mexico border, overlooking the Pacific Ocean.

ACCOMMODATIONS: There are a total of 81 rooms.

AMENITIES: Tennis courts, a swimming pool and spa, a delightful cocktail bar and restaurant, Dos Lagos, offering outstanding cuisine and spectacular views of the ocean. Bicycle rentals are also available.

GOLF: With 27 holes, there were a variety of golf designers involved – Percy Clifford, David Fleming and finally Mr. Robert Von Hagge. Lagos/Vista duo reaches out 6,968/6,295/5,712/ 4,696 yards, parring at 71. The Vista/Ocean nines combine to play a very substantial 7,145/6,610/6,089/5,175 yards, with a par of 72. The Ocean/Lagos courses stretch out 6,903/6,273/5,775/ 5,103 yards, again with a par of 71. Wind becomes the main challenge. Water comes into play on only 10 of the 27 holes. Golf is a Scottish-style links affair. There is a driving range, a chipping and putting green as well as a pro shop.

RATES: (EP) Lodgings - $116/$150. Green fees - $55/$65, including mandatory cart.

 Only soft spikes are allowed on Bajamar's courses.

ARRIVAL: By car - from San Diego, travel south on I-5. After crossing the border, follow signs that say "Rosarito Beach, Ensenada Scenic Route." This will put you on the toll road. Bajamar is located at signpost KM 77.

Cancún – Yucatán Peninsula

The Yucatán Peninsula is very deeply immersed in history. In fact, the mystery surrounding the Maya civilization is one of the greatest enigmas that has faced modern archaeologists. From 900 to approximately 1500, it flourished and, by some estimates, reached a population of some 16 million. During this six-century period, a dynamic and sophisticated society was created, with nobles, priests, artists, scribes, craftsmen, warriors, and farmers. This structured civilization built a great many Mayan cities and temples. Two questions linger on: How did they accomplish what they did with the limited equipment available during that period,

Mexico

and what happened to them? True, there are some four million descendants still speaking the Maya languages, but the once proud and magnificent cities no longer rule.

Cancún, a Mayan word, means "Pot of Gold." With an average of 240 cloudless days a year, it is little wonder the Maya people came here for a respite from the interior rain forest. Cancún is an island connected to the mainland by two bridges and is the site of several resorts, as well as two golf courses.

Golf can be played on the Pok-Ta-Pok Golf Club course. The name comes from the Mayan language and means "game played with a stick." You can't get more basic than that. The course, designed by Robert Trent Jones, Jr., has a par of 73/74, and reaches a more than respectable 6,721/6,142/5,586 yards. The clubhouse includes a pro shop and a cafeteria serving breakfast and lunch. There is also a new golf facility – the Cesar Park Golf Club. Part of the Cesar Park Beach & Golf Resort, it plays 6,641/6,102/5,246 yards with a par of 72.

Camino Real

PO Box 14, Cancún, Quintana Roo, Mexico, 77500

011-52-98-83-01-00; (800) 722-6466

ACCOMMODATIONS: The hotel is a modified pyramid-style structure with 379 rooms, including suites. The newer 18-story Royal Beach Club houses 87 of the hotel's rooms and 18 deluxe suites. The Camino literally projects out into the ocean. In fact, from a distance, it appears to be partially in the water.

AMENITIES: Four lighted tennis courts, heated freshwater pool, snorkeling, water-skiing, sailing, and deep-sea fishing; glass-bottom boat excursions can be arranged. Restaurants include the Calypso, Azulejos and the open-air Las Brisas.

 An important note: The Camino has its own water purification system.

GOLF: Guests may use the Pok-Ta-Pok golf course or the new Cesar Park Golf Club. For details refer to the above section on the Cancún-Yucatán Peninsula.

RATES: (EP) Lodgings - $260/$270/$305 and up. Green fees - $100, carts $35.

ARRIVAL: By air - Cancún International Airport (approximately 12 miles).

Casa Maya Cancún

Boulevard Kukulcan-Hotel Zone,

Cancún, Quintana Roo, Mexico 77500

011-52-98-83-05-55; (800) 207-9280

ACCOMMODATIONS: 356 rooms, including 250 suites.

AMENITIES: Two swimming pools, three lighted tennis courts, and a marina providing a variety of water activities. There are three restaurants and three bars.

GOLF: For details on the golf courses, refer to Cancún-Yucatán Peninsula above.

RATES: (EP) Lodgings - $200/$250 and up. Green fees - $85, carts $35.

ARRIVAL: By air - Cancún International Airport (20 minutes).

Hilton Cancún Resort

PO Box 1810, Reformo Lacandones Zona Hotelera KM 17

Cancún, Quintana Roo, Mexico 77500

011-52-98-81-8000; (800) 445-8667

ACCOMMODATIONS: 346 rooms in the nine-story hotel, including suites. There is also a concierge level.

AMENITIES: Two lighted tennis courts, seven swimming pools, fitness center and several shops. The resort also has five restaurants.

GOLF: For details on the golf course operated by the hotel, refer to The Cancún-Yucatán Peninsula, page 522.

RATES: (EP) lodgings - $275/$405. Green fees - $86, including cart. Golf packages are available.

ARRIVAL: By air - Cancún International Airport.

Mexico

Hyatt Cancún Caribe

PO Box 353, Cancún, Quintana Roo, Mexico 77500

011-52-98-83-00-44; (800) 233-1234; hyattcc@cancun.com.mx

ACCOMMODATIONS: 198 rooms, including 21 beachfront villas. This deluxe Hyatt was built along one of the finest secluded white sand beaches on Cancún.

AMENITIES: Swimming pool, tennis courts, and private marina. Restaurants include the Cocay Steak House, the Blue Bayou and La Concha.

GOLF: For details, refer to page 522.

RATES: (EP) Lodgings - $219/$289/$520. Green fees - $90, including cart.

ARRIVAL: By air - Cancún International Airport.

Krystal Cancún

Pasea Kukulcan, Cancún, Quintana Roo, Mexico 77500

011-52-988-311-33; (800) 231-9860

ACCOMMODATIONS: 330 air-conditioned rooms and suites, some units with private swimming pool.

AMENITIES: Two large swimming pools, lighted tennis and racquetball courts, fully equipped health club with gymnasium, Jacuzzi, sauna, and massage service. For dining there is Bogart's Casablanca Restaurant.

GOLF: For details on the golf facilities, refer to page 522.

RATES: (EP) Lodgings - $220/$240. Green fees - $90, including cart.

ARRIVAL: By air - Cancún International Airport.

Marriott Casa Magna Resort

Boulevard Kukulkan, Retorno Chac Lote 41

Cancún, Quintana Roo, Mexico 77500

011-52-988-52000; (800) 831-3131

ACCOMMODATIONS: 450 guest rooms, including 38 suites. Each unit has a mini-bar, hair dryer, TV with US cable service and, something not often found, an iron and ironing board.

AMENITIES: Ocean beach, outdoor pool, two lighted tennis courts, whirlpool, massage, aerobic classes, and weight lifting. Nearby you can enjoy scuba diving, snorkeling, parasailing, jet skiing and sailing. Tours are available to the ancient Maya ruins in Tulum and Chichén Itzá. For your dining pleasure, there is La Capilla, La Isla (poolside), Mikado (Japanese steak house), and the Bahia Club (seafood bar).

GOLF: Refer to page 522.

RATES: (EP) Lodgings - $204/$264/$380. Green fees - $86, carts $40.

ARRIVAL: By air - Cancún International Airport.

Presidente Inter-Continental Cancún

Boulevard Kukulcan KM 7.5, Cancún, Quintana Roo, Mexico 77500

011-52-988-30200; (800) 344-0548

ACCOMMODATIONS: 294 rooms, including 15 club suites (concierge level suites).

AMENITIES: Diving, snorkeling, sailing, parasailing, water-skiing, two swimming pools, five jacuzzis, tennis court, and a magnificent white sand beach. For dining there is the Mediterraneo Restaurant, El Caribeno Restaurant & Bar, and a coffee shop (Frutas y Flores).

GOLF: The Presidente is next to the golf course. Refer to the Cancún-Yucatán Peninsula section for details.

Mexico

RATES: (EP) Lodgings - $190/$220/$550. Green fees - $85, carts $35.
ARRIVAL: By air - Cancún International Airport.

Ixtapa - Zihuatanejo

Located 150 miles north of Acapulco, the area is one of tropical tranquility. While the Ixtapa resorts described here are modern and sophisticated, "Old Mexico" can be found six miles south in Zihuatanejo. A quiet fishing village of 40,000 people, it is a sharp contrast to Ixtapa. The literal translation of the word Zihuatanejo is "Land of Women." It seems that this area was, in ancient times, ruled by women.

Westin Brisas Ixtapa

Playa Vista Hermosa, Ixtapa-Zihuatanejo, Guerrero, Mexico 40880

011-52-753-3-21-21; (800) 325-3535

ACCOMMODATIONS: 428 lanai rooms, each with an ocean view and intimate, partially covered terrace. The architectural motif of the hotel might be compared to that of an Aztec pyramid.
AMENITIES: Four lighted tennis courts, and four swimming pools connected by cascading waterfalls. Or you can try a swim at the secluded beach. Sailing, scuba diving, snorkeling, windsurfing, parasailing, and deep-sea fishing trips can all be arranged. The dining facilities include El Mexicano, Le Pavilion or La Esfera.

 Camino Real Ixtapa has its own water purification system.

GOLF: About half a mile away is the Palma Real Golf Club. A Robert Trent Jones, Jr. design, it reaches 6,898/6,408/5,801 yards with a par of 72. Water becomes a factor on nine of the 18 holes. Although the course is flat, there are enough trees and traps to keep you busy. There is now another 18-hole course available as well.
RATES: (EP) Lodgings - $199/$450. Green fees - $80, carts $25.

ARRIVAL: By air - Ixtapa/Zihuatanejo International Airport (30 minutes away). Taxi service is available from the airport to the hotel.

Manzanillo

Manzanillo is 150 miles south of Puerto Vallarta. Until about 15 years ago, when a highway opened, this area was pretty well cut off. The wide, uncrowded and unspoiled beaches stretch for more than 10 miles. They provide an endless array of water activities – everything from snorkeling and scuba diving to sailing and charter fishing trips. There are a number of restaurants in Manzanillo, along with a few stores and boutiques. Accommodations include condominiums and hotels, such as Maeva, Roca del Mar, or El Pueblito. The star of the show, however, is the world-class Las Hadas. It's a place of magic, fantasy, and complete enchantment – truly the "ultimate resort."

Las Hadas

PO Box 158, Manzanillo, Colima, Mexico 28200

011-52-333-3-00-00; (800) 722-6466

Las Hadas has been judged one of our top 50 resorts. Located at the tip of the Santiago Peninsula, just across the bay from Manzanillo, the white Moorish spires of Las Hadas rise dramatically from a hilltop. One almost expects to see a group mounted on white horses and led by Tyrone Power to arrive on the scene.

This resort was the location for the filming of the movie "10" a few years back.

ACCOMMODATIONS: 220 deluxe, air-conditioned guest rooms and suites (the word deluxe is an understatement) feature marble floors, tiled private verandas, two channels of taped music and a full ystocked bar. Their graceful arched doorways and windows reflect the overall Moorish architectural motif of the resort.

AMENITIES: Two swimming pools (one with a swim-up bar), another pool reserved for adults only, 10 tennis courts (eight

Mexico

hard-surface, two clay), and a beach. All types of watersports are offered, including sailfishing, scuba diving, snorkeling, water-skiing, sailing, and trimaran cruises. The Puerto Las Hadas Marina & Yacht Club accommodates 70 vessels, and is the largest privately built marina in Mexico. There are a variety of restaurants: the Legazpi Restaurant & Lounge, El Terral and Los Delfines. At poolside, should you twitch an eyebrow, a drink is sure to appear. When the sun goes down, the action starts at the lounges and lively disco and keeps percolating until the wee hours.

GOLF: La Mantarray course, a Roy and Pete Dye design, has been rated among the world's top 100 by *Golf Digest*. Not only challenging, it is scenic as well. If you get by the first three holes without developing the shakes you have got it made. Parring at 71, it reaches out a relatively modest 6,495/5,994/5,531/4,691 yards.

    Don't let the yardage fool you – this course is tough.

RATES: (EP) Lodgings - $260/$415/$625. Green fees - $65, carts $40. Caddies - $20. Rates quoted are for the peak season, mid-December to late April.

ARRIVAL: By air - Playa De Oro International Airport. Mini-bus and taxi service is available to the hotel (30 miles).

Mazatlan, Sinaloa

Settled by the Spanish in the early 1600s, Mazatlan developed slowly over the years. Long known by sportfishing enthusiasts, this quiet fishing town was "discovered" and over the past 20 years has developed into one of the largest cities in Mexico, with a population of almost 600,000.

Mazatlan has long been recognized as one of the premier fishing areas in the world. Record catches of black marlin or sailfish are not uncommon.

There is much to do here, with beautiful beaches, watersports, shopping in many fine boutiques, back-country tours, night life activities (your hotel can direct you) and, of course, fishing and golf.

Camino Real Mazatlan

PO Box 538, Mazatlan, Sinaloa, Mexico 82100

011-69-83-1111; (800) 722-6466

The Camino Real Mazatlan is on a rocky promontory of the rugged Punta del Sabalo and a short distance north of Mazatlan. A spectacular view of the entrance to the Sea of Cortez and the Pacific Ocean extends out directly below the hotel.

ACCOMMODATIONS: Air-conditioned rooms have a view of the ocean or the lagoon; many have private balconies.

AMENITIES: Freshwater swimming pool, two white sand beaches, and tennis courts; horseback riding is nearby. Deep-sea fishing trips, water-skiing, snorkeling, and skin diving can all be arranged. The Camino's Las Terazas restaurant is a special treat and serves three meals a day.

GOLF: The nearby El Cid Country Club course has a par of 72 and reaches out 6,712/6,393/5,252 yards.

RATES: (EP) Lodgings - $137/$157/$325. Green fees - $50, carts $30. Caddies (mandatory), $15.

ARRIVAL: By air - Mazatlan International Airport (17 miles or 35 minutes south of the city). From the airport take either a mini-bus or a taxi.

El Cid Resort

PO Box 813, Mazatlan, Sinaloa, Mexico 82110

011-526-91-333-33; (800) 525-1925

ACCOMMODATIONS: The 900-acre resort has approximately 1,000 rooms and suites. Some of the accommodations front directly on the beach, while others reach inland to the country club area.

 Important note: This resort does not have a water purification plant. Each room is supplied with bottled water. By all means use it!

AMENITIES: 17 lighted tennis courts, squash and racquetball courts, and five swimming pools (one is 20,000 square feet) with waterfalls and a swim-up-bar. Additional facilities include a hot

Mexico

tub, gym, and sauna. Restaurants include El Alcazar; The Prime Rib House; La Cava Supper Club; El Corral; La Concha; and El Patio, a poolside bar and grill.

GOLF: Parring at 72, the course stretches 6,712/6,393 yards from the hombrés' tees; and 5,252 yards from the *señoritas'* tees.

RATES: (EP) Lodgings - $100/$235/$355/$490. Green fees - $50, carts $30. Caddy (mandatory), $11. Golf packages are available.

ARRIVAL: By air - Mazatlan International Airport (17 miles, or 35 minutes south of the city). From the airport take either a taxi or mini-bus to the hotel.

Puerto Vallarta, Jalisco

In recent years, road construction has made Puerto Vallarta more accessible. Now with a population of over 300,000 people, some of the finest beaches in the world, spectacular fishing and related water activities, it is little wonder it has become one of the more popular vacation destinations in Mexico. Puerto Vallarta is accessible from Guadalajara (220 miles), and from Manzanillo (160 miles).

The Marina Vallarta Club de Golf was designed by Joe Finger, a well-known American architect. It offers spectacular views of the ocean and of Bahia de Banderas with its many beautiful yachts, sailboats and ocean cruisers. Mr. Finger brought everything but the proverbial kitchen sink into play on this layout. There are lagoons, lakes, ponds, palms and waterfalls, and plenty of Mexican sand cranes. Parring at 71, the course measures 6,641/6,093/5,259 yards.

Finger was, by the way, an architectural golf genius, taking relatively flat ground and turning it into an interesting and testing golf course.

Something new has been added: designed by Jack Nicklaus a new championship golf course, parring at 72 and stretching out 6,997 yards, opened in early 2001. Ranging from gently rolling terrain to rugged arroyos, it offers spectacular views of Banderos Bay. A second course by Tom Weiskopf – also a par 72 – is scheduled to open in the latter part of 2001, bringing more adventure and better golfing to the area.

Four Seasons Resort Punta Mita

Punta Mita, Bahia de Banderas, Nayarit 63734, Mexico

11-52-329-16000; (800) 332-3442

The Four Seasons Resort in Punta Mita has been judged one of the top 50 resorts. It is located on 1,000 acres of Pacific oceanfront (justly referred to as the Mexican Riviera), approximately 60 minutes drive from Puerto Vallarta to the mouth of Banderas Bay.

ACCOMMODATIONS: 113 Casitas (guest rooms), plus 27 suites. Each unit features a private terrace or balcony with views of the beach. All have security safes, air-conditioning and ceiling fans. Some of the suites have a private soaking pool, while others are two- or three-bedroom units. All are equipped with the Four Seasons' usual assortment of amenities, including toiletries, terrycloth bathrobes, hair dryers and so on.

AMENITIES: Four Har-Tru tennis courts (lighted), free-form swimming pool and whirlpool along with beach swimming. There is also snorkeling, sailing, deep-sea fishing. During the season, whale watching is popular and spectacular. Getting back onto dry land, the resort offers the a spa and exercise room, massage treatment, steam rooms and a beauty salon. There is also a professionally supervised program for the small-fry (Kids for All Seasons), with a wading pool and other activities. The Aramara Restaurant (an outstanding dining experience), along with the Ketsi Pool Restaurant and Bar and 24-hour room service, complete the dining facilities. There is also the Tail of the Whale for poolside casual dining.

 This resort has its own water purification system – a real plus. Another extra that is so important to those traveling with young ones, not to mention the rest of us, there is a washer/dryer combination in each accommodation grouping.

GOLF: Designed by the Jack Nicklaus group, the 18-hole course boasts eight ocean-side holes, including an optional par-3

affair with the tee on the mainland and the green 199 yards away on a natural island. They also boast some 90 or more bunkers. What a horrible fate to contemplate. Reaching out a substantial 7,014/6,641/6,261/5,767/5,037 yards, and parring at 72, it is a magnificent golf course. While at first glance it appears to be a links-style layout, it has many trees forming a backdrop to the greens. With thousands of bougainvillea throughout the course, it is not only one heck of a testing golf course, but it is beautiful as well.

RATES: Lodgings - Casita rooms $495/$545/$800; suites $1,200/$2,750. Green fees - $160, including cart.

ARRIVAL: By air – Puerto Vallarta International Airport (50 km/60 minutes).

Marriott Casa Magna

Paseo De La Marina No. 5, Puerto Vallarta, Jalisco, Mexico, 48300

011-52-322-10004; (800) 831-3131

The resort is located in the Marina Vallarta complex along the Bay of Banderas.

ACCOMMODATIONS: 433 rooms, including 29 suites. Rooms include private balconies, air-conditioning and an in-room safe.

AMENITIES: Beautiful beaches for swimming and sunning, windsurfing, snorkeling, jet skiing, three lighted tennis courts, outdoor swimming pool, whirlpool, and a complete health club with sauna and massage. There is a children's "Club Amigos" to keep the five-to-12-year-old set busy. There is a baby-sitting service as well.

The hotel complex has several places to dine – Las Casitas; La Estancia; the Mikado, a Japanese steak house; and the Sixties Club, which serves up dance music from the 50s and 60s.

GOLF: You can walk to the new Marina Vallarta Club de Golf (the pro shop is just across the street). For details on this outstanding course refer to the preceding section on Puerto Vallarta, Jalisco.

RATES: (EP) Lodgings - $169/$279 and up. Green fees - $140, including cart. Golf packages are available. Rates are for peak season of January through mid-April.

ARRIVAL: By air - Puerto Vallarta International Airport (five minutes by cab).

The Westin Regina Resort Puerto Vallarta

Paseo de la Marina, PO Box 4-100

Puerto Vallarta, Jalisco 48354, Mexico

011-52-322-11100; (800) 937-8461

The Westin Regina resort is located within the exclusive Marina Vallarta community on the Banderas Bay beachfront.

ACCOMMODATIONS: There are 280 rooms, including 14 suites, surrounded by some 600 palm trees. There is 900 feet of beachfront. They also offer a Royal Beach Club Floor (called concierge level in most hotels).

AMENITIES: Three lighted tennis courts, a fitness center featuring steam rooms, sauna and whirlpool, four swimming pools, including two swim-up bars and many water sports, (snorkeling and fishing). There are also horseback riding facilities and, of course, a golf course nearby. In addition, the resort has a Westin Kids Club. There are several restaurants, including Garibaldi's and El Palmar, both delightful.

GOLF: There are two courses available to guests of the Westin: the par 72 Flamingo Country Club, a championship layout, and the Marina Vallarta Golf Club (within walking distance), an 18-hole course designed by Joe Finger. For details on the Marina Vallarta Golf Club, refer to "Puerto Vallarta Jalisco."

RATES: Lodgings - rooms $205/$215; suites $455/$570. Green fees - $160, including cart. Golf packages are available.

ARRIVAL: Air Diaz Ordaz International Airport (10 minutes). Taxi service is available.

Valle De Bravo, Edo De Mexico

Originally named by Franciscan friars "San Francisco del Valle de Tamascaltepec" (a mouthful even for the locals), the name was later changed to Valle de Bravo in honor of the renowned patriot, Nicolas Bravo. The area, situated deep in the Sierra Madres, is a popular retreat for the more affluent residents of Mexico City.

Located at an elevation of 6,000 feet, the area has a moderate climate; temperatures are in the 80s during the day and 40s at night. The hottest months are May through August, with the rainy season occurring generally during July-September.

Avandaro Golf & Spa Resort

Fracc. Avandaro, Valle de Bravo, Edo, Mexico

011-52-726-60370; (800) 223-6510

Some 80 miles west of Mexico City, nestled deep in the Sierra Madres, Avandaro has a setting much like that of the western Rockies. It was once inhabited by the ancient Tarascan Indians – a mysterious people whose history is linked to the culture of Peru.

ACCOMMODATIONS: 108 rooms, including 48 colonial-style bungalows and 60 adobe-style junior suites. All units feature a woodburning fireplace, satellite TV, a terrace, and views of either the mountains or the golf course.

AMENITIES: Seven tennis courts, an outdoor swimming pool, hiking and nature trails, hang-gliding, horseback riding, water-skiing, sailing, and fishing. A state-of-the-art spa was added during their massive renovation. For dining there is Las Terrazas, the Aquarium Restaurant, and a poolside snack shop. The nearby 400-year-old town of Valle de Bravo offers more opportunities for dining as well as many arts and craft shops.

GOLF: Club de Golf Avandaro was designed by Percy Clifford. Playing to a yardage of 6,369/5,968/5,063, it pars at 72. Enhanced by running streams, waterfalls, pine trees, bougainvilleas and wild hibiscus, this beautiful layout will enchant you. An additional golf course is located at nearby Rancho Avandaro.

RATES: (EP) Lodgings - $140/$175. Green fees - $50/$65, carts $30, caddies $15. There are many package plans available.

ARRIVAL: By air - Mexico City International Airport (two hours).

Costa Rica

1. Costa Rica Marriott Hotel/
Hotel Herradura/Melia Cariari
Golf Resort
2. Melia Playa Cochal

Costa Rica is easy to describe in physical terms: 19,600 square miles, with a population of a bit over three million people and mountains ranging up to 12,500 feet. The basic language is Spanish; however the population is approximately 80% white, with 20% consisting of a mixture of Europeans and native Indians.

A most unusual aspect of Costa Rica is their stable economy and political climate. Located in a part of the world tortured by upheaval and almost constant war, it has been described as a happy oddity in Central America – a stable democracy that has disbanded its army to preserve the peace.

San José, the capital city and located at approximately 3,800 feet, has a population of a bit over one million. Within Costa Rica are several golf resorts which are listed below.

Golf may be enjoyed on the Cariari Country Club's 18-hole championship course. Designed by George Fazio and his nephew, it came into play in 1970. Measuring 6,590/6,078/5,366 yards, it pars at 71/72. With undulating terrain, some multi-tiered greens, narrow tree-lined fairways and water becoming a factor on eight holes, it will offer all you can handle. Green fees - $35, carts $25 (not mandatory). Caddies - $10 (required).

    There is a $16.50 per person exit tax when departing Costa Rica. US dollars are easy to exchange, but that is not true for Canadian and other currencies.

Hotel Herradura Golf Resort

PO Box 7-1880-1000, Ciudad Cariari, San José, Costa Rica CA

011-506-239-0033; (800) 245-8420

The hotel is five minutes from the International Airport, 15 minutes from San Jose, in the scenic Central Valley, with a backdrop of lush green meadows and mountains.

ACCOMMODATIONS: A total of 234 rooms, including suites. All rooms feature central air-conditioning, satellite color TV and international direct-dial phone service. Safe-deposit boxes are available. It's in a spectacular setting of landscaped gardens.

AMENITIES: Three swimming pools, Jacuzzi, sauna, an equipped exercise gym, reportedly the largest casino in the country, 11 tennis courts (seven lighted). There are three restaurants and several bars, including a swim-up affair.

GOLF: For details on the golf facilities refer to the introduction under *Costa Rica* above.

RATES: (EP) Lodgings - $130/$230. MAP and FAP plans may also be arranged.

ARRIVAL: By air - Juan Santamaria International Airport (five minutes away).

Melia Cariari Golf Resort

PO Box 737-1007 (San José), Heredia, Costa Rica

011-506-239-0022; (800) 336-3542

ACCOMMODATIONS: 220 guest rooms including suites. In-room safe deposit boxes, cable TV and direct-dial phones.

AMENITIES: Eight tennis courts (two lighted), swimming pool with swim-up bar, health club and a casino. Dining facilities include Los Vitalis, featuring international cuisine, and Las Tejas, a coffee shop. There is also 24-hour room service.

GOLF: For details on the golfing facilities refer to the introductory section on *Cost Rica* above.

RATES: (EP) $175/$250.

ARRIVAL: By air - Juan Santamaria International Airport (five minutes away).

Los Sueños Marriott Beach & Golf Resort

Herradura, Puntarenas, Box 502-4005, Costa Rica

011-506-630-9000; (800) 228-9290; information@los-suenos.com

ACCOMMODATIONS: Magnificent colonial architecture, set on the Pacific Coast, surrounded by mountains and tropical rainforest. The four-story structure has 201 rooms and 12 suites

AMENITIES: Outdoor swimming pool, health club and fitness center, sauna, tennis. There is a 250-slip marina and yacht club, as well as a beach club on the property. Dining facilities include Arrecife (lunch), La Vista Casual Restaurant (breakfast, lunch and dinner), the Golf Bar & Grill (lunch and dinner) and Casa del Café (Coffee House, for breakfast, lunch and dinner) – plus 24-hour room service.

GOLF: Los Sueños Championship Golf Course, designed by Ted Robinson. An 18-hole "eco-golf course" that plays into spectacular rainforests and back to the blue waters of Herradura Bay, it stretches out 6,696 yards and pars at 72. The views, tropical flowers and wildlife make it unique.

RATES: (EP) Lodging - $250/$295 for a room; $280/$345 for an ocean- or pool-view room.

ARRIVAL: By air - San Jose's Juan Santamaria International Airport, 60 miles SW. Follow the signs to Orotina, heading in the direction of Jaco. Exist at Herradura Los Sueños and follow the signs to the Marriott.

Melia Playa Conchal

Playa Conchal, Sta. Cruz, Guanacaste, Costa Rica

011-506-654-4123; (800) 336-3542

On the Pacific northwest coast of the Guanacaste Province between the resort towns of Tamarindo and Flamingo.

ACCOMMODATIONS: There are 39 two-story buildings (each with eight suites) for a total of 308 suites, each featuring terrace and living room, satellite color TV, phone, refrigerator and safe deposit box.

AMENITIES: Free-form swimming pool, four lighted tennis courts, health club, and casino. In addition to the casino, there is a disco. With the wonderful beaches adjacent, all manner of water sports are available. Fishing, which can be arranged, is spectacular. Each night, entertainment or theme parties are offered. In addition to 24-hour room service, there are several restaurants providing a variety of cuisines.

A couple of nice extras: there is a children's program to entertain the younger group, and 24-hour medical assistance is available.

GOLF: A par-72 championship golf course stretches out a substantial 7,033/6,593/6,045/5,396 yards. It was designed by Robert Trent Jones Jr. While the terrain is generally flat, the course is tree-lined and well-trapped. Water also becomes a factor on 13 holes.

RATES: (EP) Suites - $185/$230. Green fees - $100, including cart.

ARRIVAL: By air - Daniel Oduber International Airport in Liberia (45 minutes); local airport (15 minutes). By car - from San José, it is about a four-hour drive.

Index